The

World

of

Roman

Song

ˈ *The World of* ˈ

ROMAN SONG

ˈ

FROM

RITUALIZED SPEECH

TO SOCIAL ORDER

THOMAS HABINEK

The Johns Hopkins University Press
BALTIMORE AND LONDON

© 2005 The Johns Hopkins University Press

All rights reserved. Published 2005

Printed in the United States of America on acid-free paper

2 4 6 8 9 7 5 3 1

The Johns Hopkins University Press

2715 North Charles Street

Baltimore, Maryland 21218-4363

www.press.jhu.edu

Library of Congress Cataloging-in-Publication Data

Habinek, Thomas N., 1953–

The world of Roman song : from ritualized speech to social order / Thomas Habinek.

p.   cm.

Includes bibliographical references and index.

ISBN 0-8018-8105-6 (hardcover : alk. paper)

1. Latin literature—History and criticism—Theory, etc. 2. Music and literature—History—
To 500. 3. Music—To 500—History and criticism. 4. Latin language—Spoken Latin.
5. Literature and society—Rome. 6. Latin language—Semantics. 7. Oral communication—
Rome. 8. Rome—Civilization. 9. Ritual—Rome. I. Title.

PA6019.H33 2005

870.9'001—dc22

2004023002

A catalog record for this book is available from the British Library.

CONTENTS

ACKNOWLEDGMENTS

This book could not have been completed without the generous financial support of the American Council of Learned Societies. In addition, I am happy to acknowledge the assistance of the Faculty Development program of the College of Letters, Arts, and Sciences at the University of Southern California, which made possible a number of trips abroad to conduct necessary research.

At a more personal level, I have benefited from questions and comments on the part of patient audiences at USC, UCLA, Berkeley, Yale, University of Pennsylvania, University of Minnesota, University of Texas, College of Wooster, Wellesley College, and King's College London. In particular, I would like to acknowledge specific forms of advice or assistance on the part of Brendon Reay, Kathleen McCarthy, Basil Dufallo, Clifford Ando, Peter O'Neill, Karen Dang, Phiroze Vasunia, Philip Purchase, Tricia Gilson, Ellen Finkelpearl, Leslie Kurke, Philip Hardie, Stephen Hinds, William Fitzgerald, Gregory Nagy, Carolyn Dewald, Amy Richlin, Hector Reyes, Nadja Habinek, Jacob Habinek, Joseph Farrell, Alessandro Barchiesi, Andrew Riggsby, Matthew Roller, Leah Himmelhoch, Ingo Gildenhard, Phillip Horky, Tony Boyle, and Alessandro Schiesaro. Somehow Erik Gunderson and Enrica Sciarrino each managed to find the time to read and comment on a draft of the book in its entirety: acts of generosity I cannot begin to repay. I would never have imagined that the sometimes isolated life of the scholar could have such a rich social dimension.

Finally, the editorial staff of the Johns Hopkins University Press handled the manuscript with efficiency and care, while an anonymous reader from the Press saved me from numerous errors and offered helpful suggestions for improvement.

The

World

of

Roman

Song

INTRODUCTION

Technically, every work of art comes into being in the same way as
the cosmos—by means of catastrophes, which ultimately create out
of the cacophony of the various instruments that symphony we call
the music of the spheres.

—Wassily Kandinsky, *Reminiscences,* 1913

The Latin language differentiates between everyday speech
and speech made special through meter, diction, accompanying bodily
movement, or performance in ritual context. It describes the latter with
verbs based on the root *can-,* such as *cano* and *canto,* and the related
noun *carmen.* Scholars have approached *carmen,* or song, sometimes as
an assemblage of disparate verbal genres (e.g., incantation, legal formula, oracle, recipe), sometimes as an early rhythmical form, in either
case regarding it as supplemented over time by new song types, such
as poetry, drama, and recitative, and correspondingly new metrical and
formal characteristics. In fact, it is more useful to think in terms of
a systematic distinction between everyday and ritualized speech, with
the markers of specialness or ritualization varying according to context.
The practice of ritualization, rather than any specific formal or contextual marker through which ritualization is achieved, gives *carmen* its
force. Even writing, which remains throughout antiquity the capability
of a limited sector of the population, will at times serve as a mode of
ritualization, that is, of turning speech into song and the writer into a
particular type of agent.

The double purpose of this book is to describe the Roman system
of song and speech and to develop a set of arguments concerning its social significance. Description here consists largely of the accumulation
of examples from the Latin language itself: instances in which song and

speech are differentiated, song is subdivided into song-types (including poetry), or song is situated with respect to related activities, such as play, mimicry, and craftsmanship. Also relevant are references to the agents of song—or, better, the agencies generated by the ritualization of speech—from obvious figures such as orators, priests, poets, and philosophers, to less familiar ones, such as *sodales* (co-convivialists), *vates* (specialists in both song and sacrifice), and *cinaedi* (expressive dancers, the antitypes of *sodales*). The methods used to interpret such passages, and thus, more generally, to describe the Roman system of song and speech, will be familiar to any classicist, although the conclusions drawn from the material are for the most part new. By and large, the examples I draw on are taken from what is customarily, if anachronistically, referred to as "Latin literature," specifically, texts and fragments of poetry, oratory, philosophy, history, romance, and technical treatises of one sort or another. Where possible I have supplemented such passages with reference to relevant epigraphical and visual material; but I cannot claim to have reviewed the latter categories of evidence in their entirety.

As for understanding the significance of Roman song, that entails a shift of perspective, an opening outward toward fieldwork in other traditions and toward anthropological and cultural theory more generally. If the terminology and argument of this book seem to bear some resemblance to the interpretation of Greek verbal culture advanced in recent years by Gregory Nagy, Bruno Gentili, Claude Calame, and others, that is no accident, since their work prompted my own investigation. But because of the long and complicated history of reading Roman culture as a deficient variant of Greek, I decided early on not to rely on Greek models or Greek evidence except where absolutely necessary. This avoidance was perhaps just as well, because on my reading of the Roman material, the boundary between oral and written, which preoccupies much scholarship on Greek culture, ends up being less important than the ongoing negotiation between the everyday and the special. Song in Roman culture is not coextensive with performance and orality.[1] Although performance and orality are certainly key aspects of the embodied practices of the Romans as of the Greeks, so too are reading, writing, composing, making, playing, dancing, miniaturizing, impersonating, and copying, all of which figure as well in the present discussion. The theatricalization of the everyday, a phenomenon that has rightly received special attention among Romanists, can also be understood as but a single instance of the larger pattern of ritualization that concerns us here.[2]

Ritualization has been the subject of important and wide-ranging discussion in recent years. Among the scholars of ritual whose work has been most helpful in preparation of this study are Roy Rappaport, who interprets ritual as an evolutionary response to the "chaos-inducing potential" of everyday speech; Catherine Bell, who has discussed ritualization (again, across a range of social formations) as a practice generating certain types of social agency; and Michael Taussig, who attempts (following the lead of Walter Benjamin) to reconnect ritualized language with other mimetic activities, both visual and embodied.[3] Despite differences in outlook and conclusions, all three of these scholars may be regarded as resisting the Enlightenment project of "peeling away" the semiotic from the embodied, a project that has had as one of its specific manifestations the tendency among classicists to interpret Roman literature as a free-floating system of signs and texts rather than as traces of embodied practice.[4] Perhaps not surprisingly, then, this shift of attention to practice in turns allows us to revive the neglected insights of earlier interpreters of ancient culture, such as Giambattista Vico, who insisted on the social force of linguistic creativity, and Auguste Comte, who through his study of the interconnection of verbal and visual mimesis came to the conclusion that "voluntary signs are always true social institutions" — a conclusion reinforced by the material gathered here.[5] Long before a misunderstood version of Saussure became an unexamined mantra of the intelligentsia, Comte warned that the "sign cannot have originated in arbitrary convention" and observed that, while each individual word may have an arbitrary relationship to the object or concept it represents, language in practice is never arbitrary: it is always expressed through bodies in concrete social situations.[6]

The assumption underlying this book, namely that Roman culture is to be understood as a system of practices, connects it to my own earlier research, particularly *The Politics of Latin Literature*. There I examined the macrorelations of power, such as class, gender, and national identity, that sustain and are sustained by literary production, broadly understood. Here I consider instead the microrelations, between voice and body, imitator and imitated, everyday and special, living and dead, without which (paraphrasing Bell paraphrasing Foucault) macrorelations cannot endure. Despite its fluidity, song, like its narrower subtype, poetry, is of the essence of power. The struggle among various agents to master and control song is itself testimony to this power. Ritualization provides us with a model for understanding how song's power comes to be through the constitution of agents whose ritual mastery carries over beyond the confines of the immediate ritual context. Roman singers' ritual mastery is a prototype of the large-scale relations of power (aristocrat and peasant, emperor and senate, male and female, master and slave) more commonly studied by ancient historians.

In ascribing to song what are in effect foundational powers, we are venturing into an area of inquiry inaugurated more than half a century ago by Walter Benjamin. Indeed, we might regard Roman song as a quintessential manifestation of what Benjamin described as the mimetic faculty, "the nature through which culture creates second nature."[7] Benjamin's interest in the mimetic faculty, which he saw as generating a wide array of human activities from astrology and magic through painting, poetry, and cinema, was prompted by reflection on transformation in human interaction and communication brought about by new technologies of photography, film, and sound recording in the nineteenth and twentieth centuries. He recognized that the impact of those technologies could only be explained in terms of the long history of mimesis and of struggle over the organization of its power. For Benjamin and his successors, mimesis is both a faculty with a history and a faculty whose products grant us access to history.[8] It is in the spirit of denaturalizing or defamiliarizing the mimetic practices and products of classical Rome (and, by implication, its successor regimes) that this study is conceived.

My argument concerning the relationship between ritualized speech and social order takes the form of six assertions, each developed in a separate chapter, with description of the system of song and speech interwoven throughout.

1. *Ritualization of language, that is, the transfiguration of speech into song, founds Roman culture and empowers agents within it.* This point is explored through close examination of the evidence pertaining to the rite of the Salian priests, a performance encompassing language, bodies, and ritual objects that the Romans took (with good reason) to be older than the city of Rome itself. As we shall see, the abstractions materialized by the rite, and the agencies constituted through it, are in effect definitive of Rome as a community distinct from what came before and what exists outside. Roman song makes the Roman world.

2. *The power of agents empowered by ritualization spills over from the immediate context of ritualization.* The Salian *sodales* become Salian *sodales* through the performance of the Salian rite. But *sodalitas*, the condition of "boon companionship," does not cease to have an impact once the rite is over. Instead, the ritual mastery associated with *sodalitas* spills over into other ritualized contexts, both convivial and theatrical, and into everyday existence as well. Indeed, one of the functions of sodalician song is to make of the *sodalis* the type of agent whose actions matter in other areas of Roman life. Even the narrowly poetic tradition (poetry being a subset of song) recapitulates within itself the dynamic interplay between mastery of the protocols of *sodalitas* and the creation of new strategies of ritualization.

3. *Recognition of the contrast between ritualized and nonritualized language and of the power of the former vis-à-vis the latter permeates the textual*

remains of Roman culture, informs the lore of song, and accounts for struggles over definition and mastery. The tension between song and speech is articulated in the Roman lexicon as a contrast between *carmen* and *locutio*, and the struggle over mastery of special or ritualized speech informs the interdependence of words for singing (based on the root *can-*) and words for authoritative utterance, regardless of form (based on the root *dic-*). Tracing the history of *carmina* gives us a comprehensive sense of the contexts in which language can be and is ritualized. Exploring the Roman lore of the origin of song—in metalworking, in imitation of birds, in the music of the spheres—allows us to identify a discourse whose premises closely match and confirm our earlier account of the distinctively Roman abstractions materialized by songs such as the *Carmen Saliare*.

4. *The practice of ritualization and the spillover into new contexts entail misrecognition, especially of the relationship between body and voice.* Although song, as language, is without doubt a bodily practice, an exercise of both mimetic and semiotic capacities, it is represented by Roman singers themselves as a liberated or disembodied use of the voice (in this respect the decapitated Orpheus is an emblem of both pathos and power). In particular, Roman poets struggle to represent the impossible relationship between *ludus,* or play, as an activity of the body, and *carmen,* or song, as an expression of the voice. Play turns out to be a crucial element of hegemonic Roman culture, not as a release from the labor of the everyday but as a proving ground for mastery. Those who transcend play, who carry the discipline of play into new realms, represent themselves as having transcended the body. Their liberation from the body is a social liberation as well, because the passage through *ludus* marks the free adult in contrast to the childish and the enslaved. This misrecognition or misrepresentation of the relationship between body and voice (and slave and free) underlies Rome's ability to organize mimesis as part of "the long search culminating in Enlightenment civilization."[9] In a more immediate sense, it conforms to the observation that the "'end' of ritualization" is "the production of a 'ritualized body'"[10] (or, in this case, bodies) of slaves, free men, adults, children—in short, of Romans who matter and Romans who do not.

5. *A historically accurate account of song must find ways to bring to light its incorporated and incorporating aspects.* We cannot examine ancient bodily practice directly, in the way we can examine ancient textual practice, but we can infer it, especially on the basis of analogies and antinomies contained within the texts (and text-like objects) themselves. What is singing likened to? What is it differentiated from? Exploration of likeness leads us to consider analogies between singers and nonhuman actors, especially birds, while exploration of antinomy fore-

grounds as the opposite of the singer the figure of the *cinaedus,* whose practice, paradoxically, consists precisely of exposing what is otherwise misrecognized. What is more, the elite bodily practices associated with or differentiated from birds and overly expressive dancers respectively come to light precisely at the historical moment of their transformation. Thus our investigation allows us not only to resituate bodily practice within history but also to compose at least a partial history of such practice.

6. *Ritualization is about power, but there is no power without resistance.* Hints of this paradox appear in our account of ritualization and innovation within the narrowly poetic tradition, but here we consider evidence of more generalized forms of resistance to the power constituted by the ritual mastery of song. Resistance to the disembodiment of voice can be traced in a countervailing tradition that links song to magic and sacrifice, that is, to the manipulation of bodies. Not surprisingly, inasmuch as it is free males who are disembodied in and through the ritualization of language, the countervailing tradition clusters around the contrast between male and female bodies, and male and female voices. It also manifests itself quite vividly in the context of the funeral, where different versions of funeral song (*laudatio* versus *nenia*) seem to correspond to different conceptualizations of the dead: either as prototypes to be reanimated—that is, signs given new life through mimesis—or as rival beings capable of interacting with the living on their own terms.

The preceding summary—misleading as all summaries are—frames an account of song and related practices of mimesis, play, and art as constitutive of microrelations of power. But macrorelations as well figure in our discussion, because what ends up being founded by song —at least as it survives for us—is not just the Roman community but more particularly the Roman state. State sovereignty is made manifest in the Salian rite; the state's dependence on the cooperation of *sodalitates* is theatricalized in civic drama; state rituals are constructed through mimesis of outsiders; control of the state is the ultimate prize in the struggle over mastery of special speech; *ludi* are at any given moment personal, fractional, and civic in impact; indeed, the localized misrecognition of voice's dependence on body is, if writ large, the open secret of state power, what everyone knows not to know.[11] The agents empowered by ritualization are agents of and through the state. As agents of the state, singers enter history, acknowledge a before and an after, a contrast between ritual "time out of time" and political "time after time," between death as a different mode of being and death as nonbeing. For this reason, ritual, as well as ritualization, is crucial to our discussion. The specific rituals of the *salii,* the *ludi saeculares,* and rites of passage (such as initiation and funeral) construct agents in relation to the state and make of the state itself a transhistorical agent, ascribing to it a ritual mastery whose power spills over beyond the bounds of the ritual context, beyond the bounds of context as experienced by any other agent.

And so this book is not just about practices within Rome, but also about practices through which Rome becomes what it is. It seeks to recover the cacophony of instruments through which is created not (with all due respect to Kandinsky) *the* music of the spheres, but *a* music of the spheres, that is, the song of Rome.

ONE· SONG AND FOUNDATION

S ONG ENTERS ROME IN THE CONTEXT OF RITUAL. THE EARLI-
est surviving use of the word for singing—the verb *cano,
canere*—is found in a self-referential fragment of the Salian
hymn in which the singing, dancing, armor-clanging priests
exhort one another to carry out their performance:

Seek and sing to the god: as suppliants to the god sing.

[divum] empt' akante divum: deo supplices can⟨i⟩te.
(Varro *Ling.* 7.27)

Although the text can be reconstructed and interpreted in various
ways, the use of the plural imperative of the verb *cano* is indisputable,
since it is the feature of the fragment that Varro explicitly discusses.[1] It
is also to Varro, among others, that we owe the claim that the Salian
song and rite are as old as the foundation of Rome—an ancient belief
corroborated by the modern discovery of objects resembling the Salian
ancilia or shields in Italian graves dating to the tenth and ninth centuries BC.[2]

From the standpoint of comparative ethnography, it is highly plausible that Rome had and maintained throughout its history a ritual complex that united bodily performance, display of special objects, and collective singing. Cognitive science and cultural anthropology converge
in identifying the organization and ritualization of the human capacity
for imitative action and linguistic creativity as necessary if human societies are to survive over time.[3] Both language and bodily mimesis create
the possibility of imagining alternative worlds and alternative identi-

ties that militate against coordinated activities necessary for the maintenance of a community. Language and mimesis define human beings as social creatures, yet in the absence of ritual, language and mimesis threaten to disrupt human communities and prevent their reproduction. As ritualized language, song operates in tandem with ritualized action to counter the divisive effects of "the linguistically liberated imagination,"[4] even as it assigns meaning to the objects that make concrete and material "the ultimate sacred postulates" that it articulates.[5] Although song is eventually dislodged from ritual, much as poetry is dislodged from song, still the authority of song derives from its origin both historically and pragmatically in ritual: the complex of action, object, and verbal performance, whereby, in Rappaport's bracing formulation, "the unfalsifiable supported by the undeniable yields the unquestionable, which transforms the dubious, the arbitrary, and the conventional into the correct, the necessary, and the natural."[6] For this reason we begin our study of song with investigation of its emergence in and through ritual. Each and every instance of song within Roman culture relies upon practices of ritualization analogous to those found in the Salian rite. And the Salian rite, in turn, can be interpreted as a self-referential reflection on song's role in the foundation and maintenance of social order and on song's power to transform the everyday into the eternal.

The Materialization of Sovereignty

If the Salian performance exemplifies ritual as foundational social act, what it founds is distinctive to Rome. Like all rituals, it connects the here and now with a hypostasized world beyond and, in so doing, validates certain aspects of the here and now. In Rappaport's terms, it "materializes the abstractions" of a particular community.[7]

The Romans themselves point the way to identification of the abstractions materialized by the Salian rite through their emphasis on the interdependence of the rite and the city.[8] The Salian song is said to be as old as Rome; the Salian *ancilia* are called "pledges of power" (*pignora imperii*); the armor-bearing priests dance about within the archaic *pomerium,* or city limits.[9] No doubt other songs and rituals occupied the inhabitants of Latium at the time of the emergence of Rome as a distinctive place, but it is the Salian song that is specifically assigned to that era. Narratives of the origin of the Salian priesthood attribute its establishment to Numa, the second king of Rome, the founder of all nonmilitary aspects of the city's existence and counterpart to Romulus, the general who secures the city against its enemies.[10] As cult objects, the Salian *ancilia* are said to be the responsibility of priests who are themselves "under the guardianship" of the three deities associated with Rome's enduring sovereignty, namely Jupiter, Mars, and Quirinus.[11]

Even as it acknowledges the importance of internal cohesion and appropriate use of military force in securing the city, the rite speaks to the psychological commitments that bind the Roman people together, specifically what Michael Taussig refers to as "the public secret" or "knowing what not to know." As Taussig argues, following Benjamin, Canetti, Pitt-Rivers, and others, secrecy is at the heart of power, and acceptance of power in a complex society entails not only public belief but also "public unbelief."[12] In the words of Walter Benjamin, "truth is not a matter of exposure which destroys the secret, but a revelation which does justice to it."[13] In the case of the Salian rite, the public secret is openly displayed or revealed in the form of the twelve *ancilia*. According to legend, one of these *ancilia* is divine in origin and fell from the skies into the palace of King Numa.[14] Having been informed by an oracle that the survival of the Roman state depended on the safety of the shield, Numa had a craftsman named Mamurius Veturius create eleven replicas, which, together with the one divine talisman, constitute the set of *ancilia* carried and banged upon during the Salian song and dance. What is not generally noted in scholarly discussion of the rite is the inconsistency between the story of the single *ancile* of divine origin and the repeated use of the plural (or, perhaps better, collective) expression *pignora imperii,* talismans of power, to refer to the *ancilia* as a group.[15] In a sense, this inconsistency strengthens the identification of the *ancilia* as a public secret by duplicating the deceit. First there is the manufacture of eleven false talismans, a piece of deceit made brazenly public precisely by the banging and clanging on the shields: apparently all sound and look the same, yet one is understood to be divine. But then there is the publication of the secret that the shields as a group determine Rome's fate: indeed they are hung on the walls of the Regia, and it is generally understood that should they ever move of their own accord, Rome would be in mortal danger.[16]

Comparison with an ancient Chinese legend concerning nine identical bronze tripods is instructive, for there the ritual objects are also both the source and the sign of sovereignty.[17] Whoever controls the tripods is sure to have political and military preeminence. Like the *ancilia,* the tripods are everyday objects made special through replication and the "waste" of expensive metal. As Wu Hung notes, the tripods disappear as marks of sovereignty when Chinese society has accumulated enough surplus to build recognizably monumental structures—walls, temples, and the like. But unlike the *ancilia,* which are constituted as a public secret precisely by their display, the nine tripods are generally out of sight. Their movement, rather than being observed by guardians in the temple or palace, is inferred from shifts in political and military power. In effect, the same "problem"—the need to materialize in ritual the abstract concept of a sovereign state—is solved in different yet recognizably similar ways in the Roman and the Chinese traditions. In both cases, what the community knows not to know (the identity of the true talisman, the nonexistence of the tripods) constitutes within the social world the unity that is promised by the mythic assertion of a connection between the object(s)' well-being and communal security.

In Rome, the sovereignty that is made material in the circuit of the dancers and in the double deception of the *ancilia* is linked to a transcendent cosmic order by the accompanying song. This is not to say that the song makes the connection explicit (although certainly the myth concerning the origin of the *ancilia* recounted by Ovid does, and it is not out of the question that this myth was sung as part of the rite);[18] rather, the coexistence of a song to, about, and summoning the gods, with a bodily performance and a display of objects making the abstraction "sovereignty" concrete, connects the here and now of sovereignty with the "ultimate sacred postulates" of the Roman people. Sovereignty, which, after all, is nothing but a contingent notion arising from a particular set of historical and political circumstances, is made to seem a component of an ineffable reality. It, like the eleven shields of human manufacture, is the Nietzschean artifice to which the "reality" of divine sanction has been "lyingly added."[19]

Transformation, Revelation, Composition

While the legend of the manufacture of the *ancilia* explicitly identifies them as talismans of sovereignty, it also implicitly links such sovereignty with craftsmanship, with the ability to transform raw materials into objects of a different ontological status. Ovid states that the maker of the shields, Mamurius Veturius, is rewarded by having his name included in the hymn, while other versions of the etiological legend indicate that Mamurius is driven out of Rome—a development not incompatible with inclusion in the hymn, simultaneous honor and expulsion being the fate of many a scapegoat.[20] Some scholars have suspected that the legend of Mamurius Veturius is an Augustan addition to Salian lore, perhaps designed as an explanation of the refrain *mamuri veturi* ascribed to the song.[21] But the appearance of Mamurius as artisan of a new palladium in a story assigned to the early first century BC is an unlikely coincidence and suggests either a tradition of naming craftsmen Mamurius (the way a certain kind of *vates* is regularly named Marcius) or at least circulation of the story of the Salian Mamurius prior to the end of the republic.[22] Several scholars have gone so far as to argue that the name

Mamurius Veturius is, in effect, an adaptation of the expression "crafts-man of old" or "ancient craftsman" to the form of early Etruscan per-sonal names,[23] and at least one early depiction of *ancilia* (fourth cen-tury BC) emphasizes the presence of the craftsman in the act of making the metallic shields.[24] Whether the craftsman in question was under-stood to be Mamurius Veturius cannot be known, but the rite that he made possible through his replication of the divine *ancile* shows all the hallmarks of one expressly concerned with the symbiotic relationship between craftsmanship and political power in a newly emergent state. Finally, a bronze cart from Bisenzio dating to the eighth century BC has recently been interpreted as depicting a performance that combines as-pects of a Salian-like performance with other features that resemble the Mamurralia, or ritual expulsion of Mamurius.[25]

Giuseppe Colonna, who is to be credited with making the connec-tion between the early shield disks from Norchia and Veii and the Salian *ancilia*, makes a further pertinent observation concerning the *ancilia* without fully developing its implications. He describes the bilobate *an-cilia* as products of the "metallization" of oxhide shields that would have served as the more common defensive weaponry of early peoples for whom elaborate metalwork was a rare commodity.[26] In other words, the *ancilia*, as products of specialized skills of metallurgy, would have coexisted with shields of a simpler, more everyday sort, produced by the preparation of animal hides. The metallic nature of the *ancilia* is a fact repeatedly emphasized in the ancient references to the rite: because the *ancilia* are made of metal, the Salian dancers are able to generate their characteristic ruckus, their clangor, as it is sometimes called.[27] Yet a contrast between the metallic and the organic appears elsewhere in the body of evidence concerning the ritual. At one end of the historical spectrum, the ritual cart from Bisenzio depicts a band of men banging on small disks as well as a large mammal (a bear or wolf, or perhaps a human being in the costume of a wolf?) in chains, a plowman with an ox, and the performance of animal sacrifice: if Calvetti's association of the rite with one similar to that of the Salian priests at Rome is correct, then the cart also provides evidence that the relationship between the organic and the metallic is intrinsic to the ritual complex.[28] A millen-nium later, a fourth-century AD calendrical mosaic marking the month of March seems to illustrate the Mamurralia by depicting a group of men in Salian attire striking the hide of an animal.[29] Literary testimonia contribute to the foregrounding of the relationship between organic and metallic by speaking of the beating of hides and the beating of metal shields in contexts evoking Mamurius. Servius reports that at the festi-val of Mamurius an unspecified "'they' strike a skin with branches in imitation of the craft" (*pellem virgis feriunt ad artis similitudinem*, Aen.

7.188)[30]—but which craft, tanning or metalworking? Johannes Lydus has the participants in the rite beating the *ancilia* while calling the name of Mamurius (a claim that fits descriptions elsewhere of the Salian refrain *mamuri veturi*), but then says that the common people, observing this, interpret it as marking the beating and expulsion of Mamurius himself (*De Mens.* 4.49). If nothing else, the Salian rite and the related if less well-attested rite of the Mamurralia would seem to invite comparison with widely attested rituals and myths that celebrate and mediate the impact of transformational crafts on traditional communities.

Such comparative material, from ancient Greece, the Near East, and West Africa, is the subject of a series of studies (mostly still unpublished) by Sandra Blakely, who pays particular attention to the art of metalworking, its disruptive force, and the range of ritual and mythic accommodations thereof.[31] As Blakely emphasizes, metalworking is a specialized skill. It tends to require the assemblage of materials from both near and far. Its processes are dirty and dangerous, its products extraordinarily valuable—to agriculture, to warfare, and to the development of a class system based on circulation and display of durable luxury items. One may go so far as to say that the formation of the state as a political and social entity entailing concentration of power, regulation of access to the external world, and specialization of labor is unlikely to occur without the prompting of metalworking. Metalworking is a historical disruption and an ongoing source of potential rivalry to other types of authority: hence the frequent strategy of identifying the chief or king as himself a skilled craftsman.[32]

In the Greek world, rites and stories that explore or mediate the relationship between metalworkers and the community center around daimonic figures, such as the *telchinoi*, *korybantes*, and *kabeiroi*, who sing and dance in company and are carefully situated with respect to political authority. As Blakely notes, the *daimones* most closely connected with the process of metal production and metalworking, namely the *telchines* and the *daktyloi*, are also most likely to be described as morally suspect or hostile to authority, whereas those associated with the products of the forge, especially the armor-bearing *kourētes*, are regarded as supportive of political leadership, as for example in the stories that present the *kourētes* as protectors of the newborn Zeus.[33] The connection Blakely establishes between sites of metallurgical activity and myths or rituals concerning the *daimones* is also applicable to Etruria and Latium, where metallurgy is well attested for the period coinciding with the development of cities, which is also the period in which Roman lore places the origin of the Salian rite.[34] Equally suggestive is the Roman inclusion of the organization of metalworkers among the foundational activities of Numa.[35] Such associations, however, need not imply that the Salian rite (or, for that matter, the myths of *daimones*) is exclusively, or even predominantly, a rite "about" metalworking or "for" metalworkers. Rather, following Blakely, we should regard metalworking as synecdoche (part for whole) for all of the transformative activities that link the inside and the outside of the community, nature and culture, historical time and cosmic cycle, and that must be managed by the king (or his representatives) in order for his authority—but also for the sovereignty and well-being of the community—to be secure.[36] As Mary Helms notes, crafting in a traditional context tends to be understood not as a creative skill used to generate a unique or original product, but as a means of "elucidating or illuminating the understanding of things . . . making manifest things and ideas already existing in another state . . . moving or communicating between qualitatively different cosmological realms."[37] In this sense, song, too, can be considered a craft, for it "makes manifest things and ideas already existing in another state," it grants access to the secrets of the cosmos, by asserting the "ultimate sacred postulates" of the Roman people. To follow the terminology employed by Rappaport, we may say that craft, like ritual, like song, imposes form upon the substance of the world.

In Greek myth, the metallurgical *daimones* are responsible for, among other things, the invention of music—a topic to which we return in our discussion of the ancient lore of song.[38] The specific connection between music—or, more precisely, song—and craftsmanship is more fully developed in the late medieval and early modern German tradition of *Meistergesang*, which provides a different sort of comparandum for the Salian rite from that offered by the African rituals. In the tradition of *Meistergesang*, guilds of skilled craftsmen compete in the creation and performance of song cycles. Many of the surviving songs manifest a construction in accordance with measure and number ("nach Mass und Zahl") that exactly corresponds to the work habits of the singers as craftsmen;[39] indeed, measure and number were relevant to *Meistergesang* not just with respect to song forms and metrical patterns, but even "in the process of the preparation of the material and the formulation of the songs' contents."[40] For the German singers, the preexistent literary tradition (interestingly enough, Ovid's *Metamorphoses*, a poem about transformations, figures prominently) constituted the raw material out of which new songs, often with a theological dimension, were fashioned, in a process analogous to the reworking of raw materials for the production of objects of everyday use.

Comparison with *Meistergesang* points to the central, as opposed to incidental, concern with singing as a process that characterizes the Salian rite, despite its equally strong interest in other forms of craftsmanship. The procedure of *Meistergesang*, whereby the aspiring singer fits words and rhymes to the tones set by the masters, helps to explain Festus's description of the Salian performers as "composing" hymns to the gods (carmina . . . quae a Saliis sacerdotibus componebantur, Fest. 3 L), a notion that would seem to contradict the suggestion that the song is handed down from generation to generation "in books" (in libris Saliorum, Varro Ling. Lat. 6.14; cf. in libris sacrorum, Fest. 124 L).[41] The verb compono in Latin means to fit words and music, or words and rhythm together;[42] as a result we can imagine a process whereby the Salian priests do in fact "compose" on each and every occasion even as they preserve the age-old song of their company. Ovid, in describing Numa's contribution to the Salian ritual, reports that

> He named them Salii from their leaping dance,
> gave them weapons, and words to sing in set rhythms.

> iam dederat Saliis a saltu nomina dicta
> armaque et ad certos verba canenda modos.
>
> (Ov. Fast. 3.387–88)

Ovid confirms the understanding of the Salian rite as tripartite (movement, objects, and words) while at the same time suggesting that the verbal performance is in effect a fitting together of language and rhythm, much like the procedure of the Meistersinger, and much, we might note, like the rhythmical hammering of metalworkers. At a sociohistorical level as well, the comparison with the Meistergesang, as with the African rituals, is telling. The close association of Meistergesang (in opposition to the courtly minnesong, which it displaced) with emerging urban culture, with coordinated activities among groups of men, with the systematization of processes of manufacturing, reminds us of the more general principle that the actions and attitudes enacted in ritual, far from constituting an escape from the everyday conditions and relations of production, tend to reinforce them. We may not want to go so far as Alan Lomax does when he connects the song and dance of a given community to the very movements "most essential to the activity of the everyday."[43] Yet it still needs to be acknowledged that the Salian rite emphasizes both the process and the product of transformation — in the realm of objects, language, and bodies — and that, in so doing, it facilitates the emergence and maintenance of a social order that, in effect, depends upon transmutability of statuses and identities and the fitting together of heterogeneous parts.

In his discussion of bodies, objects, and song as the three interrelated components of ritual, Rappaport gives relatively short shrift to objects and to the processes that produce them, grouping them with bodies as instances of the materialization of abstractions. But practices such as the African metallurgical rites and the German *Meistergesang* suggest that at least on occasion the objects themselves make a contribution to ritual that is not simply coextensive with that of body. Such seems to be the case in the Salian rite, where the carefully crafted *ancilia* call attention to the double estrangement of culture from nature (first the removal and treatment of hides, then the imitation of hides in metal) while at the same time materializing the possibility of substance's metamorphosis into a new form. In the rite, the removal of hides from animals is in effect an estrangement from nature that is overcome by yet another estrangement—the replacement of hides with bronze. Similarly, everyday language's estrangement from nature is mended by the transformation of language into song. Beyond this double estrangement, the ritual, with its foregrounding of transformed objects, articulates the possibility of transformation as achieving a new stability. There is no assembling and disassembling of the *ancilia:* even after the rite is over, they remain powerful, visible talismans of Rome's security. So too, the performance of the song, the composition or "putting together" of words and music, while it may well take place in the very performance of the rite, ends up being not so much about transformation as a process as it is about transformation as an outcome: the hymns are written down in books and transmitted from one generation to the next. Their availability for performance and reperformance is, paradoxically, the end result of the transformation of everyday language into special speech.

The association of practices resembling the Salian rite with the formation of the particular social order known as the state suggests that Rappaport's own relative neglect of objects may be due to his tendency to focus on pre- or nonstate societies. The state, what Michael Taussig has called "the most masked entity of all possible masked beings,"[44] would seem to require of its members the acknowledgment that at some point the donning of masks stops, the transformation is final. What the performers acquiesce in is the permanence of what they know to have been produced by observable processes undertaken in historical (as opposed to ritual) time. In this respect too, the Salian rite lends itself more to the interpretation of ritual song put forth by Bloch than to the critique thereof by Tambiah. Tambiah criticizes Bloch for seeking a "prior 'real world' of 'brute facts' that religion, as mystification, seeks to hide, as if there are some privileged orders of institutional facts which have a presymbolic or precultural existence."[45] While Tambiah's remarks make sense as a reflection on ritual performance in the abstract, in the case of the Salian rite (and others discussed here in passing) the rite itself establishes a notionally presymbolic or precultural existence in the "naturalness" of human productive activity, human performance, and human language, which can and must be channeled into specific forms and patterns. Even as the rite seeks to connect the here and now to a transcendent order, it acknowledges within itself—it "unconceals" in Rappaport's expression[46]—its own prehistory.

To be fair to the perspective articulated by Tambiah, the transformation materialized by the Salian rite is characterized by potential as well as by limitation. For the Salian rite and song also seem to serve as rite of passage, or initiation, for the participants, a process essential to state formation, but also illustrative of the principle of the finality of transformation. At any given moment the well-being of the archaic community depends on the proper modulation of relations between king and craftsman and between internal and external powers. Over time, its well-being depends in addition on the bringing to adulthood of the next generation of men and women. Such dependence is acute and self-conscious in the early history of the state, which implicitly lays claim to a transhistorical continuity and furthermore requires the reproduction of bodies for purposes of defensive and offensive warfare, not to mention everyday sustenance. Through initiation, young men and women become members of the citizen body; they are, in effect, transformed from one status to another, and their new status remains stable.[47] Especially in Rome, where the very word and concept of *civitas*, or statehood, is derivative of the word for citizen (*civis*)—rather than the other way around—there is no state, not even conceptually, without a means of producing full-fledged adult citizens.

Interpretation of the Salian rite as a type of initiation has been advanced, chiefly by Italian scholars, on a number of grounds.[48] For one thing, the performances of the *salii* are concentrated (perhaps exclusively) in the month of March, commencing with the beginning of the month, the traditional Roman new year, and culminating just before the Liberalia, the feast that marks the assumption of the *toga virilis*, or toga of manhood, by freeborn adolescent males.[49] The Salian rite can thus be seen as a positive counterpart to the rite of the Lupercalia, celebrated in February, also by companies of freeborn young men. The *luperci* are just leaving the wildness and chaos of the liminal period, while the *salii* celebrate initiation from the vantage point of its successful completion.[50] Like their *ancilia*, they are a finished product. Also pointing to initiation are the rare but suggestive testimonia concerning female *saliae*: the *saliae virgines* mentioned by the grammarian Festus (439 L) and the *praesula*, or female lead dancer, mentioned on an inscription at Tusculum (*ILS* 5018). Whether we regard the *saliae virgines* as an instance of transvestism (Torelli's suggestion)[51] or merely allow for a comparable ritual for young women as for young men, the presence of women in at least some Salian celebrations makes it difficult to interpret the rite in strictly military or perhaps even professional terms. But a celebration of successful completion of the rigors of initiation would be as appropriate for young women as for young men. In addition, there is evidence that aspects of the Salian rite are agonistic in character, pitting one company of *salii* against another: such competitions are themselves typical of initiatory complexes.[52] And the identification of the leader of the process of initiation as a skilled craftsman is attested in a number of traditional communities as well.[53]

Perhaps the most intriguing evidence linking the Salian rite to initiation is to be found in the content and form of the song and dance. Dionysius of Halicarnassus reports that the *salii* dance sometimes as a group, sometimes in alternating units: the term for the latter arrangement, *parallaks*, finds an echo in Plutarch's description of the crane dance, or *geranos*, that Theseus led after rescuing the Athenian youth from King Minos's labyrinth on Crete, itself an event that serves as mythic prototype for the escape of initiates from the rigors of initiation.[54] As far as can be reconstructed, choruses of *salii* danced in response to the figures set by a lead dancer or *praesul*. Their dance figures are indicated in Latin by use of the unusual word *amptruare* (also *redamptruare*).[55] This word, in turn, has been connected with the expression TRUIA written on a seventh-century BC oinochoe (wine pitcher) from Tragliatella. It seems more than coincidence that the word TRUIA is there a caption for a drawing of a labyrinth.[56]

The oinochoe from Tragliatella is a puzzling object by any measure, but in recent years great headway has been made in its interpretation.[57] Mauro Menichetti, who analyzes the images on the jug as commemorative of a ritual of initiation, notes the presence of figures with and without *perizoma*, or loincloth, perhaps a mark of transformed status, and associates the boat, the goats, the birds, and the small groups of mixed male and female figures with the legend of Theseus and Ariadne—a story that features escape from a labyrinth and performance of a crane dance by companies of free youths, all as accompaniments to ritual initiation in Greek rite and legend.[58] The oinochoe also depicts a company of shield-bearing youths being led in dance (or military exercises, the two often coinciding),[59] as well as two pairs of heterosexual couples copulating. On the latter point as evidence of the successful transition to adulthood, we might note as well the oversize and in some cases erect penises of the "*salii*" depicted on the eighth-century BC cart from Bisenzio discussed by Calvetti (they appear "col sesso maschile evidenziato").[60]

A pair of horsemen, perhaps to be understood as exiting the labyrinth, also appear on the oinochoe. The presence of horsemen suggests status differentiation between equestrian and foot soldiers, and hence between different social ranks. It has also put commentators in mind of the *lusus Troiae*, or horse dance, a ritual given great prominence during the reign of Augustus and described in book 5 of the *Aeneid* as part of the celebration commemorating the anniversary of the death of Anchises.[61] Vergil expressly likens the figure traced by the horses to the Cretan labyrinth (*ut quondam Creta fertur Labyrinthus*, 5.588) and employs descriptive language (*irremediabilis error*, 5.591) echoed in the depiction of the labyrinth on the Daedalan gates of the temple of Apollo at Cumae (*inextricabilis error*, also line final, 6.27). Indeed, Vergil goes so far as to state that the boys led by Ascanius constitute *Troia*, their line-up *Troianum agmen*, or a Trojan formation (*Troiaque nunc, pueri Troianum dicitur agmen*, 5.602).[62] In context the references mark the renewal of the city of Troy in the persons of the male youth who are successfully coming of age. But the description of the labyrinthine pattern also fits the archaic conception of *Truia/Troia* as the place from which youth must extricate themselves in order to pass on to adulthood.[63] The episode from Vergil and the myth of Theseus can be readily understood as referring to initiation, the rite of passage to adulthood for young men and, in the case of the Theseus story, for women as well. It seems plausible to suggest, then, that the oinochoe from Tragliatella and the Salian rite, which it parallels in certain details, are also concerned, at least in part, with the passage of companies of youths from adolescence to full membership in the adult community.[64] The indication of the ancient testimonia that companies of *salii* include both younger and older men[65] reinforces the point that in Rome, as founded by the Salian rite, transformation is perfective, or final in its impact. The rite depicts both the process and the outcome of initiation: and the outcome remains stable, as long as the *ancilia* remain intact in Rome and the Salian song remains secure in the priests' books.

Delegation, or Part for Whole

In objecting to the view that the Salian rite is an instance of initiation, Jörg Rüpke rightly observes that, at least in historical times, the *salii* constitute an officially designated *collegium:* in effect, a standing committee of the Roman political-religious establishment.[66] Dionysius of Halicarnassus, who provides the most detailed account of the rite, indicates that the dancers are drawn from the class of patricians (*Ant. Rom.* 2.70.1). This information, far from outweighing the evidence for initiation, points to yet another component of the Roman canon materialized by the rite: the principle of delegation, or interchangeability of part and whole. At what stage a small sector of the population came to stand for the initiates as a whole is uncertain (or perhaps delegation had always been a feature of the rite); but in its historically developed form, the rite materializes the abstraction of delegation in any of a number of ways.[67]

In the first place, patrician males stand in not only for all males but, if we understand the rite as initiatory, for females as well. Although women seem to have formed part of the Salian complex at some point,[68] most references to the rite, including Vergil's double company of young and old men, refer explicitly and exclusively to men. In addition, the sources intimate that the presence of non-Salian outsiders is somehow crucial to the completion of the rite. For example, the passage from Lucilius describing the Salian dance indicates that the *vulgus* or "mob" copies the movements set by the *praesul*, or lead dancer of the Salian company (Lucilius 348 W). Is *vulgus* just a coarse and ironic way of referring to the twelve or twenty-four or however many young patricians are performing the dance, or is there a sense that the common folk observing the rite are expected to mimic it as well?[69] Much later, the grammarian Diomedes reports that Numa "led the Salian dancers as they circulated through the city" (*induceret salios iuniores circulantes per urbem*, *GLK* 1.476). The verb *circulo* is more highly charged than the English "circulate" suggests: throughout Roman history *circuli* were small groups of nonelite citizens who gathered in fora and crossroads and were regarded by the elite as in need of careful political oversight.[70] Diomedes' use of *circulo, -are* thus takes for granted that the *salii*, in their movement around the city, either require or attract the presence of *circuli*. Lydus, too, implicates observers in the Salian ritual when he reports that it is they (*hoi polloi*, or the common folk) who interpret the striking of the *ancilia* as the beating of Mamurius himself: *hos ton Mamourion autoi paizoien hoi typtontes* (*De Mens.* 4.49).

Whatever the intention of the performers, ancient descriptions document the rite's strong visual and aural impact. Thus, Dionysius (who may be following a Latin annalist here)[71] invites any who doubt his interpretation of the etymology of the name of the *salii* to look to the nature of their dance (*Ant. Rom.* 2.70.4–5), which he describes in some detail, and furthermore justifies the association of Roman *salii* with Greek *kourētes* on the basis of the amount of noise generated by each group. Plutarch describes the dance of the *salii* as "chiefly the task of the feet, for they move gracefully, reciprocally dancing with strength and agility various figures and transformations, all in a rhythmical pattern that is both swift and complex" (*Vit. Num.* 13.5). Perhaps of relevance as well is the high degree of spectacularization, with corresponding exchange of identifications, characteristic of the related practice of *lusus Troiae*. In Vergil's account, Ascanius and his fellow youth "put on a show" (*ostendat, Aen.* 5.550), "strut their stuff . . . before the gaze of their parents" (*incedunt . . . ante ora parentum,* 5.553), who, in exchange, "welcome the anxious youth with applause and rejoice to observe them" (*excipiunt plausu pavidos gaudentque tuentes,* 5.575).[72] If, as Bell argues, "the implicit dynamic and 'end' of ritualization—that which it does not see itself doing—can be said to be the production of a 'ritualized body,'"[73] then we can understand the Salian ritual as producing a hierarchy of ritualized bodies wherein some count for all.

This relationship of part to whole (within the company and between the company and the community) seems to apply to the *ancilia,* or ritual objects, as well. Although the legend of the invention of the *ancilia* asks us to think of eleven *ancilia* as replicas of the single authentic talisman, the case is, objectively speaking, that one of twelve *ancilia* displayed during the rite (not recognizable as such) has a divine origin that the others lack. Again, a part of the body of objects has a significance that the rest acquire only by association. Yet taken as a group, the *ancilia* constitute a part of the ritual that remains significant after the ritual is over. Back in the Regia, their movement (or, ideally, lack thereof) is carefully monitored. They do not cease to be *pignora imperii* after the ritual of sovereignty has run its course. Synecdoche becomes a way of infusing the everydayness of political sovereignty with the sacredness of ritual, and more generally of implicating the population as a whole in the performance of a few. Indeed, when the *ancilia* are represented as moving, it is a movement of the group as whole, not simply the one sent from the sky. As Erik Gunderson observes, "we have an assertion of the collectivity that stands as a pledge of the one even as the one pledges the value of the whole"—a succinct statement of the principle of sovereignty, which is thus reinforced in the Roman context by the interrelated processes of transformation, delegation, and substitution.[74]

In a more general sense, each of the major components of the ritual —the song, the dance, and the objects—has the potential to evoke and even stand for the ritual as a whole. It is as if they carry within themselves a memory of ritual unity, the potent blend of unfalsifiable and undeniable, that can be reactivated on other occasions and under other circumstances. Thus, although the *ancilia,* as Borgna's impressive collection of visual evidence indicates, sometimes appear in connection with other Salian accoutrements, often enough they are depicted on their own as tokens of the entire ritual complex.[75] Borgna attempts to differentiate among *ancilia* as worn by the *salii, ancilia* as used otherwise in religious rites, and foreign shields that resemble but do not constitute *ancilia.* Such a subdivision seems unnecessary, since, in effect, the persistence of representations of *ancilia* somehow marked as foreign extends the logic of the core ritual to the realm of artistic representation. After all, the Salian *ancilia* are represented within the Salian legend as foreign in origin (whether from the heavens or Etruria), and their distinctiveness as products of metallurgy is advertised in the very performance of the rite. Indeed, their arrival from afar is crucial to their status as talismans of power,[76] a fact the inclusion of seemingly alien representations within the artistic tradition confirms rather than undermines.

As for the *tripudium,* or Salian dance step, it too is both indispensable to the rite and capable, on its own, of evoking it. When Livy wishes to describe the Salian performance in summary form, he mentions *ancilia, carmen,* and *tripudium* in one dense phrase: "They carry the *ancilia* and proceed through the city singing their songs together with the *tripudium* and holy leaping" (*caelestia arma . . . ferre ac per urbem ire canentes carmina cum tripudiis sollemnique saltatu,* 1.20.4). Yet, like the *ancilia* and the song, the *tripudium* becomes dislodged from the rite, migrating, as it were, to other religious contexts, ranging from the indigenous, such as the celebration by the Arval brothers (*CIL* 6.2104a line 32), to the exotic, as when Catullus uses the term to describe the dance of the self-castrating priests of Magna Mater (63.26) or when Apuleius applies it to the dance step of mendicant priests in the Thessalian countryside (*Met.* 8.27). Indeed, different versions of *tripudium* come to be understood as being practiced by and thus characterizing distinctly different populations: Livy speaks of the *tripudia* of the Spaniards (25.17.5) and of individual groups of mountain folk captured by Hannibal (*sui moris tripudiis* 21.41.3). Elsewhere we learn of a *tripudium* specific to the Gauls in Asia (Livy 38.17.4) and of one practiced by the Germans (Tac. *Hist.* 5.17). It is as if the association of *tripudium* with a rite of Roman sovereignty requires writers to clarify that the armed dance of foreigners, although comparable, is in fact distinct from the one that helps to construct the Roman social order. More particularly, *tripudium* takes on the connotation of dance designed to prepare the dancer for the execution of a violent or physically demanding act: Catullus's priests dance the *tripudium* as preparation for the ascent of Mount Ida; Livy's mountaineers perform it to ready themselves for gladiatorial combats staged by Hannibal; and elsewhere in Livy the dance is associated with "the incantations and ululations of those commencing battle" (*cantus incohantium proelium et ululatus et tripudia,* 38.17.4). In augural language the expression *tripudium sollistimum* is used to describe the self-locomotion of otherwise stable natural objects: thus, Appius Claudius gives as examples of this type of omen the tumbling of a solid rock or living tree that has not been cut or hit or pushed,[77] and Cicero and Livy use the phrase to describe the tumbling of grain out of the mouths of gluttonous chickens (Cic. *Div.*1.15.28, 2.34.72; Livy 10.40.4). Inasmuch as the etymology of the term *tripudium* (triple step) suggests an original application of the term to human or perhaps avian activity,[78] applications to self-propelled grain, rocks, or trees, despite their use in augural language, would seem to be extensions from the use of the term to describe human ritual, rather than the other way around.

Even late uses of the term *tripudium* that seem (to some lexicographers at least) to refer merely to dancing in general derive their force from the contrast between the dance described and the canonical ritual performance. Thus, the penultimate paragraph of Seneca's massive work on Stoic physics (*Quaestiones Naturales*) consists of a denunciation of the proliferation of dancing in the present day. The great schools of philosophy are dying out, writes Seneca, but

> The house of Pylades and Bathyllus [famous virtuoso dancers of the Augustan period] thrives through their successors. Many are the students, many the teachers of these skills. The private dance floor resounds throughout the whole city: men and women dance on it. Men and their wives compete with one another as to which displays the flank more enticingly.

> Stat per successores Pyladis et Bathylli domus; harum artium multi discipuli sunt multique doctores. Privatum urbe tota sonat pulpitum; in hoc viri, in hoc feminae tripudiant; mares inter se uxoresque contendunt uter det latus mollius. (Sen. Q. Nat. 7.32.3)

The scene described by Seneca is intended to rouse the reader not just through the contrast with neglected philosophy—"nobody pays attention to philosophy" (*philosophiae nulla cura est*, Q. Nat. 7.32.4) is the way the next, and final paragraph of the treatise commences—but also through an implied contrast with the proper performance of the *tripudium:* in public as opposed to private, with companies of men rivaling one another, not their wives. Similarly, the eunuch-priests who torment Lucius in *The Golden Ass* go about their begging rounds in what could be construed as a parody of the circulating *salii*. They wear various sorts of headgear (cf. the Salian *apices*), white tunics with purple lance-shaped designs (the *salii*, too, have embroidered tunics), yellow shoes, swords and axes (cf. the swords and shields of the *salii*), and "they leap about, stirred on by the tune of the flute, performing a deranged *tripudium*" (*euantes exsiliunt, incitante tibiae cantu, lymphaticum tripudium*, Met. 8.27) —a possible allusion to the Salian dance, also performed to the music of the flute (Dion Hal. *Ant. Rom.* 2.70.5). In Petronius's *Satyricon* four slaves rush into the dining room dancing a *tripudium* to the accompaniment of a full symphony, all for the purpose of removing the lid from a cooking vessel (36.1). Here too, the full irony implicit in the use of the word *tripudium* depends on (and perhaps reinforces) its continuing relevance as the technical term for ritual dance of the sort performed by the *salii*.

In a similar manner but on a grander scale, the practice of singing, retrospectively assigned to the foundational rite of the Salian priests, carries with itself, beyond the immediate context of the rite, the transcendent authority brought into being through the combination of song, bodies, and objects. This is why all the Roman writers who discuss the Salian rite at any length have so much invested in assigning it—in its totality—to the era of the foundation. The authority that inclusion in the rite grants song is an authority that continues to be of interest to the community throughout its historical existence. It is not simply that Salian song is associated with a specific, authorizing point of origin: rather its continued reperformance as song throughout Roman history keeps alive the interconnection of song and ritual and makes possible the "deployment" of ritual "schemes" "beyond the circumference of the rite itself."[79] Roman song, with Salian song as its prototype, must thus be seen as constructing what Bell has called "redemptive hegemony," that is, a "lived ordering of power . . . a practical consciousness of the world . . . and a sense of one's options for social action."[80] But these very options are effectively constrained by the rite's conflation of past and present, foundation and change. It creates a sense of Romanness that is always already what the dominant sector of society requires it to be. Although suggesting that the Salian rite encapsulates an "explicit ideology or a single and bounded *doxa* that defines a culture's sense of reality"[81] would be simplistic, nonetheless the rite is ideological in that it explicitly denies the contingency of present practice.

Whereas in the case of movement and objects the power to evoke the Salian rite and summon its authority is limited to one type of movement (the *tripudium*) and one distinct sort of object (the oddly shaped *ancilia*), in the case of song it is the making special of everyday speech through rhythm and other formal devices that persists, throughout Roman history, in evoking the foundational power of the particular song of the *salii*. The technical term available for the Salian song, *axamenta*, is as specific and restricted in application as the terms *ancilia* and *tripudium*, yet appears in the historical record only once (Fest. 3 L), in contrast to dozens of references to the Salian song as *carmen* or *carmina*. In other words, when the Romans analyze the ritual into its component parts, it is song that signifies the verbal performance of the ritual, the articulation of the unverifiable "ultimate sacred postulates" of the Roman social order. No wonder, then, that from the earliest subsequent references to song, the Romans are concerned with song's ability to connect the here and now with powers beyond, whether in a socially authorized manner (religious hymns, legal formulas, convivial songs, dramatic performances at state-sponsored festivals, poems, calls to arms, etc., all of which are described by the verb *cano* or the noun *carmen*) or in a way that threatens social order (incantations, unregulated vatic performances, defamatory songs directed against fellow citizens, which are also called *carmina*).

Song's capacity to be dislodged from the specific context of the ritual, from ritual "time out of time," and thus to have an impact on changing historical circumstances, is embedded in the very content and style of the ritual song. In its content, the Salian hymn is both unchanging and adaptable. Much of its language seems to have been fixed before the fourth century BC; in the early first century BC it attracted commentary by Aelius Stilo; and near the end of the first century AD an observer tells us that priests perform it without understanding what it means.[82] The song's air of fixity would seem to be crucial to the continuing foundational power of the rite. Yet we are also told of or can infer specific historical adaptations. For instance, the emperor Augustus's name was included in the Salian hymn during his own lifetime — a fact he was proud to record on the *Monumentum Ancyranum* among his accomplishments, or *res gestae* (*Mon. Ancyr.* 10.1). So too was the name of Germanicus added to the hymn, as Tacitus reports in a passage that echoes the phrasing of the Augustan declaration: "that his name be sung in the Salian hymn" (*ut nomen eius Saliari carmine caneretur, Ann.* 2.83.1). Other emperors, too, enjoyed a special relationship with the Salian rite. Marcus Aurelius, according to the *Historia Augusta,* entered the Salian college at age eight, learned and performed all the Salian songs, and held all the offices of the priesthood, namely *praesul, vates,* and *magister* (*SHA* 4.21), while the third-century pretender to the imperial throne, Marcus Aurelius Marius Augustus, an ex-ironworker, was nicknamed "Mamurius Veturius," presumably in honor of his prior occupation, but perhaps out of recognition of his imperial namesake's obsession with the *salii*.[83] The passage that describes the emperor Marcus Aurelius's commitment to the Salian priesthood also records that during its celebrations he, though a youth, received an "omen of empire" (*SHA* 4.3). In like manner Augustus's mention of his inclusion in the Salian hymn comes at the beginning of a sentence that goes on to explain that he was defined by law as "sacrosanct in perpetuity, and that as long as I live the tribunician power shall be mine" (*Mon. Ancyr.* 10.2.).

The Salian rite and Salian hymn thus continue to be associated with political sovereignty even as the nature of that sovereignty changes over time. Although only for Augustus and Germanicus do we have explicit testimony to changes in the content of the hymn, the continuing engagement of the Romans with the Salian rite — from the reorganization of the priesthood in the early republic through the possible application of the refrain to a would-be emperor — suggests a flexibility in the understanding of sovereignty as communicated by a seemingly inflexible song. The pattern of the song, consisting of *axamenta* to individual deities, together with a refrain, created opportunities for transformation within an apparently stable context that successive generations of political leadership successfully deployed to their own advantage.[84]

Acceptance and validation of change in the social order coincides with a founding and refounding of the cosmological order that is understood to make social order possible. Taken as a whole, the Salian performance illustrates the emergence of the divine from ritual. As Rappaport argues, the combination of the apparently reasonable element of language, its potential to make articulate albeit unverifiable claims, with the numinous or affective power of intense, rhythmical, group activity generates the divine as nonmaterial, efficacious, and rationally comprehensible.[85] The Salian ritual, situated at the commencement of the Roman year and associated with the ritual escape from death of the new cadre of initiates is, both verbally in the content of the song and experientially in the ecstatic (the Latin word is *exultatio*) performance of the priests, giving life to the Roman gods. Janus, Juno, Minerva, and presumably others receive their respective *axamenta,* or ritual assertions (Fest. 3 M); and Jupiter, under the guise of Leucesius or Lucetius, bringer of light, is apostrophized in one of the few easily comprehensible fragments (*FPL* frag. 2; Macr. *Sat.* 1.15.4). Ceres and Saturn also seem to figure in the hymn (*FPL* frags. 3 and 7 respectively). The self-address of the priests quoted by Varro *(Ling. Lat.* 7.27) has the Salian performers seeking within (*empetere*) and singing to (*akanere*) the god, a veritable summoning of the divine through energetic movement combined with a naming in language. The priests look inward (*em-*) and, in so doing, hypostatize the deity whom they address (*a-*) as having a separate, external existence.

In addition to the generation and naming of gods through performance of the hymn, such features as the number of priests in the Salian priesthood (multiples of twelve), the singing of the song on the first day of the year (when March is understood as the commencement of the calendar), and, as one late source puts it, "the hymning of Janus in accordance with the months of the Italian year" together identify the Salian hymn as the sort of cosmological creation song familiar from initiatory contexts worldwide.[86] Johannes Lydus's association of *salii* with months of the year gains in credibility when we join it with his further observation, attributed to the earlier writer Fonteius, that Janus, a god who figures more than once in ancient references to the Salian hymn, was worshiped on twelve altars, a piece of information that Macrobius also ascribes to Varro's study of *res divinae*.[87] As Macrobius puts it, "Varro writes in the fifth book of the *Res Divinae* that twelve altars corresponding to the same number of months were dedicated to Janus" (*Varro libro quinto rerum divinarum scribit Iano duodecim aras pro totidem mensibus dedicatas, Sat.* 1.9.16). But even without such explicitly cosmological elements, we are still left with the paradox of a song that in its appeal to permanence and its accommodation of transience confounds the neat categories ethnomusicologists have attempted to impose on song traditions.

Or perhaps it would be better to say that the Salian song incorporates or subsumes modes of song often kept separate within and between societies. In particular, the performance of the hymn seems to include what are sometimes grouped as European and African, or bourgeois and folk musical types.[88] The first type in each pair, it has been argued, "uses rhythm mainly as an aid in the construction of progression to a harmonic cadence," organizing song, like narrative, in terms of a beginning, middle, and an end. "By the time the music does return to home tonic, in the final recapitulation, the sense is clearly one of repetition with a difference. The momentum has elevated the initial material to a new level rather than merely re-presenting it unchanged."[89] The second is characterized by a type of repetition that folds back on itself, creating a "leveling effect, . . . systematically broken up by 'breaks' or 'cuts' . . . that only intensify the rhythmic flow once it is resumed."[90] With this type of music "the thing (the ritual, the dance, the beat) is 'there for you to pick it up when you come back to get it.'"[91] For James Snead, the differences between them speak to a difference in cosmological outlook, with the first focusing on and organizing movement over time and corresponding to a cosmological sense of the world as continuing to develop from an archetypal moment of origin, the other emphasizing periodic renewal of the world, the stability that derives precisely from the fact of repetition, and the use of music as a means of moving the participant out of the necessary directionality of life into a transcendent realm of permanence through repetition.[92] Whether we interpret the difference between these types of music in terms of ethnic or other cultural distinctions, it seems clear that Salian music falls simultaneously into both categories.[93] It is a song of the unfolding of Roman history from its origin in the sense that its very performance continually reminds Roman observers of the foundation of the city and its culture. But it is also a song shaped by the insistent rhythm of the dancers (the so-called *tripudium*), interrupted by lunging or leaping movements, *exulta-*

tiones, or cuts that "intensify the repetitive flow once it is resumed."[94] Its double chorus, the kinetic "call and response" of the *praesul* and *vulgus,* and the hymn's (eventual) performance by a delegation of initiates embody the dynamic forces of the periodic renewal of the Roman cosmos.

Exultation and Mimesis

According to Rappaport, ritual seeks to mend a world torn apart by the slashing effects of everyday language. Language is the source of humankind's estrangement from nature, and language, in the context of ritual, is instrumental to its reembedding in nature. We have seen how other components of the Salian rite play with the boundary between nature and culture. The rite introduces objects that are the product of art yet identical to an *ancile* of divine origin, that result from human reworking of metal yet end up resembling oxhides. So too, the characteristic bodily actions of the Salian rite—that is, the beating of shields in "imitation of the art" of either tanning or metalworking, the thumping dance that seems to mimic the hopping of birds—materialize the convergence of nature and culture that the rite seeks to effect. A similar merging of nature and culture characterizes the Salian song, a fact that becomes evident when we consider its description as *exultatio.*

In defining the word *redantruare,* the grammarian Festus explains that "it is a term used in the course of the exultations of the *salii,* 'when the lead dancer performs the figure,' that is, displays the movements, the same movements are given back to him" (*redantruare dicitur in Saliorum exultationibus: 'cum praesul amptruavit' quod est, motus edidit, ei referuntur invicem idem motus,* Fest. 334 L). Festus here uses the expression *exultationes* where we might expect *carmina* or *versus* or *libri.* No doubt he is drawn to the word *exultatio* precisely because it can refer to both language and movement, and in this instance he is defining a special term (*redantruare*) that applies to particular movements. The relationship between exultation, whether verbal or kinetic, and the Salian performance, is reinforced by Vergil's usage in his summary description of various Roman religious rituals on the Shield of Aeneas:

> Here the exultant *salii* and the naked *luperci*
> and the fleecy *apices* and the *ancilia* fallen from heaven
> he had hammered out, and the chaste matrons guiding the sacred
> > objects
> through the city in their comfortable wagons.

> hic exsultantis Salios nudosque Lupercos
> lanigerosque apices et lapsa ancilia caelo

extuderat, castae ducebant sacra per urbem
pilentis matres in mollibus.

(Verg. Aen. 8.663–66)

For Vergil, exultation is as pertinent to the *salii* as nakedness is to the
luperci and chastity is to matrons. Elsewhere the close relationship between the *kourētes* and the *salii* posited by ancient and modern observers
alike is reinforced by poetic application of the term *exultans* to the Greek
daimones: both Lucretius and Statius characterize the performance of
the *kourētes* (Latin *Curetae*) with the verb *exultare* ("The Curetae dance
and exult in rhythm" [*Curetae ludunt in numerumque exultant*], Lucr. 2.631;
and "the trembling Curetae exult around the Thunderer" [*Curetas trepi-
dos circa Tonantem exultare*], Stat. *Theb.* 4.790).

Another grammarian of the imperial era, Nonius Marcellus, suc-
cinctly defines exultation as "giving injury through action or speech"
(*exsultare est gestu vel dictu iniuriam facere*, 300.31). His definition thus af-
firms that the exultations of the Salian dancers can be both verbal and
bodily, but raises a different question: in what sense can any exultation,
much less that of the *salii* or *kourētes*, be said to "give injury" or "do an in-
justice"? Are we to dismiss Nonius's comment as irrelevant, or might it
offer insight into the role of exultation within and beyond the Salian rite?

In its appearances outside the Salian context, *exultatio* is not an
especially attractive activity. When used to describe natural phenomena, the verb *exulto* refers to a sudden gushing forth: for example, blood
spurting from a wound (Lucr. 2.195) or the leaping about of an untamed
horse (Hor. *Carm.* 3.11.10; also Cic. *De Or.* 3.36, as metaphor for a reckless, unbridled orator who "exults in brashness of language" [*exultantem
verborum audacia*]). In the human context, more often than not exultation occurs as an accompaniment to violent, uninhibited behavior. It
can be paired with madness as well as with joy (Cic. *Har. Resp.* 1, *Sest.*
95 vs. *Phil.* 13.86). In the ideologically charged language of the elite, it
comes to be associated with the common people (whom Nero, for example, accuses of exultation when they demonstrate in favor of Octavia:
[Sen.] *Oct.* 834), or with demagogic politicians (Cic. *Rep.* 1.62; *Cat.* 1.23,
1.26; *Sest.* 95). *Exultatio* is an activity bordering on the effeminate, presumably because of the implied lack of control: hence we hear of the
exultation of *cinaedi* "who make discordant clamor with raucous and
effeminate voice" (*exultantes in gaudium fractae rauca et effeminata voce
clamores absonos intollunt*, Apul. *Met.* 8.26) when they think a sex-slave
has been purchased for them, and of an oratorical style objectionable in
that it is "broken, exultant, and rather too soft for a man" (*in compositio-
nem fractum, exultantem, ac paene . . . viro molliorem*, Quint. *Inst.* 12.10.12).

Perhaps most frequently of all, use of *exult-* externalizes the emotional state of one who is engaging in violent activity on the battlefield. Cicero warns, as if by way of reciting a proverb, that "Mars often undoes the one who is despoiling and exulting over another" (*Mil.* 56). And he describes Catiline as "exulting in his impious banditry" (*Cat.* 1.23). In Vergil, the haughty and cruel boxer Dares is said to engage in *exultatio*, again in both word and action (*Aen.* 5.398); the doomed Camilla exults in the midst of slaughter (11.648); Pyrrhus exults as he appears on the threshold of Priam's palace, "coruscating with weapons and flashing bronze" (*primoque in limine / exultat, telis et luce coruscus aena*, 2.469–70), like a newly molted snake, "gleaming in its youth" (*nitidusque iuventa*, 2.474). Livy associates the term specifically with psychological preparation for combat: in an episode describing a duel between a Gaul and a Roman, he differentiates the two by observing that the latter had no need of song or exultation or the vain agitation of arms, but instead relied on a heart full of courage and of silent anger (7.10.8). The passage is striking because it expressly denies to the Roman the activities associated with the Salian rite: song, exultation, and the agitation of arms. But in a later episode exultation characterizes the courageous Italian hill people, who, having been captured by Hannibal, are given a chance to fight as gladiators. Each man who wins the lot and gets to fight "exults with joy and promptly seizes arms, dancing the *tripudium* of his people" (*gaudio exsultans, cum sui moris tripudiis arma raptim capiebat*, Livy 21.42.3).

For Livy, then, *exultatio* is a way of warming to the fight, of overcoming the human emotional resistance to killing another member of the species,[95] of abandoning the prohibitions that are otherwise definitive of human existence.[96] In Vergil and other authors, the *exultatio* both follows on and coexists with slaughter, and may thus be an expression of the same psychological need. Modern military historians have emphasized the role of posturing for the purpose both of frightening the enemy into submission without bloodshed (think "shock and awe") and of getting soldiers to overcome the human resistance to intraspecies violence.[97] This use of posturing is evident in the ancient sources, as when a Roman general is quoted telling his troops that the ululations and thumping dances and clanging of shields "have been carefully fitted together [by the enemy] for the purpose of generating terror" (*omnia de industria composita ad terrorem*, Livy 38.17.4). If the Romans but stand up to the first assault, he continues, they will see that the opponents are nothing but *molles*, softies who will easily crack under pressure of sun, dust, and thirst (*mollia corpora, molles . . . animos sol pulvis sitis . . . prosternunt*, 38.17.7). The fact that exultation is associated especially with youths and non-Romans suggests that the self-discipline of Roman soldiers and elite males makes it no longer necessary. Yet ritual exultation, in the context of the Salian hymn, continues to be celebrated by the Roman state. Overcoming resistance to violence is a task for the larger society and not just for the military. It requires spiritual as well as practical reinforcement. Then too the force of *exultatio*, once unleashed, cannot easily be restrained again.[98] Just as the organization of the mimetic faculty carries with it the risk of its proliferation, so too does the paradoxical yet necessary (from the standpoint of the state) attempt to organize "exultation."

For that is indeed what the rite of the *salii* does. It organizes and channels the mimetic faculty in such a way as to make its cultural use appear natural. It celebrates "the nature that culture uses to create second nature." *Exultatio* is a form of mimesis — of horses, or birds, or snakes as they revel in what appear to human observers to be erotic and aggressive impulses. But in the human context, exultation, whether conceived of as voiced or acted, is a means of foreclosing all resistance to the violence that subtends any community. As an aspect of Salian song, *exultatio* exemplifies key functions of song recognized by at least some ancient and modern observers, although not fully integrated into dominant theories of ritual song. As Jacques Attali contends, "primordially, the production of music [including song] has as its function the creation, legitimation, and maintenance of order."[99] It does so, in his view, by causing belief in the harmony of the world and forgetfulness of violence, but also by silencing other sounds. In Rappaport's theory we have an account of song's constructive role in the generation and transmission of an idea of the divine, of ultimate sacred postulates concerning a transcendent order, what Attali might call "the harmony of the world."[100] But Attali reminds us of the exclusionary and silencing aspect of song as well, an aspect brought to the fore in the Salian hymn generally through an emphasis on the noisiness of the performance, specifically through association with *exultatio*. As Pliny the Elder writes concerning the presence of music on the occasion of sacrifice (and we should not forget that sacrifice and flute playing form part of the Salian rite as well), "the flute-player sings lest anything else be heard": *tibicen canere ne quid aliud exaudiatur (HN 28.11)*. So too, the Salian priests exult so that no other version of social or cosmic order can get a hearing. Theirs is a cultural performance that in every aspect — the mimesis of natural form in cultural artifact, the mimesis involved in dance figures, the mimesis of divine talisman by human craft, the mimesis of predecessors by successors to power, the mimesis of one generation by the next — uses mimicry to naturalize culture. As Taussig, reflecting on the writings of Horkheimer and Adorno, argues, "the early magician signifies, as they would have it, not merely 'a yielding attitude to things' but the threshold of history, where mimesis as a practice for living with nature blurs with the transformation of mimesis into an instrument for dominating."[101] It is thus no accident that the Salian rite is placed by the Romans at "the threshold of history," both the imagined moment of the founding of the city and the renewal of history in each year, each generation, and each imperial reign.

An awareness of the complicated and, in a sense, tragic relationship between song and social stability finds expression in literary representations of the Salian rite, especially during the reign of Augustus. In the eighth book of the *Aeneid*, Vergil locates *salii* not only on the Shield of Aeneas, but even among the inhabitants of the proto-Rome of Evander. They play a key role in the celebration Aeneas interrupts when he first arrives at Evander's city, for they sing a hymn in honor of Hercules that amplifies Evander's narration of the god's rescue of the city from the monster Cacus. As a double chorus of youths and elders they contribute to the ritual festivities marking, in Evander's own words, "salvation from fierce dangers" (*saevis . . . periclis / servati, Aen.* 8.188–89). Just as the achievement of Hercules foreshadows the violent labors of Aeneas within the poem and of Augustus within history, so too the appearances of the *salii* in Evander's city and on Aeneas's shield anticipate Augustus's own special attention to their rite. In effect, their performance is both a preparation for further violence and an expression of relief at rescue from mortal danger.

Horace, too, invokes the *salii* in connection with the restoration of civic harmony through controlled violence. In *Odes* 1.37 the violence in question encompasses the battle of Actium and subsequent suicide of Cleopatra, activities whose completion, according to the opening stanza of the poem, necessitates drinking, dancing, and Salian feasts. The triple repetition of *nunc* at the outset of the ode seems designed to recall the beat of the Salian *tripudium,* and the reference to feasts puts a decidedly celebratory interpretation on the ritual dance (which is also mentioned in the immediately preceding ode, *Carm.* 1.36.12). But the *salii* operate here as more than symbols of uninhibited partying: as in the rite itself, their wild performance marks the escape of the new generation from impending doom, whether the metaphorical death encountered in initiation and symbolized by the labyrinthine *truia,* or the real death and destruction of civil warfare. At the same time, it is a mark of the distance between the needs of early Rome and the ambitions of the imperial city that the presence of the *salii* in Horace's ode anticipates not the joy of reproduction with female initiates, as on the oinochoe from Tragliatella and, perhaps, the ritual cart from Bisenzio, but the construction of homosocial solidarity through the death of the "not humble" queen (*non humilis mulier, Carm.* 1.37.32). Nonetheless, even such an adaptation of the symbolism of the *salii* would not be possible without a shared understanding between Horace and his audience of the underlying associations of the *salii* with initiation, escape from danger, and the complex social need to forget violence and silence any outcry against it.

In *Odes* 4.1 the mention of the *salii* again calls to mind rite of passage and escape from danger, now in a context that is decidedly more personal and domestic, although not for that reason less serious. Horace asks Venus not to resume the erotic wars he has left behind, but instead to divert her attention to Paullus Maximus, a young noble about to marry into the imperial household. Among the diversions she will find prepared by Maximus is a chorus of youths and maidens singing her praise twice a day while "striking the earth three times in the manner of the *salii*" (*in morem Salium ter quatient humum, Carm.* 4.1.28). The poet's request succeeds where Maximus is concerned (he gets the girl), but fails in his own case as he finds himself by the end of the ode struck with classic symptoms of unrequited love and pursuing the young man Ligurinus on the Campus Martius, at least in his dreams. Themes of warfare survived and resumed and of passage to adulthood find appropriate expression in the appearance of the *salii*. But in another sense what has been survived is the political and personal turmoil depicted in Horace's earlier poetry, as the poet presents himself as having achieved, albeit momentarily, a transcendent serenity that permits him to welcome graciously the forthcoming marriage of Maximus and Marcia. And the wedding itself—at least in theory—exemplifies the successful coming of age, through marriage, of a new post-civil-war generation of aristocrats.[102] Far removed as such sentiments may seem from the clanging and stomping of armored priests, they in fact constitute an Augustan inflection of age-old concerns with continuity, security, and social renewal. By singing of the *salii* in the opening poem of his own return to lyric song, Horace participates in the ongoing process of "making manifest things and ideas already existing in another state," of validating a particular instance of song within history through reference to a timeless prototype of all Roman song.[103] Salian song, a performance in time, thus becomes the model—and, as I have tried to argue, one source—of song's ability to relate the here and now of vested interests and contingent arrangements to the timeless order of the Roman cosmos.

TWO· SONG, RITUALIZATION, AND AGENCY

RITUAL CAN BE REGARDED AS "A MECHANISTICALLY DIS-crete and paradigmatic means of sociocultural integra-tion, appropriation, or transformation."[1] It can also be viewed as the outcome of a process of ritualization, the making special of the everyday. The latter approach, as Catherine Bell points out, allows us to observe how everyday schemes are transformed and "imposed in new form upon agents able to deploy them in a variety of circumstances beyond the circumference of the rite itself."[2] Bell warns us against reifying and, paradoxically, isolating ritual within Roman (or any other) society and, at the same time, points the way to an understanding of how ritualized practices, such as those de-scribed in the preceding chapter, can have an impact beyond the tempo-ral and spatial confines of a specific, recurrent performance. Whereas Rappaport's approach to ritual, with its emphasis on the interconnect-edness of language, gesture, and object, allows us to identify the ab-stractions materialized by a particular set of actions, Bells reminds us that such abstractions are carried beyond the confines of the immediate performance by historical agents who, although constituted as such by the very process of ritualization, nonetheless have the capacity to deploy the ritualized schemes and practices in ways not structured by the ritual itself. An emphasis on ritualization thus clarifies the impact of ritual. Be-cause, as Bell puts it, "ritualized practices constantly play off the field of action in which they emerge,"[3] ritualization and the everyday become mutually informing, not just conceptually, but as lived practices as well.

Bell's sense of ritual mastery as carrying over from the narrowly de-fined ritual context to "other ritualized activities, ordinary action deemed by the contrast to be spontaneous and practical, or both at the same time,"[4] helps us to grasp the emergence and interrelationship of various specialized or ritualized practices within a more broadly conceived Roman song culture, while also providing a model for understanding the impact of song as ritualized practice on society more generally. Although our own order of exposition follows the lead of the ancient interpreters in assigning a certain primacy to the song of the *salii*, in fact it is more appropriate to regard Salian song as informing and being informed by (i.e., "playing off") other types of song, even if concrete evidence for such types of song does not appear until a later stage of history. For one thing, it is difficult to imagine Salian song, at any stage in Roman history, operating in a vacuum independent of other instances of ritualization. Convivial song has as much a claim to being cotemporal with the city as does the choral song of the *salii*; although no evidence of dramatic representation exists as early as the foundation, certainly the surviving texts of early drama are best understood as manifestations of a long-standing tradition that integrates and situates still other traditional song types.[5] More important, all three of the song types that are both attested for early Rome and continue as lived practices throughout the rest of Roman history (i.e., choral, convivial, and civic) have in common an association with ritually constituted agents known as *sodales*. That practices should be linked by common agents is exactly as Bell's theory would have predicted, since, as she emphasizes, for all of ritual's involvement with objects and actions, songs and abstractions, it is agents who redeploy the ritualized practices (and songs and objects, etc.) in new contexts.

At the same time, while *sodales* provide the link among choral, convivial, and civic song—and thus, not coincidentally, the organizing framework of this chapter—their own constitution is hardly frozen by any or all of the rituals or ritualized practices in which they are engaged, instead being redefined and renegotiated in the course of the interaction between ritualized and everyday schemes; nor are they the only agents constituted by song. As much as the stylized song and dance of the Salian priests transform everyday schemes of social interaction (e.g., language, metalworking, military exercise, growing up), their performance of such song and dance in the special context of religious ritual (a context that they themselves are involved in generating) gives new significance to those everyday schemes, whether performed by off-duty *salii* or by members of their audience: here, as elsewhere, the relationship between the everyday and the special is mutually informing. In a similar manner, the everyday schemes of interaction among *sodales*, having been imposed in part by the Salian rite, come to be reritualized in the performance of state-sponsored comedies at official *ludi*, or public festivals. *Sodalitas* itself becomes one of the abstractions materialized in dramatic ritual's own combination of action, language, and object. And the ritual mastery exercised by the *sodales*, in choral and convivial contexts, is replaced by—or, perhaps better, expanded to include—the mastery of owner over slave.[6] Just as the Salian rite, as cultural practice, constructs the social agency of its various participants, positioning young and old, male and female, craftsman and consumer, performer and audience in relationship to one another, so comedy in effect creates the convivialist, the slave, and the *cinaedus* (among others), even as it juxtaposes (*componere*) them onstage in everyday scenarios made special through meter, costume, stylized language, and so on. This ritualization of yet another set of everyday practices is, once again, impressed "in new form upon agents able to deploy them in a variety of circumstances beyond the rite itself"—as the continuing history of *sodales* and their antitypes, briefly considered here and documented more fully in a later chapter, exemplifies.

Convivium, Conviviality, and the Constitution of *Sodalitas*

Already in the passages cited at the close of the preceding chapter a certain slippage was apparent between the *salii* as ritual specialists and the *salii* as convivial entertainment. Horace's Cleopatra Ode positions Salian dance between the festive drinking of the poet's *sodales* and the official display of the Roman gods on their couches or *pulvinaria*. In *Aeneid* 8, the *salii* sing around burning altars, but only after Evander has ordered the young men of his city to don wreaths, stretch forth goblets, "call upon the shared god, and pour wine freely" (*communemque vocate deum et date vina volentes*, Verg. *Aen.* 8.275)—classic convivial behavior, in Greece as well as in Italy. While the *convivium* is itself a ritualization of everyday eating and drinking, and much official religious activity at Rome entails public feasting, nonetheless the crossover between descriptions of the Salian rite as part of the annual cycle of official feasts and the appearance of the *salii* as cameo performers at the more ad hoc celebrations of Evander's populace and Horace's companions or at the prenuptial parties of Maximus and Marcia (*Carm.* 4.1) is striking. "Mechanistically discrete" rituals can no more contain the activities of the *salii* than can the legalistic straightjackets into which generations of scholars, starting with the compilers of the Digest, have tried to put them and other Roman *sodales*.

For *sodales* they are, as are the *luperci*, the *fetiales*, the Arval brothers, and the *titii*; members of at least some occupational *collegia*; worshipers of particular deities; poets' friends; buddies in comedy; and so on.[7] What is clear from the vast range of uses to which the term *sodalis* and its abstract counterparts *sodalitas* and *sodalicium* are put is that *sodali-*

tas describes first and foremost not an institution but a relationship—more precisely, a relationship constituted by and expressed in practice. Even the etymology of the term *sodalis,* which is cognate with the Latin reflexive-possessive adjective, *suus,* "one's own," points in this direction.[8] It shows poor understanding of the complexity of any social formation, no matter how "primitive," to speculate that *sodalitates* were "originally" members of hunting parties, or off-duty soldiers, or followers of a noble family, because they could surely have been any of these things and much else besides.[9] If there is one category of action that unites all known sodalities, it is eating and drinking together.[10] Such commensality, or as the Romans will come to call its ritualized form, conviviality, is the practice in which relationships of *sodalitas* are constituted. And one aspect of convivial practice, not surprisingly, is the putting into special language of the sodalician relationship, that is, the performance of convivial song. Scholarly debates over the content and format of Roman convivial song—and, in particular, long-standing misinterpretation of Cato the Elder's intervention in second-century BC arguments over convivial decorum and protocol—should not be allowed to obscure the substantial and growing body of evidence for ritualized performance in convivial context. Indeed, the very fact that the state comes to identify its companies of singing priests (*salii,* fetials, Arval brothers) as *sodales,* or coconvivialists, suggests an awareness of the history of interchange between *convivium* and chorus as well as of the defining role of song in convivial practice. In the *convivium* as in the Salian rite, song constitutes protection "against the disordering power of the linguistically liberated imagination."[11] At the same time, song appears to be one of the practices that turns the everyday actions of eating and drinking into a *convivium,* that is, it ritualizes them.

The term *sodalis* enters the historical record in the context of ritualized practice. It is found first on the so-called Lapis Satricanus, a commemorative inscription discovered in the foundation of the rebuilt temple of Mater Matuta on the citadel at Satricum.[12] On linguistic, palaeographical, and archaeological grounds the inscription has been dated to the late sixth or early fifth century BC. Indeed, there is a strong terminus ante quem of the decade 490–480 BC when the temple was rebuilt and the stone with the inscription placed in the foundation in such a way that the inscription was no longer visible. The destruction and reconstruction of the Satrican temple complex is almost certainly to be associated with the struggles that convulsed Latium around the time of the founding of the Roman Republic, perhaps more specifically to the defection of Coriolanus from Rome and his leadership of a Volscian assault on Latin cities on his way to Rome.[13] As it turns out, the content and original function of the inscription may have led to its reuse—or "burial" as one scholar has put it—in the foundation of the new building.[14]

The text of the inscription, which was written in *scriptio continua*, without interpuncts, is as follows:[15]

IEISTETERAIPOPLIOSIOVALESIOSIO
SVODALESMAMARTEI

The most plausible interpretation is that of Filippo Coarelli, who suggests that the text be supplemented and rendered in classical Latin "Manibus Terrae Publii Valerii / Sodales Martiales."[16] In other words, "the *sodales* devoted to the god Mars [make this dedication] to the deceased spirits of Publius Valerius." Coarelli establishes beyond doubt the acceptability of the combination *sodales* plus the dative (here *Mamartei*) to describe a company of men associated with a deity; and, something that has not been remarked by scholars, his interpretation preserves the natural word order and colometry of the Latin language. Moreover, as Coarelli himself notes, each of the grammatical constituents of the inscription forms a metrical colon of the sort employed in the Latin Saturnian meter.[17] Indeed, the second line of the inscription has been centered under the first, as if to clarify graphically its status as a distinct grammatical and rhythmical unit. In short, on formal grounds the inscription can be regarded as an early instance of Latin lyric poetry or song.

But rhetorical and metrical form are not the only arguments in favor of interpreting the inscription on the Lapis Satricanus in this way. The shape of the stone suggests that it originally served as a statue base. Given the mention of Publius Valerius on the stone and the existence of a Roman tradition identifying one Publius Valerius Poplicola as a leading figure of the earliest years of the republic (reputedly consul in 509, 508, 507, and 504), that is, not long before the "burial" of the stone, we may infer that the *sodales Martiales* had made a prominent dedication on behalf of Publius Valerius that soon became unacceptable to newly ascendant powers in Satricum.[18] Now there are several features, even of so short an inscription, that link dedication by the Satrican *sodales* to traditions of conviviality characteristic of early Italian communities.

For one thing, it is generally recognized that whereas in Greece the symposium tends to be seen as antithetical to death, as quintessentially a practice of the living and a sign of life, in Italy the *convivium* is regarded as transcending the boundary between life and death.[19] Convivial ware is a recurrent feature of graves from south Italy, Latium, and Etruria; less so from Greece. Some burial sites in Italy even mimic the arrangement of couches at a dinner or a drinking party.[20] Etruscan sarcophagi frequently depict the deceased as reclining on a dining couch.[21] This tendency to imagine the convivial setting as persisting after death seems related to the practice of postmortem laudation in which a group of evaluators is described as conducting an assessment of the deceased. Early Roman eulogy does not simply praise the deceased: it describes the process of "many" or "good men" or "everybody," or, in the case of the Lapis Satricanus, "boon companions," evaluating a member of the group.[22] Although such rhetorical practices may not derive solely from convivial procedure, they fit a scenario in which ritually constituted peers reflect on the behavior of other members of the group, living or deceased. In his fragmentary discussion of *carmina convivalia* Cato refers to such songs as praising "distinguished men" (*clari viri*).[23] It seems likely that the songs themselves constitute part of the process by which the men are rendered "distinguished," both during and after their lifetimes, while at the same time constructing the notion of distinction against which their accomplishments are to be measured. The habits of convivial song described by Cato have rightly been likened to the Attic *skolia,* some of which are embedded in a passage of Aristophanes' *Wasps,* with others preserved by the late writer Athenaeus.[24] But it is worth recalling that whereas the surviving Greek *skolia* speak directly of the accomplishments of the men being hymned, Roman *laudationes,* as just noted, incorporate reference to the praising community as well. The Roman practice, as represented by Cato, would thus seem to conform in a fairly straightforward manner to Bell's observation that ritualization produces schemes "that structure an environment in such a way that the environment appears to be the source of the schemes and their values."[25]

If the Lapis Satricanus thus seems to fit distinctively Italian (and, eventually, self-consciously Roman) practices of convivial praise, it also provides a prototype of the literary form such praise comes to assume. The Saturnian meter, whatever its origin, has two successors in the mainstream Latin poetic tradition.[26] One of these, as is well known, is the epic (and eventually satiric) hexameter of Ennius and later Latin poets, a meter whose adoption is signaled by Ennius in his polemic against his epic predecessors in the *Annales.*[27] But the Saturnian is also replaced by the elegiac couplet in the case of the laudatory inscriptions of the Scipionic *gens* dating to the third and second centuries BC. There later inscriptions, although echoing the earlier in content and tone and clearly designed to fit the same physical and ideological context, adopt elegiac couplet where the earlier had used Saturnian.[28] In other words, Saturnian can be reinterpreted as the fountainhead of both epic, in which the poet presents himself as mouthpiece of the Muses, and elegy, in which the poet presents himself as addressing a company of coconvivialists. The connection between elegy as the verse for funeral inscription and elegy as the verse for a certain type of subjective love poetry in Latin is sometimes made on the grounds of the prevalence of themes of death in the latter, especially the poetry of Propertius. But the association may also stem from the convivial setting (real or imagined) of both genres of song. Nor is this association to be disregarded, even if we accept Rüpke's argument that early Roman epic was itself performed in convivial context,[29] because it is elegy, as opposed to epic, that represents itself as concerned with relations among coconvivialists.[30]

In any event, my aim here is not to provide a definitive interpretation of the Lapis Satricanus (much less the prehistory of Latin meter) so much as to use this document as means of access to convivial practice in early Rome and Italy. The word *sodalis,* which later refers expressly to coconvivialists, seems to situate the inscription in a convivial milieu, while the particular form of the dedication and the afterlife of that form deepen the connection. If the textualization of the Satrican *sodales'* respect for Publius Valerius represents an attempt to project their sentiments forward in time (albeit an attempt foiled by history for well over two thousand years), what might the song of the *sodales* have meant when carried out as a living practice?

Here we must rely on interpretation of a complex body of material and textual evidence pertaining to convivial culture in central Italy from the eighth century BC forward.[31] What emerges from consideration of this evidence is the extent to which conviviality serves as the focus of struggle over the social and political relationships among various sectors of the population in Italian cities, particularly Rome. Such an investigation is relevant to our specific interest in song, but it can also be understood as part of a separate but related project of reintegrating archaic Rome into its broader Italian context. As Richard Saller notes in reference to postwar Italian archaeology, "archaeological discoveries have produced 'exceptional advances,' not so much because they allow us to check specifics of the literary tradition as because they allow us to situate Rome in Italy in a much fuller way than the tradition does."[32] Discoveries of convivial space and convivial ware from within Rome itself, although few in number, acquire significance when understood in the broader Italian context as represented in both archaeological and literary remains.[33]

As a widespread archaic Italian funerary practice, the deposit of items of convivial significance continues into the afterlife a culture of distinction via aristocratic display.[34] Those who could differentiate themselves during their lifetime by a convivial life-style involving conspicuous display maintain the distinction (or have it maintained by their survivors) through funeral banquet, procession to the cemetery, and deposit of goods in the burial *corredo.* The burial of convivial ware is commonplace in Etruria, Latium, and Campania from the eighth through the sixth century BC.[35] (In fact, the practice is probably much older, as recent finds exhibited in the Florence Archaeological Museum in fall of 2001 suggest.) Often identified as part of an "orientalizing" phase of Italian art (on grounds that the *convivium,* especially if it involves reclining, is an Eastern phenomenon), its internal significance as evidence of a culture of aristocratic display is too easily overlooked. The status differentiation implicit in deposit of convivial ware corresponds to differences implied by separation of wealthy from everyday graves, full-size armor and military gear versus miniature, and ritual deposit of items inscribed as part of an intercity system of gift exchange.[36] What is more, as Lotte Hedeager has argued in her study of Iron Age societies in northern Europe, differentiated burial deposits probably correspond to a period of social transformation in which hierarchies are being formed and resisted. Rather than constituting a passive reflection of a stable cultural system, the waste of prestige goods is better understood as "an active factor in social reproduction."[37] By the same token, the decline in such deposits, rather than indicating an impoverishment of the society in question (as is often assumed, for example, with respect to fifth-century BC Rome), may in fact be a mark of a stable system, one in which elite status and its reproduction over time are secure.[38] The ebb and flow of material — and I would argue other sorts of — evidence pertaining to conviviality is less a marker of the waxing and waning of participation in *convivia* than it is of social and political conflicts surrounding and shaped by such participation.

In the emergent phase of Italian aristocratic culture, conviviality (as well as its representation) intersects with other processes of social differentiation.[39] On the relief plaques from Murlo (early sixth century BC) and Acqua Rossa (third quarter of the sixth century BC), for example, we see elites and nonelites differentiated within the depiction of banquets or *convivia.*[40] One group, differentiated by hairstyle, reclines on couches eating and drinking, while another group waits on them. Interestingly, music seems to transcend the boundary between the two groups: in Murlo the harpist reclines together with the guests; at Acqua Rossa the harpist and flutist stand. In another depiction, this one on a funerary urn from the sixth century BC, it appears that some of the guests are dancing,[41] and on yet another plaque a guest seems to sing.[42] In any event, the social distinctions implied and advanced by such depictions are even more acute if we follow the arguments of scholars such as Rebecca Sinos who view the whole complex of images on the Murlo frieze plaques as promoting a differentiated aristocratic life-style of horse racing, banqueting, and, perhaps most startling, interaction with the gods. Sinos argues that the procession frieze in particular indicates that the building in which the frieze plaques were originally hung "was associated in some way with men who not only belonged to the world of aristocratic banquets and horses, as depicted in the other frieze plaques, but also sought to manifest themselves as recipients of divine honor, as indicated by the divine attendants as well as royal attributes in the procession scene."[43] A similar argument can be made with respect to the "assembly scene" plaques, which show groups of anthropomorphic figures of strikingly different sizes: are these perhaps gods and humans commingling?[44]

The attempt to associate aristocrats with gods is a strategy that recurs from time to time in Roman religious history. In Livy's text, Camillus is criticized for celebrating his triumph over Veii in a chariot drawn by white horses, "an act that seemed contrary not just to civil but even to human status" (*parumque id non civile modo sed humanum etiam visum*) because it implied an equivalence between Camillus and the gods Jupiter and Sol (5.23.5). The legend of the Etruscan tyrant Mezentius, possibly to be dated as early as the seventh century BC, has plausibly been interpreted as a warning to aristocrats who might lay claim to the prerogatives of the gods (Mezentius was punished for denying the gods the first offering of the vintage that is their due: Macrob. *Sat.* 3.5.10 = Cato *ORF* 8.1.12).[45] Livy refers to claims made by some that only patricians are entitled to make contact with the realm of the divine.[46] Perhaps the most striking instance of commingling of gods and men is the *epulum Iovis*, or feast of Jupiter, held at the *ludi plebei* and *ludi Romani*. On these occasions leading men dined in the presence of a statue of the god, while others held more private banquets at various locations throughout the city.[47] The style and function of these *epula* (they are also called *epulae*) were the topic of intense controversy in the aftermath of the Second Punic War, when the display of newly acquired wealth threatened (once again) to widen the gap between elite and nonelite sectors of the Roman population.[48] And anecdotes pertaining to the *epula* make playful yet pointed reference to the commingling of gods and men: for example, Aulus Gellius says that it seems the gods themselves were arbiters when Africanus and Gracchus (temporarily) allied at the *epulum Iovis* of 187 BC (*NA* 12.18.1–3; cf. Livy 38.57.5), while a much-repeated story about Tubero allows for the possibility that the austerity of the *epulum* he sponsored was due to his desire to have human beings eat from the same simple ware as the gods.[49]

In a sense, then, early Italian conviviality invites analysis of the sort applied to the Salian rite in the preceding chapter. For just as the Salian performance combines action, song, and objects to materialize abstractions that resonate beyond the specific performance context, so *convivia*, as the ritualization of everyday activities of eating and drinking, combine action, song, and special objects to materialize, in this case, the abstraction of *sodalitas* itself—that is, of a unified peer group entitled to a disproportionate share of the community's resources. To Rappaport's emphasis on the materialization of abstractions and the articulation of ultimate sacred postulates (among which aristocratic association with divinity seeks to be numbered), we may add an argument of Bell's that seems particularly applicable to conviviality, namely that "ritualization is first and foremost a strategy for the construction of certain types of power relationships effective within particular social organizations."[50] The extension of conviviality beyond the grave, rather than being a consequence of an unmotivated "difference in outlook" between Italians and Greeks, can now be seen as evidence of the Italian aristocracies' aggressive assertion of genealogy as the key determinant of membership. Conviviality, broadly understood as encompassing *laudatio*, procession, burial deposit, and commemorative song, constitutes *sodales* as transhistorical subjects, reanimators, as it were, of deceased prototypes. It seeks to establish power relationships among historical agents even before the (literal) coming-into-being of the agents themselves.

Conviviality at Rome thus has the potential to unite and to divide sectors of the population. It seems to figure in particular in the process of elite self-fashioning, both as a form of wasteful display and as a mark of elite connections with the world beyond the here and now—whether in the form of goods and practices imported from afar or as a locus of alleged interactions with the gods themselves. Viewed from this perspective, Cato's famous references to *carmina convivalia* performed by banqueters in generations past can be understood as an intervention in ongoing debates over appropriate convivial practice rather than simply being judged as true or false corroboration of an earlier life-style to be inferred from the material record.[51] His remarks confirm the importance of conviviality to the maintenance of certain types of power relations, but call attention to the potential contradiction between legitimation through display and legitimation through connection with an imagined austere past. By foregrounding an archaic practice of convivial song performed by guests in praise of distinguished men, Cato seeks to validate his own literary innovation (a man of affairs recounting the past in Latin) while indirectly criticizing the convivial practices of his contemporaries and rivals. As Enrica Sciarrino has recently argued, "Cato forecloses the social legitimacy of professionals in elite contexts, and yet participates in the expropriation of the cultural capital that was progressively becoming accessible through the mediations of these very professionals and imported books."[52] For Cato, the way to reconcile conviviality and civic harmony is through a convivial practice that minimizes the visible distinction between sectors of the population while implicating society as a whole in the traditions of a single class. Pauline Schmitt Pantel's observation on the Spartan *syssition,* to the effect that "the *syssition* is the efficacious tool of a power that, the better to inscribe itself in the realm of the imaginary is imposed on the everday,"[53] helps us to understand Cato's intentions as he seeks to shape the institutions of a newly ascendant Rome.[54] Cato thus works from within the framework of convivial culture to reshape that culture and, by extension, the broader array of social relations that it sustains.

Sodales on Stage

Attention to the few but tantalizing remarks of Cato the Elder has obscured the existence of a large body of early convivial song dating to a period a generation or two earlier than his composition of the *Origines* and fostering a different resolution of the tension between *sodalitas* and *civitas.* The material in question consists of the songs of the *sodales* embedded in the comedies of Plautus, which are themselves state-sponsored civic dramas. Analysis of the role of the *sodalis* and his song in Plautus will thus amplify our understanding of prior, lost convivial performances while at the same time reinforcing our sense of the ongoing significance of song as "an active factor in social reproduction." Plautine comedy presupposes complex traditions of differentiated song types in Latin even as it seeks to integrate the various voices and interests articulated by those song types into unifying civic song. If for Cato all of Rome is to listen to those who know the right way to perform at a *convivium,* for Plautus society at its best is a *convivium* writ large. For both writers, ultimately, authority resides in a hierarchical grouping of freeborn males. Where they differ, at least in part, is in the means through which that authority is to be transmitted. Cato presents connection with past traditions of song as legitimizing new strategies of explicitly literary production. Plautus, paradoxically the more traditional of the two, persists in privileging the power of song, with its full array of linguistic, ritual, metrical, and musical markers.

As luck would have it, the only extended passage of Plautus that can be directly compared with a Menandrian original contains four instances of the term *sodalis*—none of which corresponds to a word or phrase in the surviving Greek.[55] This difference provides clear evidence both of the centrality of the theme of *sodalitas* in the play in question (*Bacchides*) and of the Romanness of the relationships expressed by it. Even in a short passage of a few score overlapping lines, the Roman text repeatedly emphasizes relations between *sodales* where the Greek addresses issues of an altogether different sort. Thus, whereas the Roman father instructs his son's friend to "rescue a *sodalis* for yourself and a son for me" (*serva tibi sodalem et mihi filium, Bacch.* 496), the Greek speaks instead of rescuing the truant youth "because you have affection for a household that is dear to you" (*oikian philēn philōn*). As a Roman, the youth so charged to rein in his friend wonders aloud whether he should be more annoyed with his *sodalis* or with his *sodalis's* girlfriend (*Bacch.* 500–501); in his Greek instantiation he seems to speak only of the troublesome *hetaira.* When, later, he does explicitly compare his buddy and his girlfriend, he refers to the former not with a descriptive noun but simply with his name, Moschus (Men. *Dis Ex.* 99). And when the supposedly duplicitous adolescent, target of friendly, parental, and pedagogical concern, spots his conflicted buddy onstage, he declares in the Roman version, "can this be my *sodalis?*" prompting the response, "can this be my enemy?" (*Bacch.* 534) In the Greek play the corresponding exchange consists merely of the greeting "Hi there, Sostratus," and the conventional response "Hi to you too" (*Dis Ex.* 104). A final reference to *sodalitas* in the Latin scene (*Bacch.* 560) matches only a blank in the Greek papyrus, but the overall significance of the comparison is clear: Plautus introduces the theme of *sodalitas* where the Greek characters speak instead of personal, filial, and familial betrayal. That the term *sodalis* appears fully eight times in the fifty-some lines preceding the section of *Bacchides* that overlaps with *Dis Exapatōn* merely confirms our sense that in the murky world of Plautine source study we are unlikely to find a clearer example of a "Plautine theme in Plautus" than that of *sodalitas.*[56]

Indeed, taken as a whole, Plautine comedy stages a veritable ethnography of *sodalitas,* drawing special attention to its relationship with song and its ambivalent capacity for both inclusion and exclusion. The connection between *sodalitas* and song, which might have been inferred from the extratextual construction of sodalician practice anyway, is made manifest in Plautus by the distribution of references to *sodales.* Of forty-five occurrences of the word, only eight are found in spoken verse, the remainder in sung verse, chiefly recitative. Moreover, on several occasions, the appearance of a *sodalis* seems to prompt a transition to song. At *Bacchides* 607, for instance, Pistoclerus ponders what advice to give his *sodalis* Mnesilochus about his girlfriend, whereupon, as if on cue, Mnesilochus appears on stage and the two break into a polymetric duet.[57] At *Mostellaria* 310 Philolaches announces the arrival of his *sodalis* Callidamates together with his girlfriend (*sed estne hic meu' sodalis qui huc incedit cum amica sua*), and the two men, joined by two *meretrices,* or prostitutes, sing a complex lyric involving bacchiacs, cretics, anapest, and iambs — an intensification of song within the song that is the Plautine play.

This shift to song corresponds to or anticipates a shift from everyday life to ritualized conviviality within the dramatic framework. Thus

Bacchides opens with the characters evincing equal concern for the welfare of the absent *sodalis* Mnesilochus and for the preservation of their convivial life-style: it hardly seems coincidental that the title characters have names that allow for punning on bacchants and bacchanal (e.g., *Bacch.* 53). In *Mostellaria*, Callidamates' return to his *sodalis* signals not just an intensification of song but also an explicitly thematized return to conviviality: "That party was a drag [*taesum*]," he announces, but "now I'll go reveling [*commissatum*] to Philolaches' house, which is bound to be more fun" (*Most.* 315–18). Callidamates had worn himself out at an earlier party, which he abandoned, but meeting up with his *sodalis*, his only thought is to start drinking and partying once again. He expresses his intention through use of the technical term *commissatum*, which describes the noisy procession through the streets of drunken, singing revelers in the aftermath of (or, in this case, interval between) participation in a *convivium*.[58]

While *sodalitas* in Plautus is usually characterized as a relationship between two young, free males—for example, *Epidicus* 344, where Stratippocles and Chaeribulus are spotted as *duos sodalis* by the title character—several passages make it clear that the group can be extended in both size and age distribution. Thus when Lydus in *Bacchides* excoriates Pistoclerus for dallying with one of the Bacchis sisters, Mnesilochus defends him by saying he was doing it for a *sodalis*: he means himself, of course, but he wants Lydus to believe he is referring to a third party (*Bacch.* 475). And in *Mostellaria*, when Callidamates' *sodalis* Philolaches, who is holding his alcohol better, learns that his father is on his way back to town, he despairs that he will find the house "full of guest and girls" (*aedis plenas convivarum et mulierum*, 379).[59] Later in the play Callidamates proclaims himself "first *sodalis* of all" to Callidamates (*omnium primum sodalem me esse scis gnato tuo*, 1153), making it clear, if it weren't already, that *sodalitas* extends far beyond the pair bond. In *Casina*, the *matrona* Cleustrata describes her elderly husband's randy (and also elderly) companion as *sodalis tuos, amicus optimus*—your drinking buddy, your most excellent friend (581)—implying both that *sodalitas* is not limited by age and that an old *sodalis* may have more than one friend or buddy. Finally, in *Bacchides* and *Mercator*, where the duos of *adulescentes* are repeatedly referred to as *sodales* (e.g., *Bacch.* 175, 389, 435, 460, 467; *Merc.* 475, 621, 947), their fathers, also paired, although not explicitly identified with the term, nonetheless end up joining in their convivial celebration.[60]

If Plautine comedy thus recreates—albeit in schematic and stylized form—some aspects of *sodalitas* to be found in nontheatrical contexts and reinforces the connection (for us) between *sodalitas* and song, it also points to some of the tensions generated by the presence of *sodalitates* in a larger community. When Callidamates and Philolaches of *Mostellaria* awaken from their debauch, Philolaches indicates his fear of explaining what has happened to his father, leaving Callidamates to serve "as the only ambassador about *sodalitas:* it is I who must negotiate peace with his father" (*nunc ego de sodalitate solus sum orator datus / qui a patre eiius conciliarem pacem*, 1126–27) — which he promptly proceeds to do by inviting the father, who conveniently appears just then, to join him in yet another dinner. The *sodalitas* of young men is described as an entity that must relate to others in the community as if through emissaries (for *orator* used of an ambassador or go-between, see *Stichus* 291). In *Bacchides*, Pistoclerus's devotion to his *sodalis* (as well as to his girlfriend) requires him to substitute all the socially acceptable signs of adolescence for more suspect ones:

> instead of a discus, debt. . . .
> 　　　instead of a sword, a turtledove
> instead of a boxing glove, a tankard . . .
> instead of a spear, dice; not a breastplate but a soft *pallium;*
> not a horse but a couch . . . not a shield to lie with, but a wench!

> pro disco damnum. . . .
> 　　　pro machaera turturem
> 　　　pro cestu cantharum
> pro galea scaphium . . .
> pro hasta talos, pro lorica malacum . . . pallium
> 　　　pro equo lectus . . . scortum pro scuto accubet
> 　　　　　　　　　　　　　　(Plaut. *Bacch.* 60–72)

The list is echoed by the outraged *paedagogus* Lydus who tells the wastrel's father that if his own precepts had been followed, there would be running, wrestling, boxing, and leaping, not to mention a healthy dose of corporal punishment, in place of the love and kisses that now preoccupy the young man. In still other scenes, characters explicitly remark on the contrast between their home community and those they have encountered on their travels and, in so doing, employ the term *sodalis* to differentiate desirable from undesirable political and social traits. Thus Eutychus in *Mercator* celebrates his newfound *sodales* — life, loyalty, statehood, joy, play, and prank — in opposition to the abstractions for which he has no use (846–52). In *Persa*, on the other hand, a character identifies all the evils that threaten a city from within (envy, ambition, putdowns, etc.) as *sodales* of one another and encourages his enemy, the pimp, to join them in exile (534–62). Such metaphorical references to *sodalitas* reinforce our sense that convivial subgroups have the potential to exclude as well as include, to divide a city as well as to unite it.

In the scenes from *Mercator* and *Persa* just discussed, *sodalitas* is a metaphor for a cluster of abstractions. But the tenor of the metaphor— good and bad qualities of a successful state—does not seem randomly chosen. Proper handling of *sodalitas* is in fact essential to the well-being of the ancient state: not a dogma to be preached but a shared under- standing enacted through comic performance. In addition, the prescrip- tive listing of good and bad "drinking companions"—personal or ab- stract—may be part of the lore of the *convivium,* as convivial practice explicitly defines the agents it seeks to create.[61] In other words, the song of the *sodales,* which we have thus far considered as convivial enter- tainment in general, sometimes manifests itself in Plautine comedy in a more specific form—namely, as a set of convivial precepts, what we might term *dicta sodalium,* the sayings of the *sodales.*[62]

In one of the Plautine comedies that mentions *sodales* most fre- quently and reflects explicitly on convivial ethics—that is, *Bacchides*— the problem of precept giving and of interpretation of precepts looms large. *Bacchides,* famous as the source of an influential adaptation of the Menandrian proverb "whom the gods love dies young,"[63] contains other bits of proverbial wisdom that are not so easily ascribed to Greek sources.[64] In his initial soliloquy, wherein he both ponders the nature of friendship and *sodalitas* and relates the favor he asked of Pistoclerus, Mnesilochus begins with the general statement that "nothing except the gods surpasses a true friend" (*homini amico, qui est amicus ita uti nomen possidet, / nisi deos ei nil praestare, Bacch.* 387) and illustrates it with refer- ence to his relationship to Pistoclerus, whom he calls his *sodalis* (389). In similar philosophizing vein he goes on to remark:

> By god, . . . nothing is worse than an ungrateful man!
> It's better to ignore an injury than fail to return a favor,
> better to be called a spendthrift than an ingrate.
> Good men will praise the former, even the wicked find fault with the
>   latter.

> nam pol quidem meo animo ingrato homine nihil impensiust
> malefactorem amitti satius quam relinqui beneficium
> nimio impendiosum praestat te quam ingratum dicier:
> illum laudabunt boni, hunc etiam ipsi culpabunt mali.

> (Plaut. *Bacch.* 394–97)

The expression *pol quidem* (394) seems to be a Plautine signal that we are entering the realm of the proverbial (cf. *Bacch.* 1194). The two central lines in the quotation have the shape of a distich, in which the second verse complicates the proverbial essence of the first—a pattern common in the later proverbial collection known as the *Disticha Catonis,* and also characteristic of the surviving quotations from the *Carmen* of Appius Claudius Caecus.[65] Thus the late antique grammarian Priscian records one of Appius's sayings as running

> when you see a friend   you forget your sorrows
> when you remember an enemy   you're not so happy.

> amicum cum vides   obliviscere miserias
> inimicum si es commentus   nec libens aeque.
> (Priscian, *GLK* 2.384 = *FPL,* frag. 2)

While each phrase can stand alone, as in the central lines of the quotation from Plautus, the relationship between *amicum* and *inimicum,* as between *satius* and *nimio,* establishes a semantic connection between the individual proverbs. Although scholars have attributed Appius's sayings to Greek antecedents as diverse as Pythagoras and Philemon, the fact that a collection of proverbs of this shape seems to have been circulating at least as early as the time of Panaetius (mid-to late second century BC) makes it reasonable to assume that Plautus's audience would have heard Mnesilochus's reflections as being in the style of Latin wisdom literature—or, better, wisdom song—which itself is likely to have circulated in convivial contexts.[66] The further subdivision of each line of the distich into distinct syntactical coda may also be characteristic of proverb style: we might compare the boys' song recorded by Porphyry—*rex erit qui recte faciet; qui non faciet, non erit*—as well as the *praeceptum rusticum, hiberno pulvere verno luto / grandia farra, camille, metes (FPL* 419.16). In addition, the reference to praise and blame by the *boni* and *mali (Bacch.* 394) puts us in mind of the acculturative context of *convivium* (or the funeral, which, as I have suggested, extends convivial patterns into the afterlife) as evidenced in Cato's *Origines* and evoked in the opening of his *De Agri Cultura (ita laudabant cum laudabant,* etc.). In other words, while reflecting on his obligations to his fellow *sodales,* Mnesilochus slips into the language, style, and content of convivial performance.

In the *Mercator,* in which relations between *sodales* figure prominently in both the diction and the thematics of the play, the manner of communication between *sodales* is carefully if schematically differentiated from other speech acts and other social relationships. Here it is the speech of *sodales* that is opposed to other speech types, not convivial song in opposition to other song, but the effect is comparable: the valorization of relations between *sodales* and of the forms of communication that characterize them. The play opens with a virtual compendium of speech types, performed or described by a character who eventually apologizes for being *multiloquium,* or talkative (37). The adolescent Charinus declaims his love (*meos amores eloquar,* 2), narrates his suffering (*narrabo . . . meas nunc miserias,* 8), and paradoxically proclaims (like an auctioneer, *praedico,* 34) his verbal inadequacy. The verbal versatility he displays he in turn attributes to his father, who used to upbraid (*obiurgare,* 46), pontificate (*expromere,* 47), shout (*summo clamore*), and mutter (*mussat,* 49). The father would disavow his son in public (*conclamitare tota urbe,* 51) and make formal announcement of his fiscal irresponsibility (*praedicere / omnes teneret mutuitanti credere,* 51–52). The years of Charinus's boyhood seemed like one big flood of abuse (*convicium,* 59) intermingled with his father Demipho's hypocritical recollections of the good advice his own father gave him—"plow for yourself, harrow for yourself, sow for yourself, reap for yourself: your own labor is what will make you happy" (*tibi aras, tibi occas, tibi seris, tibi item metis, / tibi denique iste pariet laetitiam labos,* 71–72)—advice that Demipho promptly ignored as soon as his father died.

The opening of the *Mercator* thus presents the relationship between Charinus and Demipho as a raucous intergenerational battle that is only interrupted when Charinus sets sail on a merchant voyage to Rhodes, from which he has just now returned. And so the conflict that has been described in the opening monologue is now realized in the action and language of the play, in which Demipho confabs with Charinus's girlfriend (*confabulast,* 78), Charinus lies elaborately to Demipho (*proloqui mendacium,* 209), and Demipho for his part wrangles with his friend and agemate Lysimachus (*praedico,* 289, 293; *obiurgare,* 321, 322). So obsessed with violent, intemperate speech is Demipho that he even dreams of a talking monkey, one that curses and quarrels (*male precatur / convicium,* 235), and of a billy goat that not only steals his girlfriend but also issues verbal taunts and ridicule (*praedicare, inridere,* 249–50). When Demipho anticipates others' reaction to his son's purchase of a beautiful maid, he conjures up a list of annoying behaviors culminating in various types of aggressive and violent language:

> They'll look, stare, nod, wink, and whistle.
> They'll pinch, beckon, annoy, and jeer.
> They'll tag our doors with couplets smeared in coal!
> And if you think it's bad now, just wait till they start claiming
> that my wife and I are running a brothel! Who needs it?

> contemplent, conspiciant omnes, nutent, nictent, sibilent,
> vellicent, vocent, molesti sint: occentent ostium:

impleantur elegeorum meae fores carbonibus.
atque, ut nunc sunt maledicentes homines, uxori meae
mihique obiectent lenocinium facere. nam quid eost opus?
(Plaut. *Merc.* 405–9)

Demipho's world of wrangling soon engulfs his neighbor Lysimachus
as well, whom he gets to hide the girl of his (and his son's) dreams,
only to have her discovered by Lysimachus's shrewish wife, who in turn
showers Lysimachus with accusations, then has the audacity to accuse
him of directing *contumelia,* or verbal abuse, against her (704).[67]

In contrast to the violent speech, the taunting, boasting, lying, and
accusing that characterize Demipho and all he comes in contact with,
another type of speech—sober, patient, rational, dialogic—seeks to
make itself heard within the play. This other strain is specifically associated with the relationship between the younger men Charinus and
Eutychus, who are identified as *sodales* on five separate occasions (*Merc.*
475, 594, 613, 621, 995). When Charinus and Eutychus first appear together they describe their own interaction with words like narrate
(*narro,* 481, 482), listen (*ausculto,* 477), advise (*consulo,* 482), and deem
(*censes,* 483). The most verbally aggressive they become is to tell each
other to be quiet (*tace,* 491; *quin taces,* 494). What they plot together they
three times call *os sublinere patri* (485, 604, 631)—smearing the father's
face: a common enough expression in Plautus, but one that here calls
attention to the difference in verbal style between the abusive father
and the more restrained sons who seek only to be left alone. Even when
their plot seems to have failed, they speak to one another largely without abuse, asking (*rogas,* 633), announcing (*nuntias,* 610), relating (*oratio,*
607, 608). Indeed when Charinus finally does lose his temper and calls
Eutychus a *carnufex,* or hangman (618), for having brought bad news,
he immediately follows up the insult by asking rhetorically whether
Eutychus's behavior is the right way for a "good *sodalis*" to behave (*hem
istucinest operam dare / bonum sodalem?* 620–21).

In time the separate worlds of fathers and sons converge, and, as
we have now come to expect, it is the ethics of *sodalitas,* here represented by the relationship between the sons, that triumphs. The good
son Eutychus issues proverbial statements about behavior that is class-
and age-appropriate (*Merc.* 969 and 984), while the less obstreperous
oldster, Lysimachus, uses a phrase, *operam dare,* "to pay attention to"
(968), that elsewhere describes the right attitude of one *sodalis* toward
another.[68] Even Demipho lapses into the role of wise old man, accepting
punishment for injury given; seeking peace with his son (*pacem faciatis
oro,* 992; cf. the reference to peace and ambassadorship toward a *sodalitas* at *Most.* 1125–26); asking Eutychus, in his role as *sodalis* (995) to inter-

vene with Charinus on his behalf; and indirectly reminding Lysimachus of past *beneficia* he, as client, has received from Demipho (996). The social relations are reordered, and the culmination of the new regime comes not in a drunken party, as in *Bacchides* or *Stichus,* but in a declaration of a new law (*legem,* 1015), whereby anyone over sixty, married or not, who chases after prostitutes will be classified as a fool and deprived of his property. The law, applied retroactively to Demipho, prevents any future altercation over the money he lost in purchasing Charinus's girlfriend. It also reinforces comedy's general preference for young over old, and expenditure over saving, since it goes on to say that while sexagenarians are forbidden to take whores, young men are of course welcome to do so with impunity. The fantastic nature of the law is a reaffirmation of the comic ethos, yet it is proclaimed by the young son Eutychus and functions rhetorically and thematically as the culmination of his performance as the ideal *sodalis.*

Plautus's incorporation of convivial song, even in the paradoxical form of calm speech and sober wisdom, into civic comedy must be understood as part of a broader strategy whereby comedy seeks to harmonize discordant elements of Roman culture. Whereas Salian song, as argued in the previous chapter, epitomizes music's ability to move the human subject from historical to cosmic time, to link the individual to larger processes of communal and natural renewal, comedy takes advantage of a ritual occasion to address urgent concerns of the historically situated community.[69] To be sure, comedy derives its authority in part from its association with the sort of ritual occasions exemplified by the Salian rite. Indeed, at least at Rome, comedy is designed to be performed at religiously and politically sanctioned festivals.[70] And in its repeated emphasis on relations between the generations and, in particular, the coming into self-mastery of male youth, comedy constitutes a staged, civic version of earlier rituals marking the ascendancy of a new generation.[71]

At the same time, Plautine comedy enacts new and complex relationships of authority and mastery during a period in which Roman society's dependence on slave labor is growing significantly.[72] It negotiates relations between the civilian adolescent and the professional soldier in an era that witnesses Rome's transformation from a city fighting for survival to an unchallenged imperial power.[73] It thematizes generational conflict before a population differentiated by markedly different generational experiences of war and peace, of rural uprooting versus urban growth. Yet despite, or perhaps because of, its awareness of social tension and conflict, comedy holds out the prospect of reconciliation in its enactment of—and, in the finale of every performance, collapse into—convivial song. Comedy seeks to unify the disparate elements of Roman society by inviting them all to adhere to the ethics of *sodalitas*. It reverses the disruptive or factional potential of convivial culture by positing conviviality and *sodalitas* as goals of all free Roman men. Through its mastery of the schemes of ritualized conviviality, it deploys conviviality to a different end.[74]

In its exuberant rush toward the climactic *convivium* Plautine comedy seeks to submerge all other familiar song types. Over and over again, to a degree still too little recognized, comedy incorporates or parodies other forms of song. Paradoxically this process of parody and reuse preserves for the literary and cultural historian evidence of the "preliterary" song types of archaic Rome: for parody, especially in a popular genre like comedy, presupposes at least some familiarity with the object being parodied. Parody in Plautine comedy operates in a manner akin to the role Jean-Paul Cèbe ascribes to the demons and monsters of other Italian theatrical traditions. Of the latter Cèbe writes that demonic "figures of excess set in relief the elegance and beauty of the second roles," such as gods, heroes, officers, and youths.[75] So too, the deformation of tragedy, oratory, philosophy, love song, aristocratic braggadocio, funeral oration, and prayer, all of which are parodied in Plautus's comedies, sets in relief the attractiveness of the convivial song and convivial ethos.[76] Much like nineteenth-century American blackface minstrel shows, which took as the parodic targets of their olios, or mixtures, performance types ranging from opera and Shakespearean tragedy to the songs of slaves on plantations, so too Plautine comedy, also situated at a moment of massive social, economic, demographic, and cultural transformation, seeks to enhance its authority by articulating its relationship to other modes of verbal artistry.[77] By parodying other performance genres or song types, comedy (like minstrelsy) acknowledges their social significance while at the same time subordinating them to its (allegedly) more comprehensive project.

But perhaps the most important paradox with respect to comedy is its imaginative representation of social harmony unguided by the state—in the very service of the state. At state-sponsored festivals, the troupe of comic performers stages plays deeply engaged with issues of solidarity and hierarchy, authority and resistance, reproduction and sterility, exchange and investment, yet situated in what one scholar has described as a Greco-Roman fantasy land.[78] In Durkheimian terms, comedy advances an image of mechanical solidarity (i.e., the conviviality of the *sodales,* where individuals are presumed to resemble each other) for the purpose of creating the organic solidarity necessary for the maintenance of the highly differentiated social, political, and economic order of Rome in the late third and early second centuries BC.[79] Like the Salian rite, it constitutes a talisman of sovereignty, but one that, rather than being fixed in the materiality of the manufactured object, is now forever to be recreated in performance. Comedy's denial of the object (a false denial, as we shall see momentarily) destabilizes its ritual impact, creating a gap, a need that can only be fulfilled by incessant reperformance. Comedy is thus the prototype of an evolved civic culture in which every "player" must in effect perform on stage, and yet every performance is found wanting.[80]

As prototype of a new, more complex state formation, comedy lays bare two of the "public secrets" on which the state relies. One is the impossibility (yet necessity) of the convivial ideal: there is no longer any way, remotely, in which all Romans can dine at the same table, can "live together" (con-vivere) as notional equals, and yet this very ideal is, as we have seen, what comedy holds forth through its privileging of convivial song. And the other public secret is the material (as well as ideological) dependence of the new state on slavery. It is not just a question of comedy being "about" slaves because Rome now has far more slaves in its midst than it did in previous generations. (Although surely the presence of slaves in the audience shapes many aspects of comic performance.)[81] Rather the slave is constituted by comedy as the ritual object, the materialized outcome of processes of transformation, whose status continues beyond the ritual performance as a guarantor of the less stable, indeed inherently unstable, transformation of youth into adult, non-Roman into Roman. (Should the slaves, like the *ancilia*, ever begin to move *sponte sua*, of their own accord, Rome would indeed be at risk, as the Romans surely knew.) What is more, the permanence of this transformation is naturalized by its assimilation to the prior division between male and female, the prior creation of women as a separate stratum—an aspect of comedy made clear in multiple ways from the exclusion of female performers to the consistent celebration of phallic sexuality. Once again we might invoke Durkheim, this time for his representation of women as "the primary occupational caste, sub specie aeternitatis."[82] Woman's status as such is guaranteed by the very rites of passage that comedy co-opts and subsumes to its own ends—namely to objectify the slave as the open secret of Roman *imperium*.

But it is not just the objectified slave who is thrust into history at the conclusion of the comic ritual. Convivial song, too, carries forward into history the special, authoritative status granted it by comedy. While we may never have sufficient evidence to grasp the lived experience of *convivia* during the Roman Republic, certainly surviving texts point to the discursive impact of comedy's convivial song. As I have suggested, Plautus's use of convivial song mythologizes a more complicated, contingent, polemical practice; but, in so doing, it shapes the future history of conviviality. Questions of the relationship between *sodalitas* and *civi-*

tas, of the construction of free masculinity through convivial protocol, of the materiality of slaves, will reemerge time and again as Roman authors invoke the real or imagined convivial context, especially in poetry (i.e., song) that represents itself as convivial. Convivial song thus resembles the choral song of the *salii* and other priesthoods as both a point of reference and an authorizing prototype for all Roman song. For analytical purposes it may be helpful to keep in mind a difference between choral song and convivial song, between the "religious" performance of the whole community or its ritual delegates and the "secular" performance of private sodalities. But as we have seen, just as Salian song shades over from the public to the private, the sacred to the secular, so too convivial song, through its mythologization on the comic stage, becomes an aspect of public, state-sponsored performance. Conviviality as a ritualized practice is laid claim to by a set of agents (performers and audience alike) initially excluded from it. And their reritualization of convivial action and convivial song in yet another context makes both available for yet another round of reclamation. Although "ritualization is first and foremost a strategy for the construction of certain types of power relationships," nonetheless "ritual mastery . . . means . . . that the social body in turn is able to appropriate a field of action structured in great measure by others."[83]

The Redeployment of Ritualized Schemes

If comedy stages relations between *sodales* and other members of society in order to push the limits of *sodalitas* beyond the confines of the aristocratic *convivium* (or, in Bell's terms, redeploys the schemes of the *convivium* for its own strategic purposes), the aristocratic *sodales* are not above pushing back. Through its own privileging of *sodalitas* as a vision of harmonious civic interaction, comedy opens a space for *sodales* to perform as if they were coextensive with the larger community. The latter would seem to be the strategy of satire, a literary genre and social practice that the Romans saw as distinctively and completely their own.[84] Already in the heyday of civic comedy we find evidence of literary satire—associated first with Ennius, then a bit later with Lucilius. Whatever its prehistory, satire, as attested by these authors and those who retrospectively assigned them a position as originators of a satiric tradition, is a self-consciously citified (*urbanus*) genre that claims as its performance space the *convivium* and, in time, the lecture hall, a kind of alternative space of *sodalitas*.[85]

In contrast to comedy, which stages social practices, including sodality and conviviality, as if they were taking place in our presence, satire interposes the satirist between the activity described and the reader or listener. We are continually reminded of the existence of *convivia*, even, in a sense, invited into the convivial circle of the satirist and his friends, but only as eavesdroppers, or "overreaders," to use Oliensis's term.[86] Indeed Horace explicitly describes the prototypical satirist Lucilius as "entrusting his secrets to his [soon to be publicized] books as if to faithful *sodales*" (*Sat.* 2.1.30) and, in defending his own satirical practice on the model of Lucilius, assumes a convivial context for both (2.1.68–74) Satire thus replicates the structure of religious practices in which the commensality of the few is to be observed by the many, but infuses the commensality of the few with the civic-mindedness, or *pars pro toto* sensibility, assigned to it by comedy.[87] Without comedy's ritualized expansion of the range of *sodalitas*, satire could scarcely hope to present itself as offering guidance for the population as a whole. To put it another way, having constructed the *sodalis* as the prototypical citizen through its own ritualized practice, comedy is in no position to take him back if he presumes to act in a less than wholly inclusive manner.

Once we shift our attention to satire — which has a long history within Roman culture, encompassing not only Ennius and Lucilius, but Varro, Horace, Persius, and Juvenal as well — we begin to see how the process of ritualization, with its implicit dialectic of domination (i.e., enforcement of schemes) and resistance (possibility for redeployment of schemes) repeats itself within a narrowly conceived tradition. In relationship to other social practices, satire represents the redeployment of the ritual mastery of the *sodales* to ends different from the constitution of the unified citizen body, whether hierarchically arrayed, as in the Salian rite, or imagined as a collection of equals, as in comedy. Satire can thus be understood, despite its conservative ethics and aristocratic politics, as resisting the hegemony constituted by other sodalician practices. But as its own ritualized practice, whether construed as writing, reciting, circulating, or some combination thereof, satire constructs and enforces its own hegemony while at the same time creating the possibility of resistance to itself. Each author in turn seeks to establish his mastery of the ritualized practices of satiric performance (language, tropes, meter, personae, etc.) even as he uses that mastery to redefine the practice to his own advantage.

This model of ritualization and redeployment may seem self-evident when applied to the internal dynamics of a literary genre. What has not been self-evident, however, is that such a model works — for satire or any genre — because it replicates in the micropractice of a single tradition processes of redemptive hegemony, of domination and resistance, and of subject formation that are constitutive of social practice and social relations more generally. A genre does not cease to be song just because it gets written down or because its agents recognize it as a genre. As we shall see in subsequent chapters, even the most fervid advocates of individual traditions and genres within the Roman world remained aware, if only to the extent that they did not deny it, that all literature is song. In the present and the preceding chapter we have examined how song as verbal practice constituted itself in the context of ritual and how, through its simultaneous construction of agents, it plays off the field of its own creation, setting in motion an exchange of powers and positions and materializing an array of abstractions that, although not in each instance unique to Rome, nonetheless make of Rome a distinctive culture. Our focus has been on the early stages of Roman culture, in part because the evidence to be considered, although abundant, is relatively limited, in part because the Romans themselves never ceased to authorize later practices through reference to earlier. In subsequent chapters the issue of ritualization, that is, of the emergence, both over time and in time, of song's authority, will move to the background as we consider the synchronic workings of a cultural system based on a key distinction between ritualized and everyday speech and the related, mutually informing tensions between song and play, song and the body, and song and sacrifice. But it is the ritualization of language in distinctive contexts, as both a historically specific and ongoing, repeated process, that defines the power of song to make and remake the world.

THREE· SONG AND SPEECH

I N BOOK 5 OF OVID'S *METAMORPHOSES* THE MUSES, GODDESSES of song and dance, welcome Minerva graciously and tell her of their victory over the Emathides, who had dared to challenge them in a contest of song. The chief Muse describes the rebellious performance of these upstart women, who ridiculed the Olympian deities by reporting their self-transformation into animals in order to escape the wrath of the Titans. In return, the Muse Calliope had sung a politically correct but preposterously complex hymn to Ceres that included reference, among other things, to the imprisonment of Typhoeus, the rape of Proserpina, the transformation of Cyane, the origin of the newt, the blighting of the earth, the tale-telling and punishment of Ascalaphus, the creation of the Sirens, the compromise between Ceres and Jupiter, and the legend of Arethusa, in both abbreviated and extended versions. The Muses, by their own report, won hands down. Although defeated, the Emathides shouted abuse (*convicia . . . iacerent*, Ov. Met. 5.664–65). What else was to be done, except turn them into magpies? And so they remain, still chattering, making an immense effort to speak (*studiumque immane loquendi*, 5.678).

The story of the rivalry between the Muses and the soon-to-be magpies is one of several in Ovid's *Metamorphoses* that focus on the suppression of rebellious voices.[1] It seems no accident that the episode is placed at the end of the first third of the poem, which, loosely speaking, describes the formation of the Olympian order. The metamorphosis of the Emathides anticipates the story of the silencing of Arachne in book 6 and occupies a structural position comparable to the tale of Orpheus, which straddles books 10 and 11 (i.e., the transition from the second to the final third of the poem) and also concerns the power and

the limitations of song. Apart from any political or autobiographical
significance we may wish to assign to a story of divine punishment for
unacceptable song as related by the exiled singer Ovid, the episode of
the Muses and their rivals crystallizes in a few hundred lines the key
elements of the system of verbal performance that characterizes Roman culture. Implicit in the Ovidian narrative are distinctions between
song and everyday speech, as well as subtler differentiations within the
field of song between autonomous and derivative performances and
between the ritualized aspect of song and the ritual mastery of song
carried into new contexts. These distinctions, as we shall see, characterize the Roman system of verbal performance from its earliest days
onward, underwrite Roman reflections on the origins of song, and provide signposts for understanding historical struggles over verbal mastery and, as a consequence, political and social power in the Roman
world. In effect, the story of the defeat of the Emathides via a cosmological song recapitulates in miniature the larger processes of ritualization and foundation-through-song discussed in the previous chapters,
while also granting access to the inner workings of the Roman system
of verbal performance. The primary aim of this chapter is to sketch the
contours of that system in both its synchronic and diachronic aspects.
But it will not be possible to ignore the evasions or misrecognitions on
which Rome's system of verbal performance, like any social enterprise,
ultimately depends. Indeed, Ovid's own story of the Muses and their
mimetic rivals brings the central problem of song—for the Romans as
well as for their interpreters—to our attention, because it requires us
to confront the tension between the symbolic and mimetic aspects of
verbal performance or, as we shall redefine it in succeeding chapters,
the problematic implications of song as embodied practice.

A Short Lexicon of Verbal Performance:
Cano, Loquor, Dico, Canto

Let us consider how the key opposition between song (*cano*) and speech
(*loquor*) plays out in the tale told by Ovid in book 5 before examining
the precise meaning of the terms in question. Of the Emathides the
verb *cano* is used but once, precisely when their leader commences her
Gigantomacheia (319). Everywhere else their speech acts, both when
they are human and when they have been transformed into birds, are
designated otherwise. When Minerva first hears them, as birds, making
a greeting (*salutantum*), she thinks they are human, with such assurance
(or perhaps with such clear articulation) do they seem to be speaking
(*tam certa loquentes*, 296). And indeed they lament their fate (*querentes*,
298), they imitate everything as they perch on their branches (*institerant*

ramis imitantes omnia picae, 299). Although the chief Muse acknowledges that during the contest the leader of the Emathides is in fact singing (*canit,* 319), she concludes her description of the human performance with a different sort of phrase: "So far did she move her vocalizing lips to the lyre" (*hactenus ad citharam vocalia moverat ora,* 332). When the daughters of Pierus have been declared the losers of the contest, they utter abuse (*convicia,* 663), they curse (at least that's how the Muse sees it — *maledicta,* 666), they laugh (*rident,* 669), they express disdain (*spernunt,* 668), until at last, being transformed into birds, they struggle to speak (*conatae loqui,* 670), they long to lament (*volunt plangi,* 675), and they find themselves still endowed with vocal facility (*facundia prisca,* 677) and a strident garrulousness (*raucaque garrulitas,* 678). Women who began as rebellious singers end up as birds that endeavor to speak. Indeed, the final words of the episode, and of the book, seem to back away from assigning real speech to the now-transformed Emathides. The episode opened with Minerva thinking (*putat,* 297) they sounded human; it concludes with their *studium immane loquendi* (678): a great, even grotesque or monstrous, eagerness to participate in the characteristic human form of communication, speech.

The irony that birds, creatures conventionally associated with singing, can barely speak, though it plays just below the surface of the text, is reinforced by Ovid's persistent association of the Muses with precisely the power that undid the Emathides, namely the power to sing. The identification of the Muses with forms and derivatives of *cano* is relentless to the point of excess. Six times the word is used at the commencement of the report of the Muses' performance: "Perhaps, Minerva, you are not available to listen to our songs" (*sed forsitan otia non sint / nec nostris praebere vacet tibi cantibus aurem,* 333–34), suggests the Muse. "Do not hesitate, but sing to me your hymn in order" (*Ne dubita, vestrumque mihi refer ordine carmen,* 335), replies Minerva. And so Calliope strums the strings and joins songs to the lyre (*atque haec percussis subiungit carmina nervis,* 340). No sooner has she begun than she reminds us that her themes are those that must be sung to the goddess Ceres (*illa canenda mihi est,* 344), and she prays that her song will be worthy of the goddess, for the goddess is worthy of song (*utinam modo dicere possem / carmina digna deae! certe dea carmine digna est,* 344–45). And perhaps lest we forget, when the song of Calliope at last has run its course, another Muse tells us that her singing sister, "the greatest of us," did indeed "bring the song just performed to its conclusion" (*finierat dictos e nobis maxima cantus,* 662).

It is not as though the Muses only sing. When Minerva arrives, she merely addresses the Muses (*sic est affata sorores,* 255) and repeats a rumor (*fama . . pervenit ad aures,* 256). Urania takes up (*excipit,* 260) this conversational overture and confirms the rumor (*vera tamen fama est*, 262). Minerva responds, calling (*vocat*, 267) the Muses fortunate in their study and their locale. Not so fortunate, says one of the Muses, addressing the goddess (*quam sic affata est una sororum*, 268), and proceeds to tell the story of King Pyreneus's attempted rape of her sisters and herself. In what seems to be the midst of this rather jumbled narrative (asyndeton, parenthetical asides, unmotivated suicide of the king), Ovid describes the Muse as speaking (*loquebatur*, 294), only to be interrupted by the fluttering of the magpies' wings (*pennae sonuere*, 294). In other words, song and speech are not unique to particular characters; nor are they to be construed as freestanding categories or genres of discourse. Rather, they coexist in relationship to one another, with song in effect constituting an intensification — or, to use our earlier terminology, ritualization — of speech. The Muses speak as they show Minerva around their homeland but switch to song during their competition with their upstart rivals. The Emathides too are capable of song under certain circumstances, but having been turned into birds, they lose that power and must struggle to maintain the more basic ability to communicate through language (*studium loquendi*). Of course, the contest between the Muses and the Emathides and the opposition between speaking and singing are embedded in a text that represents itself as *carmen* from the outset (*Met.* 1.4), in implied opposition to the *locuta* of everyday, non-poetic, unmusical expression.

Ovid's story of the Muses and their rivals thematizes an opposition between song and speech that is at the heart of the Roman system of verbal artistry. Speech, the unmarked activity of human communication, serves to convey information or express emotion. The most basic word for speaking is the verb *loquor*, but words such as *for/adfor, queror*, and *voco* express specific aspects or versions of speech that fall short of turning it into song. As the verb used of everyday speech, *loquor* can be modified with an adverb referring to the language in which the speech is carried out, for example, *Latine loquitur, Punice loquitur* ("she speaks Latinly," "she speaks Punicly"). What might be described as metaphorical uses of *loquor* in fact retain the general sense of unmarked communication, which is then made more specific by identification of the source or semiotic system. Thus users of sign language, wind blowing through trees, and a musical instrument can all be said to engage in the activity referred to by *loquor*.[2]

Cano and its relatives *cantus, cantio, canticum, carmen*, and perhaps *occentatio*, on the other hand, describe speech made special through the use of specialized diction, regular meter, musical accompaniment, figures of sound, mythical or religious subject matter, and socially authoritative performance context: in effect, speech that has been ritualized.[3] In the case of the different speech acts of the Muses and their rivals, all of which are communicated in Ovidian hexameter, neither meter nor diction constitutes the basis of differentiation. But performance context (i.e., the competition to be judged by the Muses), musical accompaniment (the cithara of the Emathides, the *nervi*, or strings, of the Muse), and claim to authoritativeness differentiate their songs from their speeches. Indeed, the performance of the Emathides commences as song (*bella canit superum*, 319), but once its noncanonical content, ridiculing the Olympian gods, has become clear, it changes, as it were, into mere vocalization (*vocalia . . . ora*, 332). In other words, as it loses its authority, its identity as song dissipates as well. The Emathides have not fully mastered the rituals of performance; hence, both their competence and their ideology are called into question.[4]

Ovid emphasizes the paradigmatic nature of the contest between the Emathides and the Muses by including in the songs of each reference to the monster Typhoeus. The rebellious song of the Emathides describes the emergence of Typhoeus as scattering the frightened Olympians; the canonical song, after a brief invocation to Ceres, sets the scene for the rape of Proserpina by reminding us that Typhoeus had been defeated and pinned down beneath Sicily. Typhoeus, it will be recalled, was the last and greatest threat to Zeus's new world order in Hesiod's *Theogony*. His description, near the end of the *Theogony*, inverts the characteristics of musical beauty, order, and harmony ascribed to the Muses at the outset: he emits a cacophony of sounds, simultaneously bellowing like a bull, roaring like a lion, and rushing like a windstorm. In Hesiod's account Typhoeus threatens Zeus by negating the characteristics represented by the Muses and necessary to proper order, among the Olympians and on earth. By invoking the story of Typhoeus within his own story of the rivalry between the Emathides and the Muses, Ovid further clarifies what is at stake in the latter: not only the differentiation between song and speech, but also the right relationship between song and social authority. At the same time, Ovid enriches the significance of the story of Typhoeus by adding a dimension not evident in the Hesiodic account. For Ovid's Typhoeus can be understood not just in relationship to the Muses, as in Hesiod, but also in relationship to the soon-to-be birds, the Emathides, of his own story. The ancients understood human song to be an imitation and adaptation of sounds of nature, especially the song of birds. Typhoeus, too, emits the sounds of nature, but precisely those sounds that cannot be transformed into song. His presence in Ovid's story thus complicates the relationship between culture and nature in the genesis of song, adding an element of selection to the process—which aspects of nature are to be imitated and adapted?—while also representing a version of nature to which the Emathides, even as birds, can be consigned. Typhoeus, we might say, is the mimetic faculty gone haywire, lacking the element of prohibition that turns it into an agent of human culture. He is the chaos out of which both the cosmos and the work of art emerge (cf. Kandinsky), the slashing effect of everyday language against which the ritualized performance of the Muses provides protection. Not surprisingly, the Emathides who sing of his prowess are turned into mimes without limit, as they end up "imitating everything."

The episode of the Muses and the Pierides draws on and reinforces the distinction between *cano* and *loquor,* or singing and speaking, as characteristic of the Roman lexical and cultural system. It instantiates a further aspect of this system with its use of the verb *dico,* which can be translated as "to express with authority" or "to insist upon the validity of."[5] Uses of the verb *dico* cluster near the conclusion of the episode. When the Muse has completed her song, she is said, literally, to have "brought to an end the songs expressed authoritatively" (*finierat dictos . . . cantus,* 662). Thereupon the nymphs, whom both sides had accepted as judges, "express authoritatively their opinion that the Muses had triumphed through their harmonious sound" (*At Nymphae vicisse deas Helicona colentes / concordi dixere sono,* 663–64). And in the first lines of the following book, Minerva is said to have "listened to such authoritative utterances" and to have "approved both the songs of the Muses and their legitimate anger" (*praebuerat dictis Tritonia talibus aurem; / Carminaque Aonidum, iustamque probaverat iram,* Ov. *Met.* 6.1–2). The preceding remarks of the Muses can here be called *dicta* because Minerva accepts them as true and valid, that is, they are authoritative from the standpoint of the key figure in the narrative. That she is said also to approve of their songs — *carmina Aonidum* — does not mean that the songs exist independently of the *dicta:* indeed, both the reported song of the Emathides and the reperformed song of the greatest Muse constitute part of the *dicta* to which Minerva has just offered her ear. In other words, any *carmen* can be construed as a *dictum,* although not every *dictum* need be a *carmen. Dico* constitutes the agent's attempt to transfer the power implicit in ritualization beyond the confines of the rite itself.

One more term employed in Ovid's narrative requires examination. The basic nominal derivative of *cano,* and keyword of our study, is *carmen,* a word that is at least three times ascribed to the song of the Muses (*Met.* 5. 335, 5.340, 6.2), but withheld from the Emathides. But twice as well the Muses' song is called — by themselves — *cantus:* once when the lead Muse wonders whether Minerva really has time to hear a replay of their ditties (5.334), once when she announces the end of her performance of the previously performed song that had won the Muses their victory (5.662). Politeness is part of the issue here: Minerva grants the Muses the dignity of song that they seem reluctant to claim for themselves. Accuracy is at stake, too: *cantus* is the precise term for song that is reperformed, such as Calliope's song, which in its original version (5.340) was *carmen* but now, as replay, is *cantus*.[6] Although *cantus* is ritualized speech, marked in this instance by diction, context, and musicality, its authority is secondary to that of the original song, or *carmen*. When Cicero mocks contemporary poets as mere *cantores Euphorionis*, it is not just because they chant the works of Euphorion: it is because, in his view, they do not sing in their own voices, they do not authorize their own verbal productions. In the Ovidian episode, the narrating Muse defines the action of the original singer as *cano* and her repetition of the song as *canto*.

The interrelationship among *cano*, *loquor*, *dico*, and *canto* sketched here is hardly unique to Ovid. For the basic contrast between song and speech, we may consider a brief scene from Plautus's *Bacchides*. The slave Chrysobolus boasts to Nicobulus of his success as an orator (a calling that straddles the boundary between song and speech):

> CH I'm the greatest orator! I've made the man weep through castigation,
> through *curses* I cunningly contrived. NI And what'd he say?
> CH Not a word! Teary and silent he listened to what I was *saying*
> silently he wrote out some tablets, applied the seal, and handed them to me.
> He told me to give them to you, but I fear they *sing* the same old song.
> Check out the seal: isn't it his?

> CH optumu' sum orator. ad lacrumas hominem coegi castigando
> *maleque dictis,* quae quidem quiui comminisci. NI quid ait?
>   CH verbum
> nullum fecit: lacrumans tacitus auscultabat quae ego *loquebar;*
> tacitus conscripsit tabellas, opsignatas mi has dedit.
> tibi me iussit dare, sed metuo ne idem *cantent* quod priores.
> nosce signum. estne eiius?

> (Plaut. *Bacch.* 981–86)

In Chrysobolus's fanciful account (designed to get Nicobulus to hand over money to him), he presents himself as a successful orator, one who used *dicta* (in this case, authoritatively negative ones) to reduce his target to silence. While his imaginary speech was authoritative, its content can be described as mere talk (*loquebar*). But the response it elicits, in the form of a formal, written request from son to father, is represented as song—not the autonomous song associated with *cano,* but a repeated song that is nevertheless expected to have an impact on its audience. Although the contrast here between song and speech does not assume the thematic significance it acquires in Ovid, it does presuppose a way of identifying verbal performance as unmarked (*loqu-*) or marked (*can-, dic-*).

In a passage from Cicero's *Pro Murena,* formulaic, legal language is marked as song in part through its excess of speech. Cicero argues that the *iuris consulti,* or legal experts, invented formulaic expressions in order to confuse people and to make their own occupation necessary. Instead of saying "the Sabine property is mine—No, mine" (*Fundus Sabinus meus est, Immo meus*), they use roundabout formulas totaling at least twenty-five words: the petitioner, he jokes, hardly knows how to respond to so talkative a litigant (*tam loquaciter litigioso,* 26). Shortly thereafter, Cicero makes clear that the very expressions he has just ridiculed as too full of speech are in fact song: according to Cicero, the praetor issues just such a legal formula (*carmen compositum,* 26) so as to avoid having to speak of his own accord (*ne . . . sua sponte loqueretur,* 26). The legal expert's role as producer or performer of song (or both) is reinforced when Cicero likens him to a "Latin flute player" (*transit idem iuris consultus tibicinis Latini modo,* 26). But this songlike quality exists without actual music: all that is needed is a marked relationship to unmarked, everyday speech. As for the formula's identification as *carmen* not *cantus,* it seems to be the result of the special authority of the praetor: in this case, the fact that the praetor (and not someone else) applies this particular formula to the case at hand is what gives the expression its performative force.[7]

Cicero also provides evidence of the overlap in meaning between *cano* and *dico.* In his defense of Caelius, he quotes—and expands on—a citation from Ennius that appears to have been used earlier by one of the prosecutors. "At this point," he states, "I can cite [*possum dicere, Cael.* 18] the same passage that the distinguished gentleman Marcus Crassus just cited [*paulo ante dixit*] when he complained [*quereretur*] about the arrival of king Ptolemy." That the passage quoted is the opening of a tragedy (specifically, Ennius's *Medea*) in no way prevents Cicero from describing his recitation with the verb *dico.* Indeed, he engages in a game of one-upmanship with Crassus by demonstrating the relevance of the next line from the tragedy, a citation he expressly describes as song ("I'd like to extend the song a bit, if I may": *ac longius mihi quidem contexere hoc carmen liceret, Cael.* 18).

This interplay between *carmen* and *dicere*—with the first emphasizing the characteristics of song that differentiate it from speech, the second calling attention to its authority or the authority of the one who performs it or uses it authoritatively as part of his own performance — becomes something of a topos in the Latin poetic tradition. In Catullus's poem 62 the chorus of young men and young women use the verbs *dicere* and *canere* in close proximity to describe the delivery of the hymeneal song. The young men announce that the hymeneal song will be proclaimed (*dicetur*, 62.4), and then proclaim it (5). The corresponding group of women proceeds to evaluate the men's performance (*non temere exsiluere*, 9), even as the women look forward to a competition in song (*canent quod vincere par est*, 9). To which the young men respond, commenting on the preparations of the young women and expressing doubt over their own final victory: the women will now begin their challenge song (*dicere iam incipient*, 18), and it will be fitting for us to respond (*respondere decebit*, 18). The verb *cano* appears specifically in the context of the women's evaluation of the men's skills as performers. The men use *dico* (particularly in line 18) when anticipating the utterance to which they will be obliged to respond. But they are both speaking of the same kind of performance and the same kind of utterance. It is simply a question of the perspective from which their utterances are viewed. *Dico* lays claim to the power generated by language's ritualization into song without, through its very presence, necessarily invoking an immediate ritual context. At the same time, it is worth noting that neither Cicero's citation of Ennius nor the Catullan youths' recitation of the hymeneal refrain is characterized as *canto*: that is, mere repetition or reperformance of someone else's authorizing performance. In Cicero's case, the implication seems to be that he Cicero is validating the authenticity of the quotation from Ennius, while in the case of the young men it is their status as ritual agents that gives the hymeneal refrain its force: if you or I or one of Catullus's listeners were to recite it, we would be chanting (*canto*), not authorizing (*dico*).

Vergil's poetry also offers numerous illustrations of the relationship between the expressions *cano* and *dico*.[8] In the *Georgics* rural youth and others anticipate the harvest of grain by performing blood sacrifice, praying in a chorus, wreathing their temples with oak leaves, dancing, albeit clumsily, and reciting songs (*det motus incompositos et carmina dicat*, 1.350). The combination of song, recitation, dance, and chorus recurs in Vergil's description of the fortunate souls Aeneas observes in the underworld:

> Some exercise their limbs in the grassy palaestra
> competing at play and struggling in the tawny sand,
> others beat the choral tempo with their feet and chant hymns.

pars in gramineis exercent membra palaestris,
contendunt ludo et fulva luctantur harena;
pars pedibus plaudunt choreas et carmina dicunt.

(Verg. Aen. 6.642–44)

While our focus here is on the lexical relationship between *cano* and *dico*, it is worth noting that by using the terms *palaestra*, the Greek exercise ground, and *ludus* and *harena*, clear references to Roman practice, Vergil seems to suggest that the array of activities in Elysium are appropriate for Greeks and Romans alike. Indeed, the whole setting has rightly been seen as evoking the Campus Martius, site of youthful exercise and during Vergil's lifetime increasingly important locale for the monument-building activities of the Roman elite.[9]

The universality of song is at issue in another Vergilian passage combining *cano* and *dico*. In book 9 of the *Aeneid*, while Ascanius and other Trojan refugees are cowering in their fort in the absence of Aeneas, the Italian hero Numanus Remulus, brother-in-law of Turnus, taunts them for their Phrygian effeminacy. The refugees, he charges, wear embroidered finery, indulge in choral dances, have sleeves on their tunics and fillets on their turbans. Let them depart for high Dindyma, "where the flute supplies a double tune to the devotees of Magna Mater" (*ite per alta / Dindyma, ubi adsuetis biforem dat tibia cantum,* 9.618). "Leave arms to men and yield to the sword" (*sinite arma uiris et cedite ferro,* 9.620). Song per se is not the basis of the taunt, however, for Numanus's own remarks are understood as song, or rather as objects of the verbs *dico* and *cano:*

These boasts and dire songs
Ascanius did not tolerate.

Talia iactantem dictis ac dira canentem
non tulit Ascanius

(Verg. Aen. 9.621–22)

Numanus's taunts lay claim to being true (they are *dicta*) and take the shape of disturbing incantation (he sings them). What is more, the passage further exemplifies the recurrent distinction between *cano,* as song generated by the voice of a person with special access to sources of authority (fate, tradition, etc.), and *canto/cantus,* as musical performance to someone else's tune or singing of a song authorized by another singer (*dat tibia cantum,* 9.618). Part of what makes Numanus's speech such a slur is the implication that when the Trojans do sing, it is with someone (or here, something) else setting the tune.

In the *Eclogues*—a veritable treasure trove of song types and performance contexts—*dico* and *cano* recur in close proximity, each clarifying the nuance of the other. For example, at the beginning of *eclogue* 8, the poet promises to recite the song contest of Damon and Alphesiboeus:

The Muse of the shepherds Damon and Alphesiboeus—
at whose contest the heifer marveled, forgetful of her grasses,
at whose song [*carmine*] the lynxes were stupefied
and the rivers, transformed, ceased to flow—
the Muse of Damon and Alphesiboeus we will recite [*dicemus*].

Pastorum Musam Damonis et Alphesiboei
Immemor herbarum quos est mirata iuvenca
certantes, quorum stupefactae carmine lynces
et mutata suos requierunt flumina cursus,
Damonis Musam dicemus et Alphesiboei.
                                        (Verg. *Ecl.* 8.1–5)

While it is just possible that Vergil avoids the verb *cano* for variety's sake, it seems more likely that the nuance of *dico*, its association with authority or reliability, is relevant here. The poet promises to give a faithful rendition of the songs of the shepherds; his own authority validates the reperformance.

As the proem of eclogue 8 progresses, or rather digresses, into an apostrophe to an unspecified *tu* (either Octavian or Pollio), *dico* and *carmen* reappear. Will that day ever come, the poet asks, when I may celebrate (*dicere*, 8.8) your accomplishments? Will it ever be possible to bear throughout the whole world your songs (*carmina*, 8.10), alone worthy of Sophocles? We are hardly to suppose that Vergil proposes to celebrate a great man's deeds in less than magnificent poetry: the use of *dicere* indicates that he intends to do so in an authoritative and reliable manner.

Perhaps the most striking instance of the interplay of *cano* and *dico* in the *Eclogues* is to be found in the famous proem to eclogue 6. This passage, with its important statement of poetic and political principles, is shaped by the dynamic relationship between *cano* and *dico*, namely, the materiality of the utterance and its social or situational significance

When I was about to sing kings and battles

Cum canerem reges et proelia . . .
                                        (Verg. *Ecl.* 6.3)

—that is, when I was leaving behind everyday speech and taking up the composition or performance of a type of special speech, in this case epic poetry—

> Cynthian Apollo plucked
> my ear and gave me some advice: "Tityrus, a shepherd is supposed to
> keep his sheep fat, his song slim."

> Cynthius aurem
> vellit et admonuit: "pastorem, Tityre, pinguis
> pascere oportet ovis, deductum dicere carmen."
>> (Verg. *Ecl.* 6.3–5)

In other words, sheep, even when fat, still need to be fed, but a skinny song is ready to be performed: no need, then, to fatten it up. Tityrus should feel free to pronounce his song with authority, as indeed he seems to do in the remainder of the poem.

> Now I (for there will be those who long to recite your praises,
> Varus, and to pack away harsh wars)
> will practice a rural Muse on a slender reed
> I do not sing [*cano*] what I've been ordered not to.

> nunc ego (namque super tibi erunt qui dicere laudes,
> Vare, tuas cupiant et tristia condere bella)
> agrestem tenui meditabor harundine Musam:
> non iniussa cano.
>> (Verg. *Ecl.* 6.6–9)

The eclogue singer acknowledges the legitimacy of the praises others will offer Varus but interprets Apollo's advice as prohibiting him from singing certain kinds of song. And yet, even the slender song he will produce can lead to a celebration of Varus, as the imagined reader reads (which for a Roman meant "reperforms")[10] it in the pastoral setting:

> But if anyone, captured by love,
> read these works, too, our tamarisks, Varus, will sing of you,
> the whole grove will resound.

> si quis tamen haec quoque si quis
> captus amore leget, te nostrae, Vare, myricae,
> te nemus omne canet.
>> (Verg. *Ecl.* 6.9–11)

Here, as elsewhere, when placed in proximity to one another, *dico* emphasizes the validity or authoritativeness of the utterance, while *cano* points to its aesthetic characteristics and performance context. But both verbs take as their object, expressed or implied, the *deductum carmen* of the pastoral poet.

This variation in nuance seems to be heightened when other derivatives of *cano* are employed, specifically the verb *cantare* and the nouns *cantus, cantio,* and *canticum.* As a repeated or borrowed song, *cantus* invites still stricter evaluation for its aesthetic qualities, its ability to provoke pleasure in its hearers. For example, in Cicero's *De Oratore,* as part of his praise of the perfect orator, the interlocutor Antonius asks rhetorically, "What music is sweeter than a modulated speech? What song better constructed than an artful period? What actor more charming in imitating the truth than an orator in establishing it?" (*Qui enim cantus moderata oratione dulcior inveniri potest? Quod carmen artificiosa verborum conclusione aptius? Qui actor imitanda, quam orator suscipienda veritate iucundior?* 2.34). The overall performance of the actor and the orator are compared; the words *cantus* and *carmen* may well refer to the same utterance. But, *cantus* highlights melody, tempo, or patterns set in another medium, aspects of song that are otherwise only implicit in *carmen.* Later in the same work Crassus, after discussing prose rhythm, particularly the use of clausulae, explains that members of the audience need not understand the science of such matters to be able to judge their effects. Judgment of the rhythm and sound of language (*verborum numerorum vocumque iudicio,* 3.195) is innate, he argues. Audiences react to mistakes of meter (*numeri*) such as the lengthening or shortening of a vowel and to mistakes of pronunciation (*vocum,* no example given). It is through rhythm and sound (*numeri atque voces*) that our emotions are stirred. "Their greatest power is better suited to songs and musical performances, a fact not neglected by Numa, the wisest king, and by our ancestors, as the lyre and tibiae of the solemn feasts indicate, and the verses of the Salii" (*quorum illa summa vis carminibus est aptior et cantibus, non neglecta, ut mihi videtur, a Numa rege doctissimo maioribusque nostris, ut epularum solemnium fides ac tibiae Saliorumque versus indicant,* 3.197) Just as Crassus (and, through him, Cicero) regards rhythm and sound as innate aspects of oratory, so too the reference to *carmina* suggests that they are present there as well. By adding *cantibus* to the parallel, however, Cicero again seems to be calling attention to the specifically musical features of song that constitute part, but not the sum total, of its difference from everyday speech.

If *cano* and *dico* potentially describe the same activity, and *cano* describes a marked divergence from the activity described by *loquor,* then we would expect *dico* and *loquor* to be in a relationship similar to that between *cano* and *loquor*. In fact, this is the case, although the synchronic picture is complicated somewhat by the diachronic intrusion of Greek rhetorical terminology. For example, the simplex form of *loquor* stands in contrast to the simplex form of *dico* in the following exchange from the *Epidicus* of Plautus:

> AP Why don't you speak [*loquere*] as you began? EP Two other
>   women
> after me began to gossip [*fabulari*]—but I cunningly stepped aside
> just a little, to hide the fact I was listening to their chatter [*sermoni*]
> I didn't hear the whole thing, but I didn't miss out either
> on what they were saying [*loqueretur*]. PER I'm dying to know! EP
>   Well, one of them
> stated [*dixit*] to the other— PER What? EP Be quiet and you'll find
>   out!
> After they spotted the girl your son has fallen for, she says
> "I swear, it's lucky for her her lover
> wants to set her free." "Who is he?"
> says [*inquit*] the other one. She names [*nominat*] Stratippocles
> son of Periphanes. PER I'm doomed! What am I hearing?
> EP Just what happened. After I heard them talking [*loqui*] this way
> I began to approach them little by little
> as if a crush of people was forcing me back against my will. PER I see.
> EP But the one asked [*interrogavit*] the other "How do you know?
>   Who told [*dixit*] you this?"

> (Plaut. *Epid.* 236–50)

When a character refers to the activity of speaking, to the fact that a conversation occurred, the verb is *loquor*. A verb like *fabulari* specifies the type of conversation. But *dico* is reserved for instances where reliability or authority are at issue. Thus the verb *dixit* in verse 241 anticipates the direct quotation that begins two lines later; indeed, its use here seems designed to heighten the suspense for both the internal and the external audience—what exactly did she say? *Dixit* reappears as part of the internal quotation in 250, when one of the quoted women seeks verification of the other's claim to knowledge, which she in turn provides, citing tablets sent to the girl in question by Stratippocles.

Prose texts also illustrate the contrast between *dico* and *loquor*, in both striking and subtle ways. Near the opening of the surviving text of *De Otio*, Seneca presents his interlocutor as challenging the very idea of a Stoic speaking in support of leisure.

What are you saying, Seneca? Are you abandoning your party? Surely your Stoics state authoritatively [there follows a long summary of Stoic doctrine] Why do you speak to us the precepts of Epicurus in the midst of the elements of Zeno?

Quid ais, Seneca? deseris partes? Certe Stoici vestri dicunt. . . . Quid nobis Epicuri praecepta in ipsis Zenonis principiis loqueris? (Sen. *De Otio* 1)

The interlocutor imagines Seneca as accepting Stoic speech as authoritative (*dicunt*), while only reporting (*loqueris*), without implication of acceptance, the teachings of Epicurus.

Straightforward contrast between *dico* and *loquor* is exemplified by several passages from Cicero's *Pro Caelio*. For example, after asserting that Caelius had remained loyal to the Senate during the Catilinarian Conspiracy, Cicero tries to set aside the whole issue by noting that "I am talking too much about a matter that is hardly in doubt. But the following I proclaim with confidence" (*Nimium multa de re minime dubia loquor; hoc tamen dico*, 15). The use of *dico* in effect declares Cicero's authority—as Caelius's patron and as suppressor of the conspiracy—to speak on Caelius's loyalty during the crisis. Later when he wishes to convey his conviction that he has satisfactorily defended his client he uses *dico: dicta est a me causa*, "the case has been made by me." Yet during the course of his final review of the case he seeks to clarify his description of Caelius by noting: "My point does not concern wisdom, it concerns force of spirit," or "I am not talking about wisdom, I am talking about force of spirit" (*sed ego no loquor de sapientia . . . de impetu animi loquor,* 76). In contrast to *dico, loquor* merely calls attention to the act of speaking, not to the intrinsic validity of the claim.

Use of *dico* to call attention to the validity or invalidity of the referent explains also why the same verb can be applied both to assertions, as in the contrast between *facta,* what really happened, and *dicta,* what somebody said happened, and to performative utterances, *dicere sententiam,* used, for example, of the Senate declaring its deliberate assessment of a matter. The relationship between speaker and addressee implied by *dico* is usually an asymmetric one, either because the subject of the verb has information or judgment to impart to the addressee (*dic mihi, Marce Tulli*—"tell me, Marcus Tullius") or because the subject is formally in an authoritative position vis-à-vis the addressee (as when the Senate pronounces its judgment, *dicere sententiam*) or because the subject seeks through language to change the preexisting relationship, as may be the case with the phrase from Livy, *carmina in imperatorem dicta,* describing soldiers' jesting putdown of their general during a triumphal parade. In contrast, *loquor* is more likely to imply parity or interchangeability between interlocutors: hence its frequent use with the preverb *cum*, yielding the common verb *colloquor* and noun *colloquium* referring to conversation. *Condico*, on the other hand, far from referring to a mutual exchange, means "inform," "make subject of a legal action," "fix a contract." [11]

A passage from Cicero's *Orator* illustrates one of the most common meanings constructed by the opposition *dico* and *loquor*, namely the difference between oratorical and everyday speech. Cicero is trying to make the point that Atticism consists of more than one type of verbal output. "We must admit that it is possible for Attici to orate [*dicere*] in an ornate or weighty or copious manner: unless we want to claim that neither Aeschines nor Demosthenes was Attic!" (*Orat.* 29–30). As for those who would take Thucydides as their model of Attic style, don't they understand that he offers nothing of use for the courtroom or public life? Thucydides narrates history (*res gestas et bella narrat et proelia*, 30). If he deserves praise, it is as a narrator of wars in histories (*ut in historiis bella narraret*, 32). His imitators think that when they have uttered a few abrupt and choppy remarks, of the sort that even without instruction they could have formed, they're the real thing! (*sed cum mutila quaedam et hiantia locuti sunt, quae vel sine magistro facere potuerunt, germanos se putant esse Thucydidas*, 32). In Cicero's view, the true Attic orator speaks authoritatively (*dico*) in a variety of styles; Thucydides can be grudgingly acknowledged to narrate (*narro*) with skill; the would-be Thucydideans merely talk (*loquor*) without effect.

But even in a rhetorical context, *dico* and *loquor* need not refer to a difference of genre. Rather, much like *cano* and *loquor*, they constitute a pair best understood as conveying a relationship of marked (*dico*) and unmarked (*loquor*). When Quintilian is in the course of denouncing those who rely too heavily on the experience of the schools, and not enough on practice in the courts or common sense, he writes vividly of occasions on which the special speech (*dico*) of the schoolroom must be abandoned for the real world and real talk (*loquor*) of the courtroom:

> And so some who have grown old in school are stupefied by novelty when they actually come to court, and long for everything to be just as it was in their practice exercises. But there sits the silent judge and the adversary raises his voice and no rash assertion [*temere dictum*] is ignored, and if you make an assumption it must be proved and the time clock puts an end to the performance you've practiced and developed day and night, and sometimes you have to put the bombast aside and just plain talk [*loquendum est*]. Which these "experts" don't seem to know. (Quint. *Inst.* 12.6.5)

Given the clear distinction between *dico* and *loquor,* as well as the frequent use of *dico,* especially by rhetoricians, to refer to the special speech that constitutes formal oratory, we may be puzzled by the use of *elocutio* to refer to literary, especially oratorical style. (*Elocutio* is one of the five canonical "parts" of rhetoric, corresponding to Greek *lexis.*) This selection of a compound of *loquor* to translate a Greek rhetorical term seems, paradoxically, to confirm the antiquity of the use of *dico* as an expression for the claim to authority via language. As Ernout has argued, *eloquor* was used to Romanize a concept from Greek rhetoric because the corresponding compound of *dico,* namely *edico,* already occupied an important place in the Latin lexicon, serving to describe the proclamation of a binding decree by the Senate or a magistrate.[12] In other words, *edico* designates special speech that occurs in a particular context, whereas *elocutio* comes to refer to the style that differentiates one form of special speech, oratory, from other forms or from everyday speech. In addition, the prefix *e-* in *eloquor* seems to have a core meaning of transformation from one state to another (cf. *effeminare,* to transform from male to female; *exhaurire,* to transform from full to empty).[13] Hence when applied to *loquor* it conveys a sense of transformation from unspoken to spoken, a change in phenomenological status that pushes the meaning of the verb, in spite of the unmarked status of *loquor,* into the realm of decidedly special speech. *Elocutio,* or eloquence, emerges as an important rival to socially authoritative song in a way that *locutio* never could have. Like song, it describes a "transformational activity," linking the here and now of enunciation to a world of unspoken meaning somewhere beyond.

Singing, Song, and the Limits of Literary History

Thus far this chapter has presented a synchronic analysis of the meaning of *cano* in comparison and contrast with *loquor, canto,* and *dico.* Viewing the various occurrences of these terms as manifestations of a structured lexical system makes it possible to avoid the confusion that has plagued attempts to explain the meaning of *cano/carmen* in historical terms. Such accounts of *carmina* posit an early form, describing it as *"formule cadencée,"* or "rhythmical prose."[14] But these descriptions run up against the disconcerting fact that whereas some early *carmina,* for example, the *Carmen Saliare,* may be appropriately characterized in this manner, others, such as the Twelve Tables, which collectively are described by Cicero as a *carmen necessarium* (*Leg.* 2.59), or formulas of any sort (e.g., Cic. *Fin.* 5.15; Sen. *Controv.* 2.10) do not. On such an account, what are we to make of Cato's repeated use of the verb *cantare* to describe the action of reciting gibberish, such as *"moetas uaeta daries dardaries asiadarides"* or *"huat hauat huat ista pista sista dannabo dannaustra" (Agr.* 140)?[15] Other scholars are more circumspect, referring to *carmina* as "formulaic or structured utterances,"[16] or as expressions "defined by formal character"[17] without specifying in what the "structure" or "formal character" consists. But these accounts can leave the false impression that there still must be an original, or Ur-form, of the *carmen,* of which surviving examples, in all their diversity, are manifestations or even distortions. It seems more appropriate to understand the meaning of *cano, canto, carmen,* and similar words as determined by relationship to neighboring *dicta* and *locuta.* Song is only song in relationship to speech. And the appearance of song can vary in accordance with the speech to which it is being contrasted. To call attention to the formal characteristics of *carmina* is legitimate and appropriate, because use of *cano,* especially in connection with *dico,* lays emphasis on formal, in contrast to contextual, variation from the everyday. But this is a far cry from imagining that all *carmina* aspire to the same type of formal variation from the everyday.

A structuralist understanding of the meaning of song grows out of our investigation into the uses of the relevant terms in a range of classical Latin authors. It is persuasive because it helps to account for what otherwise might seem too varied a set of referents for *cano* and *carmen.* But this interpretation of the classical data has implications for the history of song at Rome as well: if the meaning of song is determined by variation from everyday speech in the well-attested classical period, there is no compelling reason to understand its meaning as having been different in earlier periods. In other words, beginning with a structuralist approach to the meaning of song allows us to avoid preconceived notions of what early Roman song must have looked like. All we can reasonably infer is that it was somehow differentiated from everyday speech. As we investigate the history of Roman song and song culture, we would do well to leave open the possibility that variation from the everyday came in as many strains in an early period as it did in later. Earlier need not mean simpler or more basic.[18]

In fact, the range of different speech types to which *carmen/cano* is applied, from the earliest data through the latest, is remarkably diverse and worth recapitulating at this point. As we have seen in earlier chapters, it encompasses ritual performance, such as that of the Salian priests and the Arval brothers.[19] Closely related is the application of the term to prayers and hymns to deities (e.g., the *Carmen Saeculare* of Horace; the hymn to Isis described at Apul. *Met.* 11.9.10). The term *carmina* also describes the responses of the *vates* (priest-prophets consulted in times of civic crisis) and the incantations of the fetial priests, ambassadors concerned with the handing over of citizens of neighboring states and the declaration of war if such diplomacy fails.[20] When Decius Mus devotes himself to the gods of the underworld for the sake of the survival of the Roman army, he does so by reciting a *carmen* (Livy 4.20.2). Equally grim is the singing of *carmina* at the human sacrifice of a Greek man and woman in the Forum Boarium, as ascribed by Pliny to early Roman history (*HN* 28.12).

In the civic realm, the term *carmen* describes the totality of the Twelve Tables, dating to the mid-fifth century BC. Within the surviving fragments of these early legal texts, the verbal root *can*-appears with reference to magical incantation (*qui fruges excantassit, Tab.* 8.8a = Plin. *HN* 28.17) as well as to public slander against a fellow citizen (*si quis occentavisset sive carmen condidisset, quod infamiam faceret flagitiumve alteri,* 8.1a Warmington).[21] The so-called Forum inscription, dated to the sixth century BC, may refer to performance of some type of civic song in the expression *kalator*.[22] When Cicero refers to the earlier republican custom of inscribing funerary praise, he speaks of *carmen incisum* (*Sen.* 61). As suggested in an earlier chapter, the practice of inscribing laudatory song may find early exemplification in the Lapis Satricanus of the late sixth or early fifth century BC and may be linked to the tradition of *carmina convivalia* attested by Cato, Cicero, and Valerius Maximus. Also ascribed to relatively early days of the republic is the *carmen* of Appius Claudius, a set of ethical precepts of a sort familiar enough to have been parodied in Plautine comedy.[23]

Within the incipient literary tradition, words based on the root *can*-continue to signify marked as opposed to unmarked speech and, paradoxically, to provide evidence of extraliterary forms of song. In Plautus's *Miles Gloriosus,* for example, a *praecantrix* (perhaps a sorceress?) is listed among the professionals to whom a harried husband must make payment in behalf of his wife; the others include a *coniectrix* or interpreter of dreams, a *hariola* or fortune teller, and a *haruspica,* or reader of entrails (690). In *Mostellaria,* the absence of the song of the flute player (*neque tibicinem cantantem,* 934) is taken by a character as evidence that a *convivium* has dispersed: the passage is both a commentary on the role of the flute player within the dramatic performance and, it seems likely, indication of the continuing use of flute players at *convivia* in Plautus's day. Similarly in the *Casina* the presence of a flute player in the commencement of her sweet song (*suavis cantus,* 799) signifies the beginning of the mock wedding but also marks a shift from trochaic long-verse to glyconic (loosely speaking, lyric) meter. And the end of the run of glyconics receives metacommentary with the remark that the singing of the marriage hymn has been disrupted (*dirumpi cantando hymenaeum,* 809). Here we have song within the song that is the Plautine play; but it is song that represents or recreates extratheatrical song as well.[24] Similarly when the father in *Trinummus* "sings" his precepts to his son (*canto,* 287), he employs a variety of song meters, while his son responds to him in trochaic septenarii (301–4.). Within the so-called *cantica,* or sung verse, of Plautine song, a further distinction between nonsong and song is made, a distinction that corresponds both to a shift between recitative and polymetric verse and to a shift from the representation of conversation to the representation of precept giving or, as in the previous example, wedding hymn, and back again. Plautine comedy also refers to the extratheatrical performance of vatic song in a scene in which the pimp Ballio shrugs off the insults of his attackers with the expression *vetera vaticinamini* — "you proclaim old news," or "you incant things that are familiar" (*Pseud.* 363) — and refers to his verbal assailants sarcastically as *cantores probi,* "fine singers!" (*Pseud.* 367). While there is nothing overtly vatic about the remarks of the other speakers, it is the case that their performance recreates that of the *flagitatio,* or public verbal assault, that seems to be the target of the Twelve Tables' injunction against *occentatio.*[25] Once again Plautine comedy illustrates the applicability of the distinction between marked and unmarked verbal performance within the marked performance of a play. The scene with Ballio also exemplifies Plautus's tendency to allude to the markedness of recognizable extratheatrical song types within the theatrical performance.

Plautus's contemporaries and immediate successors continue the use of words based on *can-* to describe a variety of types of verbal production, which now include Hellenized literary genres. A character in Livius Andronicus's play *Aegisthus* describes the dancing of dolphins to the song of sailors in the elegant expression *ludens ad cantum classem lustratur,* "sporting to the tune [the troupe] encircles the fleet" (6 W). Marine song figures in a fragment of Accius, as well, in which a shepherd likens the tune he hears from the sea to the melody of the woodland god Silvanus: *Silvani melo/consimilem ad aures cantum et auditum refert* (395–96 W = 403–4 R). A speaker in a tragedy of Pacuvius links the verbs *cano* and *dico* in reference to the practice of poets, declaring "let the poets to their own advantage sing what is false and fictive; they amplify the humble case with their assertions" (*poetae pro sua parte falsa conficta canant/qui causam humilem dictis amplant,* 336–37 W = 337–38 R). Here we have an early example of the use of *cano* and *dico* to refer to the same sort of speech act. But the passage also anticipates (or perhaps illustrates) the emerging competition between oratory and poetry for the authority invested in song; for here the poets are both singers and pleaders (*pro sua parte*); their subject matter constitutes a legal case (*causa*); and their procedure is assimilated to the rhetorical practice of amplification (*amplant*). Lucilius uses *carmina* of a tragic Orestes, but it is unclear whether the expression "songs" here refers to the tragedy as a whole or to lyric, that is, "sung" passages within the play ("a tragic actor who ruins songs as a hoarse Orestes": *rausuro tragicus qui carmina perdit Oreste,* 594 W = 567 M). If the former, then we have an early instance of the application of *carmen* to a specific Hellenic literary genre; if the latter, then a use of *carmen* parallel to the uses of *canto* and *cantus* within Plautus to mark the intensification of song within song (within song!). Elsewhere Lucilius declares, or has a character declare, "Make the battle of Popilius clang; sing the deeds of Cornelius" (*percrepa pugna Popili facta Corneli cane,* 714 W = 621 M). *Cano* here may refer to production of an epic poem; but we cannot rule out other marked, authoritative presentations of the accomplishments of the Cornelius in question (presumably P. Scipio Aemilianus who in 133 BC defeated the Numantines who had previously defeated Popilius in 138 BC). Nor can we be certain that the verb *percrepo, -are* refers to a desirable or attractive performance. Lucilius may be using *cano* as a synonym for *percrepo,* but he may also be contrasting the two, suggesting a raucous presentation of Popilius's defeat, a more heroic rendition of Scipio's victory. Other uses of *can-* by Lucilius seem sarcastic, but if so, their sarcasm presupposes the audience's awareness of more elevated applications of the term. Thus one fragment reads "they blurt out, and a dear old rustic sings along" (*deblaterant, blennus bonus rusticus concinit una,* 1034 W = 1063 M); another, taken from a parody of Q. Mucius Scaevola's trial for extortion, has a character, in what seems to be a mockery of vatic or prophetic song, declare his ability to "fore-chant" (*praecanto*) and "chant out" (*excanto*) the testimony of a witness (*quae ego nunc huic Aemilio praecanto et exigo et excanto,* 78–79 W).[26]

In time, as Latin literature develops a full-fledged system of genres, song comes to describe virtually every one of them. At the same time, *cano, carmen,* and related terms continue to be applied to so-called nonliterary varieties of song. Indeed, the same author can be perfectly comfortable applying the terms *cano/carmen* to what contemporary scholars regard as both literary and nonliterary compositions. Cicero, for example, in addition to using *carmen* of legal formulas, applies the term to tragedies such as Ennius's *Andromache* (*Tusc.* 3.46) and Euripides' *Hypsipyle* (*Tusc.* 3.59), to Simonides' lyric poetry (*De Or.* 2.352), and to his own translation of Aratus's didactic poetry (*Leg.* 2.7). For Lucretius, lyric (2.506), epic (1.117), and didactic (1.934, 6.938) are all songs; but so apparently are lullabies (5.1406). In the poetry of Propertius, the noun *carmen* describes the taunts directed at the door of an uncooperative mistress (1.16.10), the musical performance of the beloved (2.1.9), magical incantation (2.28.35), and Cynthia's funeral epitaph (4.7.83). It also describes his own elegiac poetry (2.5.6; probably also 2.10.11) and the heroic poetry he is dissuaded from composing (3.3.16; cf. 2.1.19, 2.1.28). Verbal forms of *can-* expand the realm of song in Propertius to include Vergil's performance of his *Eclogues* and *Georgics* (2.34.72, 77), the poems of Catullus (2.34.87), the elegies of Calvus (2.34.90), even the *Annales* of Ennius (3.3.7).

Such broad and diverse application of terms for song persists well into the imperial period, as exemplified by the array of song types attested in the *Institutio Oratoria* of Quintilian. For Quintilian, virtually every standard genre of poetry merits the designation *carmen*. In book 1, chapter 8, he lists the genres that the student must learn to sing (*canere*) because in fact they are song (*carmen*). These genres include epic (1.8.5), tragedy (1.8.6), lyric (1.8.6), and comedy (1.8.7). In his discussion of the appropriate reading list for the more advanced student, Quintilian ascribes the term *carmen* and the verb *cano* to the poetry of Euphorion (10.1.56) and Stesichorus (10.1.62), to epic poetry (10.1.62), to the mixture of meters in Varro's Menippean satires (10.1.95), even to the hypothetical poetry that would have been sung by Germanicus (*caneret*, 10.1.91) had care for the lands not turned him from the projects he had undertaken (*ab institutis studiis deflexit cura terrarum*, 10.1.91). Yet within the same work Quintilian refers to the Salian hymn (1.6.40, 1.10.20) and to lullaby (1.10.30) as *carmen*, and describes the activity of Iopas in *Aeneid* 1 (1.10.10), various unnamed "outstanding generals" who perform to flute and lyre (1.10.14), the combination of horns and tubas in the battlefield (1.10.14), the lays performed by Achilles (1.10.30–31), the piping of a *tibicen* at a sacrifice (1.10.32), the chanting of oracles (3.71.12), and the work song of a naval crew (1.10.6) with verbs or other nouns based on the root *can-*. Quintilian's list of songs provides further evidence of the array of performances that constitute song to the Romans while also making clear that users of Latin do not make any fundamental distinction between poetry and other song types within the category of song. In Quintilian, as throughout the tradition, the divide between song and nonsong is stronger and more meaningful than the divide between poetry and so-called sub- or paraliterary genres.[27]

Two authors represent a strain of resistance to the overwhelming tendency of users of Latin to invoke a divide between song and speech via use of the expressions *cano/carmen* and *loquor/locuta*. These authors, Ennius (in his *Annales*), and Horace (in his *Epistle to Augustus*) are noteworthy precisely because the failure of their efforts demonstrates the continuing significance of the lexical distinction between song and speech. In a sense, they are the exceptions that prove the rule.[28] Ennius is well known for his association of *cano* with the verbal productions of those he seeks to replace. Thus, he rejects those "verses that once upon a time the Fauni and *vates* used to sing" (*quos olim Fauni vatesque canebant,* 207); and his only other use of the verb *cano* is to describe the sound made by a tuba after its player has been felled in battle:

And when his head was falling, the trumpet alone finished the song.
Though the hero was dying, a raucous sound raced from the brass.

quomque caput caderet carmen tuba sola peregit
et pereunte viro raucum sonus aere cucurrit

(Enn. *Ann.* 485–86)

In place of *cano* Ennius uses the expressions *memoro* and *dico* to describe his own performance or that of authoritative figures within his poem, such as the Muses, and *poemata* to describe his literary output.[29] But *memoro* is too specific a word to be generalized to poetry or song and comes to be associated by later writers specifically with the production of poetry on grand historical themes; indeed it is used more narrowly in allusion to Ennius's achievement in writing the *Annales* (e.g., Prop. 2.1.25). And *dico,* while capable of describing the same activity or utterance as *cano,* calls attention to a different aspect, namely the authoritative nature of the utterance regardless of the performance context. Ennius's preference for *dico* may perhaps have contributed to later poets' comfort in alternating between *dico* and *cano* as terms for their activity; but it did not succeed in banishing, or even, it would seem, problematizing, *cano.* Thus when Lucretius, who greatly admires Ennius, wishes to cite him, the expression he uses is "as our Ennius sang" (*Ennius ut noster cecinit,* 1.118).[30] And, as noted, authors writing within a generation or two of Ennius employ *cano* for both nonliterary and Hellenized literary productions.

As for *poemata,* the term persists in reference to poetry, but with an emphasis on the fashioning that goes into its production rather than the authority that sustains and is sustained by its performance. Not long after Ennius, Lucilius defines the word as referring to a small segment of a larger poem or *poesis,* a usage that recurs elsewhere in Latin and seems to reflect the practice of selecting and memorizing choice bits of versification.[31] And Cato the Elder expresses his disapproval of the *ars poetica,* presumably on the grounds that it is an illiberal skill, fit for craftsmen, Greeks, and others who must earn a living.[32] Although Ennius's poetry represents an innovation within the tradition of Roman verbal performance, aspects of which were imitated by generations of writers to come, his attempt to constitute poetry (i.e., *poemata*) as a verbal performance type distinct from *carmina* failed. Poetry remains, as it had been prior to Ennius, an instance of ritualized speech capable of absorbing new markers of specialness (e.g., adherence to a Hellenistic tradition) without thereby ceasing to be Roman song.

Horace indicates his awareness of Ennius's failed attempt to banish *cano* along with the Camenae (whose name, by folk etymology, was linked to *carmen*). In *Epistles* 2.1 he joins in Ennius's deprecation of earlier verbal productions—indeed, he extends the criticism even to the work of Ennius and his contemporaries—but rather than assigning them the word *carmina*, by way of insult, he at first denies them the term altogether. Thus, when introducing his key theme, namely the Roman populace's paradoxical approval of its new leader Augustus and disapproval of new literature, Horace claims that as "fans of the old" (*fautor veterum*, 2.1.23) the people insist that the Muses themselves spoke (*locutas*, 2.1.27) the Twelve Tables, the treaties with Gabii and with the Sabines, the books of the pontiffs, and the age-old volumes of the *vates*. It is as if Horace cannot quite bring himself to apply to these ancient texts the word *carmen* or the verb *cano*, which have come to include the elegant compositions of his contemporaries, and instead reverts to the unmarked word for speech, *loquor*. Commentators note that the full expression used by Horace, *Albano Musas in monte locutas*, may recall an early judgment attributed to Aelius Stilo, that "were the Muses willing to speak Latin, they would speak in Plautine style."[33] In that phrase, however, *loquor* makes good sense, because it suggests that Plautine song was good enough to constitute everyday speech for the goddesses, a compliment and an observation on the stylistic register of Plautine comedy. But in the present context, to suggest that the Muses merely "spoke" the Twelve Tables and so on can only be taken as a deflating anticlimax. Not even the fondest fans of ancient lore could suggest that it achieves the status of modern *carmina*. Horace first uses the term *carmina* in the course of his review of literary history with respect to the writings of Livius Andronicus—thus anticipating modern scholarly judgments, which assign to him the "beginning" of Latin literature.

Despite Horace's denial of the term *carmen* to the early writings he most strongly deprecates, he does not succeed in restricting the term exclusively to work of which he approves. As *Epistles* 2.1 proceeds, we hear of the *Saliare Numae carmen* (i.e., the Salian song of Numa, 86), of contemporary *carmina* dictated at dinner parties by fathers and sons (110), of the *malum carmen* against which the Twelve Tables inveigh (153)—none of which is a verbal product of which Horace has a high opinion. Interspersed with these are references, in a positive vein, to choral prayers or hymns (i.e., *carmina*) directed to gods of the upper and lower realms (138) and to Horace's own poems (227 and 258). In other words, while Horace indicates awareness of a potentially charged and highly evaluative (or, in Ennius's case, deprecatory) use of *carmen*, he reverts to use similar to that found in the mainstream of prose and poetic authors: *carmen* signifying speech made special through the application of rhythm, melody, or special language, or through performance in ritual context.

One reason for Horace's acquiescence in the definition of poetry as song may well be the continuing class associations of *poema* and the labor that goes into its composition. Thus, in his review of the history of song (so named: note *carminibus* at Epis. 2.3.401, *carmina* at 403, *cantor* at 407, *carmen* at 408), the terms *poemata* and *poeta* only turn up in connection with the question as to whether a song is produced through nature or through art. The same implication, that "making" a poem is a not quite honorable thing to do, seems to underlie Horace's recommendation to Lollius that if a well-off friend wants to engage in the aristocratic pursuit of hunting, he should hardly stay home and "nail down poems" (*nec cum venari volet ille, poemata panges, Epist.* 1.18.40). Ultimately Horace seems to have conceded what other Latin writers took for granted: that it is by being absorbed into the world of Roman song that poetry shifts from a mere craft into a defining performance of elite Roman manhood.

The Lore of Song

In her study of ritual and society among the Mambai of East Timor, anthropologist Elizabeth G. Traube discusses the meaning and significance of ritual noisemaking. The Mambai language has a verb *keo*, which in its strictest sense "refers to one specific and recurrent sequence within a performance, the beating of sacred drums and gongs in a formal procession. In this strict usage, *keo* is opposed to *beha*, a simpler mode of ritual performed without drum or gong. Although *beha* ritual involves various forms of speaking, it is classified as 'silent' (*smera*), whereas *keo* implies that 'things play' (*sauna haha*)."[34] Traube goes on to explain that *keo* comes to function synecdochically for Mambai "ritual life as a whole" and to be translated into Portuguese as *adorar*, or worship.

While the opposition between *keo* and *beha* is not precisely the same as that between Latin *cano* and *loquor*, the close association of ritual and noisemaking implicit in *keo*'s application to both does put us in mind of the ritual connotations of *cano* and the role of noisemaking in Roman ritual more generally. Traube likens the Mambai realm of *keo* to the Hebrew Psalms, which beckon "all the earth . . . [to] make a joyful noise to the Lord," but notes that whereas in the Hebrew tradition, and Christian views descended from it, "man and nature together 'make a joyful noise' before the Lord, . . . Mambai cosmology represents nature as silent, and human beings as unique noisemakers."[35] Indeed, the ritual noisemaking referred to in the verb *keo* constitutes a gift offered to the silent cosmos, an exchange of "a ceremonially made clamor for life."[36]

The Mambai identification of human beings as "unique noise-makers" stands in contrast to the Roman view of ritual noisemaking, or song, as the product of human beings, of birds, and of musical instruments. Although Roman song forms part of a ritual process that is sometimes described with the word *munus,* or exchange, it does not seem to be the case that the song itself is in any sense exchanged for something else or offered as a gift to the cosmos. Instead, in the Roman tradition, as in the Psalm cited by Traube, the cosmos itself is full of song. It produces the music to which nature and culture, the human and the nonhuman, must attune themselves. In their rituals, the Mambai become "courtesans who speak, sing, play, and dance before a silent rock and a motionless tree."[37] To the Romans song is the means through which the order of the universe is realized in human society and its subsets, not least the body of the individual performer. The musician, or the singer, like the artist, is the one who makes perceptible to other human beings the patterns that are implicit in the cosmos.

Birds

Ancient lore has it that humans learned song by imitating birds. Thus Athenaeus, a Greek author of the Roman imperial period, reports that the archaic Greek lyric poet Alcman learned to sing from partridges (9.389)—a piece of information that may or may not have been transmitted independently of verses in which Alcman refers to "the tongued voice of partridges" (frag. 39), likens himself to sea birds (frag. 26), or declares "I know the melodies of all the birds" (frag. 40).[38] At least some *nomoi,* or musical modes, were identified with specific birds;[39] musical instruments were named after the birds they imitated (e.g., *tibiae gingrinae* or "goose pipes" and *tibiae milvinae* or "kite pipes");[40] and dances were performed in imitation of the movements of birds.[41] The Roman poet Lucretius, in the course of describing humanity's progressive movement toward civilization, places the invention of song alongside of the creation of textiles and the development of reliable food sources. As with the other two arts, so music developed through imitation of and collaboration with forces of nature. According to Lucretius, long before songs could celebrate the achievements of men, early humans had begun to mimic birdsong.

> They imitated the trilling voices of birds
> long before they were able to perform songs supple with melody
> and bring pleasure to the ears.

at liquidas avium voces imitarier ore
ante fuit multo quam levia carmina cantu
concelebrare homines possent, aureisque iuvare.

(Lucr. 5.1379–81)

But Lucretius's account of the origins of song does not stop with the invention of melody (*cantus*). He proceeds to describe how the passage of the wind through reeds taught men to pipe on hemlock stalks, and how men learned to produce "sweet laments" (*dulcis querelas*, 5.1383), "which the tibia pours out when it has been struck by the fingers of the performers" (*tibia quas fundit digitis pulsata canentum*, 5.1384). The three stages of the invention of song correspond to the three subdivisions of music summarized centuries later by Isidore of Seville in his *Etymologies*, namely *harmonica*, "which consists of the melodic flow of voices (*ex vocum cantibus constat*, 3.19.1); *organica*, "which consists of breathing" (*quae ex flatu consistit*, 3.19.1); and *rythmica*, "which gets its numbers from the tapping of fingers" (*quae pulsu digitorum numeros recipit*, 3.19.1). The narrative of Lucretius and the theory of Isidore correspond even in terminology: *voces/voces, cantus/vocum cantibus; digitis pulsata/pulsu digitorum*. Indeed, Lucretius's choice of the adjective *liquidas*, flowing, to describe the voices of birds receives unintended explanation in Isidore's discussion of the term *cantus*. "*Cantus*," notes Isidore, "is bending of the voice, for sound is [otherwise] direct (or straight); and sound precedes song" (*cantus est inflexio vocis, nam sonus directus est; praecedit autem sonus cantum*, 3.20.8). The adjective *liquidas*, as a characteristic of the voices of birds, describes the supple movement, or bending of the voice, human or avian, continuously up and down the scale.[42] (The ancients had another explanation for the discovery or invention of intervals on the scale.)

Unlike the Mambai, the ancient Greeks and Romans allowed for the possibility of singing by birds and attributed human song in part to imitation of the song of birds—a point exploited for paradoxical effect in Ovid's story of the metamorphosis of the magpies, and one that can be instantiated in rituals of individual and collective identity. Birds and their song become one of the governing analogies for humanness in the cosmology of the Romans. At the same time, the attribution of the origin of song to imitation of birds (and of the music of the spheres and of the sounds made by the hammering of metal) makes of song the quintessential manifestation of the mimetic faculty in Roman culture.

What is more, in Roman thought, the analogy between birdsong and human song runs both ways. Not only do humans imitate birds, but birds return the favor. Athenaeus tells of owls that are known to mimic certain human dances (9.391). Plutarch shares the story of a jay that could imitate trumpets to perfection, performing "their tunes with all their punctuations, modulations, and note patterns,"[43] while Pliny mentions a tragic actor who sought to acquire the power of mimesis by eating birds that had the ability to imitate human beings (*HN* 10.141–42). Cicero, in a remarkable passage in the *Brutus*, argues that one can tell that a true orator is at work if, among other things, "the members of the jury are held suspended, as it were, like a bird by song" (*ut avem cantu aliquo sic illos viderit oratione quasi suspensos teneri*, 200). The passage seems to refer to the use of decoy song by bird trappers. It also exposes the homology between birdsong and human song in the Roman imagination, not to mention the closeness between oratory and song. Vergil seems to have in mind a similar attunement of birds to human performance when in eclogue 6 he declares, "If anyone reads these [songs of mine] as well, anyone captivated by love, our tamarisks will sing of you, Varus, the whole grove will sing of you" (*si quis tamen haec quoque, si quis / captus amore leget, te nostrae Vare, myricae, / te nemus omne canet*, 6.9–11). Barring the unparalleled notion of singing trees,[44] Vergil would seem to be suggesting that the performance of his songs to Varus will be echoed by the birds that inhabit the tamarisk, even the whole grove. Not incidentally, the passage also suggests the mode of performance that Vergil deems suitable for his own bucolic song—in a melodic manner such as can be imitated by woodland birds.

Although Lucretius introduces song as a discovery, via imitation of nature, attributable to a prepolitical state of human development, he nonetheless emphasizes the place of song in the culmination of his progressivist account of societal evolution. At the time when cities came to be protected by towers, the sea blossomed with ships' sails, and alliances were struck and not long before writing was invented, in this era, according to Lucretius, "poets began to hand down accomplishments in songs" (*carminibus cum res gestas coepere poetae / tradere*, 5.1442–43). Song is to be listed with seafaring, agriculture, ramparts, laws, weapons, roads, garments, paintings, sculptures, and so on as proud accomplishments of human thought and endeavor. Not coincidentally, this process of thought and endeavor culminates not in Lucretius's day and age but in the invention of polis society. In our discussion of the Salian hymn, we concluded that song at Rome serves in practice to found and refound the community. Here, in Lucretius's account of *carmina* in history, amplified and supplemented by the other discussions cited, we find traces of an ancient awareness and conceptualization of precisely that relationship.

Metalworking

Associating the invention of music with imitation of birds helped the ancients to explain the fluidity of the musical scale. Another nonhuman source of sound, metalworking, was invoked as a means of understanding the existence of and relationship between intervals on the scale. Discovery of the relationship between metalworking and music is attributed to Pythagoras, who is said to have noticed that hammers of different weights, when used by smiths in the working of metal, produced sounds corresponding to the standard musical intervals. Burkert observes that the law Pythagoras is alleged to have derived from listening to the smiths is demonstrably false.[45] He thus argues that the Pythagorean connection between music and metalworking should be regarded not as an early instance of scientific thought but as an expression of the relationship between Pythagoras and the mythical blacksmiths, that is, the metallurgical *daimones* such as the *dactyloi* and *kabeiroi*. Burkert is surely right to resist attempts to force archaic modes of knowledge into patterns set by later scientific thought; but "explaining" the story of Pythagoras and the smiths on the basis of another story identifying Pythagoras as an initiate of the *dactyloi* begs the question of the basis of the association between metalworking and music — via Pythagoras, or *dactyloi*, or anyone else. The fact is that metal objects, when struck, do produce music, but music of a discontinuous sort, notes on a scale as opposed to the fluid music of birds. Thus the story of Pythagoras and the smiths does more than link him with mythical music makers. It also speaks to the paradoxical status of the musical scale as simultaneously continuous and composed of discrete intervals.[46] Moreover, the fact that in the story of Pythagoras and the smiths music is generated as a by-product of a different sort of activity makes of the seemingly trivial, or second-order, narrative a more profound meditation on the elements of surplus, waste, and transformation of ontological status that the ancients seem to have regarded as characteristic of culture more generally. Music is a by-product of the hammering of shields (both at the stage of production, as in the story of Pythagoras, and at the stage of use, as in the creation of an apotropaic racket by the daimonic protectors of the baby Zeus/Jupiter, with whom Pythagoras is also associated), yet it is an activity desirable and effectual in and of itself. It involves the transformation of breath and percussion into something categorically different, of words into song. In this respect it is not just the product, mythically and in some cases materially, of metalworking. It is also analogous to metalworking, which combines and transforms raw materials into usable tools, weapons, and so on. The myth offers an ancient understanding of the relationship between music and metalworking that we saw enacted in the Salian rite.

The connection between music and metalworking is implicit in much that might be regarded as specifically Greek lore. It manifests itself in more explicitly Roman or Italian contexts sometimes as replication of Greek lore, other times as creation of new stories that combine Roman traditions with Greek, especially stories linking Pythagoras to the Roman craftsman, king, and culture-hero, Numa. As instances of the first process, restatement of stories familiar from Greek sources as well, we may consider Lucretius's and Vergil's representation of the music-making of the metallurgical *daimones.* Lucretius describes the Curetes' dancing and rhythmical clanging of metal shields in order to drown out the cries of the infant Jove (2.630ff.) as mythical prototype and justification for the more elaborate music (2.619ff.) associated with contemporary rites of Magna Mater. While the language Lucretius uses to describe the Curetes refers specifically to rhythm and percussion (*quatientes, in numerum pulsarent,* 2.632, 637), their performance is seen as anticipating music that involves percussion (*tonant palmeis,* 2.619), melody (*cantu,* 2.620) and breath (*cornua,* 2.620; *tibia,* 2.622), and perhaps intervals as well.[47] Vergil too associates the pounding of shields by the Curetes with a broader notion of music when he notes in the *Georgics* that their performance led bees to the cave in which they supplied nourishment for the baby Jove; in his vignette the clashing bronze (*crepitantia aera,* 4.151) of the Curetes either constitutes or at least is part of the songlike sounds (*canoros sonitus,* 4.150–51) generated by these mythical craftsmen.

If Roman authors repeat Greek myths of the founding of music by metallurgical *daimones,* they are not willing to grant priority to the Greeks in the historical formation of their own musical traditions. In a sense, they take advantage of the distinctive yet interrelated traditions concerning the teachings of Numa and Pythagoras to validate the work and ideas of both. As is well known, the story that Numa was instructed by Pythagoras was widely challenged on chronological grounds by ancient writers. Cicero three times repudiates it (*Rep.* 2.28–30; *Tusc.* 4.2–3; *De Or.* 2.154), and Dionysius of Halicarnassus rejects it (*Ant. Rom.* 2.59.1–2), even though it might have fit his larger project of demonstrating the Greek origin of most of what is good about Rome. Plutarch refers to it and describes the similarities between the teachings of Numa and those of Pythagoras at length, only to dismiss his own digression as insignificant without commenting on the chronological problem posed by Numa's supposed tutelage by Pythagoras (*Vit. Num.* 8.10, 14.1–5). Livy also rejects the story of Numa's tutelage by Pythagoras, in his case arguing that even if Numa and Pythagoras had been contemporaries, the distance between them, geographically and culturally, makes influence of the latter on the former unlikely (1.18.2–3). Even Ovid, who inserts a lengthy speech by Pythagoras within the story of Numa in book 15 of the *Metamorphoses*, seems a bit reluctant to specify the relationship between Pythagoras and Numa. There is no mention of Numa's presence as Pythagoras's speech commences, and at the conclusion we learn only that Numa's heart was instructed "by such and other sayings" (*talibus atque aliis instructo pectore dictis / in patriam remeasse ferunt*, 15.479–80).

But if the chronological priority of Numa to Pythagoras was evident, then why do so many authors feel the need to discuss it—or, in Ovid's case, the right to finesse it? And why is it that, even when rejecting the story that Pythagoras taught Numa, ancient writers consistently proceed to discuss in some detail the close similarity between the teachings of Pythagoras and the cultural activities of Numa? One logical possibility is that the ancient writers, and modern scholars relying on them, are wrong about the date of Pythagoras (assigned with certainty by, for example, the *Oxford Classical Dictionary*, to the mid-sixth century BC). "Pythagoras" is perhaps less of an identifiable historical individual and more of a name associated with a type of teaching than is generally acknowledged in positivist historiography. Burkert himself makes the case for regarding Pythagoras as a figure associated with continuity and maintenance of traditional teachings in an emerging scientific age. If this is the case, then why shouldn't the teachings—and the teacher —be older than dates assigned to Pythagoras? Ovid may envision this scenario, as he emphasizes the representative nature of Pythagoras's speech (*talibus* at *Met.* 15.73 and again at 15.479 in contrast to the *haec* of, say, the Muses' speech in book 5), and his position as the fountainhead of a tradition (*primus*, 72; *primus*, 73; *coetus* 66—same word in Livy). Another possibility is that the accomplishments assigned to Numa actually do date to the period of Pythagoras's lifetime. This possibility seems implicit in Cicero's discussion in *Tusculan Disputations* where, after insisting that Numa lived much earlier than Pythagoras, he nonetheless lists as inventions of Numa practices that need not be dated any earlier than the fifth century BC—that is, during or after the lifetime of Pythagoras. Uncertainties of this sort led the historian Emilio Gabba to claim that all of the institutions assigned to Numa by later writers were products of the early Roman Republic, not the monarchy, and were merely ascribed by aristocrats of the early republic retroactively to Numa in order to give them an air of legitimacy.[48] This conclusion seems unnecessarily extreme and disregards positive reasons for associating at least some of the ascribed achievements of Numa to the period of the foundation of the city. But it does have the advantage (not mentioned by Gabba) of explaining how a figure like Pythagoras, whose followers were associated with a political program of aristocratic domination of south Italian city-states, could be invoked as teacher of Numa, the second of the Roman kings. Far from being a bad student, Numa can be seen to be a name attached to political structures very much in accord with, and conceivably influenced by, fifth-century Pythagoreanism.

Perhaps the simplest way to explain the recurrent and conflicted attention given to the association between Numa and Pythagoras is to regard it as expressing something that Roman (and Romanized Greek) writers of the classical period felt it was important to say about the musical culture of Rome. This would hardly be the only occasion in Roman thought in which Greek theory and Roman action came to be regarded as mutually supportive.[49] In this instance, Pythagoras provides the theoretical connection between song and metalworking, and between song and cosmos through his teachings concerning number. Numa puts such teachings into practice: through his affiliation with the craftsman Mamurius Veturius and the replication of the shields as in Ovid's *Fasti,* and through his establishment of Roman musical culture and musical modes more generally, as described by Cicero and others.[50] The unwillingness of Roman authors quite to abandon the story of Pythagoras as teacher of Numa, even as they acknowledge its chronological impossibility, speaks to their own understanding of the foundational significance of just such a connection.

The Music of the Cosmos

Part of what is articulated by the connection between Numa and Pythagoras is music's status as a "transformative activity" fostering "energizing links" between the "here and now" and the "world beyond." The persistent attachment of the name Pythagoras to musical lore can be understood as an ancient anticipation of the arguments presented in chapter 1 concerning the cosmic implications of the Salian hymn and of Roman musical performance more generally. As Walter Burkert writes with respect to the musical teachings of the Pythagoreans, "What distinguished the Pythagoreans was apparently not a special knowledge, inaccessible to others. Rather, something which may well have lost its interest for professional musicians came to be prized among them as a fundamental insight into the nature of reality. The wondrous potency of music, which moves the world and compels the spirit, captured in the net of number — this was a cardinal element of the secret of the universe revealed to the wise Pythagoras."[51] In a sense, Pythagoreanism expresses in another mode the knowledge carried by rituals such as that of the Salian priests, rituals routinely attributed by the Romans to the foundational vision of Numa.

In the more rationalistic and individualistic environment of the late republic, Pythagoreanism offers a means for the individual adherent to revitalize the energizing link between here and now and eternity. Music becomes both a means and a metaphor of this process. Thus in the *Somnium Scipionis* Cicero has Scipio describe a dream in which he is permitted to hear the "music of the spheres." Although the notion of cosmic music is familiar to traditions other than Pythagoreanism, Cicero here makes use of specifically Pythagorean arguments concerning the relationship between planetary motion and musical intervals.[52] "Those eight planets (of which two have the same force) accomplish seven distinct sounds by means of intervals, a number that is, as it were, the knot of everything. Learned men, imitating this on strings and in song, have opened for themselves a return into this place, like others who through their outstanding talents have cherished divine endeavors in human life" (*Rep.* 6.18). Vergil follows Cicero in this comprehensive view of individual achievement when he places musicians (Orpheus and Musaeus) and *vates* prominently — but not exclusively — among the souls who have successfully escaped the cycle of rebirth and found for themselves a permanent home in Elysium (*Aen.* 6.638ff.) Music is perhaps the best understood means of return to the ethereal homeland, in large part because of the recognition of concord between music and planetary movement. But its success serves as an invitation and inspiration to seek similar tempering to the music of the universe in other human endeavors. Hearing the music of the planets inspires Scipio to his great achievements. Meeting the musicians of Elysium and receiving the paternal instruction that explicates their destiny and that of others like them is to inspire Aeneas — and, by implication, the Roman audience — at the midpoint of Vergil's epic.

While both Cicero and Vergil are without doubt concerned with the well-being of the Roman state as a whole, nonetheless their adaptation of Pythagorean lore concerning music and the cosmos continues the process whereby the ritual insights of early Pythagoreanism are transformed into ethical guidelines for individuals — a process that has as one of its side effects the "disembodiment" of musical theory, which McClary, among others, has rightly deplored.[53] It takes a writer of a different sort to restore the social meaning of Pythagorean teaching concerning music as means of access to the universe. The writer in question is Manilius, whose attempt to explain the arrangements of the heavens and their impact on human life can too easily be dismissed as an exercise in the abstruse art of astrology or a technical tour de force.[54] In fact, Manilius's comments on his own endeavors, in the proem and in an important self-referential passage in book 2, make it clear that his

ambitions range wider or, perhaps better, that for him composing a refined poem about the abstruse art of astrology is in effect a restoration
of song to its full cosmic significance.

Manilius's poem opens with the word *carmen:*

> By song to draw down from the universe
> the divine skills and fate-aware constellations
> that vary the diverse circumstances of humanity
> through the workings of celestial reason:
> this is my undertaking; and to be first with new melodies
> to set in motion Helicon and the trees nodding on its green summit,
> as I bear from afar sacred matters commemorated by none
> > before me.

> Carmine divinas artes et conscia fati
> sidera diversos hominum variantia casus,
> caelestis rationis opus, deducere mundo
> aggredior primusque novis Helicona movere
> cantibus et viridi nutantis vertice silvas
> hospita sacra ferens nulli memorata priorum.

(Manil. Astr. 1.1–6)

But what precisely does *carmen* mean in this context? In a sense Manilius
assigns to the word a unity that the rationalizing enterprises of the late
republic had sought to deny. *Carmen* here is a magical incantation, such
as that used, according to legend, by witches who have the trick of
"drawing down the moon." It is Alexandrian poetry, as indicated by the
double meaning of *deducere,* "to draw down" and "to spin out." It is the
diverse Roman poetic tradition as well, as allusions to Propertius (1.1.19
for the "drawing down" of the moon; 3.1.3 for the claim of "first approach," *primus ingredior*) and Ennius (*memorata*) suggest.[55] It recalls the
power of Orphic song in its ability to make trees dance. But *carmen* is
also Pythagorean music, in its broadest sense, a means of linking the
mutable world of human beings to the order of the universe. It draws
down from the heavens all those things that constitute "the work of
celestial reason." *Carmen* too, as song, participates in that celestial reason: indeed, the word *opus,* which here strictly refers to the divine skills
and the constellations themselves, seems chosen in part for its ability
to evoke the effort of literary production.

The homology between the production of song and the order of
the universe, reinforced at the conclusion of Manilius's proem, can be
understood as the main theme of the first section of the poem. Having

first briefly alluded to the ritual character and significance of his endeavor (*hospita sacra ferens, Astr.* 1.6), Manilius develops these notions
fully by indicating that he sees fire burning on two altars, that he prays
at two temples, "enveloped by a twin passion for his song and his subject" (*duplici circumdatus aestu / carminis et rerum*, 1.21–22). While the two
features of form and content, or song and subject, can be differentiated,
neither takes precedence over the other. So intertwined are they that it
becomes virtually impossible to sort out the grammar of the last three
lines of the proem:

> certa cum lege canentem
> mundus et immenso vatem circumstrepit orbe
> vixque soluta suis immittit verba figuris.
> (Manil. *Astr.* 1.22–24).

Goold's translation, "The poet must sing to a fixed measure, and the vast
celestial sphere rings in his ears besides, scarce allowing even words of
prose to be fitted to their proper phrasing," is perhaps the best one can
do, given the requirements of English syntax and word order.[56] But the
Latin allows for multiple layers of meaning, which reinforce the sense
of interconvertibility between the production of song, the explication
of the celestial order, and the music of the cosmos. The phrase *certa
cum lege*, which Goold takes closely with *canentem*, as referring to the
poet's need to follow strict rules of versification, can also refer to the
law observed by the universe as it "strikes the ear of the *vates*" (*circumstrepit vatem*, 1.23) with its own music. And the *vates*, as he sings, is not
just struck by the concurrent music of the sphere: he is also, in a sense,
amazed at the vastness of the sphere and of his undertaking in describing it. He must fit what are otherwise words of prose (*soluta verba*) "to
their proper phrasing" (*suis figuris*), as Goold puts it, but also to the figures of the universe, the constellations and zodiacal signs that constitute
the bulk of Manilius's subject matter. The final line cited can be read
in another way as well, since *suis figuris* is grammatically either dative
(as the preceding interpretations assume) or ablative. In the latter case,
then what the universe is reluctant to let in are "words loosened from
their own proper patterns"—prose, to be sure, but prose understood
as a dissolution of the bonds of song. To compose poetry on a technical
matter like astrology is admittedly a challenge; but it is a virtual necessity, as well, according to Manilius, because the universe does not let in
or admit of words that follow no sure law, that have been loosened from
the patterns that connect them to the order of the cosmos. Manilius
takes for granted something that has only recently been acknowledged
by scholars: namely, the secondariness of prose in relation to song, its

derivative status as a loosening of the bonds, a progressive limitation of the marked elements that characterize song.[57]

Despite his technical virtuosity, his awareness of the specialized poetic traditions of Greece and Rome, his commitment to Stoic views of the sympathetic relationship between micro- and macrocosm, and his up-to-date intertextuality, Manilius advances a conception of the relationship between song and the universe that is as old as the Salian hymn, that is seen as being in need of rescue and preservation as far back as Pythagoras. Indeed his interweaving of poetry, philosophy, astrology, and religion is an act of composition that recalls the primordial "fitting together" of archaic *sodales*.[58] His is a foundational knowledge that grounds the experience of the community in the order of the cosmos. His poetry responds to the invitation of the universe, which repeatedly throughout the preface is the subject of simple declarative verbs (*favet*, 11; *cupit*, 12; *circumstrepit*, 23; *immittit*, 24).[59] Like Numa and Mamurius Veturius, who responded to the initiative taken by the heavens in hurling a magical shield to the earth, so Manilius, thanks to the dispensation of Caesar, will fashion a song that modulates the variegated fates of mankind to the order of the universe. Nor is his an imperialist song that justifies a specific political order or regime by locating authorization in the cosmos.[60] Rather, it speaks to the more basic need of any community to perceive itself as being in harmony with the world beyond; and it does so by reinvigorating and reintegrating the specifically Roman tradition of song, in all of its layered specificity. Manilius's song invokes the twin functions of sovereignty and reproduction that are as old as Roman song itself. Thus after announcing the universe's favorable outlook on his endeavor and its eagerness to "publicize the census of the heavens through song" (*et cupit aetherios per carmina pandere census*, 1.12), Manilius suggests that such superficial acquaintance is not enough (*quod solum novisse parum est*, 1.16):

> More fervently
> does it delight to become intimate with the very entrails of the
>   universe
> and to see how it rules and generates through its signs animate life
> and to bring this news back in rhythm, with Phoebus tempering the
>   tune.

>   impensius ipsa
> scire iuvat magni penitus praecordia mundi
> quaque regat generetque suis animalia signis
> cernere et in numerum Phoebo modulante referre.

> (Manil. *Astr.* 1.16–19)

Manilius imagines himself as reenacting the rite of passage of the Salian initiates, penetrating the mysteries of the universe, encountering now not the death that lurks in the labyrinth but the life force hidden deep within it, thereby securing both sovereignty (*regat*, 1.18) and reproduction (*generet*, 1.18).

Indeed, Manilius helps us to understand how the different dimensions of Roman song lore constitute variations on a single theme. As he indicates later in book 1—after recounting a progressivist view of human history and humanity's growth in understanding and awareness —the descent of song from heaven necessitates his explication in song of the form and image of the universe:[61]

> And inasmuch as song descends from the lofty heavens
> and the established order of the fates comes to earth
> first must I sing the very form of nature
> and set forth the whole universe in its own image.
>
> et quoniam caelo descendit carmen ab alto
> et venit in terras fatorum conditus ordo
> ipsa mihi primum naturae forma canenda est
> ponendusque sua totus sub imagine mundus.
>
> (Manil. *Astr.* 1.118–21)

Song descends from heaven, as the Salian shield falls to the earth, as the bird mediates between sky and land, as the craftsman transforms the raw material of nature into objects of great cultural value. Unlike the Mambai, who offer to the silent cosmos the gift of "ceremonially made clamor" in exchange for life itself, the Romans claim to adapt themselves to the rhythms and intervals of a cosmic song that their wise men, shamans, *vates*, philosophers, poets, singers, musicians, or craftsmen have the privilege of learning, the intimate secrets of the universe that they come to know and bring back to their fellow Romans. Song is understood to be a gift from the universe, through which the universe lays bare its inmost heart.

Song and Its Rivals

The political, social, and cosmic authority ascribed to song makes it necessary for other cultural practices to situate themselves with respect to it. To some extent these rival practices, especially oratory, philosophy, and dance, can be regarded as aspects of song that struggle to differentiate themselves from or within the realm of special speech. As promoters of the power of *dicta*, oratory and philosophy in particular derive their authority from the impact of ritualized language beyond the bounds of ritual, yet they use that authority to reshape the conditions of its production. It is more than the evidence can bear to insist that all of the authoritative types of verbal performance were once conceived of as a part of a unified system of song at some point in history. To do so may reflect a mistaken urge, already implicit in ancient treatises, to assign simplicity and unity to the earliest phases of culture and complexity and disunity to later periods. What we can say is that the rivalry among these art forms is well documented throughout the classical period and that each presents itself as potentially a part — in the past or in the present — of a larger realm of song. The possibility of a return to that real or imagined state of unity prompts the attempts to fortify the boundaries between the practices. In a sense, we can observe a narcissism of minor differences between closely related cultural practices. Moreover, the rivalry between and among song, oratory, philosophy, and dance becomes more acute during the wave of re-Hellenization that characterizes Roman culture in the late republic and early empire, as specialists in each field seek to legitimize their own expertise by defining it in relationship to a comparable Greek practice. Thus the tension between practices replicates broader cultural tensions between Roman pragmatism and Greek theory, and between the holistic knowledge of the Roman aristocracy and the specialized claims of Greek, or at least nonnoble experts. This confluence of ethnic, class, and ideological concerns may help to explain why the ideal of a unified world of song never quite loses its grip on Roman commentators, even those who are concerned to differentiate song from some practice of special concern to them. To marginalize or segment song too successfully would be to destroy a guarantor of Rome's uniqueness, of its own particular relationship to the world beyond.[62]

Song, oratory, and philosophy are grouped together in a passage of *Tusculan Disputations* in which Cicero seeks to demonstrate the immortality of the human soul. Cicero's particular argument is that certain human achievements can only be regarded as divinely inspired and that, as a result, the faculty that generates them cannot be regarded as earthbound, mortal, or subject to decline (*terrena, mortali, caduca, 1.62*). Whatever we may think of the logic of this argument, it leads Cicero to an impassioned praise of the grandeur of human achievements, a laudation in which he refers explicitly to the teachings of Pythagoras:

> What, finally, are we to make of the faculty that tracks down what is hidden, that is called inventiveness and contrivance? Does it seem to be composed of this earthbound and mortal nature, subject as it is to decline?*** What about the person who first — which seemed the

height of wisdom to Pythagoras—imposed names on all things, or who gathered together scattered human beings and called them to a sharing of life, or who, with a few markings of letters brought limit to the sounds of the voice, which used to seem infinite, or who described the courses, progressions, and patterns of the wandering stars?

Quid? Illa vis quae tandem est quae investigat occulta, quae inventio atque excogitatio dicitur? Ex hacne tibi terrena mortalique natura et caduca concreta ea videtur?*** aut qui primus, quod summae sapientiae Pythagorae visum est, omnibus rebus inposuit nomina, aut qui dissipatos homines congregavit et ad societatem vitae convocavit, aut qui sonos vocis, qui infiniti videbantur, paucis litterarum notis terminavit, aut qui errantium stellarum cursus praegressiones insti[tu]tiones notavit? (Cic. *Tusc.* 1.62)

Cicero reiterates the importance of the creation of the musical scale and the various achievements of astronomy and gives as an example of the latter the sphere of Archimedes, in which he replicates the structure of the universe, employing divine ingenuity to illustrate the work of a divine creator. "But there are better-known and more-illustrious practices that seem not to lack divine force," he continues,

As if I could imagine a poet pouring forth serious and full-toned song [*plenum carmen*] without some celestial instinct of mind, or eloquence without some greater force flowing along, with resonant words and rich sentiments. And as for philosophy, the mother of all arts, what else is it but, as Plato calls it, a gift, as I, an invention, of the gods?

Mihi vero ne haec quidem notiora et inlustriora carere vi divina videntur, ut ego aut poetam grave plenumque carmen sine caelesti aliquo mentis instinctu putem fundere, aut eloquentiam sine maiore quadam vi fluere abundantem sonantibus verbis uberibusque sententiis. Philosophia vero, omnium mater artium, quid est aliud nisi, ut Plato, donum, ut ego, inventum deorum? (Cic. *Tusc.* 1.64)

The intensity of Cicero's rhetoric may indicate that the divine nature of the soul, or the divine origin of song, eloquence, and philosophy, is very much under dispute in his own day. But his grouping of them together, as evidence of humanity's access to immortality, and his citations of Pythagoras and of Plato in support of his position, suggest that he is invoking a traditional, even prerational understanding of the unity or interconnectedness of sources of authority within a community.

This construction of a triad song-eloquence-philosophy also frames the grand work of Quintilian on the education of the ideal orator. In book 1 of the *Institutio,* Quintilian must defeat the claims of those who would deny the relevance of training in song to the would-be orator. In book 12 he tackles, in similar terms, and by means of similar arguments, those who would belittle the usefulness of philosophy. In defense of the study of music, he notes, following Cicero, that his aim is not the formation of an orator who has been or will be, but to conceive a mental image (*imaginem quandam concepisse nos animo*) of one who is perfect and yielding in no respect (*perfecti illius et nulla parte cessantis,* 1.10.4). For the production of such an *imago,* song, which was venerated in ancient times, and whose founders include the child of gods, is essential. There follows much discussion of the antiquity of song, and of the practical relevance of musical training (a thesis that Quintilian's long disquisitions elsewhere on rhythm and gesture will both confirm and confound), but rhetorically the argument is carried by an appeal to perfection via wholeness and plenitude. In similar manner, in the grand finale to his work on eloquence, Quintilian asserts that, inasmuch as the orator must first and foremost be a good man, he has need of philosophy. Here in book 12 he again invokes the authority of Cicero, citing him for the repeated observation that "the capacity for eloquence derives from the inmost springs of wisdom, and that for this reason for a long time the instructors of morals and of eloquence were the same people" (*testatur dicendi facultatem ex intimis sapientiae fontibus fluere, ideoque aliquamdiu praeceptores eosdem fuisse morum atque dicendi,* 12.2.6). Once again the particular defense is situated in the context of a larger claim concerning formation of the perfect or ideal orator (*perfectus orator,* 12.1.10), the construction of *imagines* (12.1.28), the perfection of an art that cannot be perfected (12.11.25).

Even in their appeals to the shared power of song, oratory, and philosophy to connect the here and now to the world beyond, Cicero and Quintilian acknowledge the distinctiveness of these practices and create hierarchies among them. In *Tusculan Disputations,* as cited here, Cicero refers to philosophy as the "mother of all skills," thus implicitly granting it precedence over song and eloquence, while Quintilian is clearly concerned to present music and philosophy (as well as geometry) as aids to the creation of ideal eloquence. The perfect orator whom Quintilian strives to create is described as a *Romanus sapiens:* that is, one who adapts the analytical powers of Greek philosophy and the Roman tradition of exhortation to the cause of eloquence.[63] Quintilian specifically rails against philosophy in its present-day form and states with finality that he has no intention of turning the orator into a philosopher (*quapropter haec exhortatio mea non eo pertinet, ut esse oratorem philosophum velim,* 12.2.6). The passage in question echoes Quintilian's remarks on contemporary music in book 1. There, after waxing enthusiastic about the historical role of music in the formation of Greek and Roman society, Quintilian belittles the music of the present age, "which having been feminized on stage and crushed by wanton modes to a great extent has lopped off whatever of manly firmness was remaining" (*quae nunc in scaenis effeminata et inpudicis modis fracta non ex parte minima si quid in nobis virilis roboris manebat excidit*, 1.10.31). Oratory takes precedence over song and philosophy because both of the latter have declined from their pristine state. A similar argument subtends Cicero's position in *Tusculans Disputations*, where song has been reduced to poetry, and eloquence has lost its privileged position through no fault of its own but due to the desperate condition of the republic.

Cicero and Quintilian thus invoke a (lost) scenario in which oratory, philosophy, and song share cultural authority. The unification of the three is an *imago*, or death mask, a haunting image from the past that perpetually challenges those in the present to revivify it through a kind of surrogation or reanimation. As Joseph Roach has argued in his account of such surrogation in later circum-Atlantic culture, the process tends to generate a strange mix of sentimentalism and paranoia.[64] The sentimentalism or nostalgia for a lost world of unified verbal authority is evident throughout the writings of figures like Cicero and Quintilian, as well as Seneca the Elder and Younger, Tacitus, and Pliny. But paranoid anxiety is manifest as well, as evidenced by the attempts—sometimes subtle, sometimes frantic—to maintain boundaries between song and the related arts of oratory and philosophy. Paradoxically, the very passages that seek to exorcise such anxiety simultaneously provide the contemporary reader with evidence of the continuing cultural potential of song throughout the classical period of Roman history.

Cicero is perhaps the most open of the Roman writers in acknowledging that oratory derives its authority at least in part from its resemblance to song, although even in his writings the dependence of oratory on song is treated as at best an awkward if open secret. Thus, Antonius, at the beginning of his long discourse in book 2 of *De Oratore*, while insisting that eloquence is not an art, nonetheless argues for its distinction (*nihil esse perfecto oratore praeclarius*, 2.34) on the basis of its similarity to song: "So great a delight is there in the very power of speaking authoritatively that nothing can be perceived more congenial to the ears or minds of human beings. I say, what melody can be found that is sweeter than a measured oration? What song better joined than an artful period? . . . It is the special property of the orator when offering advice on important matters to give an opinion that has been set forth with dignity. Proper to the same is incitement of a sluggish population and moderation of a reckless one." Antonius offers this implicit praise of song on the basis of its recognized ability to provide delight or delectation. Yet the discussion raises the issue as well of oratory's practical authority (*usum*, 2.33; *sententia, incitatio, moderatio*, 2.35). In its authoritativeness, oratory incorporates the power of music, for the very powers to incite and to moderate are those traditionally assigned to musical performance, from at least Plato onward. Nor does the matter of delectation seem an insignificant one, because it is, after all, the one to which Antonius devotes the most attention in this initial panegyric to eloquence; the attractive pleasure of oratory is a key reason offered throughout the *De Oratore* for making a study of it, and not simply speaking in a direct and unpolished way, as Cicero's unnamed and uncouth rivals would recommend.

Antonius's shift from overt to more implicit acknowledgment of the power of song is echoed elsewhere in the treatise, with respect to the second of the two features that Cicero regards as linking song and oratory, namely rhythm and vocal inflection (*numeri et voces*, 3.174, 3.196, 3.197). Whereas recommendations concerning rhythm and its relationship to song are somewhat vague in *De Oratore*, the issue of vocal inflection receives close and conflicted attention. At the end of book 3, Crassus, having covered the basic rhetorical curriculum, concludes his survey with a discussion of the role of voice (*vox*, 3.224ff.) in oratorical performance (*actio*). The discussion consists chiefly of exposition and analysis of Gaius Gracchus's custom of having a *fistulator*, or piper, accompany him at his oratorical performances "who would promptly blow a note in order to stir him up if he became lax or call him back from strained effort" (*qui inflaret celeriter eum sonum quo illum aut remissum excitaret aut a contentione revocaret*, 3.225).[65] One of the interlocutors demands an explanation of the practice, and Crassus readily obliges, explaining that the orator's voice should move comfortably up and down the musical scale, not remaining too long at the low end, where the vocal cords are relaxed, or at the high end, where they are tensed. The aim of the *fistulator* was to keep Gracchus from going too high or to low within the possible register of his own voice. Both in his introduction of the anecdote and in his analysis, Crassus draws on technical musical terminology (*remissum, contentio, acutissimus, gravissimus*, 3.225–27; cf. *Orat.* 58) to make his point. Yet he concludes the discussion by telling his listeners to "leave the piper at home, but take down to the forum the understanding that comes from this practice" (*sed fistulatorem domi relinquetis, sensum huius consuetudinis vobiscum ad forum deferetis*, *De Or.* 3.227). The recommendation encapsulates the relationship to song described and recommended throughout Cicero's rhetorical works, namely a knowing suppression of oratory's dependence on music.[66]

The example of Gracchus and the piper relates to the issue of the movement of the voice up and down the musical scale. In *Orator*, composed roughly a decade after *De Oratore,* Cicero again discusses the role of music in the formation of both vocal inflection and oratorical rhythm. "The variety of intonations is perfected in songs [*perfecta in cantibus,* 57]; yet there is even in oratory a somewhat more obscure melody, not that 'epilogus' characteristic of speakers from Phrygia and Caria, but the one that Demosthenes and Aeschines had in mind when each accused the other of 'inflexiones.'" The same and even a greater degree of attention is to be paid to rhythm (174ff.). Here again, proper technique is differentiated from that of the Asiatics (230), who are said to introduce pointless words (*inania quaedam verba*) for the purpose of filling out the measures (*complementa numerorum*), and who even fall into "an abject type of oration very close to trifling verses" (*in quoddam genus abiectum incidant versiculorum simillimum,* 230). And here again, as in *De Oratore,* an anecdote involving a professional musician and a musical instrument serves to define the boundaries between song and oratory and to demonstrate the need for oratory to maintain its dependence on music as a kind of open secret. The effort to produce rhythm in prose should be kept hidden by the use of weighty language and thoughts: it is not the presence but the absence of rhythm that will catch the notice of the audience (197). Nor is rhythm to be present everywhere in oratory, but almost everywhere. "And so an oration does not have patterns of percussion as if given by a flute player, but the total circuit and appearance of the speech is closed and given limit" (*Itaque non sunt in ea tanquam tibicini percussionum modi, sed universa comprehensio et species orationis clausa et terminata est, quod voluptate aurium iudicatur,* 198). There is no *tibicen* keeping exact time, and yet the rhythms outlined by Cicero depend precisely on the orator's ability to keep time. And although oratory is not music, nonetheless each segment of the oration must be closed and given limit, much as number closes and gives limit to the infinite range of human song, according to Pythagorean musical theory. Oratory is dependent on music. This dependence is what makes oratory a skill to be learned and cultivated, regardless of the restrictions of the Atticists. But oratory must not openly acknowledge this dependence with respect to either rhythm (*Orator*) or vocal inflection (*De Oratore*).

Among authors of the early principate, the anxiety over oratory's dependence on and contested boundary with song seems to intensify. In a crucial scene in book 11 of the *Aeneid,* Vergil has the Rutulian hero Turnus denounce the recommendations of the orator Drances as so much singing: "madly sing such things to the Trojan leader" (*capiti cane talia demens / Dardanio,* 11.399–400). From the perspective of the warrior Turnus, Drances' oratory can be dismissed as song, an impractical alternative to the military calculations of a man like Turnus. Yet within the larger framework of the *Aeneid,* singing is a positive enterprise, one reserved for the voice of the poet himself and characters who are divinely inspired.[67] Turnus's repudiation of oratorical song (especially that of Drances, which recommends a course of action that would have saved Turnus's life) is thus an ironic commentary on the rejection of all cultural authority, whether mystical or political, by those who rely on force to resolve disputes. At the same time, Vergil anticipates (although presumably does not share) the point of view that regards song as a corrupting influence on the orator or orator-in-training. Thus Seneca the Elder tells the story of Alfius Flavus who, although famous for his declamations while still a youth (*in toga praetexta*), let the force of his eloquence be "enervated by song" (*carminibus enervata,* Sen. *Contr.* 1.22). Song corrupted and limited the achievement of the orator Q. Haterius, at least according to Tacitus's brief obituary of him, which indicates that while the "exercise and hard work of others survived among posterity, Haterius's musicality and fluency came to an end together with his life" (*utque aliorum meditatio et labor in posterum valescit, sic Haterii canorum illud et profluens cum ipso simul extinctum est,* Tac. *Ann.* 4.61). Pliny describes the corrupt performances of the centumviral courts as veritable show tunes: "only cymbals and tympana are lacking to them . . . ululation there is in abundance" (*ac potius sola cymbala et tympana illis canticis desunt: ululatus quidem . . . large supersunt,* Plin. *Ep.* 2.14.13). The tendency to criticize a peer by accusing him of singing seems to go back at least to Julius Caesar, who according to Quintilian was responsible for the witty expression "if you are singing, you are singing badly; if you are reading, you are singing" (*si cantas, male cantas; si legis, cantas,* Inst. 1.8.2). The assignment of this saying to Julius Caesar, while still in *toga praetexta,* like Seneca the Elder's emphasis on Alfius Flavus's youthful success, fits a pattern whereby observation (or not) of the boundary between oratory and song becomes an indicator of one's success at mastering the conventions of Roman manliness.[68]

The most elaborate attempts to police the boundary between song and oratory are to be found in the *Institutio Oratoria* of Quintilian, who is forced to take up the issue of song, at times with a high degree of defensiveness, when he considers (like Cicero in *De Oratore* and *Orator*) the role of rhythm and intonation in oratorical style and performance. Thus in chapter 4 of book 9 he attacks those who would compose prose in the dangerously effeminate sotadean and galliambic rhythms (9.4.6), describes as tiresome (*molestos,* 9.4.53) the teachers who try to force all prose into metrical units as if it were lyric poetry, and defends Cicero from guilt by association with those who think that oratorical rhythm can be reduced to "the tapping of fingers and feet" (*ad crepitum digitorum et pedum,* 9.4.56)—all prior to analyzing prose passages on the basis of their relationship to recognized verse forms. When Quintilian declares that he is interested only in *oratorical* rhythm or *numerus* (9.4.57), he retreats from the Ciceronian acknowledgment of the musical basis of oratory, even though he does not retreat from the substance of Ciceronian teaching. The charge of consorting with music, which Quintilian issues freely against others, is one against which he must defend himself.[69]

Perhaps this awareness of the dependence of his own analysis upon music accounts for the even more aggressive stance Quintilian adopts with respect to the musicality of oratorical intonation. For example, he exhorts against the adoption of a chanting intonation in a case in which one might find oneself pleading for the right to commit suicide: lapsing into song is such a dangerous error it can keep you from being permitted to end your own life! (*cantare*, 11.1.56). This mistake, of delivering an oration as if it were a song, is widespread, we learn both here (*quod vitium pervasit*, 11.1.56) and in a subsequent passage (11.3.56), where, we are warned, it is even more repulsive than volubility, slowness, gasping, hissing, panting, or "hawking up phlegm from the depths of the lungs, like water from a well, sprinkling the nearest of the bystanders with saliva, and expelling the greater portion of the breath through the nostrils."[70] The practice of singing in court, Quintilian continues, clearly warming to his subject, puts one in mind of the stage, or of drunken revels. It corrupts the sanctity of the court with the wantonness of Lycians and Carians. Why stop with singing? Bring on the harps and flutes and cymbals! No, better to return to the Ciceronian dictum, and understand that if there is to be singing, it must be singing of a secret or hidden sort: *cantus quidem sed quod plerique intelligere nolunt, obscurior* (11.3.60).

The rhetor doth protest too much. Precisely because song and oratory potentially occupy the same cultural space (a fact understood well by Nero), and because oratory depends for its power on the song within (a fact understood by Cicero and even by Quintilian), the boundaries between oratory and song must be defended energetically. The struggle to replace the lost unity of song, to don the death mask imagined into being by the rhetoricians themselves, prompts nostalgia for lost unity and anxiety about the boundaries and identity of current practices.

Fortunately, the philosophers are a bit less defensive about their relationship to song, perhaps because in Rome they recognize that they have little chance of assuming center stage. Nonetheless, from time to time they do consider it necessary to differentiate their own enterprise from that of the original masters of special speech. Seneca in particular expresses concern, this despite his own composition of poetic dramas and his extensive quotation of classical Latin poetry throughout his prose works. To some extent his concern with poetry has to do with the way it is taught and interpreted by contemporary grammarians. Thus in letter 33 he objects to the quotation out of context of memorable senten-tiae, whether from poetry or from history, or even from the writings of famous philosophers. If such quotations are to be employed, he argues, it should be in the context of a fully developed and original philosophi-cal argument or exhortation, as his own early letters illustrate. So too in letter 88 Seneca expresses extreme annoyance at the trivial controver-sies fostered by the grammarians over the parentage of Homer or the drunkenness of Anacreon or the number of years between Orpheus and Homer, and so on. But his hostility to the *grammatici*, or schoolmasters, on at least one occasion betrays an anxiety about the authority of song itself. In letter 88 after arguing that memorizing stories and learning the principles of versification have little to do with regulating fear, or avarice, or lust (*Ep.* 88.3), Seneca acknowledges the counterclaim of the *grammatici* to the effect that Homer, for example, was a philosopher. The shakiness of Seneca's response reveals the ambivalence of his own position, for he merely notes that scholars have associated Homer with various philosophical schools — as if one cannot be a philosopher with-out adhering to a sect. Moreover, he contends, even if Homer were a philosopher, "surely he was a sage before he knew anything of poetry" (*nempe sapiens factus est antequam carmina ulla cognosceret,* 88.5). "And so, let us learn what made Homer a sage" (*ergo illa discamus quae Homerum fecere sapientem,* 88.5). Seneca begs the question of the potential authori-tativeness of poetry by simply claiming that anything philosophical in poetry belongs to philosophy and not to poetry.

More generally, and not just when quarreling with the *gramma-tici,* Seneca finds himself in his philosophical writings turning to poetry for evidence of the early and widespread impact of philosophy. In let-ter 8 he points out that even less-than-serious poetic genres, such as the mimes of Publilius, contain philosophical insight or precepts within them: "How many poets say what has been said or ought to be said by philosophers!" (*quam multi poetae dicunt quae philosophis aut dicta sunt aut dicenda,* 8.8). In letter 90 in which he engages closely with Posidonius's arguments concerning the role of sages in the formation of civilization much of his argument — for and against Posidonius — takes the form of quotations from poetry, specifically Vergil's *Georgics,* Ovid's *Metamor-phoses,* and Homer. Seneca is not merely adorning his argument with edifying passages from the poets. Rather, despite his insistence on the role of figures like Solon, Pythagoras, and Lycurgus in the advancement of civilization, he must turn to the Latin poets to provide an account of a world in transformation from golden age to history. For that matter, though he does not refer to the fact, would not the verbal productions of Solon, Pythagoras, and Lycurgus be more likely to constitute *carmen,* from a Latin standpoint, than *philosophia?*

Finally, Seneca's implicit commitment to the interconnectedness of song and philosophy is manifest not only in his own career but even in the advice he offers to the ideal pupil Lucilius who figures as his absent interlocutor in *Epistulae Morales*. For whatever we may think of the reality or fictionality of Lucilius, he manages to generate poetry that is quoted and praised by Seneca in several passages of the correspondence. Lucilius's poetry is well expressed and rather concise (*non paulo melius et adstrictius*, Sen. *Ep.* 8.10). His writing (in this case probably prose, since it is likened to Livy or Epicurus) merits praise for its manliness (*compositio virilis et sancta*, 46.2). His poem on Mount Aetna strives to match the quality of his predecessors Vergil and Ovid (79.5), while adding something new to the poetic heritage (79.6). In short Lucilius avoids the effeminacy and outré striving for effect that Seneca attributes to the wrong kind of song, especially the *carmen effeminatum* of Maecenas (101.13) and the luxurious excesses of contemporary symphonic music (51.4). It seems possible to regard Seneca's praise and instruction of Lucilius (whose name, we should recall, is but the diminutive of his own, Lucius)[71] as indirect defense of his own commitment to both poetry and philosophy. Indeed, Seneca's career as a whole, which involved early oratorical prowess as well, restores the mythical unity of philosophy-oratory-song implicitly praised by both Cicero and Quintilian.[72]

Song, Imitation, and Alterity

Let us visit once more with Ovid's magpies. Having started us on our exploration of the language of verbal performance, they have one more secret to share. As spokeswomen for mere speech, the Emathides are expressly denied the opportunity to sing. The relationship between their performance and that of the Muses helps us to understand song as an intensification of speech, a making special of the everyday. Although they are birds, they engage in the characteristic human activity of talking (*loquendi*).

While the *picae* are introduced as speakers, they are presented simultaneously as mimics. A careful examination of their entry into the narrative makes the significance of their mimicry clear.

So the Muse was speaking. But wings sounded through the air.
The voice of greeters came from the branches above.
Minerva looks up, trying to find the source of such distinct speech.
The daughter of Jove, she thinks she hears a mortal talking.
In fact, it was a bird; nine to be exact, all lamenting their fates,
magpies that had perched on the branches, imitating everything.

Musa loquebatur. Pennae sonuere per auras.
Voxque salutantum ramis veniebat ab altis.
Suspicit, et linguae quaerit, tam certa loquentes
unde sonent, hominemque putat Jove nata locutum.
Ales erat; numeroque novem, sua fata querentes,
institerant ramis imitantes omnia picae.

(Ov. Met. 5.294–99)

The contrast between the imperfect tense of the Muse's conversation
and the perfect tense of the resounding wings (*loquebatur* versus *sonuere*)
suggests that it is the ruffling of wings that catches Minerva's attention, that interrupts the chatter of the Muse. The sound of the magpies'
voices, on the other hand, returns us to tenses of incompletion, either
the imperfect (*veniebat*) or the present (*loquentes, sonent, querentes, imitantes*). Indeed, we are led to believe that the magpies may have been
perched above Minerva and the Muses throughout their opening conversation, a possibility signaled by the switch to the pluperfect tense in
the verb *institerant*. We are, in effect, asked to imagine a performance by
the magpies simultaneous with that of the Muse. It is not their speech,
which evidently coincides with that of the Muse, that attracts Minerva's
attention, but the fluttering of their wings. Only when they have differentiated themselves from Muses is their existence acknowledged. What
is more, although the narrator informs us that the magpies were "lamenting their fate," Minerva gives no indication that she knows their
story, and indeed listens patiently (as must the audience of the poem) to
the Muse's account of the arrogance of the Emathides and their defeat
by her sister Muse. In retrospect, the magpies' lamentation can have
been nothing more (or less) than an imitation of the Muse's lamentation of the fate of herself and her sisters. The narrator expressly tells us
that the *picae* "imitate everything" and, by implication, add nothing. Indeed, the only respect in which their performance would seem to differ
from the performance of the Muse is that the magpies still seem human,
a point emphasized by the close positioning of the phrases *hominem
. . . locutum* and *Jove nata*: human speech and the daughter of Jove. The
content of the magpies' utterance is indistinguishable from that of the
Muse, consisting in each instance of complaint or lament. The physical
characteristics of the *picae*—wings and voices that sound human—are
what give them away, although even here the poet seems to be playing
with a certain mix of sameness and difference, since the Muses, too, we
have just learned, have wings (*sumtis alis,* 5.288); and they, like all divine
characters in the *Metamorphoses*, speak as if they were human beings.

By emphasizing the mimetic capability of the magpies at the outset
of the episode, and calling attention to the sameness and yet difference

of their performance, Ovid raises the possibility, neither pursued nor denied in the subsequent narrative, that the magpies continue to imitate the Muse right on through the end of her song several hundred lines later. Although the magpies are emblems of speech as opposed to song, it is hard to see how their utterance differs categorically from that of the Muses, except insofar as it is uttered by them and not by the Muses, that is, by creatures with the bodies of birds and the voices of people.[73] For all that Roman culture, as described in the preceding pages, insists on the difference between speech and song and ascribes the specialness of song to comparably special performers, this passage at least suggests that anyone can sing, as long as she mimics faithfully another's song.

While Ovid's narrative is concerned with crossing of boundaries between ontological categories—human, avian, divine—it anticipates and resembles ethnographic narratives of cross-cultural mimicry. In his study *Mimesis and Alterity*, Michael Taussig discusses various accounts of "first encounters" between Europeans and indigenous peoples that call attention to the use of mimicry on both sides of a cultural divide.[74] A sentence from Darwin's journals is even more suggestive than Taussig indicates. Darwin writes of an encounter with inhabitants of Tierra del Fuego in 1832, and the Europeans' reaction thereto: "After our first feeling of grave astonishment was over, nothing could be more ludicrous than the odd mixture of surprise and imitation which these savages at every moment exhibited."[75] In Darwin's view, the "savages" were "at every moment" mimicking the Europeans, as Ovid's magpies, in a continuous present tense, "imitate everything." But, of course, Darwin's use of the term "ludicrous," from the Latin *ludus,* suggests a certain mix of playfulness, disdain, and it would seem, reciprocal imitation on the part of the Europeans as well. Indeed, as Taussig writes of the narrated encounter more generally, "they [the Europeans] get into the game too, not only as mimicry of mimicry but, so it seems to me, with a hint of parody as well—parody of sensuous capacity of face-pulling, and parody of mimesis itself."[76] Nor is the mimesis limited to bodily, as opposed to verbal, imitation. As Darwin elsewhere writes of the same encounter, "they [the Fuegians] could repeat with perfect correctness each word in any sentence addressed them, and they remembered such words for some time."[77]

Taussig reads this and other narratives of first encounter through the lens of Benjamin's account of the mimetic faculty as a yielding into the other, a desire "to get hold of an object . . . by way of its likeness, its reproduction."[78] And certainly just such a desire informs the entirety of Ovid's narrative: it is precisely the Emathides' rivalry in performance with the Muses that both gets them into trouble and grants them a kind of victory, inasmuch as, by being reduced to magpies, they generate a song indistinguishable from that of their oppressors. Another story, told as history rather than myth by Ovid's near-contemporary Livy, is even more explicit about the Roman desire "to get hold of an object . . . by way of its likeness"—namely, Livy's account of the invention of *ludi scaenici*, or theatrical performances, at Rome, in 364 BC, as an attempt to cure a pestilence that had not responded to ordinary remedies.[79] Livy describes the success of the Roman youth (*iuventus*) in imitating (*imitari*, 7.2.5) Etruscan dancers (*ludiones*), who had been "fetched" (*acciti*) from neighboring Etruria. Livy emphasizes that the Etruscan performers danced "without song, without any movement in imitation of song" (*sine carmine ullo, sine imitandorum carminum actu*, 7.2.4): he is no doubt thinking of the rage for mime, an art form entailing expressive dancing as accompaniment of song, in his own day, and making clear that the "first encounter" with the Etruscan dancers was a performance of a different sort. The Etruscans are in a sense, exempt from the chain of imitation, dancing to nothing but the measures of the flute. The Romans, on the other hand, not only "get hold of" the Etruscan performance by imitating it, but they supplement and simultaneously mock it, reciting jokes along with their imitation of the movements (*inter se iocularia fundentes . . . nec absoni a voce motus erant*, 7.2.5).

Much later, according to Livy, another Livy—that is, Livius Andronicus, whom modern scholarship represents as a "writer" of the late third century BC—effected a reseparation of the combined voice and movement that had characterized the first Roman imitation of Etruscan dance. Livius, we learn, was the performer of his own songs (*suorum carminum actor*, 7.2.9), but when his voice gave out, he sought (and evidently received, but from whom we never learn for certain) permission to have a slave "placed before the flute player for the purpose of singing" (*venia petita puerum ad canendum ante tibicinem cum statuisset*, 7.2.9), while he, Livius, danced the *canticum* (notice that it is now not the autonomous song, *cano*, but the second order *canticum*) "with motion all the more vigorous inasmuch as use of the voice offered no impediment" (*canticum egisse aliquanto magis vigente motu quia nihil vocis usus impediebat*, 7.2.9). The episode constitutes a more explicit ancient prototype of the mimetic "first encounter," a bringing to light of the desire for and absorption of "the other." But, in the episode recounted by Livy, such desire is ascribed not to subordinate creatures, such as Darwin's "savages" or Ovid's Emathides (poor humans, who hardly stand a chance in competition with the gods), but to the ancestors of the Romans themselves. Livy does couch the entire episode in moralizing language about the "scarcely tolerable insanity" (*vix . . . tolerabilem insaniam*, 7.2.13) of theatrical spectacle in his day, and makes clear, in subsequent passages of his narrative, that the imitation of the Etruscans did not put a stop to the pestilence. But embedded within this moralizing framework, this effort to contain the power of mimesis, is a story that reveals just that power, representing it as an unproblematic, even natural faculty of the Roman youth.[80] In this sense, Livy's narrative is emblematic of Rome's relationship to outsiders, in particular the relationship of elite Roman males to their "others", throughout history: a combination of instinctive imitation, distancing mockery (cf. the whole history of Roman satire), and constant ("at every moment"?) adaptation and use.

What the Romans are represented as adding to the mimetic performance — and here we return to our main theme — is voice. The Etruscans bring no *carmen*, no authoritative utterance, no speech made special, and thus the performance of the Roman youth can be safely represented as imitation without acquiescence, a "yielding into the other" without a loss of autonomy. Voice is present at the outset but only as a faculty of the Roman youth. Even as the bodily performance at the *ludi* becomes over time, according to Livy, the specialty of home-born slaves (*vernaculis artificibus*, 7.2.6), who dance to and perform more refined songs (*cantu motuque*, 7.2.7), the power of autonomous performance is reserved for the named Roman (characteristically, himself a freedman) Livius, who can only cede it to a slave when "permission has been granted."

Elite Roman authors knew full well that speech is a type of mimesis: Ovid gives away the game in his depiction of the magpies. And so they understood as well that song, as an intensification of speech, cannot escape the limits and possibilities of the mimetic faculty. Yet they sought to disconnect song from speech, to disembody the former at the expense of the latter, to capture in song the power of imitation without acknowledging imitation's implication in alterity. Passages like the Ovidian episode of the magpies and Livy's account of the origins of *ludi scaenici* make of the relationship between mimesis and alterity an open secret. We might add to them the obsessive play with terms relating to performance such as *ludus/ludio/lydus; troia/truia/amptruare; hister/histrio; Mamurius/memoria*. Are they Latin words, loanwords from other languages, "othering" place names?[81] Add as well the images of parodic performance found on early vases and reliefs and the narratives, historical and antiquarian, that place such performances among the early rites of Rome.[82] The capacity of imitation to assume the power of that which is imitated was familiar to Roman speakers, dancers, artists, and singers alike. But only the singer, it would seem, dared intimate that the power thus assumed had become his and his alone. In this sense, he plays a crucial role in the maintenance of the broader range of power relations on which Roman society is built. As Bell has written, in a terse reformulation of Foucault, "there can be no movement down from the top without a conduit from below . . . the establishment and maintenance of the power of kings or the power of capitalism [or, we might add, the power of the Roman ruling class] has to be rooted in preexisting forms of behavior, socialized bodies, and local relations of power, which could not be mere projections of central power and still effectively maintain and legitimate that power."[83] In suppressing the rebellious voices of the Emathides, in seeking to enforce an impossible distinction between song and mimesis, Ovid's Muses epitomize the relationship between the local and the global, the narrowly textual and the broadly social workings of power within the world of Roman song.

FOUR· SONG AND PLAY

TO UNDERSTAND THE WORLD OF ROMAN SONG, WE MUST also enter the world of Roman play.[1] In Roman culture, play (*ludus*) can be the context for song, as when hymns are sung at a festival or poems are chanted in school (both festival and school falling under the Roman rubric *ludus*). Play can be used to describe a type of song that is construed as less serious than other, nonplayful types—for instance, lyric poetry or satire in contrast to epic. And play, in its relationship to activities construed as serious, provides a cultural parallel that makes it possible to understand more fully song's relationship to speech, art's relationship to the everyday, and the role of both in the reproduction of the Roman social order. Play is a particular type of ritualized activity that is deemed trivial or ineffectual precisely to the extent that it is not song. Yet, somewhat paradoxically, song derives its self-proclaimed ability to transcend the embodiedness of play from its involvement in play. In song's relationship to play we find a richly documented example of the impact of ritualization beyond the ritual context and observe this impact as experienced in and carried by the social bodies of players, singers, slaves, free men, adolescents, adults, even poets—in short, the ritually constituted agents of Roman culture.

The critical, if often overlooked, aspect of play in the Roman world is that it is an expression of the body.[2] Play is a faculty of bodies in the same way that song is a faculty of voices. Song sometimes includes the play of dance and gesture, as for example the Salian song encompasses words and movement. But to the extent that the focus of the practice in question is vocal, it is song; if bodily, it is play, of which dance is a particular manifestation. The complementarity of voice and body that sustains the distinction between song and play serves to valorize voice. Voice is, we might say, the *primus inter pares* of bodily functions. It is an expression of the body, yet it is also a complement to the body. Voice achieves a cultural status that differentiates it from other "mere" bodily functions.[3] Roman culture, as expressed in the Latin language, manifests a tension between body and voice, or play and song. It makes no such distinction between, for example, body and touch or body and sight. The voice's ability to be of the body but not contained by it, song's ability to be of *ludus* but not contained by it, make of the voice and its capacity for song a bridge between the world of play and the world beyond play. Play is a self-contained activity, "executed within certain fixed limits of time and place,"[4] yet song manages to transcend those limits, to exist within and beyond the world of play. It is to this transcendence–or, better, bilocation—that song owes its authority in the Roman world. The transfer of social authority epitomized by the separation of song from religious ritual, such as that of the *salii,* is a potential outcome of each and every instance of play. Thus, when Roman poets self-deprecatingly describe their compositions as play, they are in fact affirming the special status of song. It is because song exists in the realm of play that it possesses authority in the realm of the real. The playful song of lyric and satire validates the serious song of epic and didactic. So too, the political authorities sing the real as an extension of playful song. Numa leads the chorus of the Salian priests and founds the civil and religious system of the Roman state. The consuls of the early republic combine the dance of the Salian *praesul* and the song of the *vates.* The republican orator struggles to differentiate his use of voice from that of other singers, but his voice only matters because it partakes of the specialness, the unreality of play. The emperor sings onstage not out of madness or disdain but as a display of the political authority of voice and its origin in play. For all of the Roman world's fascination with *ludus* or play, it is voice, and its special expression, song, that carry authority, not play. Yet song achieves its special status through its relationship with bodily play— both its inclusion in particular instances of play (e.g., school, religious festivals), and its ability to be separated from such occasions. Consideration of the relationship between song and play can thus elucidate the social significance of both.

Playing and Reality

Play does not exist except in dynamic interrelationship with reality. In the Latin language, there is no essential meaning to the word *ludus.*[5] There is not one type of bodily movement, one category of text, one musical performance that is intrinsically playful. (Thus the attempts to list the subcomponents of the category of play by, for example, totting up genres or practices, are fundamentally misguided.) Rather, an activity is construed as playful in relationship to some other activity that is construed as serious or real. Fantasizing is different from telling the truth, as Cicero suggests when he distinguishes between instances in which Plato played (*lusisse*) by inventing myths and those in which "he intended to tell the truth" (*id quod verum esset . . . dicere voluisse*, *Rep.* 6.4: note also the use of *dicere*). Imagination differs from reality, as a character in Plautus's *Asinaria* makes clear when he notes that he has "deluded" another character sufficiently: now it is time to tell it like it is (*satis iam delusum censeo, nunc rem ut est eloquamur*, 730).[6] Literary argument is an amusing pastime, but it cannot compare with the serious business of philosophy, a point Seneca the Younger makes on more than one occasion, using the verb *ludere* to describe the pointlessness of the former activity (*Ep.* 48.5, where *ludo* is opposed to *seria;* and *Ep.* 111.4, where *ludo* stands in contrast to *proficio*, "to make progress"). The ludic nature of fantasy, deceit, and scholarship is only recognizable as such in relationship to a similar phenomenon construed as serious or real.

Even in the sexual realm, play exists as play in relationship to business.[7] Sometimes sex is play if it is not with one's spouse (Ov. *Her.* 16/ 17.155; Sen. *Controv.* 7.5.10; Ov. *Am.* 1.3.22). Or sex with a boy might be considered play, in contrast to sex with a girl (Mart. 11.15.7: *ludat cum pueris, amet puellas*, "let him play with boys, let him love girls"). Withholding sex can constitute play, in contrast to doing the deed (e.g., Tib. 1.8.71–74: *Hic Marathus quondam miseros ludebat amantes / nescius ultorem post caput esse deum. / saepe etiam lacrimas fertur risisse dolentis, / et cupidum ficta detinuisse mora*, "Marathus used to toy with his miserable lovers, unaware that an avenging god was on his way. Often indeed he is said to have laughed at their sad tears, and to have detained an eager lover with a made-up excuse"; cf. perhaps Catull. 50 as well; also *Priapeia* 50.2: *me puella ludit et nec dat mihi nec negat daturam*, "the girl plays with me, she neither gives nor refuses to give"). But, so too, frequent sex, with girls and boys, can be understood as play, at least in opposition to the hardships of their lives otherwise: as Priapus puts it in one of his songs, "I'll gratify them with my eager tool, and ease their cares with plenty of play [*lusibus*] and fooling around" (*CIL* 14.3565 = CE 1504.5).[8]

If there is no play without reality, equally, strange as it may seem, there is no reality without play. As Jacques Ehrmann notes in his critique of Huizinga's discussion of the role of play in culture, "to define play is *at the same time* and *in the same movement* to define reality and culture."[9] The "meretricious glitter" that Huizinga regards as "lying over" the whole of Roman civilization may in fact be constitutive of that very civilization: Rome's highly developed sense of practical affairs, of the "thingness" (*res*) of the world and its equally highly developed sense of play are, in effect, two sides of the same coin.[10] A similar insight informs Donald Winnicott's account of the development of the individual psyche through the young child's construction of a boundary between internal and external reality via play. In his view, the infant requires transitional phenomena such as babbling at bedtime and transitional objects such as blankets and pacifiers as means of exploring the relationship between his body and external reality. Such transitional phenomena and objects are "not part of the infant's body yet . . . not fully recognized as belonging to external reality."[11] Even as the child's range of intersubjective contact grows, nonetheless she continues to play in "an area that is intermediate between the inner reality of the individual and the shared reality of the world that is external to individuals."[12] Without play there is no clear boundary between inside and out, between the imaginary and the real.

The Latin language seems to incorporate both the social and the psychological understanding of reality's dependence on play in various uses of the noun *ludus* and the verb *ludere*. School, especially the rhetoric school, is play or *ludus*. It constitutes rehearsal for a "real" life of enterprise in the forum or the lawcourts. Participants are reminded to differentiate between the two—indeed, a school that does not adequately prepare its students for the reality of the forum will find itself under attack. Failure to provide real-life preparation becomes a standard charge against schools of declamation. Yet what such charges in antiquity (and their repetition by modern scholars) overlook is that the authority of oratorical practice in the forum derives from the school, and not the other way around.[13] It is school that makes the ability to speak, dress, gesture—in short, perform in a certain way—the mark of a "good," (i.e., successful), high-status orator. Play, perhaps especially play in the realm of the fantastic, where much of Roman schooling takes place, serves the psychological function of providing a transitional experience between home or family and the world of the forum.[14] But such fantastic play—again precisely because of its fantastic nature—creates a reality whereby only those who have participated in such play have authority in the real world. From both a psychological and a sociological perspective, the play of school is as productive of the real as the real is productive of the play of school.

A comparable argument would seem to apply to the play of the gladiatorial school, and the play of the festivals in the arena, which both sustain and are sustained by the *ludus* or training camp. At the same time, the entire realm of gladiatorial play, whether in the gladiatorial school or in the arena, can only be construed as play in relation to some notion of reality. Despite the reality, from our perspective as well as that of the gladiators, of their exertions and sufferings, their practice is merely play with respect to the competitions their audiences endure for the sake of military, social, political, and economic gain. Huizinga makes the odd remark that the play of the arena is "depotentialized," by which he would seem to mean that it leads to no greater or nobler outcome than the death of the participants.[15] More recent scholarship, in contrast, has argued that the arena is productive — again both psychologically and sociologically — of elite male identity and hegemony.[16] True, the dominant sector of the population creates the arena in the sense that it orders captives, slaves, and traitors to fight to the death. But the arena creates the dominant sector as well. It performs the obsession with bodily integrity and celebrates the manly endurance that the elite imagines as differentiating itself from other sectors of society. And through controlled, prophylactic displays of violence, it works through and dispels the deeper and less manageable tensions that permeate society, thereby securing the continuity of the current power structure. As with school, so with the arena, play constructs reality.

The productive role of play accounts for its association with children and especially with those on the cusp of adulthood. Vergil describes the lashing of a top as child's play (*Aen.* 7.379–80) and imagines Romulus and Remus as babies playing near their lupine nurse (*Aen.* 8.632). Seneca mocks those who as adults (*adulti*) continue to goof off in the forum, as if they were boys playing among themselves (*pueri inter ipsos, De Ira* 2.12.2). But it is adolescence or young adulthood, the period between physical and social maturity, that the Romans most commonly associate with play. Cicero seeks to excuse the love affairs and other escapades of his client Caelius as *ludus* (*Cael.* 28) to be tolerated in those his age (Caelius was twenty-six at the time of his trial, and Cicero is referring to episodes from several years earlier). Catullus disparages a man who does not watch over his youthful wife but instead "allows her to play as she pleases" (*ludere hanc sinit ut lubet,* Catull. 17.17). Propertius indicates that it is inappropriate for a girl whose breasts do not yet hang down to be engaging in play (*necdum inclinatae prohibent te ludere mammae,* "your not-yet-inclined breasts keep you from playing," 2.15.21). Ovid describes the activity of Proserpina just before she is abducted by Pluto to be his consort in Hades as play (*Proserpina luco ludit, Met.* 5.392) — apparently it is only when she has been forced into a sexual relationship with an adult male that things turn serious. Socially approved sexual play thus has both a lower and an upper chronological limit, the lower dictated by puberty, the upper by the assumption of adult sexual roles.[17] But adolescent play is not exclusively sexual play. The play of the *lusus*

Troiae, in which male children of the highest social rank perform intricate equine maneuvers, is in no overt sense sexual (although the association with the labyrinth may evoke sexual maturity).[18] The play of elegiac poetry, while apparently only available to those who have achieved sexual maturity, and generally to be left behind as one approaches social maturity,[19] is nonetheless not exclusively sexual play.[20] Adolescent play is perhaps best regarded as a liminal experience, one in which the free play of protoforms, to borrow Turner's evocative phrase, leads to the assumption or construction of (relatively) stable adult social identity.[21] Of course, there are always those who remain stuck on the threshold, lost in passage, condemned to play forever: the emperor Nero, at least in the eyes of his ancient critics, was such a failed passenger, who remained obsessed with youthful play well into adulthood.[22]

While play is thus in some respects the special property of one period of life, its recurrence at later stages recapitulates the one-time transition from childhood to adulthood. Thus Crassus, as a character in Cicero's *De Oratore,* argues that the tendency of some elite males to engage in dialectic is reversion to a pastime (*studium ludumque*) that was created for the cultivation of youth (*ut puerorum mentes ad humanitatem fingerentur atque virtutem,* 3.58). Temporary engagement in such activities due to restriction of the political sphere is acceptable, according to Crassus, just as we accept that workmen might play dice when the weather prevents their real labors. Although preoccupation with such matters "continuously and at every period of life" (*omne tempus atque aetates suas,* 3.58) strikes Crassus as at best problematical, occasional participation restores the balance between mind and action, thought and speech. Centuries later Aulus Gellius will describe conversations about literary and cultural history as *ludus* forced upon him and his companions by the length of the Attic winter nights (*NA praef.* 4). But this scholarly *ludus,* he tells us, was undertaken with his children in mind (1) and has as its aim to inspire study, stimulate the mind, improve the memory, strengthen eloquence, and so on (16).[23] In short, *ludus,* even in adulthood, replicates the experience of the child in training for a productive adult life.[24]

Among the poetic genres, satire seems to have been constructed in part to extend the possibilities of *ludus* beyond the limits of adolescence.[25] Satire can be practiced by young or old (early Horace, Persius versus Lucilius, Juvenal), aspirant (early Horace, Juvenal), or insider (Horace book 2, Lucilius). One cultural function of satire seems to be to provide a ludic space for the performance and negotiation of alternative models of elite masculinity;[26] as we saw in an earlier chapter, satire "plays off" the ritual mastery of civic *sodalitas* in comedy to construct a more exclusive sense of conviviality with a guest list drawn from a narrower social range. The satirists' rivals, or defining others, are other agents who have the potential to cross the boundaries between the ludic and the serious and the ritualized and the everyday, namely the *scurra* and the philosopher. Satire prepares the performer (and remember that a reader reperforms a literary text in ancient Rome) to assume and reassume the role of the stable, masculine possessor of authoritative voice by playing with alternative protoforms of vocal performance. It also calls attention via parody — even to a listening and observing audience — to the vulnerabilities and distinctive features of hegemonic masculinity. Satire is thus the ludic counterpart that makes possible the "real" performances of oratory[27] and, to a lesser extent, of philosophy and epic poetry. Just as Roman social structure writ large requires the ludic performances of the arena, so the elite Roman male requires the *ludus* of satire. Satire thus is always already there in the Roman world. Even in Livy's account of the origins of *satura,* the youths who perform the medleys are already mocking and mimicking (*imitari,* Livy 7.2.5) other performances; and the earliest serious procession — that of the archaic *ludi Romani* — is imagined by later Romans as having contained a mocking element within it.[28] *Satura tota nostra est,* in the famous aphorism of Quintilian: We are the best at satire, but also, there is no "we" without satire.

Body Play

The reality generated by *ludus* is a reality experienced by and carried in bodies. Thus it is no surprise that *ludus* itself is first and foremost a play of the body. *Ludus* provides an opportunity for the young body to develop its adult schemes and modulations, for the gladiator or soldier to rehearse combat. More generally, *ludus* is identified with the stylized movement of bodies, or dance, whatever the purpose of the dance (entertainment, ritual, sexual seduction, mime, military training, etc.). In this respect, Walter Benjamin, with his emphasis on the physicality of the mimetic faculty, comes closer to recapturing the spirit of Roman play than the more abstract analyses of Huizinga, Caillois, and even their critic Ehrmann. The mimicking of outsiders discussed in the previous chapter, or of animals and birds, to be considered in the following chapters, illustrates the overlap between the concepts of dance, play, and mimesis. Even when construed as dance, play involves "yielding into" something outside the player.

In Plautine comedy characters dance — and comment on themselves as dancers. In such contexts they refer to their actions as *ludus.* For example, the title character of the *Curculio* boasts of his ability to clear the crowded city street of all kinds of passersby. No general or tyrant will get in his way. Greeks who strut about with their books and their gift baskets, who converse, who stop to drink in local bars: all will take a licking if they obstruct him. Even the dancing slaves, he proclaims, will not get in his way:

> The slaves of *scurrae,* as they dance reciprocally in the road,
> whether givers or makers, all of them I will knock to the ground.

> tum isti qui ludunt datatim servi scurrarum in via,
> et datores et factores omnis subdam sub solum.

(Plaut. Curc. 295–96).

The passage as a whole refers to the physical performance of various characters, their self-presentation as emphasized by triple repetition of the verb *incedunt* (289, 291, 294), which seems to mean something like "present through stylized gestures on stage." At the culmination of the list are the slaves of *scurrae* whose "play" (*ludere*), especially when modified by the expression "reciprocally" (*datatim*)[29] and supplemented with what are probably technical terms (i.e., *datores* and *factores),* seems to consist of a kind of challenge dance in which some "give" steps or poses and the others "make" them in return.[30] Just as other brief passages in Plautus presuppose and give insight into a vast song culture of the early classical city, so passages like this one from *Curculio* play upon the performers' virtuosity and the audience's familiarity with respect to dance types. While the *ludus* of the slaves is best regarded as dance, it also can be understood to describe "unserious" movement that depends on and constructs the "real" movement of other figures on the city streets. That the slaves in question are slaves of *scurrae* supports this interpretation, since *scurrae* more generally are parodists of the behavior (physical and verbal) of more reputable figures of Roman society.[31]

In another Plautine comedy, the *Pseudolus,* a word derived from *ludus* occurs expressly in the context of dancing for entertainment. Here the title character reports that at a *convivium* he has just left the attendees had begged him to dance (*orant med ut saltem,* 1273). He now reperforms the dance for the audience of the play, referring to the specific meter (*ad hunc . . . modum*) and the steps (*haec incessi,* 1275a: again the verb *incedo* for self-presentation on stage). But all of this movement is carried out, he says, by way of *ludus: sic haec incessi ludibundus,* 1275a)—perhaps a less serious version of the movements that otherwise would have required careful training (*discipulina,* 1274a).[32] The audience applauds, but as he tries to do an encore, he stumbles into the lap of his mistress: this fiasco, he reports, was the dirge for the dance (*id fuit naenia ludo,* 1278a). Whether serious or comic, the actions summed up in the word *ludus* constitute a special, stylized use of the body for purposes of entertainment, namely, dance.

The association of *ludus* with dance helps to explain its use for sexual activity, since both involve stylized uses of the body, and dance is frequently an imitation of or invitation to sexual contact.[33] This dual meaning of *ludus* is apparent in a highly charged scene from Plautus's *Stichus*, one that presents two slaves celebrating their recent success in an onstage drinking party. Like good convivialists, they propose to lay aside their rivalries and drink from one tankard and enjoy the company of a single whore (*uno cantharo potare, unum scortum ducere*, 730). Stichus, the title slave, plays a word game with Sangarinus, describing at length their unanimity and potential sharing of the girl, but Sangarinus cuts him off:

> Okay, enough already, I don't want to get bored. Now I'm looking
> for a different game.

> ohe iam sati'! nolo optaedescat; alium ludum nunc volo.

To which Stichus replies:

> Should we call for a girl? she'll dance.

> vin amicam huc evocemus? ea saltabit.
> (Plaut. *Stich.* 734–35)

To Sangarinus's request for another, or a different kind of, game, that is, sex instead of talk about sex, Stichus responds with a promise of a girl who will dance.

And indeed the ambiguity between dancing and sex continues until the end of the play, as the girl, Stephanium, promises sex with both men, and both men, thrilled with the prospect, begin to dance. They become increasingly excited, so much so that they invite the flute player to perform something "sexy, sweet, and cinaedic" (*lepidam et suavem cantionem aliquam . . . cinaedicam*, 760). The cinaedic tune (*cinaedi* are expressive male dancers, see chapter 5) prompts a challenge dance between Stichus and Sangarinus, which leads to a final invitation for *cinaedi* to rush the stage, like rain drenching a mushroom (772–73). The entire scene thus involves dancing on the part of the principals. But they take up their dancing in response to a promise of sexual congress with a woman, and use their dancing as a display of sexual dominance over other men. All of these uses of the body are introduced by Sangarinus's request for "a different kind of *ludus*."

The possibility of the stylized movement that is *ludus* shading over into sexual behavior is invoked in later Latin literature as well. For example, Propertius imagines Spartan girls as "sporting" (*ludos*, 3.14.3) naked among male wrestlers in the gymnasium. He lists foot racing, pankration, and discus throwing among the exercises of the body (*exercet corpore*, 3.14.3) in which young Spartan women engage, yet the upshot of the poem is that such training makes them loyal partners to their men. When Vergil describes the young man Serranus, about to be slaughtered by Nisus and Euryalus, he reports that he, "handsome to behold" (*insignis facie*, *Aen*. 9.336) had "played most of the night" (*plurima nocte/luserat*, 9.335–36), and "now was sprawling, with his limbs conquered by excess of the god—lucky, if only he had extended his *ludus* until dawn" (*multoque iacebat/membra deo victus—felix, si protinus illum/aequasset nocti ludum in lucemque tulisset*, 9.336–38). In the eroticized atmosphere of the episode, it is impossible to say in what precisely Serranus's "play" consisted—sex or dancing or both—or for that matter which deity, Bacchus or Amor, had undone him. In eclogue 9 Vergil has the singer Menalcas beckon Galatea to join him on land, "for what sort of *ludus* is there in the waves?" (*quis est nam ludus in undis? Ecl*. 9.39), he asks rhetorically. What sort of *ludus* is there on land? she might well retort.

More generally, *ludus* continues, from the generation after Plautus and onward, to be understood as (among other things) dance. Accius has a character describe Pentheus's participation in Bacchic revels as *ludus* or *ludere*.[34] Livy's consul rejects the claim that the bacchanals are to be tolerated as "acceptable dance and wantonness" (*concessum ludum et lasciviam*, 39.15.7). Vergil describes Scythian celebrations as involving nocturnal dancing (*hic noctem ludo ducunt*, G. 3.379). For Lucretius the dance of the Curetes is *ludus* (2.631); for Varro the same can be said of the performance of armed men at the feast of the Armilustrium (*Ling*. 6.22). Servius interprets the *ludus* of the fauns and wild beasts in rhythm to the song of Silenus as dance (*Ecl*. 6.28). Horace describes the movement of feet and arms and the exchange of jests collectively as *ludus* (*Carm*. 2.12.17–19); elsewhere he alludes to the dance, or *ludus*, of a pantomime (*Epist*. 2.2.124). Valerius Flaccus describes a city given over to dance and song and marriage torches by night (*ludus ubi et cantus taedaeque in nocte iugales*, *Arg*. 5.444). According to Silius Italicus, the customs of the Celtiberians include the wailing of barbaric songs in native tongue, the striking of the ground with alternating feet, and applause in time to the rhythm (*Pun*. 3.346–48): all this activity for him constitutes "respite and *ludus* for the menfolk" (*haec requies ludusque viris*, 3.349).

Such stylized use of the body need not always be frightening or exotic. Cicero refers to the exercise and practice that "we" (Romans) enjoy on the Campus Martius as *exercitatio ludusque* (*Cael*. 11); and Livy speaks matter-of-factly of the Roman general Valerius's involvement in military exercise: "He was easygoing and companionable when it came to the type of military exercise in which men of similar age entered contests of speed and strength" (*in ludo . . . militari, cum velocitatis viriumque inter se aequales certamina ineunt, comiter facilis*, 7.33.2). One of Seneca the Elder's declaimers fantasizes that the imaginary *convivium* at which Flaminius has a condemned man killed in order to gratify the curiosity of a *meretrix* is marked by other types of *ludi*, specifically dance and a competition in sensuous display: "Why should I bother to recount, judges, the different kinds of *ludi*, the dances, and worst of all that shameful competition between the praetor and the prostitute, as to which could move more enticingly?" (*quid ego nunc referam, iudices, ludorum genera, saltationes et illud dedecoris certamen, praetorne se mollius moveret an meretrix? Controv.* 9.2.8). But Seneca the Younger expressly notes that dance as *lusus* need not be at all effeminate, if it is conducted "as old-time heroes were accustomed to during play and festive times, three-stepping in manly manner" (*ut antiqui illi viri solebant inter lusum ac festa tempora virilem in modum tripudiare, Tr. An.* 9. 17.4). Indeed, a passage from Petronius suggests that any unusual arrangement of the human body can be interpreted as a *ludus*. During the course of the banquet of Trimalchio, the narrator Encolpius reports that while the host Trimalchio was butchering the *cantica* of Menecrates, some of the other convivialists were "attempting to lift rings from the pavement with hands that had been bound or while kneeling to bend their heads behind their backs and touch the tips of their toes" (*alii autem [aut] restrictis manibus anulos de pavimento conabantur tollere aut posito genu cervices post terga flectere et pedum extremos pollices tangere, Sat.* 73.5). Encolpius and company leave these guests "to their own devices" (*dum illi sibi ludos faciunt*) and instead go down to the *solium* that was being prepared for Trimalchio. Encolpius's description of the guests' gyrations as so many *ludi* may be a way of dismissing them as pointless activities; but it also suggests that *ludus* can be used to describe any stylized movement or arrangement of the human body, whatever the purpose.

Roman authors' use of *ludus* to refer to dance, sometimes shading over into sexual activity, sometimes into military practice, corresponds to Livy's account of the introduction of *ludi scaenici*, or theatrical entertainment, to the Roman world—a passage to which we have already referred more than once. In reporting the arrival of *ludiones*, or Etruscan performers at Rome in the year 364 BC, Livy explicitly describes a performance involving bodily movements and the melodic playing of the flute, but no song (*sine carmine ullo, sine imitandorum carminum actu*, 7.2.4). The youth of Rome (and Morel is surely right to see in the term *iuventus* a reference to the organized company of free adolescent males)[35] mimic the movements of the dancers, while at the same time reciting jokes in verse. From this spontaneous and simple beginning Livy traces the evolution of the now (in his view) overwrought and scarcely tolerable cycle of Roman *ludi scaenici*. While the passage in question holds important clues for the understanding of the history of Roman song generally, and drama and satire in particular, it also makes clear the primary association of *ludus* with stylized bodily movement.[36] The Etruscan *ludiones* display their decorous movements (*haud indecoros motus*) while dancing to the rhythms of the flute (*ad tibicinis modos saltantes*, 7.2.4). Indeed it would seem to be this central element of bodily movement that allows for the *ludi scaenici* to be considered *ludi* at all: the display of stylized bodily movement is what the *ludi scaenici* share with the older *ludi circenses* and with the *lusus Troiae*, both of which display stylized bodily movement (in the latter two cases, of animals as well as humans). Moreover, Livy's association of the invention of *ludi scaenici* with the use of jokes (*iocularia*) and verbal expressions similar to the (often obscene) Fescennine verse (7.2.7), together with his express description of the movement of the Etruscan dancers as "not indecorous," leaves open the possibility of a not entirely suppressed sexualized performance on the part of the Roman *iuventus*. Finally, while Livy does not call attention to the fact, the *iuventus* he refers to is to be understood as the cadre of young men of military age—hence, their interest in dance is a reminder of the role of dance in military training.[37] Whether Livy's association of the *iuventus* with early drama draws on Greek traditions linking drama with *ephebeia* or not, it fits a larger pattern of Roman associations linking dance, sexual maturity, and military preparedness, all within the realm of *ludus*.[38]

One other element of *ludus* as stylized movement emerges from a survey of its occurrences, namely the close association between the *ludus* of animals and that of human beings.[39] When Menalcas in eclogue 9 of Vergil describes Galatea's sport in the waves as *ludus* (*Ecl.* 9.39), he may well be assimilating her behavior to that of dolphins and other sea creatures, whom the ancients regarded as playing or dancing.[40] Indeed Latin authors use the suggestive verb *exsultare* (already familiar from our discussion of the Salian song and dance) to describe the movement of an array of animals, including fish, rabbits, and seals.[41] When Ovid in an early love elegy describes Jupiter's relationship with Leda, he indulges in a triple pun on the verb *ludere: quam fluminea lusit adulter ave*—"whom he tricked in the guise of a river bird" (*Am.* 1.3.22). *Ludo* here refers to the fact that Jupiter, as a swan, had adulterous sex with Leda (the offspring being Helen and Clytemnestra, Castor and Pollux). It also describes the treachery, or unreality of his appearance as a swan. And it may refer as well to the mimetic dance through which an actor might perform the part of "swan." Elsewhere Vergil (*Aen.* 1.397) refers to the "play" of swans as *ludus;* in his reference to the *ludus* of bees (G. 4.105), it is not entirely clear whether their movement is the tenor or the vehicle of the metaphorical connection between human and apian performance.

In many societies, dance movements are based on imitation of animals—and certainly Roman lore contains its share of references to humans performing as animals. The specialized art of hand gestures, which the Romans eventually adopted from Hellenistic Greece, entailed the imitation of animals through coded movement of the hands,[42] while the repertoire of mythological themes required of mime dancers would have involved more than a few animal roles for the performance of mime.[43] Apart from any drama of species differentiation implicit in such performances, there is the simpler fact that *ludus*, as stylized movement, can constitute disguise or impersonation. Two of the most striking instances of transformation known to ancient mythology can be understood (and in one case definitely was understood) as dance: the second-century AD Greek writer Lucian tells us that the mythical figure Proteus was the prototype of the mimetic dancer.[44] And Ovid's depiction of Erysichthon's daughter, who repeatedly changes shape in order to escape from those to whom her insatiable father has sold her, may well recall a bravura dance performance.[45]

The Play of Images

The connection between *ludus* and disguise accounts for some of the most complex and uncanny uses of the term. Consideration of these instances allows us to identify a personal or psychological grounding of the social significance of *ludus* while also bringing us back to the theme of the parallel development of verbal and plastic art through processes of ritualization. *Ludus* has an impact beyond the confines of play through the disembedding of both voice and image. While voice is our chief concern here, the analogous relationship of the *imago* (understood as both image and death mask) to play is used by Roman singers themselves in their accounts of the development of autonomous voice and, by extension, autonomous personality. The emergence of the poetic persona from the context of playful performance, or *ludus poeticus*, can be seen as a particular expression of the broader social processes through which *imago* is disembedded from lived practice, the adolescent liberated from the confines of childhood play, and the free male subject effectively separated from slaves through the constitution of autonomous legal personhood. Precisely because poetry as a manifestation of song in a culture of oral performance must struggle with the tension between body and voice, or the mimetic and the semiotic, we should not be surprised to find the public secret of disembodiment so clearly exposed within it. If Ovid's story of the Muses and the magpies serves as a representative anecdote for the struggle between the mimetic and the symbolic within the Roman system of verbal performance, Horace's *Carmen Saeculare*, a song performed by free youths at a ritual devoted to the renewal of the Roman people, crystallizes, as we shall see, the strategies of self-formation through play that inform a wide range of texts and practices.

Ovid's triple pun on the *ludus* of Jupiter as adulterous swan (*Am.* 1.3.22) directs our attention to the interrelationship of play and disguise. But Jupiter is not the only god to deceive with false appearances. This is exactly the charge that Aeneas makes once he realizes that the attractive young huntress he has met in the Carthaginian hinterland is none other than his mother Venus:

> She spoke, and as she turned her dewy neck shimmered.
> Ambrosial locks breathed divine aroma from her head.
> Her robe cascaded to the bottom of her feet.
> Her gait gave her away. Aeneas, once he recognized
> his goddess mother, pursued her thus (although she fled):
> "Must even you be cruel? Must you always trick your son
> with false appearances? Why can we not clasp hands
> and speak and hear words that are true?"

> Dixit et avertens rosea cervice refulsit,
> ambrosiaeque comae divinum vertice odorem
> spiravere; pedes vestis defluxit ad imos,
> et vera incessu patuit dea. ille ubi matrem
> agnovit tali fugientem est voce secutus:
> "quid natum totiens, crudelis tu quoque, falsis
> ludis imaginibus? cur dextrae iungere dextram
> non datur ac veras audire et reddere voces?"
>
> (Verg. *Aen.* 1.402–9)

Venus's appearance as a huntress had been a staged performance, a falsification of her divine body, the imposition of a new, human presence.[46] The impact of the revelation of the true goddess (paradoxically through the staginess of her gait, *incessus*) is drawn out of the performer of the text by the unusual use of hiatus between *dea* and *ille* in line 405. The reciter must catch his breath, as it were, in the face of the divine apparition. Venus's playacting, her game of concealment and revelation, has elements of sexual seduction about it, as indicated by earlier allusions to her erotic encounter with Aeneas's father, Anchises.[47] In Aeneas's view Venus has disguised herself for no good reason in an act of cruel deception. His accusation (*incusat*, 1.411) of play with false *imagines* echoes Venus's own description of Pygmalion's deception (*lusit*) of loving Dido (1.352), which was corrected, made real, by the ghostly appearance (*imago*, 1.353) of Sychaeus. Yet given the Roman understanding of *ludus* as rehearsal for the real, one wonders whether Aeneas could have grasped the true identity of Venus without the initial exposure to her disguise—Latin never uses *imago* to describe a manufactured image of a god, *simulacrum* and *signum* being the preferred terms.[48] In connection with his emphasis on play as the transitional phenomenon that allows the child to construct a boundary between self and external reality, Winnicott also develops a theory of "the good enough mother"—one who, whatever her limitations, creates the conditions for her child to engage in productive play. In the *Aeneid*, Venus, through her own play, sets the stage for Aeneas's dalliance with Dido, a transitional experience that, whatever its cost to the Carthaginian queen, prepares the way for Aeneas's encounter with the reality of his destiny.

From Aeneas's standpoint Venus's impersonation of a huntress relies on "false images" (*falsis imaginibus*, 1.407–8) and is part of a larger pattern of cruel deceptions (*totiens, tu quoque*—multiple on Venus's part, with other cruel ones drawn into the accusation as well). Vergil draws on the familiar Roman use of *imago* to mean death mask, specifically the death mask of an officeholding ancestor that is housed in the family *atrium* and worn by impersonators at subsequent family funerals.[49] We are reminded that such impersonations, as stylized uses of the body, can be understood as a type of *ludus*, yet a *ludus* that is itself constitutive of Roman reality. Although the term *imago* is usually taken to refer to the waxen death mask and then, by extension, to all portrait busts, regardless of material, a perusal of the testimonia gathered by Flower and by Daut[50] makes it clear that the *imagines* are regarded, especially in the republic and early principate, as the agents or subjects of verbal action. They "stir up" (*suscitare*), "set in motion" (*commovere*), "dissuade" (*depreci*), and "lead" (*ducere*).[51] The mimesis of the deceased seems to be the core meaning of *imago*, with the death mask serving as but a reminder of that performance, a carryover or residue from the realm of *ludus* to that of *seria*. This fact helps us to understand why, at least in Cicero's use of the term, *imago* is never the target of an aesthetic judgment: the emphasis is less on its materiality than on its character as prompt for revivification. *Imago* thus occupies a relationship to the embodied performance of the *ludus* similar to that of voice: it is an aspect of play that survives in the realm of the real and acquires its authority from precisely this double existence. (The same is presumably true of the *ancilia* in the Salian rite: it is not because they are self-activating talismans that they are carried in the rite, but because they have been carried in the rite they come to serve as self-activating talismans.)

The double status of the *imago* is manifest as well in its potential to refer to the face alone (the usual case) or the whole body: for example, in Plautus's *Amphitryo* where the slave Sosia, on encountering the god Mercury disguised as himself, describes the latter as "possessing the entirety of my *imago*" (*nam . . . omnem imaginem meam . . . possidet*, 458). Similarly, as a manufactured object, an *imago* can represent a face, a head, or an entire body, although by far the most frequent reference is to a depiction of the face or head alone.[52] Somewhat as the elite singer lays claim to the voice as the bodily faculty that survives the transition from play to reality, so the elite household develops an obsessive attachment to the *imago*, as the remnant of play, and, in the process, redefines *imago* as replication of facial features at the expense of the rest of the body. In any event, through imitation of the ancestors successive generations of the aristocratic family acquire and exercise authority within the household and the larger community.[53] Part of Aeneas's problem, from a Roman standpoint, would seem to be that the dominant *imago* at this stage of his life is maternal, rather than paternal. Thus Venus's performance, while true to her role as mother, necessary as a transition between human and divine realities, and evocative of the movement from play to reality in the lived experience of the Roman aristocrat, can nonetheless by described as "false": it is, in effect, a misrepresentation of the "true" Venus Aeneas longs for, albeit a true manifestation of the wrong parent.

The ludic *imago* appears again in a playful yet serious ode of Horace, an appeal to Galatea upon her commencement of a trip abroad.[54] After citing various possible negative and positive omens for her trip, Horace turns to the mythological exemplum of Europa, a woman whose journey on the back of a bull turned out to be a different sort of experience than the one she had anticipated. Play appears twice in the ode, once as the activity of Jupiter, once as the activity of Venus: here again it is as if the gods are only accessible to human beings through transitional objects or phenomena, through bodily falsifications, a situation that can have both tragic and comic consequences. Within the ode, Horace represents Europa as apostrophizing her absent father, all the while unsure as to the reality of what is happening to her:

As soon as she touched down in Crete potent
with a hundred towns, she declared, "Father, O
abandoned name of daughter and sense of duty
conquered by madness

From where and to where have I come? A single death is light
    punishment
for the sin of virgins. Do I, while awake, weep for commission
of a shameful crime, or does an *imago* play with
innocent me

a vain one that brings a dream as it escapes
the ivory gates?"

quae simul centum tetigit potentem
oppidis Creten, "pater, o relictum
filiae nomen, pietasque" dixit
"victa furore!

unde quo veni? levis una mors est
virginum culpae. vigilansne ploro
turpe commissum, an vitiis carentem
ludit imago

vana, quae porta fugiens eburna
somnium ducit?"

(Hor. *Carm.* 3.27.33–42)

In a singularly disturbing use of the present tense, Horace imagines Europa crying out (*ploro*, 3.27.38) while she is being ravished. As
Jupiter rapes her, she wonders aloud whether she is actually being violated, hence committing a shameful act (in the misogynistic logic of
traditional shame culture), or if instead an empty image (*vana imago*)—
that is, an impersonation of reality rather than reality itself, a dream,[55]
as she will go on to suggest—is playing (*ludit*) with her, befuddling her,
but of course also having sex with her, imposing a schematized use of
the animal body upon her.[56] *Ludus* as deceptive representation, *ludus* as
imitation of an animal, *ludus* as sex, *ludus* as transition to reality: all are
present in Europa's deranged outcry. Present as well is the invocation of
imago as death mask, as real remnant from the realm of play, as parental
image either rejected, if in fact her rape is real, and replaced by that of
her bull-god rapist, or still respected, if Jupiter's impersonation is only a
dream. Europa's use of the term *ludit* confirms by negation the function
of *ludus* as transition between the individual subject and the world beyond. Her inability to recognize whether she is involved in *ludus* can be
understood as psychic response to and manifestation of Jupiter's bodily
violation of the boundary between Europa and external reality. At the
same time, her use of the term *imago,* precisely in the context of an apos-

trophe of her absent father, cannot fail to call to mind, as in the case of Aeneas and Venus, the ancestral *imagines* of the elite household. In a sense Europa has already substituted the *imago* of her rapist-husband for that of her father. Yet, in true Freudian fashion,[57] the rejected object-cathexis becomes the content of her ego ideal, which manifests itself a few stanzas later as her father, who, still internal to her own thoughts, urges her to commit suicide for her shameful act.[58]

As Europa externalizes, through language, her psychic drama, a laughing Venus and Cupid make their divine appearance (*aderat,* 3.27.66) and, in so doing, announce the completion of play.

> Soon when she had played enough, she said
> "Refrain from anger and hot quarrel,
> now that the bull you despise lets you
> mangle his horns.
>
> You do not know that you are the wife of unconquered Jove.
> Give up your sobbing, learn to bear well your great
> fortune. A section of the earth will take
> your name."

> Mox ubi lusit satis, "Abstineto"
> dixit, "irarum calidaeque rixae,
> cum tibi invisus laceranda reddet
> cornua taurus.
>
> Uxor invicti Iovis esse nescis:
> mitte singultus, bene ferre magnam
> disce fortunam; tua sectus orbis
> nomina ducet."

(Hor. *Carm.* 3.27.69–76)

While incidentally confirming that Europa has been ravished (you *are* the wife of Jove, not you *will be*), the lines also introduce the idea that all that has happened is play. Now it is not absolutely necessary that the subject of the verbs *lusit* and *dixit* ("played" and "said") be taken as Venus, although that is the easiest interpretation. The final speech may also be Europa's own acknowledgment of her situation, perhaps in response to the laughing presence of Venus. Whether we read the final lines as a divine manifesto or as Europa returning to sanity, they supply a retroactive interpretation of what has preceded as *ludus:* either the "toying" of the gods with the hapless Europa or, following the more common use of *ludere* as "impersonation, schematized use of the body,"

Europa's own participation in sex, followed by impersonation of her father, and imagination of herself in various scenarios. Whatever the exact referent of *ludere* here, it has come to an end, and the end of play is presented as the beginning of reality. Now that her *ludus* is over, Europa really is the wife of Jupiter and the eponymous heroine of a continent. Yet only through the experience of *ludus* has she achieved this status.

The appearance of an *imago*, whether vain and dreamlike or not, has been crucial to Europa's experience—not only the *imago* of her father, carried from reality into the experience of play with the bull, but also Jove's successful deployment of the *imago* of a bull, which has led her from the play of youth to the reality of rape and wifehood. Again, as with Aeneas's encounter with Venus, so here *imago* is the feature of play that persists when playing has been completed. It seems more than coincidence that the first application of the term *imago* to a sculpture containing more than one figure is Varro's description of Europa and the bull "whose egregious *imago* Pythagoras [made] from bronze at Tarentum" (*quorum egregiam imaginem ex aere Pyt⟨h⟩agoras Tarenti, Ling.* 5.32). To Daut, the unprecedented use of the term *imago* to describe a sculptural group, together with the novel application of an adjective of aesthetic evaluation to the term, signals a shift toward use of *imago* to describe artistic depiction, or *Kunstbild*.[59] Whether such arguments are valid or not (admittedly the adjective *egregius* may refer as much to size as to quality), the artistic depiction is nonetheless the trace of a set of practices or performances: Jupiter's transformation into a bull, the abduction and flight of Europa, and Pythagoras's design and casting of the sculpture. It is the real or serious residue of a set of ludic processes. The artistic *imago* is the equivalent of the ritual objects (e.g., *ancilia*) that maintain their religious force long after the rite in which they appeared has been completed. One wonders whether Horace had the Pythagorean *imago* of Europa and the bull in mind in composing an ode that is also a meditation on the relationship between *ludus* and *imago*. As in Roman culture more generally, so in Europa's nightmarish reality, those who organize the mimetic activity of play through the skillful deployment of images, whether fathers, gods, aristocrats, or perhaps even artists, are in a position to manufacture reality.

Replication and Reanimation

We can expand our consideration of *imagines*, or death masks, as manifestations of the mimetic faculty at Rome by briefly considering them in relationship to two other sets of material objects previously discussed in this study, namely the Salian *ancilia* and the miniaturized everyday objects found in late Bronze Age and early Iron Age graves in central

Italy.[60] Consideration of these objects helps us to understand the duality of mimesis, both as it applies to what comes to be known as art and as it applies to verbal performance, whether play or song or both.

One aspect of mimesis brought to light by the objects in question is that of replication—the single divine shield multiplies to reach a total of twelve; the miniatures recreate, in smaller form, everyday objects such as shields, razors, loom weights, and huts; and the death masks reproduce the features of the various ancestors. In each of these instances we have a fairly straightforward exemplification of Helms's claim that in early societies craftsmanship consists not of original creation but of elucidating what is already present in another form. (In this sense, too, Ehrmann's objection to the use of "mimesis" as a synonym for "play" seems to have some validity—play is not so much a matter of imitating as it is of enacting.)[61] At the same time, the replication of such objects might be regarded as constituting a kind of waste: certainly there is no need for eleven additional *ancilia*, especially when they are all paraded around in public, an odd and wasteful way of protecting the identity of the magic shield that constitutes the talisman. The miniatures are wastes of materials and the effort of production because they cannot be used to fulfill the function of the original they replicate and will be buried with corpses anyway. Disposal in graves seems to be their primary function. The wastefulness of the *imagines* is perhaps less clear, although they are eventually put to use in funeral ceremonies whose own wastefulness needs to be restricted through sumptuary legislation. In any event, like play and song, as viewed from one perspective, the characteristic material productions of early Rome constitute a squandering of excess energy, an "accumulation of transformations made in time."[62]

At the same time, *ancilia, imagines,* and probably miniatures enable a type of mimesis that Thomas Mann describes as "the explicit reanimation of prototypes." As he writes with regard to the Freudian ego:

> We are to envisage the ego, less sharply defined and less exclusive than we commonly conceive of it as being so to speak "open behind": open to the resources of myth which are to be understood as existing for the individual not just as a grid of categories but as a set of possibilities which can become subjective, which can be lived consciously. In this archaising attitude the life of the individual is consciously lived as "sacred repetition," as the explicit reanimation of prototypes.[63]

The Salian *ancilia,* let us recall, are not only moved about by the performers; they also are capable of movement themselves, at least when the security of Rome is threatened. Their very existence animates the divine prototype, and they figure in a ritual that reanimates, as it were, the very prototype of Rome. So too, the archaic miniatures, as likely marks of initiation, would seem to invite reanimation of ancestral prototypes on the part of their bearers while alive. As part of the burial *corredo,* they make possible the future reanimation of the deceased, supplying him or her with everyday needs.

The death masks in particular clarify (and probably serve as the source of) Mann's concept, for they are expressly used in rituals of reanimation of the ancestors, as living members of the household or actors mimic the gait, appearance, and gestures of the ancestors while wearing them. They invite the young funeral orator and others of his generation to "reanimate the prototypes" of the ancestors — that is, to live up to and if possible, surpass their achievements.

This double aspect of imitation, as replication and reanimation, is relevant to the interrelated activities of play and song. Playful song is both a replication and a reanimation of a pattern or prototype set by someone else. To the extent that it is play, the emphasis is on replication and on the squandering of energy. To the extent that it is song, the emphasis is on reanimation, either of the song itself (*cantare*) or of the role of autonomous singer (*canere*).

Yet before turning to detailed consideration of the well-known yet oft-misunderstood phenomenon of *ludus poeticus,* the representation of certain kinds of poetry as play, we would do well to remember that the process of transition from playful to serious, from replication to reanimation, has as its own prototype the movement from childhood to adulthood. The miniatures, interpreted by archaeologists as mementos of initiation, may mark this movement; the Salian rite and the wearing of the death masks almost certainly do. It cannot be accidental that the revivification of the *imagines* coincides with a rite of passage for the emerging youth of the clan (recall that it is the youngest adolescent male who, according to Polybius, delivers the funeral oration to the assembled clan). As Winnicott rather startlingly puts it,

> It is valuable to compare adolescent ideas with those of childhood. If in the fantasy of early growth, there is contained *death,* then at adolescence there is contained *murder.* Even when growth at the period of puberty goes ahead without crises, one may need to deal with acute problems of management because growing up means taking the parent's place. *It really does.* In the unconscious fantasy, growing up is inherently an aggressive act. And the child is now no longer child-size.[64]

At the aristocratic funeral, the presence of the *imagines* allows the adolescent to "take the parent's place." It manages his aggression through a ritual that simultaneously revives and lays to rest the young man's predecessors.

A further citation from Winnicott is relevant to an understanding of the *imagines* at the aristocratic funeral and more generally:

> It is only here, in this unintegrated state of the personality, that that which we describe as creative can appear. This if reflected back *but only if reflected back,* becomes part of the organized individual personality, and eventually this in summation makes the individual to be, to be found, and eventually enables himself or herself to postulate the existence of the self.[65]

The *imagines* are the parents that must be replaced, the roles that must be filled. They are also the reflectors, the re-presentations that enable the individual (the clan, the community, etc.) "to postulate the existence of the self." Their inclusion in the world of play, of playacting, their association with art as a wasteful replication of the everyday, their appearance as figures of dream, fantasy, even delusion, identifies them, paradoxically, as creators of the real. Winnicott's language is strikingly close to that of another interpreter of play, the German philosopher Eugen Fink. For Fink, the "play world" created by play is an illusion closely akin to a reflection or a mirror image; as such it constitutes "an autonomous category of Being and embraces something specifically 'unreal' as a constitutive element of its reality."[66] "Playing," he continues, "is a real mode of behavior, which contains, so to speak, a mirror image derived from behavior in the real world: play behavior as structured by the roles of the play."[67]

Despite the anguish they inflict on Europa and Aeneas, then, despite the sense of seriousness, even awe, that pervades ancient descriptions of them, *imagines* are of the essence of play. They enable the transition to the real, even as they "embrace something specifically 'unreal.'" At the same time, the final emphasis in the relevant poetic passages on authoritative utterance (*dixit* at Hor. *Carm.* 3.27.70 and Verg. *Aen.* 1.402; *voces* at *Aen.* 1.409, even *suadet* in the case of Pygmalion at *Aen.* 1.357) as ending the experience of play while fixing its meaning clarifies for us the hierarchical relationship between body and voice, play and song, to which we now return. As the voice is to the body, or the text is to the song, so the *imago* is to the ancestral performance: an authoritative survival, a realization in historical time of the experience of play in "time out of time." *Imagines,* conventionally understood as part of the political self-representation of the aristocratic elite, in fact, through their incorporation in the texts of prose authors and poets alike, participate in the microrelations of power without which the macrorelations could not be sustained.

Ludus Poeticus Reconsidered

The interrelated phenomena of song and play converge in the literary theme of *ludus poeticus,* or poetic play. If Huizinga's study and critiques thereof provide a useful, if problematical, starting point for consideration of play as a general cultural phenomenon, Henrik Wagenvoort's short article on *ludus poeticus* supplies a touchstone for discussion of song as play within the literary tradition.[68] Wagenvoort reviews the instances in which Latin authors refer to their own or others' poetic productions as *ludus* and concludes that *ludus poeticus* is not an essential but a relative or, we might say, metaphorical concept. In other words, to call a poem *ludus* is to suggest that it stands in a contrastive relationship to another kind of poetry or another activity in general that is to be taken more seriously. The implied contrast might be between early poetry and late, short and long, lighthearted and profound. Or use of the term might contrast the *ludus* of poetry with the *seria* of philosophy, politics, or business. Wagenvoort is rightly keen to emphasize that calling poetry *ludus* implies no hostility toward it; rather it associates the poetry in question with relaxation, culture, and the arts in general.

My aim in this section is not so much to correct and revise Wagenvoort as to deepen and enrich his analysis on the basis of a more precise understanding of both song and play in Roman culture. Certainly Wagenvoort is correct that *ludus*—poetic or otherwise—implies and depends on *seria,* and that in many cases the identification of a poem as ludic seems to associate it with an aspect of extrapoetic reality that can itself be considered ludic, such as youth and love (to which we might add conviviality, a frequent association with *ludus poeticus* that is not noted by Wagenvoort). But it does not seem quite right to say that poetry called *ludus* is akin to the arts in general, since such a claim carries with it the implication that nonludic poetry (e.g. epic, tragedy, and didactic) is somehow not akin to the other arts, a claim that Wagenvoort himself surely would not wish to endorse. Nor is it quite satisfactory to suggest that *ludus* is always and only relative. If that were the case, then we would expect more uses of *ludus* to differentiate, say, a mature epic poem from an immature one, when in reference to epic there seems to be only one surviving use of the term *ludus,* which has a rather different significance altogether. Instead, I would like to suggest that the concept of *ludus poeticus,* like the other instances of *ludus* in Roman culture, carries with it a strong connotation of corporeality, either in the sense of engaging in a specific movement of the body or its parts (modulating via the vocal cords, writing with the hand, dancing along to a song) or in the sense of adapting language to externally imposed schemes, specifically meters and their antecedent dance steps. *Ludo* (like *dico*) can and frequently does describe the same practice as *cano*, but (like *dico*) it describes that practice from a different perspective. *Ludo* places emphasis on the physicality of the performance and its relationship to other physical patterns of movement, rhythm, and action. When assigned to poetry it describes a vocal performance, but a vocal performance that is in transition, between the demands of the body and the independent, autonomous voice. It is as if in the case of *ludus poeticus* the body is the external reality against which the voice must learn to define itself, much as the child learns to recognize itself as a self through exploration of external reality in the context of play, with its constraints and limitations. *Ludus poeticus* is the poet's rehearsal. It is certainly not trivial, any more than play is trivial in the life of a child or *ludus* is trivial in the production of the reality of Roman civilization. It is a transitional phenomenon, but what it is transitional to is the liberation of the voice, the autonomy of authoritative utterance. In the Roman concept of *ludus poeticus*, such activities as dancing, versifying, and even writing constitute rehearsal for the serious business of singing. While song frequently overlaps with *ludus*, its ability to be differentiated from *ludus* is precisely what stakes its claim to special authority in the Roman world.[69]

Let us begin with consideration of one of the best-known instances of *ludus poeticus:* poem 50 of Catullus, addressed to his friend, fellow poet, and orator, C. Licinius Calvus.[70] The poem illustrates certain widespread associations of *ludus*, both within and beyond the canon of classical Latin poetry. *Ludus* is associated with relaxation (*otiosi*, 50.1), takes place in the context of a drinking party (*per iocum atque vinum*, 50.6), and is good-humored (*per iocum*, 50.6). Other features, though widely attested, receive less notice. The *ludus poeticus* involves writing (*in meis tabellis*, 50.2; *scribens*, 50.4) and entails acceptance of certain metrical constraints ("each of us was playing now in this measure now in that": *ludebat numero modo hoc modo illoc*, 50.5) — the latter being an aspect of *ludus poeticus* that recurs throughout the Latin tradition, from the satires of Varro through the late, pseudo-Vergilian *Ciris*.[71] Indeed, it seems that the poetic game described in the first portion of Catullus's poem consisted of a challenge match in which Catullus and Calvus made each other compose verses in various meters. Like any game, poetic play entails acceptance of arbitrary rules and formal requirements.

Metrical discipline, however, is not the only external constraint imposed on Catullus and Calvus. There is also the social discipline of the *convivium* and *commissatio* that permits bodily closeness but forbids sexual congress.[72] The *ludus* shared by Catullus and Calvus is the not-quite-sex, the "trivial" intimacy of the relaxed *convivium*, implicitly contrasted with more "serious" forms of contact.[73] (It may also be the "trivial" sex of a one-night-stand, of homoeroticism in contrast to "serious" sex: that is beside the point, since the poet doesn't tell us enough to be specific.) But from the vantage point of the poem, all such play is in the past. The speaker cannot tolerate the restrictions that convivial convention has imposed on him. He is not satisfied with *ludus*—poetic or personal. He is inflamed by the recollection of Calvus, cannot eat or sleep, and longs for daylight so as to speak (*loquerer*, 50.13) and be (*essem*, 50.13) with Calvus. His limbs, exhausted with labor, lie half dead on the bed (*at defessa labore membra postquam / semimortua lectulo iacebant*, 50.14–15). And so, at last, he composed this poem. He has moved from *ludus* to something else and, in the process, has left behind the discipline of the body—poetic, sexual, alimentary—in favor of the discipline of the voice: *hoc tibi poema feci* (16).

Some may argue that production of the poem in question is itself a bodily discipline, an acquiescence in the demands of meter, control of the *stilus*, and so on. But that is not the way the poet presents it. All that precedes the poem is corporeal, a submission to externally imposed schemes, play. This, what we are reading—or, better, what we are asked by the poem to imagine ourselves hearing, what we revoice in reading the poem—is what matters. The final verses of the poem abound in direct address (*cave, cave, caveto*), second-person verb forms (*perspiceres, despuas*), and words for orally performed speech acts (*preces, oramus*). The poet has broken free of the demands of *ludus*, of writing, of convivial convention, of bodily contortions on a lonely bed, and has found his voice. In so doing, he has redefined his relationship with Calvus, for he now addresses him as *iucunde* (agreeable, pleasing; 50.16)—the quintessential term of affection toward a friend, an expression of the socially validated emotional relationship between adult Roman males.[74] The poem is thus a miniature drama of the development of the ego, of the construction of the social, political, aesthetic, and psychological real through *ludus*. But it is also a drama of the liberation (or disembodiment) and empowerment of the voice. By the end Catullus can speak to Calvus and to us with full and confident authority. Dana Burgess has rightly interpreted the final lines as turning the poem as a whole into the issuance of a new challenge to Calvus to respond in kind.[75] But the challenge and the response ask these former *delicati* (note the pluperfect tense of the expression *convenerat delicatos*, 50.3) to adopt a new relationship to the production of poetry, one that makes of it not just a metrical game but also an expression of the emergent ego.

Another poem of Catullus, number 68, describes a similar transition from playful to serious. This poem as well associates the playful with the bodily and is more explicit than poem 50 in connecting seriousness with the voice liberated from the body. Importantly, it confirms the association of play and body with writing in contrast to speech. The outset of the poem presents itself as a response to a piece of writing: "You send a message that has been written out" (*conscriptum . . . . mittis epistolium,* 68.2). The written nature of the addressee's communication is noted a second time: "You write that it is shameful for Catullus to be at Verona" (*quod scribis Veronae turpe Catullo esse,* 68.25). The speaker's problem, as diagnosed by self and addressee, is complex, but it includes an inability to take pleasure in the song of past writers (*nec veterum dulci scriptorum carmine Musae / oblectant,* 68.7–8), or to reciprocate the addressee's written gifts (*munera,* 68.52) due to a lack of writings at hand ("because there aren't a lot of writers here with me," *quod scriptorum non magna est copia apud me,* 68.33; "only one carton out of many has accompanied me here," *huc una ex multis capsula me sequitur,* 68.36). While the tone of the poem is more somber, the situation is not so different from that described at the outset of poem 50: the expectation of submission to externally imposed constraints manifests itself as pressure to write in exchange for another's writing. Calvus and Catullus succeed in playing, in writing now in this meter, now in that. Catullus and the addressee of poem 68 explicitly fail: and so Catullus here speaks of play in the perfect tense — "the much I've played is enough" (*multa satis lusi,* 68.17) — a theme to which he returns at the very end of the poem in which he wishes Allius *felicitas,* or good fortune, in the home in which Catullus and Lesbia used to play (*in qua lusimus,* 68.156).

Now it would be easy, following Wagenvoort and others, to understand the references to abandoned play as a cue for a more serious kind of poetry. But this generic cue, if such it is, is combined with an emphasis on writing as writing and intersects, as in poem 50, with bodily distress. Here the phrase "warm my freezing limbs in a deserted bedroom" (*frigida deserto tepefactet membra cubili,* 68.49) signals a transition from the realm of *ludus* comparable with the discussion of loss of appetite, lack of sleep, and exhaustion of the limbs in poem 50. And even more clearly than in poem 50, liberation from *ludus* — or, perhaps better, what is carried forward from *ludus* — is the power of the voice. *Non possum reticere,* "I cannot remain silent" (68.41), is the phrase that marks the transition between the proem to poem 68 and the central narrative, between an account of failed *ludus,* abandoned *ludus,* cold bodies (Catullus's own, and that of his brother), rite of passage (*vestis mihi tradita pura est,* 68.15), and the utterance of authoritative speech (*dicam,*

68.45). "I cannot keep silent," the poet declares to the goddess Muses, "I will declare authoritatively to you and you in turn declare authoritatively to many thousands and bring it about that this sheet of papyrus speak when old" (*non possum reticere . . . sed dicam vobis, vos porro dicite multis / milibus et facite haec carta loquatur anus*, 68.45–46). Writing does not disappear from the world of song; rather it is resituated as a means to the production and transmission of voice. Yet even here, precisely because the utterance is imagined as depending on the persistence of a written script (*carta*, 68.46), Catullus does not assign it full male subjectivity, likening it instead to the speech (*loquatur*, 68.46) of an elderly woman (*anus*, 68.46). Only later is the *munus*, the exchange, that could not be completed in, through, or due to a crisis of writing (68.32–36.) at last accomplished, brought to fruition, through song: "This is the gift, accomplished through song, such as I had power to complete" (*hoc tibi, quod potui, confectum carmine munus*, 68.149). As at least one commentator has noted, the term *munus*, meaning gift or exchange, can also signify sexual intercourse — a connotation here reinforced (or activated?) through use of the participle *confectum*, "finished off," as in orgasm, and of the perfective form of the verb for potency (*potui*, 68.149).[76] Song thus constitutes the substitution for and supplement to bodily activity of two sorts: graphic and erotic.

In the case of Vergil, the drama of the liberation of the autonomous voice that we have just observed in Catullus's poems 50 and 68 is played out over the course of a career. Vergil famously issues a retroactive interpretation of his *Eclogues* as *ludus* in the concluding lines of the *Georgics*, not denying them the status of song but suggesting that they, in contrast to the just-completed *Georgics* and the forthcoming *Aeneid*, constitute ludic song: *carmina qui lusi* is his expression for the *Eclogues*, "songs that I played," in contrast to "these things I was singing" (*haec . . . canebam*, G. 4.559, framing a line) in reference to the *Georgics* (in whole or in part),[77] and *arma virumque cano*, "arms and the hero I am singing," at the outset of the *Aeneid* (note also the transition from perfect [*lusi*], to imperfect [*canebam*], to present [*cano*] tense). But it is not just that pastoral poetry can be construed as trivial in contrast to didactic and epic. Rather, the *ludus* of the *Eclogues* is a play of the body as much as of the voice. External evidence for the impersonation on stage of characters from the *Eclogues* points in this direction,[78] but more important is the internal evidence, the way in which the terms *ludo*, *ludus*, and *cano* can be seen to interact within the texts of the *Eclogues* themselves.

In eclogue 6, for example, Vergil twice differentiates between *ludo* and *cano*, once with respect to his own poetic production, and once with respect to the performance of Silenus within the eclogue. At the outset of the poem, Vergil notes that

At first my Thalea deigned to play in Syracusan verse
nor did she blush to inhabit woodlands.

Prima Syracosio dignata est ludere versu
nostra neque erubuit silvas habitare Thalea.

(Verg. Ecl. 6.1–2)

Play here refers to the relative insignificance of pastoral in comparison
to the potential epic poetry that is to be mentioned next.[79] But it is also
play according to an externally imposed scheme, that is, the conventions of Syracusan, or Theocritean poetry, conventions that we might
recognize as governing meter, diction, characters, themes, and so on.
The Vergilian imitator who wrote the *Culex* seems to have understood
the passage this way, for he alludes to it with the expression "Once we
played . . . while slender Thalia set the rhythm" (*Lusimus . . . gracili modulante Thalia, Culex* 1). Mention of play invites mention of the source
or nature of restrictions upon it.

But there is no such restriction implicit in the use of the verb *cano*
that immediately follows in the Vergilian context of eclogue 6: "When I
was attempting to sing of kings and battles" (*Cum canerem reges et proelia,*
6.3). The shift to the first person points a contrast between the dancing
Thalea, sporting to the figures of Theocritus, and the confident singer,
momentarily in control of his voice.

Of course, there is a restriction to be imposed, and it comes in the
form of an intervention by Cynthian Apollo, who instructs Tityrus to
keep his sheep fat and his song slender. But it is a restriction that, far
from forestalling the performance of *carmen*, facilitates it. The poet's
song is to be *deductum*, refined, a transformation of the discipline of *ludus* into production of a particular type of song. This merging of *ludus*
and *carmen* is figured in the immediately following verses of the poem
in which the poet describes himself as "meditating the rural Muse on a
slender reed" (*agrestrem tenui meditabor harundine Musam,* 6.8) and "not
singing what I've been ordered not to" (*non iniussa cano,* 6.9). The term
meditabor, with its range of meanings encompassing exercise, preparation, and contemplation of a performance,[80] overlaps with the preparatory aspects of *ludus* without replicating its status as oppositional to
seriousness; while the double negatives in the expression *non iniussa
cano* present the poet as backing off from the claim to song. It's as if the
eclogue poet acknowledges that Cynthius has empowered him to sing,
but he is not quite willing to lay claim to the authority to do so on his
own. Hence, he rehearses, he sings what is not forbidden.[81]

Instead, the power of song is displaced onto the fictional character
of Silenus, who encounters no limits whatsoever. He has teased (*luserat,*

6.19) Chromis and Mnasyllos with expectation of song; and once they force him to fulfill expectations, his performance prompts a *ludus* on the part of the internal audience:

> Then, to be sure, you could see the fauns and the wild beasts
> dance in time.

> tum vero in numerum Faunosque ferasque videres
> ludere.
>
> (Verg. *Ecl.* 6.27–28)

The play of the fauns and beasts consists of adaptation of the body to someone else's rhythms. Silenus, on the other hand, is all song or vocal performance—*namque canebat* (6.31), *solatur* (6.46), *tum canit* (6.61), *tum canit* (6.64), *ille canit* (6.84)—even to the point of celebrating the song of Linus and Gallus within his song (*carmine*, 6.67; *dicatur*, 6.72). Eclogue 6, which is justly regarded as a key statement of Vergilian—and, more generally, Augustan—poetics, thus illustrates the core distinction between bodily play and vocal song while also exploiting the distinction to make some fairly subtle points about Vergil's own transition from *ludus poeticus* to autonomous song. A poem about poetic inspiration and poetic initiation serves as a transitional object aiding in the development of the independent poetic ego. Or, to put it another way, the poem thematizes the emergence of voice from play, the development of voice "as a willed aspect of the body."[82] Vergil modestly refrains from ascribing such a transformation to himself, yet his evocation of Apollo in effect grants divine sanction to song. No wonder then that Silenus, who is represented as singing, sings of nothing less than the coming into being of the cosmos. He, like Gallus later in the poem, is granted what Whitman will call "the divine power to speak words," the ability, in effect, to bring the world into being through naming.[83]

On a smaller scale, the opening verses of eclogue 7 also illustrate the core distinction between *ludus* and *carmen*, with *ludus* calling attention to bodily movement and acquiescence in an external discipline and *cano/carmen* emphasizing the distinctive authority of the voice. In this poem the narrator Meliboeus explicitly states that he set aside his serious responsibilities to attend to the play of Corydon and Thyrsis: *posthabui tamen illorum mea seria ludo* (7.17).[84] This play, we have already learned, is much like the play of Calvus and Catullus in Catullus's poem 50 because it involves responsive singing in a competitive context: *et cantare pares et respondere parati*, "prepared as peers to sing and to respond (7.5)[85] The point is reemphasized at the end of the proem: "And so both began to contend in reciprocal versification" (*alternis igitur conten-*

dere versibus ambo / coepere, 7.17–18). The activity of Corydon and Thyrsis is play because it stands in contrast to the serious business of tending sheep and goats. Like play more generally, it can be construed as an age-specific activity: here the competitors are introduced as being in the prime of youth (*ambo florentes aetatibus*, 7.4). But their alternating performance is also rightfully designated play because it involves competition and acquiescence of action to constraints established by others yet accepted for purposes of the game. It is a game that involves song (*cantare*, 7.5);[86] but it is not the song per se that makes it a game. Indeed, it seems more than coincidence that Corydon, who at the end prevails as victor in the *ludus*, is the one character who uses the word song (*carmen*, 7.21) and who mentions it specifically as something to be conceded to him (*aut mihi carmen . . . concedite*, 7.21–22). Corydon, like Silenus in eclogue 6, like Vergil at certain points in his career, carries song beyond the confines of *ludus*, and indeed at the end of the poem, through his victory in *ludus*, Corydon becomes a self-authorizing figure of poetic virtuosity: "Henceforth Corydon really is Corydon for us" (*ex illo Corydon Corydon est tempore nobis*, 7.70). As Clausen puts it, "not simply Corydon, therefore, but Corydon the ideal singer."[87]

While in general Vergil, throughout all his poetry, uses *ludus* in accordance with the patterns outlined earlier in this chapter (appropriate for youth, involving the body, in contrast to serious activity, sexual overtones, etc.), two other passages reinforce the particular relationship between *ludo* and *cano*. In book 2 of *Georgics*, the book devoted to viticulture, Vergil describes the origin of dramatic rites of Bacchus in a passage that illustrates various aspects of play and song simultaneously. Vines must be protected against the depredations of heat and cold, of forest oxen and pursuing goats who play against them (*cui . . . inludunt*, 2.375). It was because of precisely such damaging play that a goat was sacrificed at the ancient dramatic *ludi* in honor of Bacchus, we are told (*non aliam ab culpam Baccho caper omnibus aris / caeditur et veteres ineunt proscaenia ludi*, 2.381–82). At such events the country folk could be found to play with disheveled verse and dissolute laughter, to put on frightening masks made from hollowed-out rinds (*versibus incomptis ludunt risuque soluto, oraque corticibus sumunt horrenda cauatis*, 2.386–87). Vergil's use of language is, as often, excruciatingly precise: he describes the verses employed in such playful situations as disheveled, *incompta*, a term not to be confused with the *incondita* of Livy's description of early satire and dancing.[88] Far from suggesting that the verses were random or spontaneous, which would not accord well with the disciplined nature of Roman play, Vergil observes that the metrical pattern of the verses was ragged—perhaps, as della Corte notes, that they consisted of saturnians.[89]

But the same country folk also would call on Bacchus through joyous songs (*vocant per carmina laeta*, 388), for which reason, according to the poet, we too

> will declaim his honor to Bacchus
> in ancestral songs.

> suum Baccho dicemus honorem
> carminibus patriis.
>   (Verg. G. 2.393–94)

Commentators tend to interpret the passage as a whole as referring to the history, or prehistory of Roman drama, following Vergil's linkage of the sacrifice of goats to the beginnings of theater (2.380–81). But Vergil's concern seems to be less with offering an institutional history of drama (unlike Livy) than with recounting the transformation of physical practices into celebratory song. The entire episode begins with a description of the physical intrusions (*inludunt*, 2.375) of wild oxen and goats and proceeds to recount the play of the *coloni* in terms of bodily mimesis. Indeed, Vergil seems to be relying on his audience's awareness of a connection between dancing or acting and imitation of animals in order to supply thematic continuity within a passage whose development otherwise depends exclusively on the presence of naughty goats, alive in the vineyard and dead at the dramatic festival. Once again, what is to be carried forward from all the play described in the passage (bestial, dramatic, and rustic) is voice. Voice transcends or survives play in the historical past (the invocation of Bacchus and the declaration of his due honor), and voice is carried from past play into the present of the poem (i.e., in the singing of ancestral songs).

In *Aeneid* 6, the coexistence of song and play transcends even the boundary between life and death, as the inhabitants of the Elysian fields contend in competition (*contendunt ludo*, 6.643), but also sing songs (*carmina dicunt*, 6.644). This seemingly incidental differentiation in fact structures Vergil's representation of Elysium. Between the description of the players and the singers, there is mention of choral dancing, an activity that shades over from one to the other, as it involves the movement of play but, at least in this case, includes the utterance of voice as well. Orpheus is introduced as both playing his lyre and singing, with equal attention given to the movement of his fingers and the modulation of his voice. All of Elysium is a kind of never-never land of boys who don't have to abandon their toys: if they liked horses in life, they have horses here. But the residents of Elysium sing as well (*laetumque choro paeana canentis*, 6.657)—a happy song in honor of a god (the paean is specifically associated with Apollo),[90] much as the old time *coloni* play in the vineyards of Bacchus. In such a context, is it any wonder we find *imagines* galore, of Romans-to-be, of father Anchises himself (*imago*, 6.695, 6.701), inviting surrogation on the part of the hero and the audience? From this dreamlike world of permanent play, the authoritative utterance of all (Roman) time emerges, Anchises' account of the transmigration of souls and the looming destiny of Rome, the longest speech of the poem (but for Aeneas's narrative of his journeys), the parental exchange (*reddere voces*, 6.689) denied by Venus (1.409), now at last provided by the human father. All of this is what Aeneas carries from the land of dreams into the world of reality, as Vergil's account of the departure from the underworld makes clear:

> These are Anchises' words as he guides the Sibyl and his son
> and sends them forth through the ivory gate.

> his ibi tum natum Anchises unaque Sibullam
> prosequitur dictis portaque emittit eburna.
> <div align="right">(Verg. <i>Aen.</i> 6.897–98)</div>

We all remember and puzzle over the hero's exit through the ivory gate. Vergil's language places equal emphasis on the verbal utterances (*his . . . dictis*) that accompany him.

And yet in presenting the emergence of the hero from the imaginary world of Elysium as analogous to the emergence of song from play, Vergil enriches — and undercuts — the simplistic understanding of song as authoritative in contrast to play. Like Whitman, who in his poem "Vocalism" moves from what Stewart regards as a definition of voice as "willed aspect of the body" to an understanding of language as a kind of lyric possession, the "archive" (in Benjamin's terms) of "the long history of the use of words, the legacy of generations of the dead and the somatic memory of living speakers," so Vergil's hero is possessed, albeit unawares, of and by the legacy of what precedes him.[91] As Whitman puts it,

> I see brains and lips closed, tympans and temples unstruck,
> Until that comes which has the quality to strike and to unclose,
> Until that comes which has the quality to bring forth what lies
> slumbering
> forever ready in all words.[92]

In effect, the Roman view of voice as superior to and freed of the body cannot escape haunting by the history of words and bodies alike.

While traces of the interrelationship between *ludo* and *cano* that we have been exploring can be found in still other Roman writers (e.g., Ovid, Statius, Pliny, Quintilian, Martial), it is perhaps Horace who makes most interesting use of the distinction. His writings confirm the association of *ludus* with conviviality, with metrical play, and with bodily discipline, sometimes in startling ways. They also acknowledge the expectation that the poet will leave the realm of play, the need of poetry to separate itself from *ludus,* however imperfectly. At the same time, his poems display an ambivalence over attempts to dissociate the voice from play and to give it, or claim for it, an autonomous authority. Throughout Horace's poetry, there are reservations about the power of song independent of *ludus* that paradoxically lay bare the more widespread pattern of the setting aside of the body in favor of the voice.

Odes 1.32 illustrates Horace's use of the vocabulary of play and song in ways comparable to those of Catullus, Vergil, and others cited previously. The ode recounts an invitation (*poscimur*—or *poscimus*—at 1.32.1) and proceeds to address the lyre, or *barbiton,* that is to join Horace in his poetic endeavor. It is structured as a kind of hymn, first recalling past collaboration, then giving some sense of the history of the lyre, addressing it in alternative invocations, and concluding with a request, albeit a simple one: "Be propitious to me as I call upon you in ritual manner" (*mihi cumque salve / rite vocanti,* 1.32.15-16). Embedded within the poem is another request, perhaps not so different in significance from the culminating prayer, but certainly different in form: "Come now, deliver Latin song, o lyre" (*age dic Latinum, / barbite, carmen,* 1.32.3-4). This request to deliver song is framed by references to *ludus,* one explicit, the other indirect. Preceding the request are the following lines:

> If at leisure beneath the shade
> I have played with you something that will survive for this year
> and for many to come . . .

> si quid vacui sub umbra
> lusimus tecum, quod et hunc in annum
> vivat et pluris

> (Hor. *Carm.* 1.32.1-3)

We might assume that Horace is merely saying that he has done lighthearted poetry in the past, but now he wants the lyre to join him in something more serious. The *ludus* to which he refers, however, consists of interaction with the lyre, that is, adaptation of his own bodily actions to external constraints. As Huizinga long ago noted, when words for play are applied to musical performance, they regularly refer to

the physicality of the connection between performer and instrument.[93]
Thus how Horace's performance with the *barbiton* could ever quite
cease to be *ludus* is not at all clear.

Indeed, there is a second allusion to such *ludus* in the phrase immediately following the request to the lyre to perform Latin song, for
now Horace describes the *barbiton* as that which was

> first modulated by a Lesbian citizen,
> who, though fierce in war, nevertheless
>
> . . . .
>
> used to sing Liber and the Muses and Venus
> and the boy always clinging to her,
> and also Lycus, gorgeous with his black eyes and black hair.

> Lesbio primum modulate civi,
> qui ferox bello tamen inter arma
>
> . . . .
>
> Liberum et Musas Veneremque et illi
> semper haerentem puerum canebat,
> et Lycum nigris oculis nigroque
>   crine decorum.

(Hor. Carm. 1.32.5–6, 9–12)

The term *modulor* again refers to the adaptation of the singer to the lyre
and the lyre to the singer. While Horace does not say so in so many
words, he seems to regard the lyric performances of Alcaeus (the Les-
bian citizen) with their convivial context (Liber and the Muses) and
erotic content (Venus and Cupid and Lycus) as simultaneously *ludus*
and *carmen*. In fact, the poem would seem to celebrate the dependence
of the lyric poet on the lyre and on the ludic play of adaptation to the
constraints imposed by the instrument, both directly and perhaps indirectly as a metaphor for the discipline imposed by the complex meters
of lyric song. The singing done by Alcaeus, the *carmen* requested of the
barbiton, and the poem performed by Horace all belong to the realm of
song, are all expressions of voice, yet are not for that reason freed of,
released from, or thrust out of play.

Much later in his lyric career, in *Odes* 4.9, Horace again brings to
light the tension between *ludus* and *carmen,* confirms (some of) the
meanings we have identified for them, yet pulls back from announcing
the transcendence of song over play. The poem is an attempt to praise
the somewhat dubious achievements of Lollius while at the same time
reassuring him that praise in lyric poetry will stand the test of time. Here
instead of drawing on the resources of song to proclaim the renown of

Lollius, Horace holds back, and although he makes a case for the significance of lyric poetry, it is for such poetry as everything but song. Horace
speaks ironically or self-deprecatingly of his own prior poetic accomplishments with the expression *verba loquor*, to employ words (4.9.4).
The words, to be sure, are fitted to chords of the lyre (*socianda chor-
dis*, 4.9.4), an expression that puts us in mind of the lyric modulation
of *Odes* 1.32 and elsewhere. And indeed, among the poetic antecedents
Horace cites in this ode are Pindar, Simonides, Alcaeus, and Stesichorus,
all of whom are invoked as characters seeking to avoid the shadows of
Homer rather than as singers or performers. Only Anacreon receives
a verb associated with verbal production, namely *lusit*: "Whatever he
played, time has not erased" (*nec si quid olim lusit Anacreon / delevit aetas*,
4.9.9–10). With the use of the verb *deleo* for the destruction that has not
occurred, we encounter again the association of *ludus* with writing. Era-
sure, rather than silencing, is the avoided threat to Anacreon's survival.

The poem continues with mention of Sappho, and of all those Hel-
ens and Teucers who were never celebrated in verse. Idomeneus and
Stheneleus, we are told, were not the only heroes who fought battles
"worthy of celebration by the Muses" (*dicenda Musis proelia*, 4.9.21).
There lived many brave men before Agamemnon, but they go unla-
mented "since they lack a sacred *vates*" (*carent quia vate sacro*, 4.9.28). By
this time Horace has thoroughly blended the language of writing and
the language of speaking, of trivial, bodily *ludus* and inspired, prophetic
song. Perhaps it is not surprising then that the culmination of the defense of lyric immortality is an expression that continues to combine
these different categories of performance:

> I will not permit you
> to be silenced in my pages
> nor will I allow jealous forgetfulness
> to prey upon your numerous labors
> with impunity.

>   non ego te meis
> chartis inornatum sileri,
> totve tuos patiar labores
> impune, Lolli, carpere lividas
> obliviones.
>   (Hor. *Carm.* 4.9.30–34)

It is a bit difficult to tell what exactly is being promised to Lollius here,
but whatever it is, it is not the transcendent voice that we might expect
on the basis of the pattern familiar from Catullus, Vergil, and others. Yet

the issue of voice is foregrounded, as if Horace cannot escape the expectations set by the cultural synergy between *ludus* and *carmen*, for it is silence, the opposite of voice, that Horace promises to avoid. With the mention of pages, *chartae*, we are in the realm of *ludi*, at least as other poets interpret it, with writing serving as rehearsal for song. There is indeed something trivial in what is offered Lollius, at least in contrast to the proud song that opens book 3 or closes book 4 (*carmina, canto,* 3.1.2, 4; *carmine, canemus,* 4.15.30, 32). And there is something slight about the form in which he receives his praise, a genre that, while it guarantees immortality, is forever in the shadow of Homer. But perhaps this evasion of song is precisely the point of the poem: Lollius himself will forever be in the shadow of Augustus, will never quite assume autonomous authority, will never find his voice. At best he will persist as a figure of writing and of play, lucky to have chanced upon a decent *vates,* forever defining Roman reality by contrast with his own ineptitude.

Or not. *Epistles* 2.2, addressed to one Junius Florus, makes a similar move, only now it seems as if Horace wishes to emphasize the power of silence, of choosing not to speak, not to exercise the voice as itself an expression of psychological, social, and perhaps political autonomy. At the crucial transition point of the poem, as Horace moves from explaining why he is not sending poems (*expectata . . . carmina,* 2.2.25), to a discussion of what he in fact is now doing—studying, thinking, and writing philosophy—he invokes the image of the *ludus:*

> It makes sense to be wise, lay off the nonsense,
> leave the fooling around to boys.
> Stop chasing words to fit to Latin strings,
> instead get to know the numbers and measures of real life.

> nimirum sapere est abiectis utile nugis,
> et tempestivum pueris concedere ludum,
> ac non verba sequi fidibus modulanda Latinis
> sed verae numerosque modosque ediscere vitae.
> (Hor. *Epist.* 2.2.141–44)

The passage—indeed, the poem as a whole—recapitulates the broader cultural understanding of *ludus* as submission to arbitrarily imposed conventions in the spirit of nonserious play. The play that is to be conceded to boys is assimilated to *nugae*—trifles, often trifling poetry. But it also includes Horace's own proudest poetic achievement, his *Odes,* or *carmina,* here interpreted as well as a type of *ludus,* inasmuch as they entail submission to the rhythmic and musical discipline of lyric versification in Latin. Horace retrospectively interprets his career as that of a dancer to others' tunes. Just before this passage, after listing all the work that a good poet must do (*at qui legitimum cupiet fecisse poema*, 2.2.109), including acting as a kind of censor, selecting words carefully, pruning back excess, softening what is too harsh, he sums up such efforts with a simile expressly drawing on ludic dance:

> He'll contort himself, like a dancer who mimics
> first a Satyr, then a rustic Cyclops.

> ludentis speciem dabit et torquebitur, ut qui
> nunc Satyrum, nunc agrestem Cyclopa movetur.
>
> (Hor. *Epist.* 2.2.124–25)

The aesthetic discipline of poetic composition is likened to the adaptation of dance movements and bodily schemes appropriate to a mimetic dancer. *Ludus* is not a metaphor or a statement about the relative insignificance of one kind of poetry with respect to another but a precise description of the poetic activity in which Horace has engaged and excelled.

Ludus becomes for Horace in this epistle a practice akin to enslavement. In the transitional passage in which Horace proposed conceding play to boys (2.2.142), my translation skirted over the double meaning of the word *puer* in Latin: boy (who might grow into a man) or slave (who will never have the autonomy of a man regardless of age and training). Horace does not permit us to escape this duality. Certainly, there are enough instances in Latin literature where play is associated with the young, and so in that sense it is not inappropriate to take the reference to *pueri* in the same vein. But this particular poem has opened with the disturbing image of the prospective sale of a slave:

> Florus, faithful friend of good and famous Nero,
> if by chance someone were trying to sell you a male slave
> born at Tivoli or Gabii . . .

> Flore, bono claroque fidels amice Neroni,
> si quis forte velit puerum tibi vendere natum
> Tibure vel Gabiis
>
> (Hor. *Epist.* 2.2.1–3)

Horace proceeds to imagine the vendor describing the strengths and weaknesses of the human merchandise in question: his training, his unschooled talent for singing (*quin etiam canet indoctum*), the fact that he once stopped working and hid under the stairs to avoid the expected whipping (*semel hic cessavit et, ut fit,/in scalis latuit metuens pendentis habenae, Epist.* 2.2.14–15). The exemplum offers a kind of allegory of Horace's own relationship to Florus, in effect telling the latter that he knew Horace's limitations already when he (Florus) was setting out on his travels (*dixi me pigrum proficiscenti tibi,* 2.2.20).[94] Horace had stopped (presumably writing lyric poetry, since that is what Horace says Florus wants from him) once before.[95] Can Florus legitimately be upset if he has failed to write yet again?

But the passage, by invoking the figure not only of the candid slave vendor but also of the slave himself—handsome, homegrown, ready to be fashioned in whatever way his master pleases (*candidus . . . pulcher . . . verba . . . argilla quidvis imitaberis uda,* 2.2.4–8)—anticipates and makes more disturbing the later references to *ludi.* The slave is like an adolescent ready to be disciplined to the rhythms of life: only not in a type of play that will be transcended but through a permanent loss of autonomy. The "hilarious self-depreciation" that Oliensis detects in the passage puts one in mind of the frequent representations on wall paintings of *deliciae,* or sex slaves, as charming *amorini* engaged in various forms of sport.[96] And the readiness of the slave to be fashioned to whatever ends, like wet clay, resembles Ovid's later depiction of Erysichthon's daughter as in effect a slave—someone who must change shape repeatedly at another's bidding.[97] At one level, Horace surely wants his slave-owning readers to recognize, in the slight hint that for him too writing what others want has become a kind of enslavement, a potent defense of his current course of action. At the same time, the image establishes a pattern, developed throughout the poem, and, I believe, culminating in the climactic rejection of *ludus,* of contrast between bodily discipline and personal autonomy.

Following the exemplum of the slave for sale comes the story of a soldier, who, having lost all his possessions, fights ferociously and succeeds in leading the conquest of a city (2.2. 26–40). When encouraged to do so again, he tells another to take his place: he will do it, says the soldier, who has also lost his purse (*qui zonam perdidit,* 2.2.40). What else is a soldier but one who submits to bodily discipline, sometimes in play, sometimes in all seriousness: as one ancient observer puts it, soldiers do in battle what they have rehearsed in play. And Horace himself, we are told, has passed through a similar rite of passage, feeling himself obliged, after taking the losing side in civil war, to make a name for himself. But the passing years have snatched much from him—jokes, sex, *convivia,* play (*iocos, Venerem, convivia, ludum,* 2.2.56)—can poetry be far behind? Indeed, the life of the poet even in his prime constituted a different kind of *ludus,* a submission to social convention, to the niceties and stress of aesthetic rivalry. Horace presents his relationship with an unnamed elegist (usually understood to be Propertius) as a kind of slow-motion duel (*lento . . . duello*, 2.2.98), a poetic competition that puts us in mind of the ludic rivalry of Cordyon and Thyrsis in Vergil's eclogue 7, or perhaps even that of Catullus and Calvus. Is it any wonder, then, that he is ready to concede play to the slaves or boys and to get on with the discipline of real life?

Having established the need and opportunity for leaving *ludus*, Horace announces his recovery of speech: "And so I speak to myself and keep records, but in silence" (*quocirca mecum loquor haec tacitusque recordor*, 2.2.145). It is zero-degree speech, silent speech, but speech nonetheless. Horace relies on the commonplace understanding of letters, *epistulae*, as half a conversation.[98] Indeed while in the first 140 lines of the poem (up to the abandonment of *ludi* in favor of the rhythms of real life), he mentions the practice of writing at least eight times (*epistula*, 22; *mittam*, 25; *scribere*, 66; *scripta*, 67; *scriptorum*, 77; *scribo*, 103; *scripsere*, 108, *scriptor*, 126; cf. *libris*, 83), in the section subsequent to his abandonment of *ludi* he makes no such mention at all. The rest of the poem, following on the *haec* of line 145, is devoted to the delivery of philosophical precepts and exempla. This latter section, while not identified as a *carmen*, is no longer *ludus* either. It seems to constitute Horace's own contribution to the attempt by philosophy to claim the space of *carmina*, an attempt apparent in the writings of Cicero and Seneca discussed in an earlier chapter. Although Horace's advice takes the form of a versified epistle, it presents itself as unconstrained speech. What is more, the life-style it recommends is itself noteworthy for its rejection of external constraints:

> I sail all the same
> whether the boat is big or small.
> No billowy masts or gusting winds set my course:
> no adverse conditions either.
> In strength, talent, looks, courage, station, and wealth
> I'm the last of the first yet well ahead of the last.

> ego, utrum
> nave ferar magna an parva, ferar unus et idem.
> non agimur tumidis velis aquilone secundo,
> non tamen adversis aetatem ducimus austris,
> viribus, ingenio, specie, virtute, loco, re,
> extremi primorum, extremis usque priores.
>
> (Hor. *Epist.* 2.2.199–204)

Here psychological restraints are presented in the language of physical subjection to the buffetings of the winds and the challenge of the racecourse. Horace depicts himself as in effect impervious to both and invites Florus to join him in this new condition.

By the end of the poem Horace is able to proclaim *lusisti satis*: you have played enough (2.2.214). The expression is addressed to Florus, to the potential philosophical initiate and, it would seem, to Horace himself. It recalls the statement of the chorus of young women in Catullus's poem 61 (*lusimus satis*, 61.25) who use it to mark both the end of their choral performance and the transition to adulthood signified by heterosexual sex and sexual reproduction. It recalls as well Catullus's own description of his own rite of passage, marked by his assumption of the *toga virilis*, his grief over the death of his brother, and his adoption of a new poetic voice (*multa satis lusi*, Catull. 68.17). And it also recalls Venus's declaration to Europa, her signal that impersonation, sex outside marriage, dreams, and youth must all come to an end as she accepts her role as wife, *uxor*, of Jupiter (*ubi lusit satis*, Hor. *Carm* 3.27.69). For Horace in *Epistles* 2.2. it constitutes in its immediate context an invocation to be ready to leave life to those who know how to live it.[99] The expression that just precedes it—"If you don't know how to live properly, then leave it those who are capable" (*vivere si recte nescis, decede peritis*, 2.2.213)—recalls Horace's earlier admonishment to "concede play to boys" (*pueris concedere ludum*, *Epist.* 2.2.142). The final image of the poem is of youth now scorning one who is drunker than is right (*ne potum largius aequo / rideat et pulset lasciva decentius aetas*, 2.2.215–16). The phrase "you have played enough" is not an invocation to acceptance of death so much as it is an invitation to a different kind of life, one interpreted as free of external pressures and obligations and depicted in verse that presents itself, however inadequately, as simple, unconstrained, speech. The sense of autonomy implicit in the new poetry and the new life of Horace and his addressee is reinforced by a final tacit reminder of the slave with whom the poem opened. The laughing youth and the inappropriately drunken old man who has not yet given up on *ludus* are, of course, stock characters from comedy, much as the capable yet unreliable dancing slave is. The unstated contrast between the slave and all the characters at the end of the poem—Horace, Florus, readers, youth, drunkard—is that they at least have the choice to leave *ludus* behind, to cross the boundary between playful and real, disciplined and autonomous, and to carry with them from one realm to the other the power of the unconstrained voice, the power even to remain silent.

Centuries after Horace, Walter Benjamin will describe the fragile status of the mimetic faculty due to the development of technologies of mass reproduction. This fragility led him to reflect on the importance of mimesis throughout history and to recommend a reclaiming of "presubjective embodied agency" as a means of resisting "the seductions of disembodiment projected by contemporary reproductive and virtual technologies."[100] For the Romans, the omnipresence of slaves fostered an overabundance of mimetic activity, and a desire, on the part of the free, to deny or transcend the mimetic basis of song, to privilege language precisely as an archive of "nonsensuous" or noncorporeal similarity. We might attribute to the reliance on slaves a mimetic crisis in ancient Rome comparable with the one Benjamin ascribes to modernity's employment of new, nonhuman modes of reproduction—a mimetic crisis made especially acute for poets, who depended on the labor of slaves, past and present, for the success of their enterprise, not to mention their daily needs.[101] As Benjamin emphasizes, while mimesis is a natural human capacity, it also has a history—both in the development of the individual subject and within society writ large. The proliferation of slaves must be understood as a key component of the history of mimesis in ancient Rome, again in both the "ontogenetic" and "phylogenetic sense." The tensions we have traced thus far in Latin poetry between celebration of mimetic play and valorization of escape therefrom lay bare free Romans' anxieties over their own ceding of the capacity for mimesis to other human beings who are, in effect, their tools. The impossibility of their attempt to reduce language to its semiotic, as opposed to its embodied, mimetic dimension finds expression in the ghostly dicta that follow Aeneas from the underworld, in the *imago* that terrorizes Horace's Galatea, in the figure of the slave that haunts Horatian autobiography down to what may well be the final words of his poetic career.[102]

Play, Ritual Mastery, and Assent:
The Case of the *Carmen Saeculare*

No consideration of *ludus poeticus* or of the relationship between song and play more generally can be complete without discussion of Horace's *Carmen Saeculare*.[103] Here we have a song composed to be performed at *ludi*, in this case the *ludi saeculares* of 17 BC, yet taking on an existence of its own among the poetic texts of the Horatian corpus. In a straightforward sense, the *Carmen Saeculare* manages both to participate in *ludus* and to transcend it. We might wish to regard the *Carmen Saeculare* as a confirmatory illustration of the larger argument we have been developing in this chapter concerning the relationship between song and play. Indeed, Denis Feeney has recently used the *Carmen Saeculare* to make the case that distinctively literary interpretation of religious practice is an important part of Roman religious discourse.[104]

But before jumping to the conclusion that the *Carmen Saeculare* itself is thus best understood as part of an autonomous literary system (a conclusion understandably congenial to those readers trained exclusively or predominantly in literary scholarship), we would do well to consider just how deeply embedded this song is in the particulars of the *ludi saeculares,* and just how rich are its interconnections with the broad traditions of Roman song. The *Carmen Saeculare* acknowledges and in its textual history attests to the autonomy of song within the Roman world. But that autonomous song serves ultimately to confirm the reality constructed by the *ludus* of which it is part. Much as the *Carmen Saliare* celebrates the role of music in modulating the Roman state to the rhythms of the cosmos, the *Carmen Saeculare* concerns itself with the role of song in securing the reproduction of the state over time. Naturally the *Carmen Saeculare* offers a different perspective on the events of the *ludi saeculares* from that implicit in the official, political *acta* or in the fragmentary accounts of ancient historians. But its perspective matters and its interpretation counts to the extent that they arise from within the traditional context of the *ludi.* Following Rappaport's analysis of ritual, we can understand that there is no secular rite without the *Carmen Saeculare:* actions and words are coconstitutive of the ritual, and the latter cannot simply be segmented off as "decoration."[105] Following Bell's discussion of the relationship between ritual mastery and the possibilities of resistance, we can see that Horace as composer, the youths as singers, and the political authorities as commissioners of the song make their own contribution to the ritual's meaning and effect only insofar as they master the roles the ritual requires of them.

One argument that has been made to disconnect the *carmen* from its context is that while the *ludi saeculares* of 17 BC, according to the *acta,* were presented in honor of Jupiter Optimus Maximus, the hymn is sung in honor of Apollo and Diana, with only a brief, anonymous reference to Jupiter and Juno.[106] Such an approach presupposes that the substance of the *carmen* should somehow be coextensive with other components of the ritual—a presupposition hardly sustained by other surviving ritual *carmina,* such as the *Carmen Saliare,* which names many gods even as the *sodales* who perform it are associated with only a few among them. Moreover, it ignores the evidence that links the *ludi saeculares* in their earliest presentation to the god Apollo. As Coarelli notes, the *ludi saeculares* almost certainly date to 509 or 504 BC, with 249 BC being the date they are transformed from a celebration sponsored by the *gens Valeria* to a state ritual.[107] Coarelli bases this conclusion on (among other things) the language of the *precatio* preserved in the Augustan and Severan *acta,* which asks that "the Latin always obey" (*utique semper Latinus obtemperassit*), a request that makes most sense in an era when the Latins were deeply troublesome for the Romans.[108] This crucial piece of information coincides with other testimonia, such as the

etiological story recorded by Plutarch in his life of Valerius Poplicola.[109]
While we need not accept every detail of Coarelli's reconstruction, his
suggestion that the *ludi* originally had a connection with Apollo, due
to their attribution (as Plutarch records) to a Delphic oracle, makes a
great deal of sense. While Plutarch sometimes seems to retroject early
imperial ideology onto archaic Roman history,[110] there would be no
reason for him to invent a detail about the oracle especially since the
Augustan *ludi* were attributed to a different prophetic source, namely
the books of the Erythraean Sibyl.[111] Interestingly, Plutarch's etiological story also indicates that the Valerii were prompted to take action
because of widespread difficulties with childbearing among the Roman
population. Again, such information may constitute an after-the-fact
attempt to explain the inclusion of deities of childbearing in Horace's
hymn, but an alternative explanation of the story is that it might be true:
that is, that in response to a demographic crisis, the Valerii sought advice from Apollo who instructed them to establish (or renew, as Plutarch would have it) games celebrating—what else?—the periodic
replenishment of the population of Rome. In other words, Horace's
celebration of Apollo and Diana, his invocation of Ilithyia, even his mention of Augustan legislation designed to encourage sexual reproduction
(*Carm. Saec.* 18–20), far from constituting an addition to previous performances of the rite, serve as a reconnection of the Augustan state rite,
with its earlier antecedents—"an explicit reanimation of prototypes."
Horace works from within the tradition of the *ludi* to generate a song
that will carry meaning beyond the conclusion of the sacred time (*tempore sacro,* 4). In so doing, he composes in accord with the Sibylline
verses (presumably also made public through official action) that call
for the performance of Latin paeans at the *ludi,* the paean being traditionally sung to Apollo or to Apollo and Artemis.[112]

A further reason for the emphasis on Apollo and Diana, rather than
Jupiter and Juno (the latter of whom are surely to be included, however,
among the gods "to whom the seven hills have been pleasing," *Carm.
Saec.* 7), is the song's concern with the *ludus* as, among other things, a
celebration of passage. Apollo and Diana, not Jupiter and Juno, are the
deities associated in myth and cult with the transition of young men
and women to adulthood, and their presence here both explains and
is explained by the appearance of a chorus of boys and girls of good
birth with surviving parents (*patrimi et matrimi,* as the *acta* put it, *CIL*
6.32323.148) as singers of the hymn. Like the *Carmen Saliare,* so the *Carmen Saeculare,* while not exclusively a celebration of initiation into adulthood, nonetheless links the moment of festive renewal and play with
just such transformation in the life of the individual adolescent and of

the supportive community as well. Such a connection is not surprising in view of the associations of *ludus* with youth, sexuality, and the playful acquisition of the proper bodily modulations for the next generation of citizens. The privileged association of the *patrimi* and *matrimi* with *ludus* makes them the appropriate transmitters of praise and request to the gods of Rome.[113] In the ninth stanza (*Carm. Saec.* 33–36), which is rightly seen as rounding out the first half of the hymn with a return to the mention of Apollo and Diana, the two deities are explicitly asked to listen to the company of boys and company of girls, respectively: as the special protectors of the transition of free youth to adulthood they are the gods most appropriately invoked as part of a general prayer on behalf of Roman society. As our analysis of the relationship between *ludus* and *carmen* has made clear, the ability to carry song forward from the context of play is figured as a mark of adulthood, of the abandonment of childishness and the merely physical in favor of the voice of the free, autonomous Roman subject. Like the poets struggling to sing, indeed like all of Roman society starting afresh with the *ludi saeculares* after the passage of some hundred years, so the *pueri puellaeque* of the *Carmen Saeculare* give voice to their new status and, in turn, are given voice by it.

Recognition of the song's relationship to ritual passage helps to explain the otherwise puzzling transition between the ninth and tenth stanzas of the hymn, with the ninth asking Apollo and Diana to listen to the prayers of the boys and girls, and the tenth (followed by the eleventh) referring to the transition of Trojan squadrons to Etruscan shore, the movement of part of the population to a new city, and the escape of Aeneas *sine fraude* (without fraud, *Carm. Saec.* 41) through burning Troy. Feeney is certainly right to see reference to the narrative line of Vergil's *Aeneid* here, but that is hardly the only appropriate cultural intertext for the hymn, especially the hymn performed (or recollected as performed) in ritual context. Troy had, as far back as the seventh and sixth centuries BC, served as metaphor for the travails of rite of passage, much as the labyrinth had.[114] To escape Troy (as Ascanius's own *lusus Troiae* in *Aeneid* 5 seems to indicate) is to pass safely to adulthood. The departure from Troy is, in effect, the foundation of Rome—a connection made clear by the positioning of the word *Roma* at the commencement of the tenth stanza. The twelfth stanza of the *Carmen Saeculare* confirms this connection with passage while broadening the scope of significance of both the hymn and the *ludi*.

Here the chorus sings as follows:

> Gods and goddesses, grant good morals to youth who have been
> trained well.

Grant rest to peaceful age.
Grant resource and offspring and every kind of beauty
to the people of Romulus.

di, probos mores docili iuventae,
di, senectuti placidae quietem,
Romulae genti date remque prolemque
    et decus omne.

                                        (Hor. *Carm. Saec.* 45–48)

The stanza recapitulates the cultural significance of *ludi* in the form of a
request to the gods—as first heard, any and all gods "whose concern is
Rome" (*Roma si vestrum est opus,* 36), but, in the sequence of the hymn,
more particularly the Capitoline deities.[115] The youths are to be supplied
with good morals: the Latin word used here, *mores,* has as its most basic
meaning the concept of "measure."[116] This is what youths are to learn
from play: the proper measures of life. Moreover, these "measures" entail probity, good behavior generally, but more specifically sexual behavior oriented toward reproduction of citizens. So the measures to be
developed through the *ludi* have, as often, a sexual aspect to them. The
youths who learn these measures are said to be "docile," *docilis,* a word
that means, in effect "subject to instruction." In the context of a sung
performance, the instruction referred to is that of a chorus. The fact
that the youths have learned and are performing the measures of the
song at the *ludus* is itself an indication that they will be docile henceforth: this association of performance by initiates with performance of
adult responsibilities informs initiatory dance in a wide range of traditional communal settings.

    While the youths are to receive appropriate morals, measures, and
patterns of behavior, the older members of society are to receive peaceful—or, perhaps better, pleasing—rest. That is to say, their movements
have abated. The energetic performance of the youth serves to differentiate them from the now-becalmed elders. More generally, the whole
Romulean people is to receive possession and offspring and all aesthetic
beauty. The phrase *Romulae genti* is no random circumlocution for "Romans" but seems to acknowledge the gentile history of the rites, which
now belong not to one *gens* within Roman society, but to the Roman
people, falsely but usefully thought of as members of a single clan, or
blood association, as implied by the term *gens*. This *gens* is to receive
possession, or wealth, or, we might even say, reality (*res*), in the sense
of a recognizable cultural inheritance, and offspring, who will come to
possess the *res Romana*. It is also to receive *decus omne,* a superfluity of
beauty, a waste of energy in the creation of the more-than-real, in the

"transfiguration of the commonplace" into art and song—the very song being sung and performed by the chorus before us.[117] If for the youthful participants the autonomy of voice is what is carried forth from the ceremony, for the society as a whole it is the bodies of the offspring and the beauty exhibited in their performance that constitute the ritual objects created by the *ludus,* a materialization of the abstraction "prosperity" echoed in the final stanza, where "hope" and "home" stand side by side, one the objective correlative of the other.

In the thirteenth stanza (49–52) the chorus extends its prayer, asking in effect that the good things just sought after be obtained as much through kindness to defeated enemies as through warfare. Its song refers specifically to the sacrifice of white oxen, which the Sibylline oracle had advised be made to Apollo, Diana, Jupiter and Juno, but which the *acta* record as offered to Jupiter and Juno alone. Feeney makes much of this fact, together with the failure of the hymn to mention Jupiter and Juno by name at this point, as evidence of the song's attempt to "eclipse" the old Capitoline deities.[118] Again, considering the hymn in the broader context of *ludi* and *carmina* allows us to avoid such a radical conclusion. It may be that the chorus at this point in the hymn directs attention to Jupiter and Juno without naming them, but it does so not in an effort to eclipse them, but because it is saving the name of Jupiter for its own climactic utterance at the end of the song. Just as the return to Apollo and Diana closes the first half of the hymn, so the return to Jupiter (and from Jupiter) closes the hymn and, in its second performance on the Capitoline, the whole festival.[119] The structure of the song *as part of a ritual occasion* forms a chiasmus with the sacrifices that precede it. According to the *acta,* there were sacrifices to Jupiter and Juno on the second night of the *ludi,* to Apollo and Diana on the third, whereupon (*sacrificio perfecto, CIL* 6.32323.147),[120] the *pueri* and *puellae* sang the hymn, first (presumably) on the Palatine and then, "in the same manner, on the Capitoline" (*eodemque modo in Capitolio, CIL* 6.32323.148). In other words, far from eclipsing the Capitoline deities, the hymn—as part of the overall ritual performance—integrates elements particular to Apollo and Diana, especially the waxing of a new generation, with celebration of the sovereignty of Rome, as associated with Jupiter and Juno. Its seeming emphasis on Apollo and Diana, at least in its first half, flows from its initial performance in their presence. And its culminating reference to Jupiter fits its reperformance on the Capitoline, in an act of circumstructure for the *ludi* as a whole every bit as striking as the circumstructure created within the first half of the hymn by the double reference to the Palatine gods.

Every singer at Rome potentially lays claim to a special connection with the world beyond, as defined by time, space, and ontology. Song, as we learned in chapter 1, is a "transformative activity" that links the world of the here and now to the world that is historically past, geographically distant, and metaphysically or ontologically distinct (i.e., the realm of the gods). As the *Carmen Saeculare* progresses, the attention of the singers is redirected outward, no longer to the other Latins who prompted anxiety at the foundation of the ritual, but to the Medes, the Scythians, and the Indians (*Carm. Saec.* 54–55). The singers confidently assert that such peoples will fear the "companies powerful on sea and land" together with "the Alban axes" (*iam mari terrasque manus potentis . . . Albanasque timet securis,* 53–54). They allude to the virtues of the past (*Fides et Pax et Honos Pudorque,* 57), calling them ancient or ancestral (*priscus,* 58), and to virtue more generally, describing it as neglected (*neglecta,* 58), and indicate that these abstract qualities now dare to return. In so doing, the members of the chorus invoke golden age mythology familiar from contemporaneous Latin poetry. But they also assert the ability of the inspired singer, dating as far back as Homer and Hesiod, to know the past, the present, and the future, due to a special connection with the gods, especially with the Muses, daughters of Zeus (Jupiter) and Memory.

And so the hymn returns to the gods: to Apollo, as patron of the arts, welcomed by the nine Camenae (62), ready to lighten weary bodies and to assist Rome and Latium, whose conflict informed the original *ludi,* to flourish together (63–66); to Diana, of the Aventine (in Rome) and of Algidus (in Latium, 69); and, in the final stanza, to Jupiter and all the gods. As the collective chorus sings:

> Jupiter and all the gods decree these things.
> Such is the good and certain hope I carry home
> as chorus trained to sing the praises
> of Phoebus and Diana.

> Haec Iovem sentire deosque cunctos
> spem bonam certamque domum reporto,
> doctus et Phoebi chorus et Dianae
> dicere laudes.
>
> (Hor. *Carm. Saec.* 73–76).

The ultimate source of the authority of the song, according to the final stanza, is not the chorus itself, not Apollo or Diana, not the Camenae: but Jupiter and with him the collectivity of the gods. They are the ones whose solemn declaration (*sentire*) is celebrated, they are the ones who approve of what Apollo and Diana are being asked to do. And the members of the chorus are confident of this, are in a position to "carry back" this news—from their own experience of initiation, from their own encounter with the deadly and the divine—because they have been taught to perform as a chorus. Their song and their dance, their participation in the "transformative activity" of song, in the reality-generating experience of *ludus,* gives them a connection with the world beyond, secures the "energizing links" between past and future, near and far, human and divine. Indeed, as we also recall from chapter 1, their use of ritual language (and not, we might add, their participation in an autonomous literary system) articulates what is at stake in the bodily activity of the *ludi:* the intense activity of the three days leading up to the performance of the hymn, together with the hymn's evocation of an apparently reasonable and orderly, yet ultimately unfalsifiable, realm of the gods, generates the experience of the divine, from which they "carry back" the happy news of their own and Rome's prosperity. For a moment the girls and boys of the chorus share with the divine king, the Salian dancers, the inspired poet, the orator, and others the full power of song. From within the realm of *ludus,* from within bodies newly disciplined to right measures, they project a message that will persist long after the sacred time has ended and the enabling constraints of play have been removed. If their song has meaning, if in its virtuosity it has something to contribute to the religious and social experience of the Roman people, it is because it is embedded in and emerges from the bodily practice of play.

FIVE· SONG AND THE BODY

SOCIETIES TRANSMIT THEIR MEMORIES THROUGH TEXTS, broadly understood to include literature, documents, inscriptions, and even artifacts that can be interpreted on analogy with texts, and through bodies, in activities ranging from everyday dress, deportment, and gesture to civic or communal rituals. Following Paul Connerton's terminology, we may attribute the former to "inscribing activities" or "inscribing practices," and call the latter "incorporating practices." Social reproduction takes place both through practices that have been inscribed and through the inculcation of certain patterns of bodily presentation, what José Gil has called "bodily exfoliations" and Connerton refers to as "bodily automatisms."[1] Gil describes the radically different modes of bodily presentation that characterize tribal versus state societies, whereas Connerton focuses on incorporating practices apparent in more recent periods of history—from the development of table manners, crucial to Elias's description of "the civilizing process" in early modern Europe, to differences in body language between members of various communities observable on the streets of any culturally diverse metropolis.

While the distinction between inscribing and incorporating practices is a relatively straightforward one, the way the two categories relate to one another in specific cultural contexts is inevitably complex. Ancient Rome is no exception to this rule. One of the challenges involved in understanding Roman song is that it plays a crucial role in the transmission of social memory as both an inscribing and an incorporating practice. Song leads to the production of texts, both directly in the case of poetic *carmina* and indirectly, as I have argued, in the case of prose genres such as oratory and philosophy that derive their authority in part from their conflicted relationship with song. As inscribing practice, song "reaches . . . its fulfilment," to borrow Connerton's expression, "in the formation of a canon."[2] This canon preserves and transmits the memories of the dominant sector of Roman society and allows "Rome," in all of its geographical, cultural, linguistic, and temporal diversity, to conceive of itself as a single entity with a shared, albeit contested, memory worth transmitting.[3] The canon of Latin literature preserves the memory of Rome to the present day, long after the bodily community of ancient Romans has diminished in size and significance.

At the same time, analysis of classical Latin literature allows us to infer a set of incorporating practices that can be generally understood as song. Such practices range from the ceremonial and formal, as in the case of the Salian ritual or the choral performance of Horace's *Carmen Saeculare,* to the less formal, more commonplace, such as the mutual scribblings of Catullus and Calvus, the convivial singing and dancing of *sodales,* the vocal modulations of orators-in-training, the give-and-take of the poetic recitation. As incorporating practice (or, more accurately, set of incorporating practices), Roman song seems to find its fulfillment in the liberation of the voice, the privileging of the authoritative utterances of elite males who regard themselves as having transcended the bodily discipline and subordination implicit in play or *ludus.* The fact that the incorporating practices of song, culminating in the authoritative use of voice, must be inferred from texts does not thereby make them less significant or less real. It only makes them more difficult to study. As Connerton puts it, "inscribing practices have always formed the privileged story, incorporating practices the neglected story, in the history of hermeneutics."[4] The irony of this situation is that incorporating practices' resistance to study (and therefore to critique) is the key reason why they are so powerful as mnemonic devices. Texts carry with them an implicit acknowledgment of their own constructedness and hence are open to deconstruction. Incorporating practices succeed as carriers of memory precisely to the extent that they seem natural. In Connerton's words, "they are not easily susceptible to critical scrutiny and evaluation by those habituated to their performance."[5]

The inertia associated with incorporating practices does not mean that they are without history. Incorporating practices, including the incorporating practices of song, can and do change over time; they interact with and sometimes succumb to political, social, and economic developments of various sorts. Indeed, it is precisely when incorporating practices are in a process of transition that their constructedness as practices becomes apparent — either to participants in the practices or to the scholarly observer or to both. Not surprisingly, Connerton's account of incorporating practices begins with a consideration of the radical change in practices brought on by the French Revolution: changes in dress, demeanor, and gesture as well as in formal ritual. So too, it is through their distance from present-day practices and in their moments of radical transformation that the incorporating practices of Roman song become apparent as such. Thus it is inevitable in our consideration of song as bodily practice that we discuss simultaneously continuity and change, the social inertia fostered by the maintenance of shared practices of song over many centuries together with the moments of transformation, crisis, and fissure that bring such practices to light for us and revise them for their practitioners. No doubt, too, it is pressure on our own incorporating practices—technological pressures that affect habits of communication, and the wide array of pressures that affect the bodily performance of gender, ethnicity, and class—that make us alert to the continuities and changes incorporated by other peoples at other times.

Birds of a Feather

The 1957 classic of Russian cinema, *The Cranes Are Flying*, depicts the sacrifices of everyday Russians during the heroic struggle against fascism.[6] The story is focalized through the experiences of a young woman Veronika, whose lover Boris departs for the front with other young soldiers and is subsequently killed in action. At the beginning of the film Veronika and Boris spot cranes flying in formation over Moscow, and Veronika cannot resist singing and dancing to a short song about cranes, which gives the film its title. At the end of the film, the cranes reappear just as the surviving soldiers of Boris's company return home to a welcoming crowd, including the distracted, forlorn, but ultimately accepting Veronika.

The association of flocks of birds with departing and returning soldiers is an old and widespread image. Cranes are especially popular in this regard due in part to their size (some species are over five feet tall when standing on their legs) and in part to their seeming anthropomorphic characteristics: they appear to dance, they have a variety of songs, they bond in pairs, and they migrate.[7] A notable passage in Peter Matthiessen's account of the demise, and in some few cases, recovery of crane populations in recent years describes the "accidental paradise" of the Korean demilitarized zone, where the absence of human activity has created an opportunity for cranes to flourish. Matthiessen's description inadvertently echoes the association of cranes and other large, migratory birds with young soldiers that can be found in works as varied as Homer's *Iliad* and Kalatazov's film. Matthiessen writes:

> Watching these great and ancient birds flying through the mists in a damp cold where so many young soldiers quaked in fear and wretchedness, watching them stalk these silent winter fields veined with so much human blood, one is beset by somber, confused feelings. . . . To protect these birds as harbingers of peace and morning calm—how respectful that would be, however late, to the young soldiers on both sides.[8]

More is at work in Matthiessen's description than a vague sense of the unity of life or an idealization of nature as pacific. Throughout his book on cranes Matthiessen discusses human emulation of these birds: the repetition of their calls with voice or musical instruments and the imitation of their movements in a wide variety of dances. In northern Australia crane dances "are performed by men only—a solo or paired dance, or a group of dancers in a circle or in a line, 'advancing with bird-like hops, arms oustretched like wings. The chirping sounds made by the dancers intermingle . . . with the bird-call refrains of the singers.'"[9] Among the Ainu of Hokkaido, "only the women danced the slow ceremonial step, while a chorus of their sisters clapped and sang in imitation of the marsh god's cries."[10] In eighth-century China, according to legend, Prince Yi of Wie "welcomed cranes as revered guests, awarding them their own coaches, haute cuisine, and even a handsome stipend; all had the rank of civil servants, and some were promoted to generals"; the voice of the crane even inspired music for the lute.[11] For Matthiessen the return of cranes to a land they had once nearly abandoned is a reminder of the impossibility of return on the part of the dead soldiers. The similarity of bodily practice between birds and soldiers prompts reflection on the difference in their fates.

I am less concerned here with the natural history of cranes (fascinating as it is) than I am with illustrating the widespread tendency on the part of human beings to assimilate their activity to that of other animate creatures and exploring the particular significance of birds, especially large, migratory birds, in such a practice. Mimicry of animals makes it possible for a group of people to adopt a new set of bodily practices without submitting to the regime of outsiders (i.e., by being enslaved or conquered). At the same time, attribution of such practices to the natural world (whatever their real source) displaces anxiety over the power of their human promoters. Young people learn to dance and sing like cranes or swans, with all that such performance implies about relations between individual and group, fight and flight, rather than expressly learning to dance and sing like another person who happens to be moving in a pattern or singing a song that resembles that of a crane. Crane dances (and other organized imitations of animals) exemplify both the mimetic faculty ("the nature that culture uses to create second nature") and the tendency on the part of society to organize that faculty, while pretending not to. As José Gil explains, exteriority of origin banishes "the very idea of human creative intervention."[12]

In the ancient world assimilation of the activities of companies of young men (and to a lesser degree young women) to the song and dance of cranes, swans, and the like serves to naturalize a set of practices that is every bit as constructed as any other human institution.[13] It makes the loyalty to the band or company or state seem a part of nature — and a rather elegant and appealing part at that, if we are to trust the reaction of authors from Homer through Ovid and beyond. At the same time, the recurrent association, in literature, art, and ritual, of young men, warfare, and sexual maturity with the song and dance of birds such as cranes and swans allows us to infer a set of incorporating practices and metaphorical projections that we might otherwise overlook in our study of antiquity.[14] Even more, the rupture or transformation of the association between birds and young soldiers, from emphasis on the company to emphasis on the solitary virtuoso, allows us to situate changes in the nature of Roman song within larger changes in the Roman social and cultural order. As incorporating practice, song (again in its broad sense encompassing music, poetry, and dance) is a repository of "the values and categories" that Roman society is "most anxious to conserve."[15] The change in the incorporating practice of song can thus be read as both symptom of and contributor to the changing values of Roman society, especially of the elite males whose experience is most fully accessible to us.

We may begin our analysis of Latin literature's assimilation of human song and dance to that of birds by returning to a passage already discussed in the preceding chapter. In the first book of the *Aeneid,* the goddess Venus appears to her son disguised as a young maiden huntress. Aeneas, upon recognizing his mother, chides her for "playing with false images" (*falsis / ludis imaginibus,* 1.407–8). The encounter puts us in mind of play as a preparatory activity supervised by the mother for the benefit of the child. It alludes to the role of *imagines* in Roman culture, and underscores the Roman understanding of maturity as what Connerton calls "the capacity to reproduce a certain performance" or what Mann regards as "the explicit reanimation of prototypes."[16] Aeneas, in lamenting the absence of a true or real encounter with Venus, calls attention to the illusory quality of play even as Venus's playful performance provides him with the information and encouragement that will allow him to make his way in the new world of Carthage.

Embedded in the narrative of the playful encounter between Venus and Aeneas is another kind of play, the play of birds. When Aeneas explains his distress at not knowing the fate of his comrades' ships, Venus points out and interprets an omen:

> Look, she says, twelve swans rejoice in battle formation
> though Jove's eagle, swooping from on high
> tried to dislodge them from the open sky. Now in a long line
> you can see them reach the land or look down on the land that
>   others have reached.
> Like returnees they dance about with noisy wings
> spiraling around the axis of the heavens chanting songs.
> Just so do your ships and the young men of your people
> either hold port already or approach the river mouth with full sail.

> aspice bis senos laetantis agmine cycnos,
> aetheria quos lapsa plaga Iovis ales aperto
> turbabat caelo; nunc terras ordine longo
> aut capere aut captas iam despectare videntur:
> ut reduces illi ludunt stridentibus alis
> et coetu cinxere polum cantusque dedere,
> haud aliter puppesque tuae pubesque tuorum
> aut portum tenet aut pleno subit ostia velo.
>
> (Verg. *Aen.* 1.393–400)

Venus excitedly describes the activity of the swans as it occurs: their flight in formation; the disturbance by an eagle; their successful regrouping and gradual descent to earth; their play upon the shore; their spiraling upward on air currents; their joyous song. The sequence of events seems to correspond to the disruption of Aeneas's ships in transit followed by their subsequent return to the safety of shore. The passage is the first of many omens in the *Aeneid,* and as such it has been studied by commentators for its plausibility and accuracy, for the message it might or might not be conveying about the reliability of the gods, natural signs, and their interpreters. It is also a striking instance of Roman poets' powers of observation and description of the natural world: the image of swans spiraling or wreathing "the pole" would seem to describe the common phenomenon of birds "spiraling upward on thermals" with *polus* here meaning, as often, the tip of an axis.[17]

At the same time, the passage asks us to imagine young men in their sexual maturity (*pubes tuorum*), formed in a battle line, undergoing attack, regrouping, dancing, singing, swirling: just like birds. Like a flock of birds, the individual ships of Aeneas's fleet, but also the individual soldiers who constitute the collective *pubes tuorum,* must both fend for themselves and operate as part of a collective. This tension between countable individuals (there are after all, twelve and only twelve swans) and the collective body implied by terms like *agmen, ordo, pubes* is what the "irresistible analogy" (to use Bourdieu's term) between birds and young soldiers attempts to negotiate and perhaps even blur.[18] This tension has been at the heart of the training of companies of soldiers throughout history. The director of *The Cranes Are Flying* exploits and exposes it too in his use of the imagery of flying cranes: although from a distance the flight of the cranes at the end of the film looks just like the flight at the beginning, in reality the company of returning soldiers is not the same as the company that departed. Many men, and in particular Boris, the lover of the heroine Veronika, have died and cannot return.[19]

The fraught relationship between the individual and the flock informs Vergil's other references to swans and their song and dance. For example, in the seventh book of the *Aeneid,* during the description of the gathering of Italian forces in support of Turnus against the newly arrived Aeneas and his allies, Vergil recounts the arrival of Messapus and his followers, who are of diverse ethnic background. Messapus rules over a peaceful, multiethnic community, peoples long settled (*iam pridem resides populos,* 7.693) and unaccustomed to war (*desuetaque bello,* 7.693). Nonetheless they gather at his call—Fescennines, Aequi, Falisci, and others.

> They marched forth made equal by the rhythm and they celebrated
>   their king in song:
> Like snow-white swans among the gleaming clouds
> come back from feeding, chanting song
> from long necks. The stream resounds and the Asian marsh
> echoes afar.
> No one who saw them would think that bronzed battle-lines were
>   assembling
> in so great a swarm, but rather that an airy cloud of raucous birds
> was being driven from the high seas in the direction of the shore.
>
> ibant aequati numero regemque canebant:
> ceu quondam nivei liquida inter nubila cycni
> cum sese e pastu referunt et longa canoros
> dant per colla modos, sonat amnis et Asia longe

pulsa palus.
nec quisquam aeratas acies examine tanto
misceri putet, aeriam sed gurgite ab alto
urgeri volucrum raucarum ad litora nubem.

(Verg. Aen. 7.698–705)

The common translation of the expression *aequati numero* as "in equal
ranks" or "equal in number" is both vague and misleading. Did each of
Messapus's subject peoples just happen to contribute the same number
of troops? Did Messapus send surplus troops home to keep the number balanced? If taken literally, though, as "made equal by rhythm,"
the expression can be seen to describe the very process through which
Messapus's diverse subjects are transformed into peers, namely marching (*ibant*) together and celebrating their king in song (*regem canebant*).
"Keeping together in time" makes of Messapus's soldiers (as of any
group of soldiers) a single entity, a fact underscored by the reference
to a swarm (as of bees) and to a singular cloud (as of birds).[20] Who can
identify an individual within a mass of bees, or a flock of birds, or an
army marching in rhythm? Again there is an illuminating parallel in *The
Cranes Are Flying:* one reason for Veronika's distress throughout the film
is that she failed to say farewell to Boris in person at the soldiers' assembly site. She was delayed by a line of tanks heading for the front, and
by the time she arrived at the assembly site for the infantry, the recruits
had already begun to march in formation and to sing, thereby making
it impossible for her to locate the individual Boris among the moving,
resounding mass.

If birds provide a seductive image of soldiers in formation or legitimately at ease, of individuals coalescing into a single company, so too
can their behavior illustrate the consequences of a breakdown of group
cohesion. Thus in the eleventh book of the *Aeneid,* Vergil again likens a
community to a flock of birds, this time emphasizing the chaos and confusion that reign in King Latinus's city as Aeneas and his soldiers draw
near. In particular, it is the noise of the birds, their raucousness in contrast to their potential for song, that draws the poet's (and the reader's)
attention:

Trembling they insist on being armed, the youth cry out for arms,
the elders weep and groan. Here, from every side, a great uproar
rises on the wind in mingled discord:
no different than when companies of birds settle in the treetops
or raucous swans chatter and squabble
midst the still waters of abundant Padusa.

arma manu trepidi poscunt, fremit arma iuventus,
flent maesti mussantque patres. hic undique clamor
dissensu vario magnus se tollit in auras,
haud secus atque alto in luco cum forte catervae
consedere avium, piscosove amne Padusae
dant sonitum rauci per stagna loquacia cycni.

(Verg. Aen. 11.453–58)

The words *poscunt, fremit, flent, mussant, clamor, dissensu, sonitum,* and *loquacia* all describe the chaotic noise made by birds and humans alike. Against the backdrop of similes highlighting the similarities between harmonious flocks of singing, playing birds and companies of young men, the description of Latinus's people as a discordant flock of birds illustrates the disruptive impact of Aeneas and his troops.

This potential of the analogy between birds and soldiers to cut in more than one way is critical to an understanding of the all-but-final bird omen of the *Aeneid,* one that answers to the omen interpreted favorably by Venus in book 1. At this point in the narrative, Aeneas and Turnus have agreed to settle their dispute through single combat. A battle between the leaders will prevent the destruction of countless followers. But the Rutulians are struck by the unfairness of the match: Turnus is but a youth (*iuvenali in corpore,* 12.219), his cheeks just showing the first signs of manhood (*pubentesque genae,* 12.219). His sister Juturna disguises herself as a fierce warrior and starts to stir up the assembled mass of Rutulians. They, or at least the young men among them (*iuvenum sententia,* 12.238), respond, and a murmur (perhaps recalling the rustling of the birds in book 11: cf. also the similarity between *arma volunt,* 12.242 and *arma . . . poscunt,* 11.453) slinks through the battle lines (*serpitque per agmina murmur,* 12.239): apparently the followers of Turnus have remained in formation all along. At this point Juturna sends an omen: according to the narrator, it is the most vivid (*quo non praesentius ullum,* 12.245) ever to disturb and deceive Italian minds:

> For a tawny bird of Jove flying in the ruddy upper heavens
> was harrowing shore birds and the resounding crowd
> of the winged battalion, when suddenly, swooping down to the sea
> he seizes in his curved talons a magnificent swan.
> The Italians bristle at attention, but all the other birds—
> an amazing sight!—whirl about with an outcry.
> Massed together they hide the heavens with their wings and chase
>   the enemy through the open air
> until at last, overcome by their force and by the weight of his prey,

the eagle hurls the swan from his clutches
down into the water and makes his getaway into the clouds.

namque volans rubra fulvus Iovis ales in aethra
litoreas agitabat avis turbamque sonantem
agminis aligeri, subito cum lapsus ad undas
cycnum excellentem pedibus rapit improbus uncis.
arrexere animos Itali, cunctaeque volucres
convertunt clamore fugam (mirabile visu),
aetheraque obscurant pennis hostemque per auras
facta nube premunt, donec vi victus et ipso
pondere defecit praedamque ex unguibus ales
proiecit fluvio, penitusque in nubila fugit.

(Verg. *Aen.* 12.247–56).

The augur Tolumnius interprets the omen as a sign that Aeneas will
be driven off from the shores of Italy, and rushing forward, he hurls a
weapon at the opposing forces. The battle resumes, at enormous and
pointless cost to both sides.

This episode of the rescue of the captured swan repeats features
from Vergil's earlier descriptions of birds, highlighting the relationship
between an assembled flock and a group of young men leaving for or
returning from war. Just as the flock can mass on a moment's notice to
support its leader or to ward off a threat, so too can it whirl in an in-
stant and start a battle where none is needed. So powerful is the analogy
between birds and young soldiers by this point in the epic that Vergil
presents the Rutulians as in essence becoming birds. Like the birds of
book 11, they murmur and rustle at signs of distress. When the eagle in
the distant sky snatches the swan, it is they, the Italians, who spring to attention (*arrexere animos,* 12.251). In his discussion of military tactics, the
Roman writer Vegetius ascribes to the legions the qualities of speed and
surprise, the ability to change direction on a moment's notice.[21] In Vergil's narrative the proto-Roman followers of Turnus have, in effect, absorbed the lessons of military training well; they have become a venge-
ful flock of birds, indistinguishable as raindrops in a cloud—until they
die, one by one, in the subsequent passages of the poem. The flocking
birds of the *Aeneid,* whether they struggle with eagles or sing and cavort,
are images of young men in their sexual and military prime, ready to
protect and preserve the sovereignty of the community. Vergil's use of
the image of flocking birds both honors and laments the loss of indi-
viduality that military combat entails.

In his stress on the collective activity of birds, Vergil represents one of the key incorporating practices of the ancient—and, until quite recently, the modern—state, namely the disciplining of young male bodies to the requirements of military service.[22] Odd as it may seem, birds, rather than more ferocious creatures, are most frequently associated with soldiers during the period of state formation in the ancient Mediterranean. In his study *Art and the Greek City State*, archaeologist Michael Shanks notes the frequency with which birds and soldiers appear together on proto-Corinthian aryballoi (of roughly late eighth and seventh centuries BC) and interprets this phenomenon in the light of Homeric similes linking birds and soldiers, as well as Homeric representations of the gods as birds. In archaic Greek thought, birds constitute a fourth realm, distinct from gods, humans, and beasts: as the soldier constitutes a separate sector of society, so he may be associated with a distinct component of the nonhuman world.[23] Vergil seems aware of this separate classification of birds, for in the omens of swans and eagles that frame the *Aeneid*, he is careful to place the swans among the breezes of the lower atmosphere, while the eagle, avatar of Jove, swoops down from the ethereal realm beyond (i.e., *aperto caelo* versus *aetheria plaga* at *Aen.* 1.394–95 and *rubra aethra, aethera* versus *litoreas, per auras, facta nube* at *Aen.* 12.247–54). As mediators between the land and the sky, birds carry a knowledge of the world beyond: hence their significance as omens and as messengers or avatars of the divine.[24] In similar manner, the warrior must communicate between the here and now of a peaceful community (like the dancing birds on the Carthaginian shore) and the distant place of battle. Birds migrate and, under the right circumstances, return: so too young men who set off to fight.

The archaic association between birds and soldiers is not limited to the Greek mainland. It characterizes various objects from early Italy, which in turn expand the range of associations that flow from and reinforce the link between the avian and the military realms, especially in the context of the early state. For example, bi- or trilobate shields from Norchia and Veii of the tenth and eighth centuries BC that were discussed in chapter 1 as analogs of *ancilia* are decorated with images of birds—files of identical birds that follow the circular contour of each disk.[25] So too, the oinochoe from Tragliatella, whose decoration Menichetti interprets as integrating the myth of Theseus into local rituals of initiation, contains a number of avian figures. Particularly striking are those depicted on the shields of the horsemen.[26] The images on the oinochoe together remind us of the connection between birds and soldiers; of the association between readiness for military service and sexual maturity; of the role of dancing in the training of soldiers; and, perhaps as well, of the role of organized companies of young men— as soldiers and as dancers—in maintaining "energizing links" with the world beyond, since the escape from TRVIA, if it calls to mind Troy, would fit the larger iconological program of Etruscan art of this period, which associates the emerging power center of Rome with its legendary Trojan founders.[27] The escape from TRVIA energizes the community represented on the oinochoe as well as the community united through the ritual of the *convivium,* at which the oinochoe presumably was featured and put to use.[28]

The combination of images linking the tenth- and eighth-century shields with the seventh-century oinochoe may even find expression in the heart of Rome itself, namely in the decorative program of the so-called Third Regia, dated to about 570 BC. There we find among the architectural terracottas that probably adorned the building's cornice one that depicts felines flanking a minotaur, another that depicts a feline and a bird, "either an ostrich or a crane."[29] Are these merely figures designed to inspire awe in the eyes of the observer?[30] Or do they speak to a deeper connection between escape from the labyrinth, the song and dance of birds, and rites and symbols of initiation, sovereignty, and social reproduction? Recall that, according to later sources, the Salian dancers deposited their *ancilia* in the Regia, a practice that came to be commemorated in a later stage of Regia decoration, namely the reliefs from the reconstructed Regia, or Regia Calviniana, of 36 BC.[31]

Neither the literary nor the visual record allows us to establish unbroken continuity between representations of birds in archaic or regal Rome and the imagery exploited so brilliantly by Vergil. Yet it does not seem farfetched to suggest that an incorporating practice linked to sovereignty, initiation, and formation of military cadres is likely to have remained steady over an extended period of time. As citizen-soldiers, young men would have been required to conceive of their bodies as simultaneously free and coerced, as autonomous entities and participants in collective action. For our purposes, what is striking about the collocation of images and ideas found in "texts" as diverse as tenth-century Etruscan shields, a seventh-century oinochoe, and Vergil's epic poem is that they manifest a shared connection with song and dance, *carmen* and *ludus.* The shields resemble the *ancilia* of the Salian rite and song; the oinochoe depicts dancing and may commemorate a ritual of initiation; the birds of the *Aeneid,* apart from flocking and fighting, also sing, dance, and play. The degree to which the bodily practice of song remained consistent over hundreds of year of regal and republican history is an open question. That song is to be understood as incorporating practice, however, seems undeniable. The assimilation, in poetry as in art, of human song to birdsong is evidence of the practice itself as well as of its significance.

The representations of birds considered thus far tend to call attention to their capacity for collective action. In still another passage, though, Vergil indicates awareness of a different way of structuring the relationship between human and avian performance. Among the heroes depicted as accompanying Aeneas as he sets out for battle is one Cupavo, who wears swan feathers on his helmet as "an emblem of paternal beauty" (*formaeque insigne paternae*, 10.188). It turns out that Cupavo's father Cycnus (whose name means swan), in lamentation for his beloved Phaethon,

> while singing and consoling sad love with music,
> took on the whiteness of old age in the form of soft plumage
> and leaving the earth behind sought the heavens through his song.

> dum canit et maestum Musa solatur amorem,
> canentem molli pluma duxisse senectam
> linquentem terras et sidera voce sequentem.

(Verg. Aen. 10.191–93)

Cycnus turns into a swan, his song of lamentation for his beloved Phaethon constituting the swan song that marks his own departure from the earth.[32] Rather than a shared experience of war, the relationship between Cycnus and Phaethon is figured as one between lover and beloved, with the older figure becoming unmanned—note the softness or effeminacy of his plumage—at the death of the younger. The asymmetric relationship between the two stands in pointed contrast to the peer group bonding between Cupavo and his colleagues, as implied in the narrator's remark that "the song brings as companions in his fleet bands of peers" (*filius aequalis comitatus classe catervas*, 10.194). Cycnus's story is distinguished both by its eroticism (younger and older being Vergil's standard construction of male-male desire)[33] and by the virtuosity of its hero: it is through his solitary song, his own voice, that he makes his way among the stars.

A generation after Vergil, this emphasis on virtuosity at the expense of camaraderie characterizes Ovid's bird similes and bird images that in other respects resemble their Vergilian antecedents. For example, in book 5 of *Metamorphoses*, in the course of the Muse Calliope's long hymn to Ceres, which is in fact a reperformance of her successful competition piece against the Emathides, the Muse locates the site of the rape of Persephone near a Sicilian pool called Pergus:

> The river Cayster hears no more
> songs of swans than that place does in the midst of its gliding waters.

non illo plura Caystros
carmina cycnorum labentibus audit in undis.

Stephen Hinds is no doubt correct to describe these verses as a "proud
programmatic claim" on Ovid's part, one celebrating the poet's own
successful transfer of the story of Persephone and Demeter from Asia
Minor to Sicily as well as placing the Muses' own song, internal to the
Metamorphoses, in a tradition of respectable poetry.[34] As Hinds notes,
most references to singing swans in Augustan poetry (the passages from
the *Aeneid* just discussed being the obvious exceptions) contain "clear
evocations of 'poets and other literary men.'"[35] The poet's virtuosity is
celebrated, but then so too is that of the Muses, since the entire episode
recounts the contest for supremacy in song between the Muses and the
daughters of Pierus or, more precisely, a contest over the right to perform song, since by the end of the encounter the losers have been reduced to chattering magpies. They, in contrast to Vergil's soldier-swans,
or the swans of Pergus, are quintessentially birds without a song, pos-
sessors of a mimetic faculty that is without semiotic significance.

This contrast between singing and songless birds reappears in a
later episode of Ovid, one that also differentiates the magpie from the
swan, and the soldier from the virtuoso. The episode involves the character Picus, totemic hero of the early Latins, a figure whose name is
often translated as "woodpecker" but is in fact the masculine version of
pica, the type of bird the Emathides become when they lose their power
to sing. This Picus, as it turns out, has all the characteristics we might
expect of a Roman youth or *iuvenis*—birth, wealth, reliable comrades,
a horse he uses for war and hunting, and an eagerness to combat wild
boars (*Met.* 14.320ff.) It is as if he has stepped right off the Tragliatella
oinochoe into Ovid's recitation space. Picus's incorporating practices
are those implied by the bird images of Vergil and of Vergil's predecessors in archaic art. What Picus lacks, however, is song: specifically the
maiden named Canens, or "singing one," who is handed over to him in
marriage (14.335–43).

Canens's devotion to Picus, together with her power of song, attract the jealous attention of the witch Circe, who creates a phantom
boar that lures Picus from his comrades. When he nonetheless resists
Circe's advances, she turns him into a woodpecker: of the original Picus
nothing remains except the name (*nec quicquam antiqui Pico, nisi nomina,
restat,* 14.396). Canens's rage and grief surpass exemplum; like a mad-
woman she races through the fields of Latium, going without sleep or
food for six days and six nights. On the shores of the Tiber

she wept and poured forth words modulated by sorrow itself
with a delicate sound, as sometimes
a swan on the verge of death sings its own funeral songs.
At last, liquefied by sorrow, she melts her tender innards
and little by little vanishes into thin air.
Renown has marked the place, which the Camenae of old,
from the name of the nymph have properly dubbed "Canens."

illic cum lacrimis ipso modulata dolore
verba sono tenui maerens fundebat, ut olim
carmina iam moriens canit exsequialia cygnus.
luctibus extremum tenues liquefacta medullas
tabuit, inque leves paullatim evanuit auras.
fama tamen signata loco est: quem rite Canentem
nomine de nymphae veteres dixere Camenae.

(Ov. Met. 14.428–34)

Canens, who is introduced as a paragon of the cosmic singer, with
the power to set the world a-dancing to her tunes (in effect, a female
counterpart to Orpheus), delivers a final, bravura performance. Restricted by no conventions, she modulates her song to her heartfelt emotion alone. Her virtuosity matches that of the legendary swan song, and
she dissipates into the breezes, the realm of birds in their role as inter-
mediaries between human and divine. Song has been feminized and
individualized, its separation from the masculine enterprises of warfare,
hunting, and initiation figured in the story of Canens's frustrated devotion to the young man Picus. (In his association of virtuosity with the
female, Ovid anticipates a regendering of vocal performance under the
principate.) A different kind of song, the destructively utilitarian incantation of Circe, has prevailed. But the final words in the story of Picus
and Canens describe Canens's song and her assimilation to the virtuoso
swan.

Just as Vergil's commitment to the imagery of singing soldiers is revealed by his exploration of both the positive and negative implications
of their assimilation to birds, so too Ovid's representation of the virtuosity of the birdlike singer is fully apparent only through explicit negation. He too, in yet another episode from the *Metamorphoses,* tells the
story of a hero named Cycnus, not the lover of Phaethon who turned
into a constellation, but the great warrior, son of Neptune, a hero
whose only legitimate rival is Achilles himself (for Cycnus's accomplishments, see *Met.* 12.71ff.). Being invulnerable to attack (like Achilles),
Cycnus boasts that he wears armor not for protection but for decoration: "These weapons are only for show," he proclaims; "Mars, too, dons

armor for this reason" (*decor est quaesitus ab istis / Mars quoque ob hoc ca-
pere arma solet*, 12.90–91). Achilles attacks ferociously, hurling his spear
and slashing at Cycnus with his sword, but to no avail. At last he knocks
his impenetrable rival to the ground and strangles him with his helmet
straps, thus depriving him of life — and, we might add, a swan song. Yet
swan song or no, just as Achilles is getting ready to strip Cycnus of his
weapons, the god intervenes and turns him into a bird, specifically a
swan:

> The god transformed his body into a white
> bird of the sea, which assumed the name he recently bore.

> corpus deus aequoris albam
> contulit in volucrem, cuius modo nomen habebat.
> > (Ov. *Met.* 12. 144–45)

As if to emphasize the absence of song in an episode about the death
of the swan-man, Ovid proceeds to describe the sacrifice and feast that
followed upon Cycnus's metamorphosis by describing the conventional
musical accompaniments that it lacked:

> There was no playing of the lyre, there were no songs
> nor did the long flute bring delight.
> Instead they pass the night in conversation, and virtue
> is the substance of their talk.

> Non illos citharae, non illos carmina vocum
> longave multifori delectat tibia buxi
> sed noctem sermone trahunt: virtusque loquendi
> materia est.
> > (Ov. *Met.* 12.157–60)

The terms *loquor*, "everyday speech," and *sermo*, "conversation," that
here describe the replacements for the missing song are repeated, as if
for emphasis, in subsequent lines of the narrative (*Met.* 12.162, 163, 165).
In his recounting of the story of Cycnus, Ovid confirms the earlier associations of warriors, birds, and song even as he pointedly denies their
relevance to his own narrative.[36] In the continuation of the story, Cycnus is replaced by a different kind of performer, namely Nestor, a virtuoso of loquaciousness, whose storytelling (not singing) occupies the
feast after the death of the hero, not to mention the next four hundred
or so verses of Ovid's poem.

Whether or not we accept the possibility of continuity between the archaic material and the Vergilian, it does seem clear that Vergil represents, except in his account of the virtuoso Cycnus, an archaic system of thought and practice in which song and the warrior, in ritual performance and in imagery of birds, secure the well-being of the community, especially of its sovereign. In contrast, Ovid, echoing and expanding the ramifications of the Vergilian Cycnus, presents the almost literal deconstruction of that system, as birds cease to sing, Singing or Canens fails in her mission, and swan-man is denied his song. The transition between Vergil and Ovid may be regarded as marking a transformation in bodily practices, an incorporated revolution of the sort ascribed by Connerton to late 1780s France. In revolutionary Rome, as in revolutionary Paris, the rupture in practice makes the practice evident as such. Classicists who have noted the apparent "crisis in masculinity" that accompanied the failure of the Roman Republic and emergence of the principate have directed at least some attention to the ramifications of this crisis in law, ideology, and textualized psychology — that is, the "inscribed practices" of Roman history.[37] My contention here is that this crisis — or, more accurately, redefinition — of masculinity, one not so different from that undergone in Western countries in the last generation or so, has bodily or "practical" ramifications as well.

Because the changes under consideration, even if brought to our attention through the minutiae of textual practices, are of far-reaching importance, it will help to adopt a broader perspective in seeking to describe and understand them. In his study, *Metamorphoses of the Body*, anthropologist and philosopher José Gil, describes the different ways in which the body can be used in different social and cultural contexts. His term for the different schemes or uses of the body is "exfoliation," chosen to suggest how the same body can branch out or leaf out in different directions in its relationship to external reality, and so seem like a different body, depending on its particular relationship to the environment, its exfoliation, in different circumstances. As an anthropologist, Gil is especially interested in the regulation of bodily exfoliations imposed by the transition from what we might loosely call tribal to state society. In other words, like Connerton, he seeks to understand how historical change is carried by the experience of bodies. And, although his imagery of exfoliation is drawn from the realm of organic plant life, the processes he describes can also be understood from the vantage point of Benjamin's "mimetic faculty" and its transformation and reorganization.

Of tribal societies Gil writes as follows:

The forms of education one encounters in tribal societies show how from a very young age children come into contact with crowds of other bodies, are touched by many hands, nursed by ten women, confronted with a thousand parental images, identified with a thousand other children and adults. This play of a whirling multiplicity liberates infantile singularity by breaking the capture that would result from primary identification to a sole image. The body of the child becomes a sort of articulatory receiver where other bodies are imbricated and disentangled in a dynamic plurality of connections and corporeal influences. In this way the children learn their proper rhythms by learning to modulate those of others in themselves. . . . The singularity of the 'individual' . . . [is that of] a body in communication with the whole of nature and culture, and all the more singular to the extent that it allows itself to be traversed by the greatest number of natural and social forces.[38]

With the transition to the state, according to Gil, the bodily exfoliations are limited, boundaries are imposed between individuals, only to be weakened in moments of intense group activity. The soldier-citizen, I submit, is the locus of a particularly powerful struggle between autonomy and immersion in the group, needing at times to stand alone, on other occasions to operate as one with his comrades.[39] This dynamic underlies the connection between birds and soldiers, the use of birds as patterns for structuring the exfoliations of the young soldier-to-be. Observation of other creatures provides a way of thinking through the strengths and limitations of different exfoliations, or automatisms, of the human body, and those observations and exfoliations can be put in practice either through the play of dance, or ludus, or in the different but related activity of war.[40] But we must add to this recognition of the metamorphoses of the body in the movement from tribe to state acknowledgment of the role of song, in its specific sense of special speech. Song, by making connection with the world beyond, by creating "energizing links" between the natural realm of birds and the man-made realm of musical instruments in the bodily performance of the singer, reorients not just the singer, but the audience as well. As Attali reminds us, song calms or excites, unifies or disperses.[41]

The concentration of energy in the body of the singing warrior, the fixing of its exfoliation in the play of the swan or crane, is a foundational act that must be repeated and transmitted from generation to generation and from body to body. Only when the body has made the performance its own does the performance become impervious to critique. Because of the need to found and refound Rome, to transmit the bodily practices from one generation to the next, the rite of the salii, even when not fully understood, is preserved at Rome, as a bodily (including vocal) performance. At the same time, the successful transmission of such practices can account for the concinnity in ideology between archaic art and Vergilian epic. The epic poet still imagines the bodies of men as the bodies of warriors, is still interested in the tension between the male body employed in war and the male body as means of reproduction of the people, in the relationship between the singular body, especially as object and subject of erotic attraction, and the corporate body, as agent of history. For Vergil, it is still a question of "founding" the Roman state.

For Ovid, obvious as it may sound, bodies are in flux. Their metamorphoses follow the metamorphosis of human figures in dance; they raise the possibility of a new range of bodily exfoliations or automatisms, new patterns for imitation.[42] But the dance of Ovidian bodies is not that of individual and chorus, soldier and company, initiate and troupe, bird and flock; rather it is the dance of the virtuoso performer, who, as Lucian puts it in his treatise on the dance, must master all the transformations from Chaos to Cleopatra—that is, loosely speaking, the table of contents of Ovid's poem.[43] Moreover, this Ovidian transformation of the archaic-to-Vergilian imagery of birds seems of a part with other aspects of what has been called a Roman cultural revolution: transformations in sexuality, class structure, patterns of authority, domestic and social architecture, the personhood of women, the practice and rhetoric of empire.[44] More precisely, Ovid's reconceptualization of the male body, as figured in his reworking of the metaphorical relationship to birds, closely parallels changes in military recruitment and conscription that take place during his lifetime, specifically between the time of composition of the *Aeneid* and the time of composition of the *Metamorphoses*. One of the key political and military developments of the Augustan period is the drastic reduction in number of citizen legions (from about sixty to about twenty-five) and corresponding increase in reliance on auxiliary units manned by noncitizens.[45] According to Cassius Dio, a major reason for this change was the desire of Augustus and his followers to end conscription, particularly among Italians.[46] Modern military historians hypothesize that the number of legions approved by Augustus was the result of a fine balancing act between the military needs of imperial rule and the political desire not to use conscripts.[47] While it is true that Augustus and successive emperors retained the legal right to draft citizens, it was a right that was exercised only rarely; the steady decline in Italians as a percentage of legionary soldiers, as documented by prosopographers of the Roman military, is evidence of the rarity of conscription of citizens.[48]

Finally, lest we regard it as unlikely that such changes could occur so swiftly, especially given the tendency toward inertia in incorporating practices, we would do well to recall, once again, the observations of Paul Connerton. In discussing social memory in general, he writes:

It is an implicit rule that participants in any social order must presuppose a shared memory. To the extent that their memories of a society's past diverge, to that extent its members can share neither experiences nor assumptions. The effect is seen perhaps most obviously when communication across generations is impeded by different sets of memories. Across generations, different sets of memories, frequently in the shape of implicit background narratives, will encounter each other; so that although physically present to one another in a particular setting, the different generations may remain mentally and emotionally insulated, the memories of one generation locked irretrievably, as it were, in the brains and bodies of that generation.[49]

The generation of Ovid was spared the experience of civil war, even (for the most part) the experience of military conscription.[50] Much else changed as well in the transition from republic to principate, with such changes inscribed in the epigraphical, historiographical, and legal canons of the time. Incorporating practices must have changed too, and some of the particulars of those changes, at least as they pertain to song, are to be inferred from the surviving texts.[51]

Comrades and *Cinaedi*

During much of Roman history, elite male practice is by and large one of camaraderie. Such camaraderie is itself incorporated through practices of singing, dancing, military training (which overlaps with singing and dancing), religious ritual, public spectacle, and conviviality. While none of these practices disappears from the record with the transformation of republic into principate, nonetheless they change sufficiently to expand the masculine ideal to include expectations of virtuosity — rhetorical, literary, philosophical, musical, sexual, and so on. Traditional ideals of camaraderie continue to exert their influence in later periods, and virtuosos can be found among the figures of republican cultural history. But the trend over time is from the one to the other.

Among comrades a line is drawn between acceptable and unacceptable behavior, particularly with respect to sexual interaction. The male body that must accept the possible penetration of weapons in war must reject penetrative sexual intercourse.[52] As a means of policing relations among peers, Roman culture, like many others before and after, develops a scare figure, a monstrous other whose characteristics define by opposition those that are to be sought or rejected by members of the mainstream group. In Rome, the defining other is a figure of song and dance, namely the *cinaedus*.[53] The bodiliness of the *cinaedus* — his identification as a certain type of dancer and certain type of participant in sexual intercourse—completes our understanding of the figure of the *sodalis* by helping us appreciate him as a figure of embodied as well as textual history. And observing the history of the *cinaedus,* his transition from musical performer to essentialized (in the view of his opponents) sexual renegade, expands our sense of the history of incorporating practices more generally. Explicitness, which is the mark of cinaedic behavior in republican Rome, comes to be associated with virtuosity more generally under the empire. The threat posed by the *cinaedus* bifurcates into a public threat, summed up in the figure of the expressionistic virtuoso, and a private threat, epitomized in the second-century astrologer Firmicus Maternus's anxiety about hidden or secret *cinaedi* and the signs through which they can be identified.[54] This change occurs as ideal manliness comes to be located in individual as opposed to corporate performance. The history of the *cinaedus* thus provides a different, but corroborative, perspective on the transformation inferred from the Ovidian rewriting of Vergilian imagery.

In Plautus, whose texts preserve the earliest representations of *cinaedi* at Rome, the *cinaedus* appears both explicitly and implicitly as the antitype of the *sodalis.* The *sodalis,* through his convivial antics, his song and dance on the comic stage, is always on the verge of becoming a *cinaedus.* This possibility is repeatedly toyed with, only to be rejected. Firmicus Maternus provides us with the tantalizing piece of information that some *cinaedi* "constantly dancing, mime the outcomes of the old plays" (*qui veterum fabularum exitus in scaenis semper saltantes imitentur, Mathesis* 6.39). Firmicus might be referring to a contemporary practice of having silent dancers mime alongside of other kinds of performances; but given the evidence of parodic dancing at Italian spectacles as far back as the sixth century BC, we cannot rule out the possibility that *cinaedi* performed in connection with early Roman comedic presentations as well.[55] As we shall see, one Plautine comedy specifically invites *cinaedi* to take the stage at its conclusion. Firmicus's comment reminds us that our reading of the textual traces of Plautine comedy must be informed by an awareness of how much bodily practice is lost to us: brief references in terminology or meter were no doubt amplified through gesture, costume, deportment, and the like, and the nature of such amplification could vary with varying occasions and context of performance. Firmicus's remark also invites us to consider whether *cinaedi* might not be more integral to the incorporating and textual practice of Roman comedy—and with it, Roman conviviality—than has previously been assumed.[56]

An episode from Plautus's *Menaechmi* gives us a sense of the performance qualities and social resonance of cinaedism. In the scene in question (III.ii = 466ff.) the parasite Peniculus has just spotted the second

Menaechmus leaving a *convivium* with the *palla* of first Menaechmus's wife in hand. Outraged at the failure of the man he mistakes for his patron (the Menaechmi are identical twins who have been separated for years) to invite him to the party, Peniculus proclaims Menaechmus's misdeeds and his own plans for vengeance against him. Peniculus's list is drawn up in the epigraphic style of successive ablative absolutes: "the meal finished up, the wine drunk down, the parasite locked out" (*confecto prandio, vinoque expoto, parasito excluso foras*, 469–70).[57] Even Peniculus's remark, "By god I am not who I am, unless I avenge this injury and myself—prettily at that" (*non hercle is sum qui sum, ni hanc iniuriam / meque ultus pulchre fuero*, 471–72) depends for its comic force on a rhetoric of self-promotion that equates a sequence of achievements, including vengeance, with high status in the community. As if to mock Peniculus's indignant declaration, Menaechmus II—who of course hasn't a clue as to Peniculus's imagined relationship to him—celebrates his own deeds in language reminiscent both of Peniculus's list and of funeral laudations of Roman nobles, historical and fictional alike:

> I ate. I drank. I had sex. I stole
> this [*palla*] which no one will inherit after this day.

> prandi potavi scortum accubui apstuli
> hanc quoiius heres numquam erit post hunc diem.[58]
>
> (Plaut. *Men.* 476–77)

The sequence of simple perfects to describe great deeds puts us in mind of passages as varied in provenance yet similar in tone as the epitaph of Scipio Barbatus (*cepit / subigit . . . abdoucit, CIL* 1[2].7.5–6), the suicide speech of Dido (*vixi . . . peregi . . . statui . . . vidi . . . recepi*, Verg. *Aen.* 4.653–56), the *Res Gestae* of Augustus, not to mention the classic pronouncement of Julius Caesar, *veni vidi vici*: all proud statements of accomplishment structured around a series of unmodified perfective verb forms.[59] Menaechmus's words seem to pick up in particular on the appropriateness of such a retrospective list at the end of one's life, because he proceeds to use the otherwise peculiar term *heres*, heir, to describe potential future owners of the *palla*.[60] Of course, Menaechmus II is far from dead: he has merely finished off an especially pleasant and profitable day. But even in his conflation of day and lifetime, he may be parodying other Roman habits, such as the totting up of losses and gains at the end of each day or the representation of banquet and life as metaphors for each other.[61] The latter habit of thought and speech seems linked to the custom of funeral banquet, a custom cited in turn by Peniculus when later in the same scene he confronts Menaechmus II directly over his failure to invite him to the *convivium:* "You've held a funeral without my presence at the banquet: how dare you when I'm an equal heir with you!" (*fecisti funus med apsenti prandio / qur ausu's facere, quoii ego aeque here eram? Men.* 492–93) Peniculus's words both underscore the eulogistic aspect of Menaechmus's self-presentation and emphasize the foolishness of Peniculus's own pretensions, pretensions summed up in his parting threat to Menaechmus to tell of his wrongdoing to his wife: "All of these contumelies of yours will fall back on you. I shall bring it about that not unavenged did you eat your chow today" (*omnes in te haec recident contumeliae / faxo haud inultus prandium comederis,* 520–21).[62]

The scene between Peniculus and Menaechmus II is worth dwelling on because it introduces two additional song types, one perhaps unique in the Plautine corpus, the other — the cinaedic — constitutive of a great deal of comic effect in a number of plays. When Peniculus has brought his charge of wrong dining against Menaechmus, Menaechmus understandably and truthfully declares that he has no idea who Peniculus is and even asks him his name. Of Peniculus's response (*etiam derides quasi nomen non gnoveris,* 499) Gratwick has written that the *figura etymologica* (*nomen nosco*) and unusual cadence "give a weighty contrast with the rapid run of short syllables in the first half of Men[aechmus]'s exasperated reply."[63] This weightiness is continued in Peniculus's next response to Menaechmus's continued denial: *Menaechme, vigila,* which is arguably an echo of the cry of the priests who seek to rouse the inattentive god by bursting into the temple, rattling shields, and crying, *vigilasne Mars, Mars vigila!* ("are you awake, Mars? Mars, wake up!")[64] If so, it exemplifies Plautus's use of both general and specific allusion to religious *carmina.*[65] In a different vein, yet one arising from the context of conviviality and conflict over elite male ethics, the next exchanges between Peniculus and Menaechmus II refer to the song-and-dance routine of the *cinaedi,* a type of *carmen* Plautine comedy routinely seeks both to exploit and to differentiate itself from. Frustrated at Menaechmus's repeated denials, Peniculus inquires: "Didn't I see you go outside wearing a *palla?* " to which Menaechmus responds, inferring an accusation not of theft but of transvestism or perhaps sexual deviance, "to hell with you! just because you're a *cinaedus* doesn't mean everyone else is" (*vae capiti tuo! / omnis cinaedos esse censes quia tu es,* 512–13). At one level this jibe may seem to be the customary use of sexual putdown in the context of male competition, but the passage is also more specifically metatheatrical, or metamusical, in its allusion to the onstage antics of *cinaedi.* While only briefly evoked in the exchange between Menaechmus II and Peniculus, the dance of the *cinaedi* is as important a component of Plautine comedy as tragedy, boasting, and epitaph.

Moreover, in this particular passage, reference to the *cinaedus* occurs in a context that raises—albeit in comic and parodic manner—questions of appropriate convivial behavior on the part of elite males.

Although it is customary in modern discussions of Roman sexuality to refer to *cinaedi* as men who enjoy the receptive role in anal intercourse, in fact the term enters Roman discourse in reference to the performers of a particular kind of lascivious dance.[66] As Lore Benz has recently argued, Plautine comedy is deeply rooted in Greco-Roman mime, with dancing *cinaedi* constituting an important element of that performance genre.[67] In Plautus, *cinaedi* appear as performers of a particular type of song. Their performance is, to be sure, often sexual in nature, with their sexuality construed sometimes as specifically receptive, more generally as exaggerated or farcical. For example, at *Miles* 668 the old man Periplectomenus, who is eager to join the antics of the slave Palaestrio and the youth Pleusicles, assures them that he can perform any role they require. "Do you need a harsh, irascible advocate— here I am! A gentle one? I can be gentler than the sea is silent and liquidier than the wind is windy. How about a fun-loving banquet guest? . . . a parasite? . . . a butcher? Why, no *cinaedus* is as supple for dancing as I am" (*tum ad saltandum non cinaedus malacus aequest atque ego,* Plaut. *Mil.* 668). Periplectomenus understands cinaedic dancing to be a theatrical role comparable with that of performing as a parasite or a cook. He is also, like the parasite and cook, an accoutrement of the convivial lifestyle. In *Poenulus,* when the soldier and *adulescens* are trading insults, the young man's intimation that the soldier is itching to perform fellatio ("isn't it the case, young man, that your cheeks or at least your teeth are itching?" *num tibi adulescens, malae aut dentes pruriunt?* Plaut. *Poen.* 1315) is matched by the soldier's comeback: "When you speak like that you should carry a tympanum, for I think you're more a *cinaedus* than a man" (*nam te cinaedum esse arbitror magi' quam virum,* 1318). Performance type (playing the tympanum, which is expressly associated with *kinaidos* song in the text of the Charition mime, *P. Oxy.* 3.1903.413) and sexual category here implicate each other.[68]

A particularly striking evocation of the song of the *cinaedi* occurs in a passage in which the word *cinaedus* is never mentioned. In his entrance song in the *Amphitryo* (153ff.), the hero's slave Sosia laments the fact that he has been sent on a mission at night. Roaming alone, he worries aloud about being thrown into prison by the *tresviri*—and brought out, or "uncorked," next morning for the purpose of being whipped (*depromar ad flagrum,* 156).[69] His fantasy continues: he won't be allowed to mount a defense, and as a punishment he will be seized by eight strong men "who will beat him like an anvil" (*ita quasi incudem me miserum homines octo validi caedant*, 160).[70] Such, he sings, is the fate of the slave of a rich man:

Night and day enough and beyond
whatever he needs in word or deed—you get no rest.

noctesque diesque adsiduo satis superque est
quod facto aut dicto adest opus, quietu' ne sis.

(Plaut. *Amph.* 168–69)

As Maurizio Bettini has noted, these last two lines as well as three more that follow have the metrical shape of catalectic sotadeans—that is, the kind of sotadean employed in the *kinaidos* songs of Sotades of Maronea, a Greek writer of the first half of the third century BC.[71] Bettini points out that sotadeans fall into two types, with one group being used by Sotades, in Ennius's *Sota,* in the Charition mime (*P. Oxy.* 3.1903.41–56), in Petronius's *Satyricon,* and in the song of the *retiarius* to the *murmillo* in the arena; while those of a slightly different metrical shape are employed for philosophical reflection in the sotadeans falsely ascribed to Sotades by Stobaeus (Greek) as well as in the didactic sotadean poetry of Accius (Latin). What the first group, so-called pure sotadeans, have in common, besides shared meter, is a shared association with performance that is enticing and lascivious: *mollis et lubricus* in the words of Marius Victorinus (*GLK* 6.131.8ff.). The second type of sotadean is associated with the tamer content and a didactic tone. With respect to the passage in *Amphitryo,* Bettini rightly sees that the use of this lascivious meter at this point in Sosia's song hints at the use to which he is put by his master Amphitryo: night and day enough and beyond whatever the master needs. The sexual dimension of Sosia's night fright has already been cued by the imagery of the opening lines of the song, with the extraction or uncorking of Sosia and the pounding he gets by eight strong strangers expressed in language that is at least potentially sexual in nature. The implicit accusation against Amphitryo is not a new strain but the metrical and thematic climax of Sosia's song: the poor slave is screwed if he goes out at night and screwed if he stays home.

While the Roman audience may understand the nature of Sosia's fear and complaints from his language alone, the full effect of the song depends on recognition of the cinaedic song-type embedded within it. Centuries later, Pliny the Elder will speak of "hearing comedies, watching mimes, reading lyrics, and comprehending sotadeans" (*et comoedias audio et specto mimos et lyricos lego et sotadicos intellego, HN* 5.32), as if the last-mentioned deliberately hide their sexual content beneath a more decorous surface.[72] Bettini's analysis of the passage from the *Amphi-*

tryo thus supports the view that, like tragedy, love song, and laudation, cinaedic song is familiar enough as such to Plautus's audience to be deployed strategically for comic effect. Sometimes the allusion to cinaedic song is incidental, part of the give-and-take of the comic exchange; elsewhere the possibility of comedy crossing over into *cinaedia* seems to structure an entire episode, even an entire play. The versatile, would-be *cinaedus* of the *Miles* (Periplectomenus) exemplifies the incidental or local reference: although a *senex,* he raises the possibility of dancing like a *cinaedus,* perhaps even does a little vamping, but the comedy moves on to other issues and targets.

In a particularly obscene passage from *Asinaria* (623ff.), the accusation of being a *cinaedus* puts an end to an argument between two slaves bickering in the presence of the *adulescens* Argyrippus and the *meretrix* Philaenium. When the *meretrix* greets the trio with the conventional expression "may the gods grant what you wish," one slave retorts, "how about a night with you and a sack of wine." The *adulescens* intervenes —"be careful what you say, scoundrel [*verbero*]"—and the slave backs down: "I was wishing those things for you, not me." "Then what do you wish for? Tell us please." "I wish—to flog [*verberare*] this one," pointing to the other slave. The second slave defends his honor: "Who on earth would entrust this to you, *cinaede calamistrate* [*cinaedus* curled with a curling iron]? Are you going to give a flogging, when you enjoy getting flogged for lunch? [*tun verberes, qui pro cibo habeas te uerberari?*]" (629). The sexual nature of the exchange becomes clear when we recognize that *verbero, -are* "to flog," can be a metaphor for assuming the penetrative position in sexual intercourse.[73] The master uses the noun, *verbero,* scoundrel, as an insult. The first slave puns on the noun *verbero* and the verb *verberare* to propose that if the *meretrix* is off limits he'll gladly have his way with his fellow slave. And the second slave points out that, as a *cinaedus,* the first couldn't have his way, even with a willing partner, because his preference is the receptive role, especially, it would seem, during oral sex.

In *Aulularia* both the sexual and theatrical aspects of the *cinaedus* become manifest in a scene involving the old miser Euclio and the cook Congrio, who has entered the house to start preparations for the wedding feast of Euclio's daughter. Congrio rushes out of the stage building yelling for all in the audience to get out of his way. He's fleeing a beating with cudgels (*fustibus,* 414) by Euclio, who assumes he is in the house in order to steal the hidden pot of gold. Congrio's song makes a big deal of the beating he is receiving, likening himself to a punching bag for Euclio, admiring the skill with which Euclio has offered him wood (*ligna . . . praeberi . . . pulchrius,* 412). When Euclio arrives on stage, he proposes to turn Congrio over to the *tres viri*—the same figures Sosia feared would detain him — on the grounds that Congrio is wielding a knife (*cultrum,* 417).

> *C* But it's the right prop for a cook *E* Then why have you
>   threatened
> me with it? *C* I think you've been done badly, since I didn't poke you
>   in the flank.
> *E* No man is alive today more shameful than you!
> And there's nobody I'd more gladly do badly than you!
> *C* By Apollo though you're silent, what's happening is completely
>   obvious. The matter is its own witness.
> I've been softened up by cudgels better than any *cinaedus.*

> *C* coquom decet. *E* quid comminatu's
> mihi? *C* istuc male factum arbitror, quia non latu's fodi.
> *E* homo nullust te scelestior qui vivat hodie,
> neque quoi ego de industria amplium male plus lubens faxim.
> *C* pol etsi taceas, palam id quidem est: res ipsa testest;
> ita fustibus sum mollior magi's quam ullu' cinaedus.

(Plaut. Aul. 417–22)

As in *Amphitryo,* here in *Aulularia* the reference to the *cinaedus* (there through rhythm, here through the word itself) culminates and, at least for the text-bound modern reader, clarifies the series of sexual and theatrical gags. The association of Congrio with a *cinaedus* is intimated from the first mention of cudgels (*fustibus*) because cudgels are elsewhere associated with *cinaedi* (e.g., *Poen.* 1320, where the *adulescens* tries to show he isn't a *cinaedus* by having the soldier beaten with cudgels by his slaves), like brickbats used against clowns in later comedy. But the beating of the *cinaedus* is metaphorical for the sexual pounding he's used to taking, as the exchange between Congrio and Euclio soon makes clear. When Euclio asks why Congrio is waving a knife, Congrio answers with the perfectly ambiguous expression *quia non latu's fodi:* because I haven't stuck it in your side, *latus* being the untranslatable but all-purpose Latin word for the sexual regions.[74] Euclio gets the jab and turns it back on Congrio, saying he would gladly "do him badly" — picking up on Congrio's expression *male factum* and perhaps capping it, by punning on *male* (badly) and *malus* (ream or post) — a common wordplay in Plautus, at least according to Gurlitt.[75] Congrio in effect announces that he's already been manhandled by Euclio: thanks to his blows, he's turned him into a *cinaedus* — both a sexual submissive and the suggestive dancer of theatrical or musical tradition.

Perhaps the most elaborate evocation of the *cinaedus* — and again

one that relies on both the sexual and the theatrical aspects of the role —
is the culminating scene of the *Stichus*. The title character Stichus, who
has been granted a day off and a cask of wine by his master on their
return from a successful journey abroad, plans to celebrate with his
fellow slave Sangarinus and their shared girlfriend Stephanium (430ff.).
The singing and dancing of the two slaves emphasizes their exaggeration of the convivial norm of equality to the point that they will share
everything. "Here's a good jest, for two rivals to love each other, to
drink from one cantharus, to enjoy one wench. This is worth remem-
bering: I am you, you are me, we are both together, we both love one
girl, when she's with me she's with you too; and when she's with you,
she's also with me; neither of us will envy the other. . . . Let's call her
out . . . she'll dance!" (729–35). The girl appears but apparently doesn't
dance for free. She says she's bathed herself, just as a prostitute does to
please her customers (745–47); what is more, she expects the slaves to
give a drink to the flute player (757). Stichus and Sangarinus, who long
to dance and sleep with Stephanium, announce they're smitten with
her and say farewell to their hard-earned savings (749ff.) But they —
and we — get something special out of the flute player, for Sangarinus
instructs him to "swiftly take up a different song, seductive [*lepidam*],
sweet [*suavem*], and fit for *cinaedi* [*cinaedicam*] — so that we can itch all
the way down to our toenails" (760–61).

And so, after a pause while they refresh themselves (in senarii) and
the *tibicen* has a drink, they take up "a new song for old wine" (768). The
rhythm shifts, not to sotadeans but to a mix of iambic long verses,[76] and
the two slaves proceed to sing:

> SA Which ionic or cinaedic is there who could do such as this?
> ST If you've beaten me with that verse, provoke me with another.
> SA Do it this way. ST No you do it this way. SA babae! ST tatae!
>   SA papae! ST pax!

> SA Qui Ionicus aut cinaedicus⟨t⟩, qui hoc tale facere possiet?
> ST si istoc me vorsu viceris, alio me provocato.
> SA fac tu hoc modo. ST at tu hoc modo. SA babae! ST tatae SA papae
>   ST pax

(Plaut. Stich. 770–72)

Again the rhythm shifts, now to reiziani, and Sangarinus sings:

> Now both together. I call all *cinaedi* out against us.
> There aren't enough for us any more than there's rain for a
>   mushroom.

nunc pariter ambo. omnis voco cinaedos contra.

satis esse nobis non magis poti' quam fungo imber.

(Plaut. *Stich.* 773-74)

These lines can only mean that Sangarinus and Stichus are sexually provoked by the idea of *cinaedi*—perhaps even by the presence of *cinaedi* who appear on stage as part of the finale. While they begin their final dance being sexually enticing themselves, they end it being aroused by others.

The *Stichus,* perhaps more than any Plautine play, is a wild party waiting to happen. As one handbook of Latin literature puts it, "This plot has an unusually modest development and but little tension."[77] Father wants daughters to divorce absent husbands, husbands return, parasite wants to attend party but is ridiculed and rebuffed, slaves get a holiday and hold a party of their own. The final party is described and represented in rather explicit detail. We learn that the slaves have already eaten, thanks to the efforts of Stephanium (681); we know where they got the wine—indeed the *cadum,* or wine flask, is probably a visible prop from the first appearance of Stichus (425); various characters throughout use the technical vocabulary of the *convivium*—*propino* (425, 468, 708, 712), *condixi* (432; cf. *Men.* 124), *conviva* (478), *lectis sternendis* (678), *munditiisque apparandis* (678), *comissatum* (686), *scaphium* (693), *cantharum* (693, 705, 712), *cyathus* (706). We witness a guessing game to determine position on the couch (*mica uter utrubi accumbamus,* 695), the mixing of wine and water (Fons vs. Liber, 696ff.), the selection of the *magister bibendi,* here called a *strategus,* or general (702). Even a snippet of a Greek drinking song (*cantio Graeca*)—in Greek—is introduced (707). What is lacking is explicit reference to entertainment, until Stephanium shows up halfway through the party scene and insists that the flute player be given a drink. In return he plays the cinaedic song that ends the play. In other words, Stichus and Sangarinus turn themselves into entertainment at their own *convivium,* but only long enough to make possible the arrival of the *cinaedi* on the scene. The play almost but not quite collapses into cinaedic song, and the slave-hero turns himself into a *cinaedus,* albeit momentarily. The *Stichus* thus raises in a fairly explicit manner questions that are implicit throughout Plautus: how does comedy differ from cinaedic song and how do male characters of comedy—singing and dancing for the pleasure of others—differ from the *cinaedi* they routinely insult? Why the cudgel for some and not for others?

The presence of *cinaedi* on the Plautine stage, figuratively or literally, defines by contrast the proper behavior of the *sodalis. Cinaedi* take the camaraderie of the *convivium* too far by allowing themselves to become objects of erotic attraction and sexual action. They make explicit the subjection to scourging, slashing, and cudgeling that characterizes slaves as well as wayward soldiers. The *cinaedus* is the goof, the punk, the clown whose ineptitude and virtuosity together define the norm. He is inept in that he is chased about the stage under a shower of blows and fails to carry out sex acts in the socially approved manner. He is a virtuoso in that he dances gracefully and enticingly. The softness (*mollitia*) of the *cinaedus* is not the softness of effeminacy (whatever that is, anyway), but the compliance of the entertainer who adapts to his audience's desires, of the sexual player who submits to the demands of another. He sings—we know of *kinaidologoi* in both Greek and Latin,[78] and the potential *cinaedi* in Plautus's plays break into song as readily as the would-be *sodales*—and he dances. He is part of the textual and the embodied history of Roman manhood.

The implicit tension between the *sodalis* and the *cinaedus* that structures the conviviality of Plautine comedy becomes explicit in the poetry of Catullus. In the Catullan corpus the term most frequently applied to the poet's friends is *sodalis,* and the sharpest insult directed against his enemies is *cinaedus.* The positive associations of *sodalitas* are clear. In poem 12 Catullus requests return of a dinner napkin, not, he says, on the basis of its expense (*aestimatione,* 12.12) but because it is a memento of his *sodalitas* with Veranius and Fabullus.[79] Not incidentally, the behavior of the thieving Asinius Marrucinus, although carried out at a *convivium* (*in ioco atque vino,* 12.2) places him outside the charmed circle of *sodalitas.* In poem 35 Catullus describes the "gentle poet" (*tenero poetae,* 35.1) Caecilius as his *sodalis* (*meo sodali,* 35.1) and orders his papyrus to fetch him back, presumably to the convivial circle, where he can get the advice of still another friend of both men. Even the language with which Catullus jokingly recalls him—*si sapiet, viam vorabit,* 35.7—has a convivial flavor, since *sapio* is the technical term for convivial knowledge, and *vorabit* ("he will devour") mixes metaphors of traveling and dining. The poem seems to link the poet's separation from Catullus and the unnamed friend with the incompleteness (*incohata,* 35.13, 35.18) of his poem on Magna Mater. The convivial circle, with its atmosphere of admiration and constructive criticism, not to mention homosociality, is implicitly accepted as the appropriate context for poetic production.[80] Poem 47 bemoans the exclusion of Catullus's *sodales* Veranius and Fabullus (so described here, as in poem 11) from *convivia,* while Piso's henchmen are living it up.

> Piggy and little Socrates, sidekicks
> of Piso, mange and hunger of the universe:
> has that horny Priapus really preferred you

to my dear Veranius and Fabius?
You enjoy sumptuous banquets
every day, while my drinking buddies
are out cadging invitations in the crossroads.

Porci et Socration, duae sinistrae
Pisonis, scabies famesque mundi
vos Veraniolo meo et Fabullo
verpus praeposuit Priapus ille?
vos convivia lauta sumptuose
de die facitis, mei sodales
quaerunt in trivio vocationes.

(Catull. 47)

Setting aside the question of just how complimentary the poem is (or isn't) to Veranius and Fabius, it is clear that their identification as *sodales* (47.6) is intended to stand in contrast to their exclusion from the elegant *convivia* enjoyed by Porcius and Socration. Finally, in poem 100 Catullus identifies Caelius and Quintius as *sodales* of a sort, and plays off the proverbial observation (known to us from Cicero) that *sodales* should behave like brothers.[81] According to the poem Caelius and Quintius have themselves fallen for a brother-sister duo, the flower of Veronese youth, Quintius for the boy and Caelius for the girl. "Well," the poet comments "this really is that well-known proverbial expression, 'sweet, brotherly sodality'" (*hoc est, quod dicitur, illud/fraternum vere sodalicium*, 100.3–4).[82] Because Caelius and Quintius appear elsewhere among Catullus's poems as confidant (poem 58) and devoted friend (poem 82) respectively, it seems reasonable to regard *sodalicium*, once again, as an approbative term, one that links the two addressees and the poet in a bond of conviviality.[83]

In contrast to Catullus's loyal *sodales* stands the treacherous Alfenus, "unremembering and disloyal to his buddies of one mind" (*immemor atque unanimis false sodalibus*, 30.1). The list of Alfenus's crimes—betrayal, neglect, desertion, forgetfulness—reads like an inversion of the virtues of *sodalitas*. His words and deeds count for nothing, in contrast, it would seem, to those of the loyal, true, and like-minded *sodales*. Although the poem is not expressly about poetic production (except to the extent that it conjures up the circumstances of its own creation), the association of *sodales* with "memory" and "one-mindedness" links them to the literary "Muses of one mind," daughters of Zeus and of Memory. By violating the compact of *sodalitas*, Alfenus makes himself the enemy of the god Fides, as indicated at the end of the poem, but also

the target of the creative energy unleashed by the remaining *sodales* —
as evidenced by the fact of this poem itself.

For Catullus the term *sodalis* describes an individual who belongs
to a well-defined group, even if it is just a group of two. The term *cinaedus* sometimes functions in the same way. Thus in poem 57 Catullus
addresses both Mamurra and Caesar as *cinaedi:*

> How nicely the shameless *cinaedi* fit together
> Mamurra and bottom-boy Caesar.
> No wonder — equal stains on both,
> the one in town, the other out in Formiae.
> Their vices are ground in and can't be washed away
> they're equally sick, the two of them, like twins,
> two smartasses on one couch.
> Neither is a more voracious adulterer than the other,
> comrades and rivals for all the darling girls
> How nicely the shameless *cinaedi* fit together!

> Pulcre convenit improbis cinaedis,
> Mamurrae pathicoque Caesarique.
> nec mirum: maculae pares utrisque,
> urbana altera et illa Formiana,
> impressae resident nec eluentur:
> morbosi pariter, gemelli utrique,
> uno in lecticulo erudituli ambo,
> non hic quam ille magis vorax adulter,
> rivales socii puellularum.
> pulcre convenit improbis cinaedis.

(Catull. 57)

While it is possible, I suppose, to imagine either Mamurra or Caesar as
a *cinaedus* on his own, Catullus seems to want to emphasize their like-
mindedness in opposition to the like-mindedness of himself and his *sodales.* The *cinaedi* become the antitype of the *sodales* both formally and
ethically, much as bandits and senators become antitypes in Ciceronian
political rhetoric.[84] Moreover, the poem makes it clear that their cinaedism is carried by their bodies: they are stained and sick, they commit
adultery together, they share a couch, they "fit" together. In contrast to
the vocal production of the *sodales* — poems, oaths, dicta — the *cinaedi*
here are all body, even in spite of their erudition (*erudituli,* 57.7).

In poem 16, try as they might to express an opinion hostile to Catullus, Aurelius and Furius, described as *pathicus* and *cinaedus,* can do no

more than think (*putastis*, 16.3, 16.13). For this offense alone, because their thoughts are inimical to Catullus's poetic production, they are to be subject to anal and oral rape: whether both each, or one punishment per perpetrator, is left unclear. In any event, the aim of the punishment is surely to deny voice to the victims—literally in the case of oral rape, figuratively in both instances since to be so victimized would humiliate Aurelius and Furius and make any future speech worthless.[85] The poem thus situates the *cinaedus* (as well as the *pathicus*) at least implicitly as antitypes to the poetic *sodales:* hostile to the values of this particular *sodalitas* and excluded from the activities that reinforce the bonds among its members.

In poem 25 the exclusion of the *cinaedus* takes place before our very eyes (or ears, as the case may be). Thallus is addressed as a *cinaedus* from the outset, and his softness compared with that of a rabbit's head, a goose's inner down,[86] an old man's penis, and a spider web. Yet despite his attempt to emphasize softness as a quality of sensation, Catullus ends up acknowledging Thallus's alacrity, his nimbleness as well.[87] For it turns out Thallus has managed to steal Catullus's *pallium* or Greek-style cloak, his special Spanish handkerchief, and some paintings from Bithynia. (We might recall that it was in the context of an apparent theft that Menaechmus II found himself charged with *cinaedia*.) Catullus further suggests that Thallus might have gotten away with the crimes, had he not been so inept (*inepte*, 25.8) as to flaunt the booty publicly, as if the stolen goods were his own ancestral possessions. Return what you have taken, Catullus demands, lest

> inflamed whips make ugly marks
> on your downy flank and gentle little buttocks[88]
> and you squirm mightily, like a tiny ship caught
> on the great big sea, as the mad wind rages against you.

> ne laneum latusculum manusque mollicellas
> inusta turpiter tibi flagella conscribillent
> et insolenter aestues, velut minuta magno
> deprensa navis in mari, vesaniente vento.
>
> > (Catull. 25.11–14)

Thallus is exactly characterized by the lubricity associated with the ci-naedic dancer. His moves are supple, so much so as to allow him to remove substantial objects from Catullus's home. Was he there as a co-convivialist, a violator of the bonds of *sodalitas?* He is lubricious in another sense as well, for his moves arouse the passion of Catullus. His softness starts as a basis for insult but turns erotic and enticing by the end of the poem: his downy flank, his tender buttocks, his squirming body. Thallus's performance, like that of the Plautine *cinaedus,* is a (relatively) public one: indeed, his flaunting of his booty gets him in trouble. But again, by the end of the poem, Catullus has threatened to isolate him, as the image of the tiny ship caught on the wide sea makes clear. Thus the final words of the poem, *vesaniente vento,* take on a double meaning, referring to both the fury of Catullus's revenge, prompted by Thallus's cinaedic performance, and the madness of his lust, also prompted by Thallus's cinaedic performance. On either reading, *cinaedus* Thallus, although removed from the larger social context, remains a lubricious body, bending to the will of one more powerful.

Thus far we have considered the *cinaedus,* in Plautus and Catullus, as the antitype to the *sodalis.* His behavior carries convivial camaraderie too far; it constitutes the kind of explicit, sexually suggestive dancing that invites the hostility of orators and others who maintain a pose of upholding conventional ethics. It advertises hungers that mainstream ideology insists be kept in check. As his association with thieving and gluttony suggests, he wants more than his share of the communal goods. But the *sodalis* is himself nothing more (or less) than the citizen-soldier at ease. His convivial camaraderie matches and carries into peaceful times and places the camaraderie of the soldier with other members of his company. Thus it is not surprising to find the *cinaedus* differentiated not only from the *sodalis* but also from the soldier, or *miles.* As noted, one punishment for soldiers who abandoned their comrades under duress of battle was beating to death with *fustes,* or cudgels: the same punishment is humorously applied to comic *cinaedi.* When the *adulescens* at *Poenulus* 1320 has his slaves beat the soldier with the same *fustes,* he not only turns the accusation of cinaedism against his tormentor: he simultaneously lays claim to proper military identity at the wretched soldier's expense. Some years ago Jack Winkler clarified the rhetorical opposition between the hoplite and the *kinaidos* in Greek oratory and political invective.[89] The same opposition is implicit in Roman literature as well; not, I would argue, because the Romans read the Greeks (although they did), but because similar issues of honor, boundary limitation, and appropriate use of the body were being worked through by elite Roman males as by elite Greek males. Yet the Roman use of the *cinaedus* figure does seem to differ from the earlier Greek uses described by Winkler both in the tendency to situate the *cinaedus* as a threatening figure within the convivial, as well as the military, context and in the emphasis throughout the Roman (or Roman-era Greek) material on the bodily flexibility and expressivity of the *cinaedus.*

The rhetorical function of the *cinaedus* in describing proper military behavior is evident in what is perhaps the most famous (and complex) use of the term by Catullus, namely poem 29, in which he twice addresses *cinaedus* Romulus. Romulus is the founder of Rome, but he is also a military leader: an *imperator*, winner of the *spolia opima*, protector of the city from external invasion. As military leader he stands in contrast to the peaceable second king Numa.[90] During Catullus's lifetime Cicero had made extraordinary use of the military associations of Romulus in his orchestration of senatorial and other opposition to the so-called Catilinarian Conspiracy.[91] And in his own poem Catullus moves quickly from invocation of *cinaedus* Romulus to address of Caesar as *imperator unice* ("one and only general," 29.11), thus linking Romulus as a (cinaedic) general to Caesar. Catullus challenges *cinaedus* Romulus for seeming to witness and yet endure the hoarding of plunder from various provinces by a single aristocrat, Mamurra: "*Cinaedus* Romulus, will you see these things and will you bear them?" (*cinaede Romule, haec videbis et feres?* 29.5, 29.9). As *cinaedus*, Romulus is the opposite of what he should be. Even the simple word *feres*, meaning "will you bear?" hints at his debased status, as it refers not only to toleration or endurance but also to the physical burden the *cinaedus* bears when the weight of a dominant male or the pressure of cudgels is loaded on him (cf. the phrase *onustum fustibus* in Plautus).

Catullus uses other terms of sexual and bodily degradation to describe anyone — in addition to Romulus — who might tolerate the situation: "Who can see this, who can suffer it, besides a wanton and a glutton and a gambler?" (*quis hoc potest videre, quis potest pati, / nisi impudicus et vorax et aleo?* 29.1–2). At first glance the words *impudicus, vorax,* and *aleo* seem to suggest an equivalence between the one who tolerates Mamurra and Mamurra himself, because Mamurra will be seen to violate sexual ethics through his rampant adultery and to devour the resources of various provinces. But the words can also apply to the cinaedism of the "bearer" of Mamurra's burden: for a *cinaedus* can certainly be described as sexually wanton, voracious (Catullus elsewhere uses the term *vorax* specifically to describe the rectum of the *cinaedus* Vibennius junior, 33.4), and a gambler.[92] The irony of the situation is that it is Mamurra whose real behavior would seem to mark him as a *cinaedus*: he is the one who "proud and overflowing ambles through the bedrooms of all, like a little white dove or Adonis himself" (*et ille nunc superbus et superfluens / perambulabit omnium cubilia / ut albulus columbus aut Adoneus?* 29.6–8). Mamurra's commission of theft and adultery is bad enough, but there is something decidedly theatrical and overly expressive about his performance as well. As a dove or an Adonis, he turns himself, although a male, into an object of sexual desire.[93] Indeed he performs the very figure from mythology — Adonis — who, along with Ganymede, is con-

nected to cinaedism in Plautus's *Menaechmi* (*Men.* 144–45) and seems to
serve more generally as a figure of male attractiveness.[94] Mamurra's behavior, specifically his refusal to share booty from the provinces and his
disrespect for other men's sexual property as evidenced by his wanton
adultery, violates the ethics of *sodalitas* as well as of military camaraderie. For this reason he is a *cinaedus*, but then so too, at least potentially,
are those who tolerate him, including Caesar, Pompey, Catullus himself, in short everyone who aspires to live up to the example of Romulus. The poem clearly situates cinaedism and proper elite male behavior,
especially but not exclusively in a military context, as defining opposites
without specifying who, finally, owns each role.

Virtuosity and Its Discontents

Thus far we have been considering cinaedism as depicted in texts from
republican Rome, specifically the songs of Plautus and Catullus. The
very fact that the term *cinaedus* does not appear in classical prose, where
charges of sexual and convivial misconduct are nonetheless bandied
about with great frequency, suggests that the *cinaedus* remains, at least
to some degree, a figure of song: a performer of song and dance or a
social type to be reckoned with in theatrical and convivial contexts.[95]
The *cinaedus* is available for sexual penetration, but this is not the only
respect in which he threatens the integrity of the homosocial group,
whether military or convivial. He is also a thief and a glutton.[96] Most
striking, but also most difficult to comprehend, is the *cinaedus*'s persistent association with expressivity, even in the republican period. It is as
if the *cinaedus* gives away the game of conventional incorporating practices. His ability to mimic various characters and assume various sexual
roles, and his bodily pliability expose the constructedness of the incorporating practices of mainstream soldiers and *sodales*. This emphasis on
pliancy is apparent in the language applied to *cinaedi* — *mollis, malacus,
lubricus* — but also in some of the specific circumstances that generate
charges of cinaedism. In the *Menaechmi*, for example, Menaechmus II
assumes that Peniculus is charging him with cinaedism when he says
he saw him exit a *convivium* with a *palla*. The possibility of a charge
of cinaedism is overdetermined: theft of garments from a *convivium* is
grounds for the charge in Catullus's poem 25; the fact that a *palla* is a
woman's garment raises the issue of sexual protocol. In addition, this
particular scene inevitably puts the viewer in mind of the earlier scene
in which Menaechmus I had indeed appeared on stage with a *palla*.[97] In
that instance he tells Peniculus that he is imitating mythological paintings of the eagle's theft of Catameitus (Ganymede) or Venus's theft of
Adonis:

Tell me, have you never seen a painting on a wall
where the eagle snatches Catameitus or Venus takes Adonis?

dic mi, enumquam tu vidisti tabulam pictam in pariete
ubi aquila Catameitum raperet aut ubi Venus Adoneum?

(Plaut. *Men.* 143–44)

In the exchange that follows it is never quite made clear whether Menaechmus regards himself as resembling Ganymede (Catameitus) and Adonis, or the eagle and Venus, or both. He simply insists, repeatedly, that Peniculus acknowledge that he, Menaechmus I, is a "very appealing guy" (*dic hominem lepidissumum esse me,* 147). Both the explicitness of the imitation and the possibility that what Menaechmus is imitating is a pair of mythological males who are the object of sexual desire and sexual aggression, contribute to the association later in the play of Menaechmus II (confused with Menaechmus I) with a *cinaedus.* The passage also invites us to consider the relationship between cinaedism and slavery. As Eleanor Leach has noted, the image of the handsome Ganymede painted on the wall reminds us that the Romans could and did surround themselves with *deliciae,* both figuratively and literally.[98] The *cinaedus* is thus one who willingly chooses the self-exposure imposed upon the "handsome foreigner abducted by a potentate" — whether as a decorative addition to a dinner party or a commodified body in the slave market.[99]

The expressiveness of the *cinaedus* seems to account for Catullus's unexpected use of the adjective *cinaediorem* ("rather *cinaedus*-like") to describe the behavior of a woman. In Catullus 10 the poet describes a trip to the Forum to check out Varus's new girlfriend, whom he describes as "not without charm or sex appeal" (*non sane illepidum neque invenustum,* 10.4). Both Varus and the girl ask after Catullus's success in the province of Bithynia, specifically whether he has acquired a set of litter bearers. To make himself look more prosperous in the girl's eyes, he lies and boasts that he brought back eight strapping guys (*octo homines rector,* 10.20); whereupon the girl, "as befits one who is a rather *cinaedus*-like" (*ut decuit cinaediorem,* 10.24), asks if she can borrow the team and litter to take her down to the temple of Serapis. If we simply regard *cinaedus* as an all-purpose term of abuse, then it is easy enough to understand why Catullus describes the girl's behavior as *cinaedus*-like: she has called his bluff and successfully embarrassed him in front of his friend. He doesn't like her and showers her with insults, calling her now a *cinaedus,* later tasteless (*insulsa,* 10.33) and annoying (*molesta,* 10.33). But it seems worth noting that the specific characteristics that prompt the charge of cinaedism are that the girl takes Catullus literally and uses her sexual attractiveness to get her way with him. In both respects she undercuts his self-presentation as a good ol' boy, a *sodalis*. Indeed, the term *sodalis* shows up in his bogus explanation that she can't have the litter because his *sodalis* Cinna has it. He even appeals to the ethics of *sodalitas* as justification for his inability to lend her the litter and for his false claim of ownership:

> My buddy
> Gaius Cinna—actually, he bought it for himself.
> but what difference is it to me whether it's his or mine?
> I use it the same as if I had bought it for myself.

> meus sodalis
> Cinna est Gaius, — is sibi paravit.
> verum, utrum illius an mei, quid ad me?
> utor tam bene quam mihi pararim.
>
> (Catull. 10.29–32)

Of course, Catullus's assumption that *sodales* share and share alike perhaps exposes his real motive in going down to meet Varus's charming and sexy girlfriend: he wants a share of her, too. But by acting the *cinaedus* the girl has in effect exposed his desire, his posturing, and the insubstantiality of his claims of participation in *sodalitas*. Through the explicitness of his imitation or the literal-mindedness of her interpretation of an offhand claim, the *cinaedus* reveals the artificiality of the posturing—physical and verbal—of the *sodalis,* the mainstream male, and serves as a reminder that *sodalitas* is just as much a pose, just as much a bodily or verbal construct or performance as cinaedism. In this sense, it hardly matters whether the *cinaedus* is a genuine, historical "gender deviant," to use Craig Williams's phrase, or simply a theatrical and discursive scare figure: either way he has the power to threaten mainstream gender protocols, not necessarily directly, through open resistance, but through his exposure of the fact that they are protocols at all. The *cinaedus* lays bare the "public secret" that normative masculinity is itself an artifice. He uses the mimetic faculty not to produce second nature but to expose the operations of mainstream culture in its attempt to create second nature.[100]

Under the empire the social function of the *cinaedus* in elite discourse changes somewhat. Certainly there are still *cinaedi* who sing and dance and entertain at dinner parties: Pliny contrasts his own elegant entertainment, which consists of a comic actor, a professional reader, and a lyre player (*Ep.* 9.17.3; cf. 1.15.2) with that of other elite Romans who opt for "something pliant from a *cinaedus*, sarcastic from a *scurra*, and stupid from a buffoon" (*molle a cinaedo, petulans a scurra, stultum a morione, Ep.* 9.17.2). The context makes clear that the *cinaedus* is a professional entertainer, presumably a dancer of the sort "provoked" at the end of Plautus's *Stichus*. Martial seems to have a similar professional role in mind when he lists a *cinaedus* among the biological fathers of Cinna's many children: the others include a cook, a wrestling coach, a flute player, an overseer, and a buffoon (6.39.12).[101] The *cinaedus* is also associated, at least sometimes, with expressivity. For example, Aulus Gellius relates the story (which he attributes to Plutarch) that when the philosopher Arcesilaus spotted a rich man who, despite his reputation for sexual integrity, nonetheless had a voice that was subdued, hair that had been arranged artistically, and eyes that were playful and full of enticement and pleasure, he declared "It makes no difference by which body parts you are *cinaedi*, those behind or those in front" (*"Nihil interest,"* inquit, *"quibus membris cinaedi sitis, posterioribus an prioribus,"* Gell. 3.5; cf. Plut. *Quaest conv.* 7.5.3). The point of the story seems to be that the rich man, even though he never engages in shameful sexual intercourse, nonetheless is a *cinaedus* due to the overwrought and overly expressive nature of his voice, hair, and eyes.

Among the physiognomists, expressivity, and what we might call disarticulation of the body, are key signs of latent cinaedism or effeminacy. Thus Adamantius says that the androgynous man "moves all of his limbs" (*kineitai panta ta mēla, Scriptores physiognomici graeci et latini,* Forster 1.416.1–2) and "juts out" (*epithrōiskei,* F.1.416.2), while Polemon observes that such a man "frequently agitates his joints, as if everything were loose" (*et artus frequenter agitantem, tamquam si omnes laxi sint,* F 1.276.18–19). An early Greek physiognomist writing in the Peripatetic tradition notes that *cinaedi* are "knock-kneed" (*gonykrotos*) — an expression that seems to build upon Aristotle's identification of women as characterized by such a walk.[102] Interestingly, the Latin adapter of the treatise renders the expression *gonykrotos* as *genu flexibilis,* with flexible knee, which seems to fit the Roman notion of *cinaedi* as having particularly supple or pliant bodies. And then there is the peculiar belief that a *cinaedus* reveals himself by the fact that he scratches his head with a single finger: an action which some have read semiotically as a signal from one member of a subculture to another, but which might also be understood as the disarticulation of bodily performance into its smallest components.[103]

Despite such similarities in identification of the term *cinaedus* between republic and empire, as a term of abuse the word comes to be used in a very different way. Under the empire the charge of cinaedism, rather than being directed at a violation of performance guidelines, functions more as an attempt to reveal or expose the true *cinaedus* within.[104] Certainly this is the point of the physiognomists' list of signs by which true but hidden *cinaedia* can be unmasked. A man who is a *cinaedus* can be identified by bodily deportment as readily as one who is brave, timid, well-born, shameless, spirited, bitter, wrathful, gentle, ironic, cowardly, and so on (all from the Peripatetic treatise, chapters 13ff. = F 1.26ff.; most repeated in later essays by Polemon, Adamantius, etc.). Juvenal acknowledges familiarity with such categorization when in his second satire he denounces a philosopher who masquerades as a true man but in reality "is the best known ditch among the Socratic *cinaedi*" (*cum sis / inter Socraticos notissima fossa cinaedos*, 2.9–10). Juvenal's rhetorical assault begins with the general rule that you just can't trust facial expression (*fronti nulla fides*, 2.8), the implication being that one has to examine other aspects of bodily structure and practice. Phaedrus writes two poems, the point of which is to show that a person can look like a *cinaedus* but not in fact be one. In one the poet Menander seems out of place in a line of men drawn up in military formation (*extremo agmine*, Fab. 5.1.14). The tyrant Demetrius mocks him as a *cinaedus* until he learns his true identity, whereupon he describes him as "very handsome" (*formosior*, 5.1.18). The point seems to be that signs can be misread, but only because a person has a true identity behind the signs, against which their message is to be tested.[105] So too in appendix 10 Phaedrus describes an apparent *cinaedus* who turns out to be a great soldier (albeit still a thief). The point again seems not to be that cinaedism is a performance role rather than an identity but that looks can be deceiving when it comes to judging identity. By and large, though, looks are not deceiving, and as far as Martial is concerned (Martial being the source of the majority of poetic slurs against *cinaedi*), who is and who is not a *cinaedus* is pretty obvious, and no one ever crosses over from one side of the divide to the other.

This concern in the literature of the empire with the identification and belittlement of true *cinaedi* goes hand in hand with other changes in the construction of sexuality that characterize the Roman cultural revolution of the early principate, such as an emphasis on privacy as the context for sexual behavior, a concern with sexual technique, and a belief (close to that characterizing the late modern era) that sexual preference is determinative of personal identity.[106] Now, under a revamped or, in a sense, newly created system of sexuality, to be a *cinaedus* is not simply to step out of line at a *convivium*, to ask an overly literal question, to steal a garment as a bad joke: to be a *cinaedus* is to be radically and unalterably different from being a "real," heterosexual, penetrative man. Paradoxically, while the *cinaedus* continues, at least on occasion, to be overly expressive, under other circumstances he is virtually indistinguishable from a normative male. The great challenge for writers concerned with *cinaedi* is to expose them, to identify and call attention to the traits that reveal the true *cinaedus* within. No doubt there is still an element of game playing, of posturing, of shoring up images of masculinity in these charges of cinaedism. But there is also a newly developed sense of an essential difference between *cinaedi* and *viri* (the latter understood as *sodales* and *milites*), a difference that is particular to an individual and not just or even chiefly to a set of behaviors.[107] Cinaedism is as definitive of a person's character—and as important to know about in interacting with a stranger—as are courage, timidity, high birth, greed, malevolence, and all the topics that interest physiognomists, poets, fabulists, historians, and declaimers alike. In this sense the discourse of cinaedism comes to resemble the discourse of homo- and heterosexuality that emerges in the industrialized West in the late nineteenth and early twentieth centuries: not that the *cinaedus* is a homosexual but that the widespread belief in "true" *cinaedi* is a manifestation of a wider and deeper redefinition of subjectivity and identity.

This shift in the discourse of cinaedism is what makes the *cinaedus* less useful as a means of commenting on right and wrong self-presentation in the public sphere, that is, right and wrong performance of song, dance, or oratory. The *cinaedus* as "songster" is marginalized by his very professionalism, but the issue that cinaedism had raised in Plautus and Catullus—specifically expressivity as a challenge to the claim of "naturalness" as applied to the bodily practices of the dominant class —is still a serious one. Only now the issue of expressivity, or, better, overexpressivity, is itself carried by a different, more explicit sort of discourse. And so texts that approve or disapprove of song performances of all types come to focus specifically on questions of restrained, or traditional, versus expressionistic performance style. Indeed, every instance of individual performance, whether dance, or song, or literary recitation, or declamation, or oratory, is open to criticism for its expressivity (often in language similar to that used to identify *cinaedi,* terms like *fractus, mollis, laxus*) or praise for its restraint and discipline (with terms such as *severitas* or *diligentia*). This shift in focus (individual performance) and grounds (expressive or not) for evaluation is not just the result of the change in the conceptualization of the *cinaedus.* It is also a response to the change in the conceptualization of the performer as well, the very shift from corporate to individual performance made manifest in the changing body imagery we have traced in the poetry of Vergil and Ovid. Once again, song is both an indicator of and a contributor to the transformation in bodily practices that constitutes such an important, if neglected, component of Roman cultural and social history.[108]

As Nevio Zorzetti observes, any treatment of expressionism as a performance style must include consideration of the chapter on dancing in Macrobius's *Saturnalia* (314.4–15).[109] Macrobius adopts a position hostile to all dancing, and the examples he adduces of dancing aristocrats in the late republic are presented in order to problematize claims about the superior ethics of earlier Romans. But the language he uses — and, more important, the language he cites — make it clear that already in the middle and late republic, performances were judged by at least some Romans on a scale ranging from severe, austere, dignified (all good) to overwrought, flowing, luxurious, expressive (all bad). Macrobius quotes Sallust's disapproval of Sempronia not for dancing, but for dancing very well (*non quod saltare sed quod optime*, 3.14.5). He cites Scipio Aemilianus Africanus's expression of outrage at his discovery that freeborn youths and maidens are attending a dancing school. Not just any dancing school, mind you, but one also frequented by *cinaeduli*, one that teaches the performance of others' songs (*cantare*, i.e., to sing what another has composed) and dancing with expressive use of castanets.[110] And his criticism culminates in paraphrase and quotation of Cato the Elder's attack on Caelius, a senator, whom Cato nonetheless describes as a "traveling showman and a Fescennine performer" (*spatiatorem et Fescenninum vocat*, 3.14.9), on the grounds that

> "He gets down from his nag, and right there strikes little poses and
>   tells jokes."
> And elsewhere he [Cato] alleges against the same Caelius,
> "What is more he sings expressively wherever he feels like it, he even
>   performs Greek verses, he declaims jokes, he tries out different
>   voices, he strikes little poses."

> descendit de cantherio, inde staticulos dare, ridicularia fundere
> et alibi in eundem
> praeterea cantat ubi collibuit, interdum Graecos versus agi, iocos
>   dicit, voces demutat, staticulos dat.[111]
>
> (Macrob. *Sat.* 3.14.9 = *ORF* 8.114, 8.115)

Rather than indicating a generalized disapproval of dancing on the part of the Romans,[112] passages like these point to a persistent critique of an overly expressive performance style. The passage from Cato groups with Caelius's striking of poses his singing imitatively, his performance or enactment of Greek verses, and his adoption of different voices, as well as his unseemly telling of jokes. Although a senator, a man who of all men should enact the proper bodily habitus, Caelius, at least according to Cato, reveals the unnaturalness of aristocratic comportment by adopting a variety of poses, voices, perhaps even characters. A similar critique seems to underlie Scipio's attack on the dancing children: yes, he intimates that they are being exposed to improper sexual influences or temptations; but he is also concerned that they are not learning the bodily practices, automatisms, and rhythms appropriate to the "upright," "dignified," "severe" Roman male. Many passages indicate the acceptability of dancing on the part of elite Romans—but it must be a type of dancing that resembles that of the Salian priests, either the specific movement of the *tripudium,* or the manly style of performance.

The concern with proper modulation of bodily rhythms that is implicit in the early texts cited by Macrobius is made explicit in Cicero's *Laws.* The relevant passage draws heavily on Plato's treatment of music, but the fact that Cicero has adapted Plato's suggestions to the specifics of the Roman situation makes it clear we are dealing with Cicero's considered judgment and not just with reliance on Greek precedent. In proposing laws for the ideal Roman state, Cicero specifies:

> At public celebrations such as take place without chariot races or athletic competitions, let them moderate the joy of the people in song and lyre playing and flute playing and unite it with respect for the gods.

> loedis publicis quod sine curriculo et sine certatione corporum fiat, popularem laetitiam in cantu et fidibus et tibiis moderanto eamque cum divum honore iungunto. (Cic. *Leg.* 2.22)

In his explication of the proposed law Cicero makes it clear that its aim is to inculcate the proper bodily schemes and movements of the people through music. He discusses at some length the potential of music both to calm and to excite assembled crowds and contrasts the "pleasing austerity" (*severitas iucunda*) of the measures of Livius and Naevius with reaction to contemporary music, which prompts audiences to "jump about and twist their necks and eyes along with the twists of the measures" (*illud quidem video quae solebant quondam conpleri severitate iucunda Livianis et Naevianis modis, nunc ut eadem exultent et cervices oculosque pariter cum modorum flexionibus torqueant,* 2.39). Jumping about (*exultatio*) may not in itself be a problem, since it is the standard movement of the Salian priests. But exultation on the part of a large crowd, combined with a close adaptation of bodily movement to inappropriate music is unacceptable, to such a degree, according to Cicero, that the Greeks of old punished such behavior severely (*graviter olim ista vindicabat vetus*

illa Graecia) because they understood that it led the way to the other-
throw of entire states (totas civitates everteret, 2.39). Cicero's remarks en-
capsulate a widespread ancient understanding of the relationship between musical measures and bodily deportment, one found as well in
the legends describing great musicians' ability even to alter the movement of trees, rocks, animals, and birds. At the same time, he provides
us with a terminological distinction that obtains in various later discussions of proper and improper performance styles, namely the contrast
between severitas and flexiones. Severitas becomes a key term of approval
for acceptable performance style in music, dance, oratory, and poetry;
while flexio/flectere joins such terms as mollis and lubricus to describe inappropriate, overly expressive performance modes of the various arts.[113]

We get a clear sense of the approbatory tone of the term severus
from Aulus Gellius's story of the actor Polus who returned to the stage
after the death of his son with a performance of Sophocles' Electra.
As the female character Electra, he managed—as always—to perform
with skill and austerity (scite atque asseverate, NA 6.5.2). Gellius illustrates
this skill and austerity by telling how Polus's wailing over the fictional
ashes of Orestes "filled everything not with simulacra and imitations,
but with true and vibrant grief and lamentation" (opplevit omnia non
simulacris neque imitamentis, sed luctu atque lamentis veris et spirantibus,
6.5.7). Polus is clearly a virtuoso (he performs scite, knowingly), but his
virtuosity, rather than exposing the artificiality that characterizes any
and all performance, is matched by the authenticity of his emotion.
Gellius implicitly acknowledges the specialness of this situation: how
many times can a favorite son die, after all? Still, the anecdote points
toward a deeper desire on the part of imperial Romans to have the performance and the true sentiment somehow correspond, for knowing-
ness and dignity or austerity to reinforce one another.[114]

The desire for a virtuoso performance that is dignified rather than
overly expressive is specifically attributed to (some of) his Roman contemporaries by the Greek author Plutarch. One of the problēmata, or
questions, posed in his collection of table talk concerns the right type
of entertainment for a dinner party (Quaest. Conv. 7.8 = Moralia 711a–
713f). Plutarch's friend Diogenianus, a sophist named Philip, and Plutarch himself all participate in the discussion. Diogenianus announces
a preference for a new type of entertainment now gaining popularity at
Rome, namely the dramatic performance of Plato's dialogues by trained
slaves.[115] Interestingly, his praise of this new fashion focuses more on
the performance style than on the content of the dialogues, as he com-
mends the "fitting of the presentation to the character of the participants
in the dialogue" (hypokrisis prepousa toi ethei, Mor. 711c), the molding
(plasma, 711c) of voice, and the use of "bodily scheme and delivery that

follows what is being said" (*skhēma kai diatheseis hepomenai tois legomenois*, 711c). It is as if Diogenianus (or Plutarch) recognizes that he is coming dangerously close to a description of an effeminate, submissive sort of performance, one in which the supple, disarticulated body of the actor is made to do another's bidding, and so he clarifies that this type of presentation is welcomed by "men of dignity and charm" (*austēroi kai kharientes*, 711c) and rejected by those who are "unmanly and enervated" (*anandroi kai diatethrymennoi* [cf. *fractus*], 711c) and "lacking in musical culture and experience of beauty" (*di' amousian kai apeirokalian*, 711c). Indeed, he argues, if the innovation does not take hold, it will be because "womanliness is overpowering" (*epikratei gar hē thēlytē*, 711c).

As the episode progresses, we learn of Diogenianus's distaste for the vulgarity and explicitness of Old Comedy and his affection for the subtle eroticism of Menander—a poet whose verses can appropriately be read to men "shortly going home to their own wives" (*meta mikron apiousi para tās heauton gynaikās*, 712c). Plutarch himself chimes in, praising the lyre and the flute, but only as accompaniment for words. Indeed, he suggests, the satyr Marsyas (the quintessential figure of popular culture in Roman myth and art)[116] was punished by the gods for daring to offer instrumental music as rival to the combination of song and lyre (713d). The episode thus illustrates a careful negotiation among elite males in a convivial context between the appeal of virtuosity and the implicit potential for unmanliness in all virtuoso performance. That the discussion focuses on performances by slaves does not diminish its relevance for the self-construction of the elite male, who, after all, is himself called upon over and over again to perform for the approval and pleasure of others.[117] In Diogenianus's view mimetic performance in a style that pleases the austere ones in the audience (with *austēroi* here doing the work of the Latin *severi*) is acceptable. Plutarch observes that in the final analysis, the words in the performance matter, with melody and rhythm serving only as a sauce or relish (*hosper opson*, 713c) on them, and he infers as well that skilled mimesis of Plato is acceptable at least in part because it is mimesis of Plato and not of some less authoritative figure. The elite figures of the dialogue want to have their cake and eat it too: that is, they seek to incorporate the virtuosity of the *cinaedi* in a presentation that reinforces the traditional primacy of voice. The blustering interjection of the sophist Philip to the effect that Plato of all people should not be employed in this way (711d) seems to be introduced for the express purpose of being ignored. Indeed, it is in part the authority of Plato's *logoi* that legitimizes the pleasure derived from the submissiveness of the virtuoso mimesis.

A second episode from Plutarch's table talk further illustrates the conflicting claims of traditional manliness and expressive virtuosity as well as the assertion of the authority of language as a means of reconciling the two. In this short narrative we hear of a symposium at which a flute player in effect hypnotized his audience with his evocative playing and licentious movements. He sought, in Plutarch's words, "to do with them what he pleased" (*Mor.* 704d)[118] and created a situation in which the guests "were no longer content to shout and clap from their places, but finally most of them leapt up and joined in the dancing, with movements disgraceful for a gentleman, though quite in keeping with that kind of rhythm and melody" (704d). When the guests have settled down, they are subjected to a series of lectures by the host Callistratus, by Plutarch's brother Lamprias, and by Plutarch himself. The gist of these critiques is that such reactions to music are characteristic of beasts, not free men; that they demonstrate conquest of the body and the mind by an outside force; and that the proper way to enjoy music is to turn to the works of Euripides and Pindar and Menander. It is not music per se that is problematical, but music that is not restrained by language, "holy and august writings, noble songs and poems and discourses" (706e). Plutarch revives the Platonic-Socratic argument concerning the power of certain types of music to foster inappropriate mimesis, but now he seeks to address the problem not by banning musicians or types of music but by regulating music through language. The ability of unaccompanied music to "corrupt our judgment" (706b) concerns Lamprias, especially because it is available free of charge in public places, with therefore no anxiety about expense to counterbalance the pleasure it provides. As a result, according to Lamprias, "when we fall among Sirens," we must take refuge with the Muses (706d).

Recognition of the role of virtuosity in both presenting and fostering a breakdown of traditional patterns of bodily comportment underlies many of the episodes of theatrical history at Rome. For example, Velleius Paterculus argues that it was due to the *severitas* of the state that Rome so long resisted the construction of a permanent theater (1.15.3). Historians suggest that the long-standing preference for construction and dismantling of the theater on an annual basis made clear the connection between the theater and the ruling class, which could give it or take it away of its own volition.[119] Such is certainly the case, but Velleius's use of the suggestive word *severitas* indicates another, related motive: the potential for virtuoso performance to move from traditional restraint to expressivity, as it did at Callistratus's symposium, and with comparable consequences. This seems to be what Cicero has in mind when he describes the inappropriate movements of crowds in the theaters in *De Legibus,* and it is a possibility exploited by the emperors and others who organized claques of rhythmic clappers, whose performance led others to succumb to their *numeri.*

Such submission — to the rhythm of the flute or clappers, to the demands of mimetic storytelling, to another's sexual forays — can constitute a type of play, as we have seen. If regulated by larger social patterns
of play and seriousness, rehearsal and reality, slavery and freedom, it can
be considered acceptable, as Plutarch's table-talkers implicitly acknowledge. The conceptual opposite of such play can be *seria,* but it can also be
severitas — both seriousness and the (etymologically) related concept of
severity. The relationship between the two (play and severity) structures
one of the fables of Phaedrus, entitled "De Lusu et Severitate," which recounts Atticus's encounter with Aesop as he played among some boys.

> When a certain Atticus spotted Aesop in a crowd of boys
> playing with nuts, he stopped
> and laughed at him as if he were insane. But the old man,
> more derider than derided, as soon as he sensed what was going on,
> placed a taut bow in the middle of the street.
> "Come over here, egghead, and explain what I just did."
> A crowd gathers. Atticus torments himself for a long time
> but he cannot understand the basis of the challenge that has been
>   posed.
> Finally he concedes. The victorious sophist declares:
> You'll break the bow quickly if you always hold it tensed,
> but if you let it relax, it will be useful when you want it to be.
> Similarly, play ought to be given to the mind from time to time
> that it might better return to cogitation when you so desire."
>
> Puerorum in turba quidam ludentem Atticus
> Aesopum nucibus cum vidisset, restitit
> et quasi delirum risit. Quod sensit simul
> derisor potius quam deridendus senex,
> arcum retensum posuit in media via:
> "Heus!" inquit "sapiens, expedi quid fecerim."
> Concurrit populus. Ille se torquet diu
> nec quaestionis positae causam intellegit,
> Novissime succumbit. Tum victor sophus:
> "Cito rumpes arcum semper si tensum habueris;
> At si laxaris, cum voles erit utilis.
> Sic lusus animo debent aliquando dari,
> ad cogitandum melior ut redeat tibi."
>   (Phaedr. *Fab.* 3.14, "De Lusu et Severitate")

The fable follows the pattern of many Aesopic stories, with the man
of the people outsmarting his condescending social superiors, often,

as here, with an action that can best be described as a performance.[120]
There is some attempt on Phaedrus's part to update the traditional context to one more specifically Roman: the foiled *sapiens* of the fable is
identified as *quidam Atticus*, either "a certain man of Attica" or, "a certain Atticus" — Atticus being of course the name of Cicero's close friend,
whose bloodline became mingled with that of the Julio-Claudian emperors. The fable seeks to legitimize *ludus*, but only as an activity that
contributes to more serious enterprise, in this case cogitation.[121] Indeed,
the net effect of the poem is to marginalize *ludus* in the realm of boys,
nuts, and street-corner preachers: like *ludus* itself, all useful, but only up
to a point. The concept of *severitas*, never mentioned in the poem except in the title, nevertheless remains the unchallenged mark and goal
of proper deportment.

If the texts that express elite male ideology with respect to performance styles sometimes acknowledge the competing attractions of
submission and severity or of tradition and expressivity, in other cases
they are ferocious in their invective against the submissive or expressive
style. Seneca, Juvenal, and Tacitus all associate such expressivity with
womanliness and criticize it in the harshest terms, especially when they
observe it in other members of the elite. For Seneca, in letter 114, the
target is Maecenas, in both his life and his oratory. While acknowledging that oratorical style can be either too inflated or too broken, it is
the latter possibility that draws his attention. The expressions *infracta*,
"broken into pieces," and *in morem cantici ducta*, "fashioned in the manner of song" (*Ep.* 114.1), used to describe the bad oratory that will draw
Seneca's wrath throughout the letter, not only mark a dangerous crossing of the boundary between oratory and song; they also associate bad
oratory with a particular kind of musical performance. The term *infractus*, together with its simplex form *fractus*, shows up repeatedly in descriptions of *cinaedi*, and the use of the expression *ducta*, "having been
led," describes a style that has been made to submit to external constraints — in this case, someone else's rhythmical or melodic pattern.[122]
In opposition to appropriate style, which is healthy, composed, serious, temperate (*si ille sanus est, si compositus, gravis temperans*, 114.3), bad
style is the expression of a spirit that is languid (*animus elanguit*, 114.3),
that drags its limbs and moves its feet sluggishly (*trahi membra et pigre
moveri pedes*, 114.3). "Don't you see," Seneca challenges his reader, "that
if the spirit is effeminate, its softness is apparent even in a man's gait;
if it is sharp and fierce, his pace will be agitated?" (*Non vides, si animus
elanguit, trahi membra et pigre moveri pedes? si ille effeminatus est, in ipso
incessu apparere mollitiam? si ille acer est et ferox, concitari gradum?* 114.3)
All you have to do, according to Seneca, is read some of the surviving
writings of Maecenas to conjure up the image of a man who pranced

(*incesserit*,114.6) around the city with his tunics untied (*solutis tunicis*, 114.6), who appeared in every public gathering with a *pallium* covering his head, except for the ears, as if he were the fugitive slave of a wealthy man in some mime (*in omni public coetu sic apparuerit ut pallio velaretur caput exclusis utrimque auribus, non aliter quam in mimo fugitivi divitis solent*, 114.6). A tender and flowing style is to be expected of one born a wimp (*delicati tenera et fluxa*, 114.20).[123]

> But what you see those guys pursue, who pluck or interpluck their
>   beards,
> who shave their lips a little too closely
> and scrape what's left, even down below
> who don raincoats of shameless hue
> who wear see-through togas!
> who are unwilling to do anything that would escape the eyes of
>   mortals:
> they provoke those who look at them and turn them against
>   themselves
> they wish — mark my word! — to be seized/rebuked
> even as they are stared at.
>
> That's the style of Maecenas!
>
> quod vides istos sequi qui aut vellunt barbam aut intervellunt
> qui labra pressius tondent
> et adradunt servata et summissa cetera parte
> qui lacernas coloris inprobi sumunt,
> qui perlucentem togam,
> qui nolunt facere quicquam quod hominum oculis transire liceat:
> inritant illos et in se avertunt
> volunt vel reprehendi
> dum conspici.
>
> Talis est oratio Maecenatis . . .
>
>   (Sen. *Ep.* 114.21)

Seneca's description of Maecenas makes it clear that the polarity between severity and expressivity is not unique to musical performance: it informs, as here, descriptions of oratorical style, delivery, indeed everyday life. In the process of rebuking this shameful corruption, Seneca reinforces our sense that what is disturbing about it is precisely its visibility, its making open to scrutiny the structures of language and bodily presentation best left mystified, bound up, obscured. Seneca draws upon the diagnostic technique of the physiognomists, who can tell a person's character from his demeanor, and directs their insights against a real, historical individual, one who fashioned himself a virtuoso of sorts and a patron of other virtuosos. The ostensible topic of Seneca's letter is right and wrong literary style, but its focus, inevitably, I would argue, given literature's status in Roman antiquity as both a textual and a bodily practice, is on the body of Maecenas as well as on his text. For Seneca, Maecenas is the *fons et origo* of the very problem of virtuosity that plagues him and fellow elite Romans. And while Seneca's tone is entirely scornful, it is a scorn that perhaps in spite of itself acknowledges the attraction of the scorned performer. Everything about Maecenas is open for scrutiny, according to Seneca. His toga is transparent (*perlucentem*, 114.21). He does nothing that he does not wish to have pass before the eyes of others. He stirs them up but also encourages them (the word *irrito* has both meanings). He turns them *in se*, against himself but also toward himself. His desire, expressed in the Latin verb *reprehendo*, is to be rebuked, but also, as the word indicates, to be laid hold of, even as he is gazed upon. In a sense, Seneca's description of Maecenas recapitulates not just the imagery but also the movement of Catullus's poem about Thallus *cinaedus* (a man, it should be noted, who also made off with the *pallium* of another, 25.6): what starts out as an attack ends up an acknowledgment of the desirability of all that has been laid bare, disarticulated, languidly presented.[124]

If Seneca acknowledges, perhaps unintentionally, the appeal of the expressive style even as he denounces it, Juvenal and Tacitus appear to be made of sterner stuff. In the case of Tacitus, the language of dissolute, fluid, disarticulated performance is concentrated in his account of the empress Messalina, especially her behavior at Rome during the fateful days of Claudius's journey to Ostia.[125] He presents her flowing toward unfamiliar lusts (*ad incognitas libidines profluebat, Ann.* 11.26.1). She violates the decorum of the *convivium*, lying together with the consul designate, embracing and kissing him, in anticipation of a night of conjugal license (11.27). She perverts religious ritual with a simulacrum of a harvest festival (*simulacrum vindemiae*, 11.31.2), with a flirtatious chorus resounding all about (*strepente circum procaci choro*, 11.31.2). The latter scene combines elements of theatrical performance (Silius's *cothurni* or "buskins," the presence of the chorus) and of religious ritual (the women in attendance are said to resemble bacchants either sacrificing or going insane), with Messalina as the virtuoso at the center of attention. With her all is fluidity: she is loosened by luxury (*solutior luxu*, 11.31.2), lakes (of grape juice!) flow (*fluere lacus*); her hair flows too (*crine fluxo*).[126] Even her colleague Vettius Valens's remark that he spied a ferocious storm coming from the direction of Ostia is said to have slipped (*lapsa*) from him. Whether Messalina's marriage to Silius was real or not, the expressivity of her performance, both in content and style, demands restraining action on the part of her husband. As Tacitus puts it, in a curious reminiscence of Plutarch's Diogenianus (*epikratei gar hē thēlytē*), there was to be no mercy "because the deformity of the crimes was prevailing" (*nulla cuiusquam misericordia, quia flagitiorum deformitas praevalebat*, 11.32.3). The sensual beauty of Messalina's performance becomes, under the gaze of imperial ideology, a hideous manifestation of criminality. Unlike Thallus and Maecenas, whose bodily practice, while despised, draws the attention and the desire of their observers, Messalina, though within sight of Claudius and his advisers (*in adspectu*, 11.34.1), cannot get him even to listen to her. Indeed, he averts his eyes from a notebook her accuser presents that details her lustful acts (*simul codicillos libidinum indices tradidit, quis visus Caesaris averteret*, 11.34.2). As the narrative progresses, she vanishes from the scene while her colleagues in vice are dispatched. Claudius, at his wine, seems to be softening in his anger (*languescere ira*, 11.37.2), and so the freedman Narcissus bursts forth (*prorumpit*) and gives the order for her execution. Messalina is found in the Lucullan gardens, poured forth (*fusam*) on the earth, with her mother beside her, and dispatched by the tribune. The news is delivered to Claudius — still at dinner (*epulanti*) — and he neglects to ask for details, instead proceeding with his *convivium* as is his custom (*poposcitque poculum et solita convivio celebravit*, 11.38.2). Messalina's interaction with Silius is retroactively interpreted as a kind of convivial entertainment, one rejected despite — or perhaps because of — the expressivity, the fluidity of its style. The story of her downfall confirms the importance of bodily presentation as a subject of history.

In his second and sixth satires Juvenal develops distinctive variations on the theme of male desire aroused by sensuous performance. Satire 2 features males who choose to make spectacles of themselves and thereby arouse one another. Satire 6 denounces female spectators who succumb to the allure of expressive male performance. Although the focus in both satires is on what Juvenal wishes us to regard as a perverted performance style, each — as is to be expected in satire — implies the existence of a morally preferable (i.e., traditional) alternative. Somewhat paradoxically, while both satires argue for the naturalness of traditional sex roles and traditional performance styles, in their detailed description of widespread adoption of alternative roles and styles, they end up confirming the artificiality of all such postures. The overwrought tone of Juvenalian satire, especially in its attack on the sexual aspect of public performance, is itself evidence of the instability of elite incorporating practices in his day and age. And the performance style his text invites us to imagine, the blend of the indignant diatribist and the mocking *scurra,* to the extent that it is presented as performance, projects a sense of knowing awareness of the constructedness of bodily practices as itself a distinguishing characteristic of elite masculine identity (i.e., Juvenal is hip). Juvenalian satire inverts the long-standing relationship of playful and real, making playfulness the characteristic stance of the authoritative male, the possessor of autonomous voice.[127]

Satire 2 announces a desire to avoid all those who lecture on morals, pretending to be Curii (i.e., traditional Romans) while living Bacchanalia. The satirist picks a fight — as often — with his competitors for the moral high ground, philosophers, and in the process differentiates between two life-styles, one traditional, the other wanton. The distinction between life-styles quickly turns into a distinction between styles of bodily performance. The satirist exempts from his critique those who are self-evidently "sick." At one level, he seems to be suggesting that the tried-and-true signs of cinaedism, demeanor and gait (*vultu . . . incessuque,* 2.17), are no longer adequate for uncovering the latent sensualist: his poem will represent an advance in the craft of physiognomic detective work. But there is also a suggestion that some *cinaedi* are so by nature, whereas others are by choice (on those who are born *delicati,* cf. the remarks of Seneca, *Ep.* 114.20). Juvenal expresses pity for the *simplicitas* and *furor* of Peribomius (*Sat.* 2.18), for a performance that is true because inborn (*verius . . . magis ingenus,* 2.15–16), but has only disdain for those who speak of virtue while flexing their ass muscles (*de virtute locuti / clunem agitant,* 2.19–20). The gist of the satire seems to be that such "wannabe" perverts should either keep it to themselves (i.e., adopt a different performance style) or return to traditional patterns of masculinity, as figured in the exempla that dot the poem: the Curii (2.3, 2.153), Cato (2.40), the Marcelli and Fabii (2.145, 146), Catulus (2.146), Paulus (2.146), Fabricius (2.154), Camillus (2.154), and the countless youth who lost their lives at Cremera and Cannae (2.155) or who prevailed in the conquest of Britain (2.161) and the defense of the Armenian frontier (2.164). What infuriates and frustrates the speaker of the satire is the ability of present-day *cinaedi* both to hide and to flaunt their difference. At times, we are told, their numbers protect them from the harsh punishment of the Scantinian law. Their wives can be bought off in order to keep their secrets (*arcana,* 2.61). They don fancy jewelry in private (*domi,* 2.84) and carry out secret orgies (*talia secreta coluerunt orgia taeda,* 2.91). And yet their actions are known precisely because they are so numerous, because they discuss their plans to attend a same-sex wedding in earshot of others (2.132ff.). What hasn't yet been made public will be soon enough (*fient / fient ista palam,* 2.135–36). Their life-style — and their performance style — is one of expressivity, indeed of flaunting. Creticus, we learn, likes to plead cases in a transparent gown (*multicia,* 2.66, 76;

perluces, 2.78). Even when on military assignment, men like Otho carry mirrors, worry about their fingernails, put on face packs, and speak in those weakened, crushed, mincing voices (*fracta voce,* 2.111).

As for the women of satire 6, Juvenal is concerned less with questions of secrecy and exposure and more with reveling in the details of their masculine lustfulness. The male desire that cinaedic performance has sought to foster from Plautus onward is now projected onto women; women's adoption of the male perspective is what makes of them monstrosities. Nor is the eroticism associated with expressivity limited to a single type of performance. Here, perhaps more clearly than in any other ancient text, expressivity is presented as a potential characteristic of virtually every performance genre. Bathyllus performs a supple pantomime (*molli saltante,* 6.62) of the myth of Leda: Tuccia loses control of her bladder and Apula moans in orgastic ecstasy (6.63–64). Urbicus does a rendition of Autonoe in an Atellan farce, and Aelia falls in love with him (6.72). A comic actor, a singer, a tragic performer all receive the amatory attention of lustful women (6.73–74; cf. 379, 396). A *citharoedus,* a *choraules,* a *murmillo* all are potential cuckolders of good Roman males (6.76–81). The language used to describe these male performers or their female counterparts is the language familiar from descriptions of cinaedic performance throughout the ages. They dance and speak in a supple, subtle manner (*molli saltante,* 6.63; *dicas haec mollius,* 6.198; *vox mollior,* O 23), they incite the loins of their listeners (*lumbos incitat,* 6.314–15); they challenge others to rival their sensuality (*provocat,* 321; cf. Plaut. *Stich.* 770, where *cinaedi* are called to a challenge dance); they move their haunches enticingly and in a fluid manner (*fluctum crisantis* 6.322). Indeed, they are worse than the *cinaedi* of old, for none of what they do is done by way of play, everything is serious:

> Nothing there will be performed as play, everything will take place
> as true and real. In this way Priam frigid with age
> or the jug of Nestor can be heated up.

> nil ibi per ludum simulabitur, omnia fient
> ad verum, quibus incendi iam frigidus aevo
> Laomedontiades et Nestoris hirnea possit.

> (Juv. *Sat.* 6.324–26)

Against the overly expressive performer—male or female, named or unnamed, overt *cinaedus* or inflamed convivialist—stands the responsible, dignified Roman male. In Juvenal's poem 2 he comes under a variety of names, all from the distant past. In poem 6 he moves closer

to the present, appearing in the form of a brief reference to the orator
and teacher of rhetoric, Quintilian:

> Urbicus gets a laugh during an Atellan farce
> with his imitation of Autonoe, impoverished Aelia falls in love with
>   him.
> The fly of a comedian is undone, for a high price at that,
> and many a woman wants Chrysogonus after he's sung.
> Hispulla gets off on a tragedian: do you really expect Quintilian to be
>   loved?

> Urbicus exodio risum movet Atellanae
> gestibus Autonoes, hunc diligit Aelia pauper.
> solvitur his magno comoedi fibula, sunt quae
> Chrysogonum cantare vetent, Hispulla tragoedo
> gaudet: an expectas ut Quintilianus ametur?

(Juv. *Sat.* 6.71–75)

Quintilian seems to have been selected as a representative not just of a
different genre of performance but of a different style or mode as well.
No see-through tunic or mincing voice for him — as anyone would know
who had the least familiarity with Quintilian's obsessive rules concerning management of all aspects of delivery.[128]

But perhaps the most compelling and well-rounded exemplum of
the dignified elite, male performer is the one Pliny the Younger creates of himself, particularly in his numerous references to his participation in literary recitations. Little chance of Pliny appearing as heir
of the republican *cinaedus:* instead he works hard not to fall into the
opposite extreme and instead to temper severity with sweetness. Pliny's
self-presentation complements the negative accounts of Seneca, Tacitus, and Juvenal (one could easily add Persius to this list) with a nu-
anced depiction of an up-to-date yet acceptable performance style. It
also allows us to see the recitation of standard "literary" genres as subject to the same protocols of evaluation that characterize other types of
song. Once again we are reminded that even literature is a bodily practice in ancient Rome, and that for all of the efforts by its proponents to
differentiate it from popular or musical culture, it remains part of that
culture and benefits from interpretation as such.

We get a sense of Pliny's sense of the ideal recitation in his description of the young Calpurnius Piso, whom he had the good fortune of
hearing at his literary debut, a presentation of a poem on an astronomi-
cal topic (*katasterismon, Ep.* 5.17.2). Piso's poem is written in elegiacs —

a dangerous move, given their potential association with softness—but an appropriate one, in view of the performer's youth.[129] The language Pliny uses to describe the poem is at first worrisome: flowing, gentle, and free from knots (*scripta elegis erat fluentis et teneris et enodibus*, 5.17.2). We may well wonder how this performance differed from that of the much-abused Maecenas of Seneca's letter. Have standards changed? Or is something else underway here? The answer comes quickly, for Pliny informs us that the performance was in fact an artful but varied presentation (*apte enim et varie*, 5.17.2: the terms can apply to both the literary style of the poem and the performance style of the reciter). Young Calpurnius managed to combine lofty with low, thin with full, cheerful with severe, all handled with equal skill (*excelsa depressis, exilia plenis, severis iucunda mutabat, omnia ingenio pari*, 5.17.2). His voice was very sweet, but the sweetness was tempered with modesty, much vigor, much care in his face—both great accessories for a reciter (*commendabat haec voce suavissima, vocem verecundia: multum sanguinis, multum sollicitudinis in ore, magna ornamenta recitantis*, 5.17.3). Pliny responded with many and long kisses, and he urged him on with praise that he might continue as he had begun (*multum ac diu exosculatus adulescentem, qui est acerrimus stimulus monendi, laudibus incitavi, pergeret qua coepisset*, 5.17.4). As Florence Dupont notes, the passage suggests that the *recitatio* has replaced the funeral *laudatio* as the occasion of a noble youth's debut.[130] Certainly Pliny reminds us of this fact when he concludes the letter with reference to *gloria* (5.17.6), an aristocratic type of renown, and with the desire that noble homes henceforth contain something beautiful besides their death masks (*mireque cupio ne nobiles nostri nihil in domibus suis pulchrum nisi imagines habeant*, 5.17.6).

But the passage suggests another type of institutional surrogation as well (i.e., besides the substitution of *recitatio* for *laudatio*), for the occasion of the *recitatio* has come to resemble that of the *convivium*. Here, instead of poetry being composed on the spot, as for example in Catullus 50, a prepared text is recited, but the reciter is expected to have the mix of qualities—severity and charm, sweetness and modesty—that characterizes the right kind of convivialist or *sodalis* throughout the ages. And just as the *sodalis* of earlier times ran the risk, with the wrong kind of behavior, of being perceived as a *cinaedus*, so here Calpurnius Piso is an object of erotic attraction, an expressive performer, but within limits. Unlike Catullus, who crosses a crucial boundary in longing for Calvus after the *commissatio*, Pliny is satisfied with kisses—albeit many and long-lasting ones (*multum ac diu exosculatus adulescentem*, 5.17.4). And if there is any stimulation going on, it is not so much Calpurnius enticing the audience (although this possibility plays just below the surface, for example, in Pliny's use of the term *pulchrum*, 5.17.6), as the audience, in the person of Pliny, inciting (*incitavi*) Calpurnius to pass the torch, as it were, from his ancestors to his heirs (*lumenque quod sibi maiores praetulissent posteris ipse praeferret*, 5.17.4). The reference to ancestors and heirs, together with the later optimistic prediction that the current *saeculum* will not be sterile or effete (5.17.6), again marks the episode as a rite of passage, celebrating the sexual as well as the literary coming-of-age of the young Calpurnius. As it has long been, song is here both a part of the rite and the expression of the passage that has in effect already occurred: Calpurnius has indeed found his voice. He has become the ideal singer. He has passed from *ludus* to *seria* under circumstances that demand of him a certain autonomous, individual virtuosity. And he has exercised that virtuosity, pressed the limits of its potential for expressivity and erotic appeal, without succumbing to cinaedism of any sort.[131]

While Pliny is too tactful to say as much directly, several passages that describe his own participation in recitation make of him a grown-up Calpurnius, one who successfully and continually negotiates the boundaries between text and body, body and voice, play and seriousness, virtuosity and severity. In letter 2.19, for example, he describes the inherent difficulty attendant on reciting an oration. There is a forcefulness and heat to the oratorical setting (*impetum . . . caloremque*, 2.19.2), one that is matched by the stance and gait, the discourse, in effect, "the vigor of the body consonant with all the movements of the soul" (*omnibusque motibus animi consentaneus vigor corporis*, 2.19.2). In the recitation hall, on the other hand, there is the danger that the audience will languish (*relanguescit*, 2.19.4), that it will long for something sweet and resonant rather than austere and compressed (*potius dulcia haec et sonantia quam austera et pressa*, 2.19.6). To respond to the challenge of the recitation hall, the sitting (*sedentes*) reciter has bodily resources, specifically eyes and hands (*oculi, manus*, 2.19.4), but Pliny is not certain that these will be enough to meet the demand for blandishment and piquancy (*blandimentis . . . aculeis*, 2.19.4). In effect, Pliny tells us, the recitation hall invites an expressivity and sensuality of behavior that its very conventions make it difficult to supply. A similar challenge and similar resources confront Pliny when illness makes it impossible for him to carry out a planned recitation of some poetry (9.34). He proposes to have a freedman read in his place, but expresses uncertainty whether he should sit rigid and mute, like one with nothing to do,[132] or whether, as some do, he should accompany the recitation with vocalization, eyes, and hand (*an, ut quidam, quae pronuntiabit, murmure oculis manu prosequar*, 9.34.2) The passage reminds us of the corporeality of performance, of the expectation of expressivity fostered by audience and at least some performers (*ut quidam*) alike. Yet it also presents Pliny as valiantly rejecting the temptation: "I think I dance no less badly than I read" (*sed puto me non minus male saltare quam legere*, 9.34.2) is his reaction to the possibility of accompanying the recitation with a dumb show or, in effect, a mime of the professional mimes. Here, as in *Epistles* 2.19, the possibilities and expectations of recitation are set over against the instincts and inclinations of the appropriately dignified elite male.

Yet Pliny does recite — orations (*Ep.* 7.17.2.), including his *Panegyricus* in honor of Trajan, spread out over three days (3.8); verse in varying meters (8.21.4); lyric (5.3.2); and elegy (7.4.7). We learn much about Roman practices of literary performance from his descriptions, including the fact that some of his works were sung (*legitur, describitur, cantatur etiam*, 7.4.9), even (although not by him) to cithara and lyre (7.4.9; 4.19.4). Pliny's tone in describing his custom of reciting such works is repeatedly defensive, as he refers to unnamed others who "criticize" his behavior (*quosdam qui reprehenderent*, 7.17.2; *quosdam qui . . . reprehenderent*, 5.3.1), or offer arguments in support of his custom. Yet the arguments he offers, both explicit and implicit (i.e., through the terminology he applies to his habits), are of vital importance. In essence, they illustrate his ability to negotiate the Scylla and Charybdis of expressivity and severity and to express his longing by so doing to resituate the virtuoso and his song among the convivial *sodales*, even, it would seem, to close the (imagined) gap between oratory and song.

Consider *Epistles* 3.18. Here Pliny describes his reperformance, in the context of recitation, of the *Panegyricus* that his consular position obliged him to deliver in honor of the emperor Trajan. So thrilled are his friends with his performance that they oblige him to extend it to a third day. And Pliny is thrilled in turn, by their zeal but also by their judgment (*cum studium . . . tum iudicium*, 3.18.7). He does not say in so many words whether the audience verbalized their judgment, but he can tell from their reactions that the most austere aspects of his performance pleased them the most: *animadverti enim severissima quaeque vel maxime satisfacere* (3.18.8). And indeed by the end of the letter he finds himself praying that the sweetness and gentleness of his work will give way to the austerity and severity demanded by his discerning audience (3.18.10). We have here a celebration of a quality, *severitas*, that is ordinarily troublesome in the context of recitation. The shift in valuation seems to be justified by the significance of the topic, namely the greatness of the current emperor. And it is as if the magnitude of the subject matter invites an equally magnanimous gesture on the part of Pliny, for within the letter he links his oratorical recitation with the theatrical performance of song:

And as once theaters used to teach musicians to sing badly, now I am
led to hope that it might possibly come to be that the same theaters
will teach musicians to sing well.

ac sicut olim theatra male musicos canere docuerunt, ita nunc in spem
adducor posse fieri, ut eadem theatra bene canere musicos doceant.
(Plin. *Ep.* 3.18.9)

Pliny alludes to the arguments that popular demand and taste have corrupted music (e.g., passages from Cicero and Plutarch discussed earlier),
and suggests that now popular demand, namely, that of his audience,
will lead music to improve itself. But this self-congratulatory compliment depends on ready acceptance of the very equivalence of music and
oratory, theater and audience, that ignited the anxieties of rhetoricians
from Cicero through Quintilian and Tacitus. In effect, Pliny imagines
himself as reconciling the long-standing divide between *carmina* and
dicta, singer and speaker, at least when it comes to the severe performance on the part of the consul as he offers thanks to the princeps.

Pliny's interest in and receptivity to the judgment of his audience,
at least in the context of recitation, subjects even the marathon performance of the *Panegyricus* to the standards of the *convivium.* For it is in
the convivial context, as clear from Catullus, Horace, Ovid, and others,
that the writer receives the criticism and evaluation that guarantees the
quality of his work. In letter 3.18 Pliny alludes to without articulating
the nature of such evaluation, speaking of the satisfaction the audience
communicates, the lessons it provides for him as *musicus.* Elsewhere he
is less circumspect. Indeed, in letter 5.3 he expressly defends recitation
on the grounds that it improves the work being recited.

The many listeners give many pieces of advice. And even if they don't
advise openly, still, what each listener thinks is apparent from his countenance, eyes, nodding, hand gesture, murmuring, or silence.

Multa etiam a multis admonetur, et si non admoneatur, quid quisque
sentiat perspicit ex vultu oculis nutu manu murmure silentio. (Plin. *Ep.*
5.3.9)

And again in letter 7.17 he describes a process of multiple recitations, to
smaller and larger groups, with the aim both of pleasing the audience
and of improving his text by noting their reactions. What earlier poets
accomplished in the context of the *convivium,* Pliny undertakes through
recitation.

But is *recitatio* really so far removed from the *convivium*? Is the virtuoso so different from the *sodalis*? In letter 8.21 Pliny introduces an account of a recent recitation with the general observation that it is "very elegant and very cultivated to mingle severity with geniality" (*pulcherrimum et humanissimum existimo severitatem comitatemque miscere*, 8.21.1). This he tells us is the reason that even in his more serious compositions (*graviora opera*, 8.21.2) he includes playful matters and jokes (*lusibus iocisque*, 8.21.2). But the rest of the letter suggests that recitation itself is, in effect, the insertion of playfulness and jocularity into the serious business of life. And so he gathers his friends, when they are at ease, into his dining room (*triclinio*, 8.21.2) to hear him recite (*recitaturus*, 8.21.3). On this occasion he clearly expects his gathered friends to offer input that will help him to improve his writings. "I read aloud everything, the entirety of the work in question, so that I might emend everything," he observes (*lego enim omnia ut omnia emendem*, 8.21.4). He runs the risk of boring his friends because he loves them and perceives that he is loved in turn: after all, what good would *sodales* be if they gathered together (exclusively) for their own pleasure (*alioqui quid praestant sodales, si conveniunt voluptatis suae causa?* 8.21.5). Without identifying it is as such, Pliny asserts the convivial ethic of shared criticism, shared pleasure, shared affection. No wonder, then, that in precisely this context he reverts to the technical term for coconvivialist, namely *sodalis*.

The language of convivial play, and of its twin but opposite risks of severity and, in this case, cinaedism, shapes letter 5.3 as well. While much of the letter is taken up with the citation of illustrious precedents for Pliny's practice (Cicero, Calvus, Asinius Pollio, all the way through Verginius Rufus, as well as the emperors Julius, Augustus, Tiberius, and Nerva), the argument of the letter is also carried by Pliny's use of the language of appropriate convivial behavior that is now familiar to us. He tells us that he is interested in a wide variety of literature, and the list ranges from his composition of verses that are not at all severe (*facio non numquam versiculos seueros parum*, 5.3.2) to an interest in Sotadeans (*et Sotadicos intellego*, 5.3.2). Apparently Pliny does not take the risk of performing sotadean song, with or without its cinaedic gestures, yet he makes it clear that he is familiar with it, thus identifying the boundary against which elite behavior presses, but through which it must not pass. He is not in the least bothered by (the again unnamed) others' objections to his practice, for he would rather err along with those "who consider it praiseworthy to portray not only what is serious but also what is playful" (*quorum non seria modo verum etiam lusus exprimere laudabile es*, 5.3.5). The word here translated as "portray" (i.e., *exprimere*) is nicely chosen for it can refer either to the composition of serioludic works or to the performance of serioludic subject matter: a reminder that Pliny is simultaneously defending both his authorial (in our sense) and his recitative customs, his inscribing and his bodily practice. And the custom defended is one that enacts the authority of the voice to reconcile the difference between *seria* and *ludus,* to move from one to the other and back again, to leave the ludic context of the *convivium/recitatio* and carry on the "serious" business of making history.

Finally, in letter 7.4, Pliny reviews and defends his entire poetic career, as both a composer and a performer, as one who lives the anxieties of the man of the empire while finding precedent in heroic figures of the past. His addressee Pontius, he tells us, has expressed surprise that Pliny writes hendecasyllables, inasmuch as he (Pliny) seems to be an austere man (*severus*). Pliny repudiates neither the hendecasyllables nor the austerity, although he prefers the expression "not a buffoon" (*non ineptus*) to "austere one." He proceeds to explain that he has been involved with poetry since childhood, having written a tragedy at age fourteen, Latin elegies while on his way back from military service (i.e., around age twenty), later heroic poetry, and now hendecasyllables. The proximate cause of the hendecasyllables was his recent birthday, for during that holiday he chanced upon some books by Asinius Gallus that contained a comparison between Gallus's father and Cicero. And within these books, it seems, were suggestive epigrams by Cicero, addressed to his slave-secretary Tiro. Inspired by the exemplum of "the greatest orators," Pliny sets out to do the same, that is, to compose poems celebrating homoerotic desire, and he shares with his addressee (and his readers) one that he came up with:

> When I was reading the books of Gallus, in which he dared to give
> to his father
> the victory branch in a competition with Cicero,
> I found some foolish business of Cicero, playful
> yet worthy of such a talent. There he hid serious matter
> and there he showed that even the minds of great men
> take pleasure in human wit and much and varied charm.
> For he complains that Tiro defrauds his lover
> by withholding at night kisses promised at dinner.
> Having read these things I ask myself
> "Why then do I keep my loves hidden
> and, out of fear, reveal nothing in public and admit nothing
> of the tricks of Tiro, nor that I too know the fleeting
> blandishments of Tiro and the secrecy that adds new fuel to the
> fire?"

Cum libros Galli legerem, quibus ille parenti
ausus de Cicerone dare est palmamque decusque,
lascivum inveni lusum Ciceronis et illo
spectandum ingenio, quo seria condidit et quo
humanis salibus multo varioque lepore
magnorum ostendit mentes gaudere virorum.
Nam queritur quod fraude mala frustratus amantem
paucula cenato sibi debita savia Tiro
tempore nocturno subtraxerit. His ego lectis
"cur post haec" inquam "nostros celamus amores
nullumque in medium timidi damus atque fatemur
Tironisque dolos, Tironis nosse fugaces
blanditias et furta novas addentia flammas?"

(Plin. *Ep.* 7.4.6)

When he had returned to the city, he proceeded to compose some
elegies as well, which he recited to his approving *sodales* (7.4.8). He continued writing in a playful vein, ultimately producing a whole book of
hendecasyllables, which, as we have earlier noted, came to be recited,
and transcribed, and sung (*cantatur*) — even to the cithara and lyre. Now,
he admits, he should perhaps apologize, not for writing and performing such poetry, but for boasting of it. Yet, he notes, it is not his judgment but that of others that he reports. "Whether they judge [properly]
or they err, it gives me pleasure. One thing I pray, that posterity too
either err or judge in like manner" (*qui sive iudicant sive errant, me delec-
tat. Unum precor, ut posteri quoque aut errent similiter aut iudicent,* 7.4.10).

Here we have the now familiar evocation of convivial context, with
the mention of *sodales* for whom Pliny recites, perhaps too with the
mention of musical accompaniment by cithara and lyre.[133] And the convivial context finds it antecedent in the Ciceronian context as well, for
the poetry of Cicero embedded within the poetry of Pliny speaks of
kisses after a nighttime dinner, while the language Pliny uses to describe
that poetry is reminiscent of the convivial song of Cicero's contemporary Catullus.[134] Convivial ethics, too, are invoked, as Pliny replaces
identification as a *severus,* or austere man, with acknowledgment that
he — unlike many of Catullus's poetic targets — avoids ineptitude. Pliny
even manages to slip in a reminder of his youthful military service: not
due to conscription to be sure, but taken on, one imagines, as a precon-
dition for the distinguished political career Pliny had long hoped for. His
indulgence in elegy as a reprise from military service is a reminder of
the elegiac poets' own tendency to contrast a poetic career with a military one, and perhaps too of the particular association of elegy with a
period of youthful playfulness.[135] The *sodalis,* we should remember, is a

coconvivialist, but as such he is always also a potential soldier or mate. Pliny's acceptance of new models of virtuoso manhood goes hand in hand with military service, rather than replacing it. Indeed, the entire letter can be read as a mediation of all of the conflicts and anxieties generated by changing textual and bodily practices brought on by the transition from republic to empire. Though a virtuoso, Pliny is also a veteran. As a *sodalis*, he is "not goofy" as opposed to "austere." He seeks pleasure from his comrades, in the form of praise or blame of his poetry, yet he toys with the idea of seeking pleasure through more intimate contact. He makes himself the center of attention, the target of the approving gaze. But he is no *cinaedus:* his literary production consists of "plowing" (*exaravi*, 7.4.5) in verses, a phrase that evokes the metaphor of *stilus* as phallus.[136] And the entirety of his performance finds both its origin and its justification in the career of Cicero, who becomes, in effect, the *imago* that Pliny playfully dons, the role he seeks to surrogate in order to become fully himself. In so doing, as his final words indicate, he prays that he too will survive, whether to be praised or blamed scarcely matters, into posterity.

SIX· MAGIC, SONG, AND SACRIFICE

ROM AS EARLY AS THE TIME OF THE TWELVE TABLES, SONG includes activities later interpreted as magical in nature. Certainly the regulation against the "singing out" or *excantatio* of crops from one plot of land to another suggests belief in the possibility of just such action.[1] And the prohibition against defamatory song, or *occentatio*, while customarily interpreted as applying to a different category of activity, makes sense only when at least some portion of the population believes that reputation can be diminished through song as well.[2] It is a problem of semantics whether such theft of reputation through song constitutes magic: certainly it, like the enchantment of crops, is in the modern view a different type of activity from the authoritative use of voice by poets, orators, and priests that has chiefly been our concern in this study. And yet the Romans categorized such activity (e.g., enchantment, defamation, incantation) as song—not just in the Twelve Tables but throughout the history of the language, in all genres and periods. As we saw in our discussion of Ovid's story of Picus and Canens, for all that Canens seems to represent a socially acceptable type of song, the possession of which completes Picus as a prototypical Roman *iuvenis*, her verbal production is described in exactly the same terms as are applied to the "witch" Circe, whose jealous use of incantation leads to the destruction of both Picus and Canens. Without concerning ourselves unduly over the politics of the term "magic," we can see even from these few examples that a contemporary, "commonsensical" differentiation between song and magic is likely to be as difficult to apply to the Roman material as are the fraught distinctions between religion and magic or magic and science.[3]

At the same time, part of what interests us about song as a category of practice in the Roman world is that it does include elements we might not expect to see grouped together. The aim of the present chapter is to use the problem of magical and other nonhegemonic song types as a way of reminding ourselves just how much remains to be explored before we can achieve a comprehensive account of song in the Roman world.

In studying the unexpected, the marginal, the nonhegemonic aspects of song, here or in any projects that grow out of this one, we might take a cue from Raffaela Garosi's remarks at the beginning of her own pathbreaking work on Roman magic: "[O]ur [meaning our modern, Western, bourgeois] concept of magic is always at hand, no longer as an instrument of reduction, but as a point of reference and comparison."[4] So too our expectations with respect to song and, in particular, its tendency to diversify into such areas as magic, law, rhetoric, and poetry inevitably shape our inquiries but cannot be allowed to blind us to countervailing practices and forces that would resist the disembodiment of song and the peeling off of the symbolic from the mimetic. Over and against the narrative of song emerging from play, free voice from disciplined body, Roman culture provides a conflicting narrative, based on a competing set of practices that would restore song to the body and send the initiates, as it were, back to the labyrinth. To a large extent, this alternative narrative is represented by the sources (whether texts or rituals or images) as female in origin and nature, as entailing female divinities, female singers, and female bodies. But this gendering of song and song types, this rendition of women as "the eternal irony of the community," in Hegel's terms, is itself nothing but a trace of Roman men's self-constitution as masters of the rites of reading, writing, and transmitting. Their mastery spills over into other contexts; but then so too does the ritual mastery achieved by women, freedmen, outsiders, and slaves. As Bell reminds us, "ritualization is a strategic arena for the embodiment of power relations."[5] If in the preceding chapters we have considered the flow of power from the top down, that is to say, the paradoxical embodiment of disproportionate power in the disembodied voice of the elite male, here we examine the flow of power upward, the resistances without which domination would, again in Bell's words, "undo itself."[6]

Carmentis, or What the *Vates* Knows

It is no accident that the one performer of magical song already mentioned in this study is female. To Circe we could add a long list of female enchantresses and prophetesses familiar to the Romans. Many of these are borrowed from Greek myth or cult (e.g., Medea); others, like Dido, draw on a mix of Roman and non-Roman traditions;[7] some seem to be the product of an individual poet's imagination (e.g., Canidia of Horace's *Epodes*), while others, such as the unnamed *vates* who populate the works of Livy, Lucretius, Cicero, Tacitus, and so on (and whose gender is not always specified) are represented as real inhabitants of the Roman cultural landscape. One such female singer who crosses boundaries between Roman and Greek, mythical and historical, religious and literary, socially disreputable and socially acceptable, is the eponymous goddess of song herself, Carmentis, or, as she was known to at least some Greek writers, Carmenta.[8] As it turns out, what little we can glean of the cult and legend of Carmentis is highly suggestive with respect to recurrent yet incomplete efforts on the part of different sectors of the Roman population at different periods of history to divide song into distinctive categories based on social location or gender of the singer, or on intended relationship to the "world beyond" (in essence, instrumental versus revelatory uses of language). At the same time, the path of inquiry on which Carmentis leads us complicates and enriches our understanding of the metaphysical, social, psychological, and political ramifications of Roman song. Some aspects of the investigation will be familiar but will appear in a new light when viewed with particular attention to questions of gender, social location, and intentionality.

As with the legend of the fabrication of the Salian *ancilia,* so again it is Ovid who, in his *Fasti* (1.461–636), provides the most comprehensive surviving narrative of the goddess Carmentis, her attributes, and her accomplishments. Ovid (with the overwhelming majority of the tradition) represents Carmentis as the mother of Evander, who accompanies him on his flight from Arcadia, consoles him on his undeserved statelessness, and gives him guidance in selecting the site of his settlement along the Tiber.[9] She is on the scene during Hercules' visit and confrontation with the monster Cacus and ends up prophesying the hero's future deification. She also prophesies various events familiar from the *Aeneid* (the arrival of the Trojans, the death of Pallas, the victory of Aeneas) as well as political transformations of Ovid's lifetime, namely the reign of Augustus, the accession to the throne on the part of Tiberius, and the importance of Livia, here called Julia Augusta (Ov. *Fast.* 1.536). Scholars have not failed to note the flattering reference to the new emperor's mother or the politically convenient parallelism between the pairs Carmentis-Evander and Livia-Tiberius evoked by the whole episode.[10] The rising tide of panegyric raises all boats, for just as Julia Augusta is proclaimed "a new divine power" (*novum numen erit,* 1.536), so Carmentis, who in other accounts is at best a nymph, here becomes a full-fledged goddess:

But the lucky prophetess, as she lived most pleasing to the gods,
so as a goddess she possesses now this day [i.e., January 11] in the
    month of Janus.

at felix vates, ut dis gratissima vixit,
possidet hunc Iani sic dea mense diem.

(Ov. Fast. 1.585–86)[11]

While the reference to Tiberius and Livia has caused some to regard
much or all of the Carmentis episode as a late edition to the *Fasti*, the political appropriateness of Carmentis's story by no means suggests that
Ovid invented it or her out of whole cloth.[12] The festival of Carmentis, the Carmentalia, is well established as part of the Roman religious
calendar. The goddess (or nymph) had a *flamen* named after her (albeit
a "minor" one), and the locale sacred to Carmentis figures in at least
one story associated with a much earlier period of Roman history (i.e.,
Livy's account of the Gallic invasion of 390 BC). Moreover, in Ovid's rendition, as in other testimonia, Carmentis is linked with Janus, a god attested as early as the fragments of the Salian hymn. One might argue
that this is to be expected given the date of her feast (January 11), but
in fact, the close association in function between Janus and Carmentis leads to their calendrical proximity and not the other way around.
In other words, Ovid is not taking advantage of a calendrical accident
when he places Carmentis at the beginning of the story of Rome. Details may have been added to get her prophecies to mesh with the current political situation, but she receives attention near the beginning of
Ovid's versified account of the religious year because she deserves it.

One of the details that Ovid may well have added or changed or
selected to suit contemporary needs—apart from Carmentis's prophecy of the coming of Livia—is his presentation of Hercules as founder
of his own cult. As Ovid tells the story, no sooner had Hercules felled
Cacus than he sacrificed a bull to Jupiter and then proceeded to establish the Ara Maxima for himself (*constituitque sibi, quae maxima dicitur,
aram*, 1.582). Vergil limits Hercules to the slaughter of Cacus, and attributes the annual rite and establishment of the Ara Maxima to Potitius
and the Pinarian clan (*Aen.* 8.269–70). Strabo (*Geog.* 5.230) and Dionysius of Halicarnassus, (*Ant. Rom.* 1.40.1–2), however, make Evander the
initiator of the sacrifice and founder of the cult of the Ara Maxima, in
each case under the guidance of his mantic mother. There is a certain
logic to the latter version of the story, because it is the prophecy that
Hercules (or Greek Herakles) will in time become divine that makes
it legitimate to establish a cult in his honor even while he lives. Dionysius further explains that after the initial sacrifice by Evander, Herakles

made additional sacrifice and entrusted the annual celebration of the rite to "two distinguished households," namely the Potitii and Pinarii (*Ant. Rom.* 1.40.3–4). Versions of the story thus differ with respect to the degree of involvement of Carmentis and Evander in the establishment of the cult to Hercules at the Ara Maxima, with Ovid making her an awkward sideshow to the main event ("nor was the mother of Evander silent, but she predicted the time was at hand when the earth would have had enough of its Hercules": *nec tacet Evandri mater, prope tempus adesse, / Hercule quo tellus sit satis usa suo, Fast.* 1.583–84), Vergil writing her out of the establishment, but Dionysius and Strabo presenting her as the figure who set the chain of events in motion. This seemingly minor shift in emphasis becomes more suggestive when we recall that the Ara Maxima was, in historical terms, crucial to the development of a permanent settlement at the site of Rome. As Coarelli puts it, review-ing the recent archaeological work in the area of the Forum Boarium, the Ara Maxima was a sanctuary established to protect "a precolonial Greek establishment."[13] Whatever the origin of the story of Carmen-tis (and with Carandini, Sabbatucci, and others I am inclined to regard it in its basic framework as quite old), it lays bare conflicting attitudes toward the nature of Roman identity, the social function of song, and the foundation as gendered activity. With her two key performances, one identifying the site of the precolonial settlement, the other naming its god, we might say that it is Carmentis who sings the city into being. She is the foundress before the founder (whether that founder is con-ceived of as Evander, or Hercules, or Romulus, or even Numa), but one whose story is always on the verge of being effaced.

What exactly did Carmentis found? According to the legend related by Dionysius, Vergil, and Ovid, she directed Evander to a site at the foot of the Palatine. This is an important point because it seems from other evidence that the Porta Carmentalis and *fanum* (or shrine) of Carmen-tis were actually at the foot of the Mons Saturnius, or Capitoline. Thus it is unlikely that the association of Carmentis with the founding of the Palatine settlement is simply a retrospective interpretation of geogra-phy on the part of late republican antiquarians. In fact, the site that Car-mentis indicates to Evander is closer to the Forum Boarium, location of Greek remains possibly as old as the eighth century BC,[14] and, more important, at the center of the circuit formed by the surrounding hills of Rome. Indeed at least one scholar has suggested that the name of the Palatine is etymologically connected with *pol-* as in *polus:* the axis linking the earth to the heavens, around which circles the rest of the city.[15] The location of the settlement of Pallanteum, on the west side of the Palatine, is emphasized in different ways by each of the main tellers of the Carmentis legend. Thus Dionysius writes of Themis's (Carmentis's) insistence that the Arcadians settle at the Palatine, which, he adds, "is now virtually in the center of the city."[16] As the first stop on his tour of proto-Rome, Vergil has Evander show Aeneas the gate named after Carmentis, "who was the first to sing the coming of the great people of Aeneas and noble Pallanteum" (*cecinit quae prima futuros / Aeneadas magnos et nobile Pallanteum, Aen.* 8.340–41): from there they examine sites located on the Palatine and Capitoline and either proceed to or at least observe, the Ianiculum across the river. Ovid has Carmentis in a veritable frenzy, stretching her arms toward the shore, banging the ship's deck with her cane, threatening to leap to land unassisted, so sure is she of the proper location for the new settlement. She cries out to the gods of the new locale, to the rivers and springs and groves and forests, then turns to the hills encircling her and asks:

> Am I wrong? or will not these hills become huge ramparts?
>> will not the rest of the earth seek laws from this earth?
> The whole world is promised to these mountains.
>> Who could believe the place to have so great a destiny?

> Fallor? an hi fient ingentia moenia colles?
>> iuraque ab hac terra cetera terra petet?
> Montibus his olim totus promittitur orbis.
>> Quis tantum fati credat habere locum?
>>>>> (Ov. *Fast.* 1.515–18)

In Carmentis's vision the natural ramparts of the hills anticipate the Romulean foundation via construction of walls. Her foundation song links the city to the rest of the cosmos both spatially (the encircling rampart of hills) and temporally (the prophesied growth of Rome).

Another cosmological aspect to the story and cult of Carmentis has been observed by a number of commentators: the Roman calendar places her festival in the month of Janus.[17] As a goddess associated with the passage from nonbeing to being—whether the founding of a city or the birth of a child—she is a good match for the two-faced god, lead recipient of sacrifice, according to Cicero, and (probably) first god invoked in the Salian hymn.[18] Janus is a god of passage, of coming into being, and Carmentis is the female counterpart to his male, paternal status.[19] As Sabbatucci notes, her festival is the first of a series of festivals at the beginning of the year that commemorate deities associated with the creative power of the human voice and limitations thereon: first Carmentis, in the middle of January, then Faunus in February 13, finally Tacita Muta on February 21.[20] As the anthropologist Roy Rappaport argues, language estranges human beings from nature, and ritual (including ritual language) reunites them with it.[21] Carmentis's cult thus speaks not only to the particulars of the founding of Rome (or proto-Rome) but to more general, abstract issues of entry into life (she is a birth goddess) and into human self-awareness.

For the Romans, as for the Greeks, the practice that unites diverse cults and, in so doing, provides the imagery and vocabulary for explaining any of a number of foundational activities is sacrifice.[22] Dionysius tells us that the Romans made annual public sacrifices to Carmentis (*Ant. Rom.* 1.32.2), but her connection with sacrifice may have a different dimension as well. To found a city is, among other things, to found its religious practices. In the most widespread version of the founding of Rome, this aspect is concentrated in the figure of Numa (who, like Evander, has a knowledgeable female adviser).[23] Numa both performs sacrifice and gives instruction for the repetition of ritual over time. While no source explicitly says as much, I believe that Carmentis's role as foundation-singer, her identification as *vates,* the etymology of her name and perhaps certain of her attributes identify her as one knowledgeable in the art of sacrifice. Her sacrificial expertise both confirms her cosmological significance and points to yet another way in which song "founds" the Roman universe.

Vergil explicitly identifies Carmentis as a *vates* (*vatis fatidicae,* Aen. 8.340). For him this means first and foremost that she has prophetic powers.[24] But where do those prophetic powers come from? The Sibyl, as *vates* (so called at *Aen.* 6.65, 78, 82, 125), instructs Aeneas in the proper expiatory sacrifice for the unburied Palinurus (6.149–53). Helenus, as *vates,* gives Aeneas guidance in appeasing Juno through sacrifice (3.433–40) The epic singer apostrophizes *vates* as a group immediately after describing Dido's consultation of the "seething entrails" (*spirantia exta*) of sacrificial victims (4.60–66). During the plague described in book 3 of the *Georgics,* animals collapse on their way to the altar, and even when a priest does manage to slaughter one in the ritual manner:

> The altars do not blaze, although entrails have been heaped upon
> them;
> the *vates,* when consulted, are powerless to respond.[25]

> inde neque impositis ardent altaria fibris,
> nec responsa potest consultus reddere vates.
>
> (Verg. G. 3.490–91)

The passages from Vergil thus imply a connection between the *vates'* power to foretell the future and their ability to interpret the entrails of sacrificial victims and to give instruction in ritual.

A similar nexus of ideas shapes Livy's numerous references to *vates*, especially in his discussion of the early years of Rome. For example, when the Romans and the Sabines are contending over the proper location of a temple to Diana and thus the "headship of affairs" (*caput rerum*, Livy 1.45.3), someone chances upon a she-ox "remarkable in size and beauty" (*miranda magnitudine ac specie*, 1.45.4). It was regarded as a prodigy, and the *vates*, having been consulted, "sang out that whichever state's citizen sacrificed it to Diana, that state would have dominion" (*et cecinere vates cuius civitatis eam civis Dianae immolasset, ibi fore imperium*, 1.45.6).[26] In another episode, when Rome is wracked simultaneously by internal strife and external struggle with both Veii and the Volscians, the *vates* seek to calm the terrified minds of the people by pointing out, on the basis of their consultations, "now of entrails, now of birds," (*nunc extis, nunc per aves consulti*, 2.42.10) that "sacrifices were not being performed properly" (*haud rite sacra fieri*, 2.42.10). When on yet another occasion (427 BC) a combination of drought and pestilence drives the rural folk into the city, and both bodies and minds are afflicted, the people turn to "new rites of sacrificing introduced by the vatic singing" (*nouos ritus sacrificandi vaticinando inferentibus*, 4.30.9). Finally, during their ultimate struggle with Veii, the Romans, confronted by the prodigy of the Alban Lake, rely on the advice of a captured *vates* in order to placate the gods. And what they learn, apparently from the *vates*, is that "certain ceremonies had been neglected and a solemnity allowed to lapse" (*neglectas caerimonias intermissumve sollemne*, 5.17.2). *Vates* can foretell the future because they can read the signs of the universe, chief among them the entrails of sacrificial victims. Having this knowledge, they can shape the future as well, first and foremost by offering advice on proper ritual procedure.[27]

The power of the *vates* to import new rites, already alluded to in the episode describing the crowding of the country folk into the city (4.30.9), is most famously addressed in the account of the suppression of the Bacchanals in 186 BC (39.8–18). The arrival of the new, disruptive cult is attributed to a "low-class Greek . . . a mere sacrificer and *vates*" (*Graecus ignobilis . . . sacrificulus et vates*, 39.8.4). Men who have joined the cult "with crazed tossing of their bodies sing like *vates*" (*cum iactatione fanatica corporis vaticinari*, 39.13.12). The consul, in explaining the measures taken to suppress the cult, emphasizes that it is a foreign importation, and explicitly links the prevention of new religious practices (*uti sacra externa fieri vetarent*, 39.16.8) with the banning of the *sacrificuli* and *vates* and the confiscation and burning of their books (*sacrificulos vatesque foro circo urbe prohiberent, vaticinos libros conquirerent comburerentque*, 39.16.8). Fritz Graf may well be right when he suggests that in this context Livy uses the phrase *sacrificulus ac vates* as a translation of the Greek *agyrtēs kai mantis,* and in so doing refers to a kind of itinerant magician other-wise unknown among the Romans.[28] But this transference from Greek to Latin does not change the fact that Livy and his Roman readers appar-ently understood the term *vates* to refer to, among other things, those who provided instruction in cult practices. Here, as often, Livy may be writing more carefully than scholars like to admit, for the development in his description of *vates*, from the early books to the later account of the suppression of the Bacchanalia, seems to reflect a progressive tighten-ing of control over religious practices by the state as it grows in size and strength. The skills attributed to the *vates*, the domains of their knowl-edge, are the same in Vergil's poetry as in Livy's prose, in Livy's account of early Rome and in his account of more recent eras. What is under-stood to have changed is the social location of those described as *vates*.

Are the skills of the *vates* those of Carmentis? Here we have little choice but to consider the etymology of her name. The ancients them-selves linked *Carmentis/ta* with *carmen*, imagining her as a goddess of song, even as they associated her with childbirth as well.[29] An alterna-tive ancient etymology identifies her as "crazy," from *caro, carere* (to lack) and *mentis* (mind).[30] While this second etymology has found no sup-port among modern scholars, it nonetheless fits our picture of a god-dess and power always at risk of being cast out of the mainstream. (As we shall see, the *neniae*, or funeral lamentations of female mourners, were also associated with mad ravings, or *deliramenta*.) Modern schol-ars have also tended to dismiss the etymology from *carmen*,[31] usually without offering clear alternative explanations. Peruzzi's attempt to de-fend an etymology from *carmen* on the basis of a parallel with *cruentus* ignores the structure of the root *can-*, although to his credit he explains the variation *-tis/-ta* as "characteristic of rustic and technical terms that are securely ancient."[32] Pettazzoni's connection of *Carmenta* with *car-penta* is no more than a revival of a folk etymology based on the inci-dent in which women were forbidden to be drawn to temples in carts known as *carpenta*.[33] Perrot, who offers a comprehensive discussion of nouns ending in *-men* and *-mentum*, notes that the most common nouns in *-men* (*agmen, carmen, crimen, flumen, limen, lumen*) lack counterparts in *-mentum*,[34] an observation that may argue against the early coexistence of *carmen* and *Carmentis* as nouns derived from the same verbal root. He also considers the possibility that *carmentis* is to *carmen* as *sementis* (sea-son for sowing, *semailles*) is to *semen* (seed), but rejects it, apparently on the grounds that the semantic relationship is not equivalent in the two pairs.[35]

More promising is the approach of Radke, who starts from the ob-servation that *Carmentis* is to the well-attested *Carmentalia* as *parentes* is to the feast of *Parentalia*, as **larentes* would be to *Larentalia*.[36] On this interpretation, the root of *Carmentis* is neither *can-*, as in *cano,* nor *carmen,* but **carm-* (unattested) or, better, *carn-* as in Latin *caro, carnis* or Oscan *carneis,* meaning "part." In that case, Carmentis is not a personification of song but the abstraction for "that which procures or brings allotment."[37] Radke goes on to associate this meaning of Carmentis's name with her role as birth goddess and seer, but neglects to mention what is perhaps the most commonplace use of the root *carn-*in Latin, namely *caro, carnis* the word for flesh, more specifically the portion allotted in a sacrifice.[38] Indeed, as John Scheid observes, Varro (*Ling.* 6.25) uses the expression *carnem ex sacris petere* in the very context (the distribution of meat at the sacrifice on the Alban Mount) in which Dionysius of Halicarnassus employs the Greek terms *moira* and *meros* (Dion. Hal. *Ant. Rom.* 4.49.2).[39] Carmentis would thus seem to be a figure associated both with sacrifice (through the etymology of her name and her association with allotment) and with prophecy (a fact that led to, rather than derived from, the folk association with *carmen*). She is, in effect, the quintessential *vates.*

If the words *carmen,* meaning song, and *Carmentis,* the goddess of allotment or distribution, however, do not share an etymology, this in no sense suggests that the association of Carmentis with song is somehow a late fantasy of Hellenizing authors. The connection between sacrifice and song is a perfectly logical one for a community to make at a very early stage, at least if we follow Rappaport's argument that language alienates humanity from nature, while ritual (including the making special of speech in song, as well as sacrifice) restores the connection. I have already suggested that the association of sacrifice and song was made manifest by the Romans in their recognition of the manifold power of *vates* to establish religious, especially sacrifical procedure, to foretell the future, and to read signs, including the entrails of sacrificial victims. The song of the *vates* is about the restoration of humanity to nature; it looks inward (think of Dido peering at the entrails, or Manilius exploring the innards of the universe) in contrast to the (eventual) mainstream of song, that is, the song of elite males, which looks outward, to other sources of authority, such as the realm of the gods, the world outside the community, and the distant past.[40] The *vates* may be male or female; he or she often operates as part of a group, and thus seems to draw on a knowledge of and evince a respect for the human body that is more comprehensive than that of the later poets or orators. (Or perhaps it is just the case that masculinist ideology assigns the bodily and, therefore, "inferior" knowledge of the *vates* to the realm of the nonmale.)

In any event, the connection between song and sacrifice that we have identified in the story of Carmentis and in the social role of the *vates* can be found elsewhere in Roman culture — specifically in further details of the Carmentis story and in the practice of regarding song as a sacrificial offering to be carved and consumed.

Recall that Dionysius of Halicarnassus gives Carmentis's Greek name as Themis. The identification might point to Carmentis's (like Themis's) oracular power. But Themis is also a founder, as her name makes perfectly clear. And indeed Dionysius attributes to the Arcadians guided by Themis a number of remarkable achievements upon their arrival in Italy, including the introduction of Greek letters and of music performed on lyre, trigon, and aulos, as well as the establishment (*thesthai*) of *nomoi*: in short, they "transformed men's mode of life from the prevailing bestiality to a state of civilization."[41] The *nomoi* that the Arcadians established might be laws, but they can equally well be musical modes or sacrificial procedures pertaining to distribution (cf. the derivation of *nomos* from *nemein*). In the Greek concept of *nomoi*, sound is conceived of as an offering that is distributed according to specific patterns. Dionysius takes for granted that a similar nexus of ideas can be associated with Carmentis even in her Latinate manifestation as a goddess named after *carmina*, or song. He thus makes of the Arcadians originators—or, perhaps better, prototypes—of the song culture of archaic Rome, with its interrelated "laws" of musical, religious, and political behavior.

In Greek texts, the representation of a song as a sacrificial victim is relatively common.[42] An anecdote tells of Pindar bringing a paean to be sacrificed at Delphi; in the Homeric Hymn to Hermes the god's lyre and the music it produce are considered worth fifty cows; Aeschylean tragedy is famously described as "slices from the banquet of Homer"; and Philodemus notes, apropos Pindar's promise to "sacrifice a dithyramb," that "thanks to poetry, the honor of the gods is augmented."[43] The technical language used to analyze song, poetry, and prose abounds in reference to disarticulated body parts: *melos* (limb), *kōlon* (also limb), *komma* (cutoff piece), *oura* (tail), *akephalon* (headless, as when the first syllable of a meter is missing), and so on. Latin, too, preserves some traces of such a connection, certainly in its technical vocabulary, which may be regarded as simply translated from or calqued upon the Greek: for example, *membrum, incisum, coda*; perhaps too in reference to style as *gracilis* (slender), *gravis* (weighty), as having or lacking *nervi* (sinews).[44] But a few passages suggest an indigenous tradition of equating song with sacrifice, or at least an adaptation that responds to the particulars of Roman practice.

For example, the *acta* of the Arval brothers for the year AD 218 indicate that the priests, having left the temple, took up *libelli*, and "while carving up the song, danced the *tripudium* to the following words" (*carmen descindentes tripodaverunt in verba haec*).[45] The exact action taken by the Arval brothers has received varying scholarly interpretation: do different brothers take different parts of the song? Do they all in some sense "scan" the song, breaking it into its rhythmical components? Whatever the precise meaning, their action is construed as a type of cutting, or carving, comparable with what one might do with meat (e.g., *obsonium scindere* at Sen. *Vit. Beat.* 17; *aves in frusta scindere*, Sen. *Brev. Vit.* 12).[46] Indeed, the use of the compound in *de-* suggests that the Arval brothers not only disassemble the song but in some sense reassemble it—that is, through cutting return it to its original form.[47] The phrase *carmen descindere* thus suggests a certain similarity between animal sacrifice, with its cutting and assembling of portions, and ritual song and dance. Such a meaning is reinforced by the context, since the *acta* describe the brothers as performing blood sacrifice of *agnae opimae* just before the "carving" of the song. Surely Philodemus's words, although written in Greek with respect to Greek texts, are relevant here as well: through song (as through sacrifice) the honor of the gods is augmented.[48]

A second example of the application of sacrificial language to poetry is more playful, yet seems to make sense only if the underlying seriousness of the equation is respected. Poem 90 of Catullus reads as follows in its entirety:

> Let a magus be born from the unspeakable union of Gellius and his
>> mother
>> and let him master Persian divination
> for (as the saying goes) a magus is born from mother and son
>> if the impious religious belief of the Persians is true
> so that welcome he might venerate the gods with a pleasing song
>> while liquefying the fat omentum in the flame.

> nascatur magus ex Gelli matrisque nefando
>> coniugio et discat Persicum aruspicium
> nam magus ex matre et gnato gignatur oportet
>> si vera est Persarum impia religio,
> gratus ut accepto veneretur carmine diuos
>> omentum in flamma pingue liquefaciens.

(Catull. 90)

The poem has been cited as evidence of Roman interest in Persian religious beliefs and practices, and the final line interpreted as referring to the sacred fire of Zoroastrian worship.[49] Even so, as a recent commentator has noted, the final line seems to make a rather feeble ending to an otherwise strong invective accusing the hapless Gellius (yet again) of incest.[50] Why should the poem reach its climax in an irrelevant reference to blood sacrifice? Thomson seems to be on the right track in suggesting that the final two lines may refer not just to sacrifice but to the destruction of Gellius's own poems.[51] He builds his argument by referring to a passage of Suetonius that includes a certain kind of *omentum* among writing materials used in previous eras.[52] But it is also worth noting that *omentum*, the fatty layer encompassing the entrails, is a part of every blood sacrifice.[53] In other words, with or without the reference to writing material, and with or without interpretation of the fire in the last line as Zoroastrian, we may well have an equation of *carmen* and *omentum*. Indeed, such an equation gives greater force to the participle *accepto* as applied to *carmine* in the penultimate line, because *acceptum* is the word used of an "acceptable" sacrifice to the gods. Thus, the song and the *omentum* are offered up together.

Our third example of the Latin equation between song and sacrificial victim is no doubt the most famous. In the course of defending himself against charges of being a dangerous poet, Horace makes the argument that, as a satirist, he is not a poet at all. True poetry, he writes, is not a matter of fitting words into patterns of verse (that, as we know from chapter 4, is the task of *ludus*). For true poetry "fierce breathing and life-force" (*acer spiritus ac vis*, *Sat.* 1.4.46) must be present as well. As for Horace's compositions,

> If you were to snatch away
> the set rhythms and measures, and the word that was sooner in
>   order
> you put later, placing the last before the first,
> you wouldn't—as you would if you were to break apart "postquam
>   Discordia taetra
> Belli ferratos postis portasque refregit"—
> find even when dismembered the limbs of a poet.

> eripias si
> tempora certa modosque, et quod prius ordine verbum est
> posterius facias, praeponens ultima primis,
> non, ut si solvas "postquam Discordia taetra
> Belli ferratos postis portasque refregit,"
> invenias etiam disiecti membra poetae.
>
> (Hor. *Sat.* 1.4.57–62)

The image of dismemberment is a complex one, as commentators have recognized. In one sense Horace is simply differentiating between the allegedly serious poetry of Ennius and his own conversational description of the world around him. Even if the meter were dissolved, Ennius would still be something of a fire breather (or at least a living sacrifice), whereas meter is all that differentiates Horace's satire from everyday conversation. At the same time, Horace seems to allude to the myth of Orpheus, the legendary singer torn to pieces by those he had offended: such a fate might await an Ennius who gave offense, although it is hardly an appropriate response to Horace.[54] But the reference to dismemberment brings to mind the carving of a sacrifice as well,[55] a point anticipated by the two allusions to rendering just a few lines earlier: *dissolvas* (1.4.55) and *solvas* (1.4.60). Indeed, the differentiation between poetry and conversation with which the whole section commences relies on a confusion between animate poet and inanimate text, as Horace categorizes as something other than poetry verbal production "where fierce breathing and life-force are present neither in words nor in subject matter" (*quod acer spiritus ac vis / nec verbis nec rebus inest*, 1.4.46–47). This same crossing of poet and poem characterizes the final reference to "limbs of a dismembered poet" (*disiecti membra poetae*, 1.4.62): are they in fact the limbs of the poet or the *membra* (the technical term for the subdivision of a sentence, as well as body parts) of the poetic passage cited? The whole passage from Horace thus relies on an equation of poem and sacrificial victim or offering to achieve its effect. Indeed, it is precisely the nonsacrificial nature of satire, its disconnection from the world beyond and its focus on the here and now, that makes it, at least in this instance, something other than song. Horace works hard to desacralize a genre that is, after all, named after a type of food and repeatedly features scenes of banqueting. But in so doing he provides evidence for the latent connection between sacrifice and song, in Roman culture as in Greek.

Nenia, or Laying Down the Dead

For all that Roman poets play with the possible equation of song and sacrifice, no surviving texts are quite so blunt as the story of Pindar bringing a paean to sacrifice at Delphi. Just as the goddess Carmentis is marginalized, her legend and rite never quite coalescing into a foundation song as powerful as that of the *salii*, just as the *vates* she represents are imagined over time as farther and farther removed from the center of Roman power,[56] so too the skills that Carmentis and the *vates* unite, skills of prophesying, singing, and sacrificing, while occasionally acknowledged as coextensive, are more often than not treated as characteristic of performers separated by gender, social location, or ascribed intention. In a simple sense, *vates* can be (and have been) defined as singers whose song is not (in itself) recognized as authoritative by the state (although the songs of some *vates* can be given state sanction on some occasions).[57] But such a definition ignores the reasons for state disapproval and the mutually reinforcing strategies of gender differentiation, specialization, centralization, and marginalization that characterize the history of song.

We gain further insight into these processes by considering what is perhaps the most widely attested type of song associated with women (but, again, not exclusively women)—namely, the *nenia*, or funeral dirge led by the *praefica*.[58] This type of song, too, is conceptualized in sacrificial terms. According to the late antique author Arnobius, *nenia* is the Latin word for the end of the intestines, including the *anus*. It constitutes one part of the *augmenta*, or add-ons, boiled with the main entrails in animal sacrifice.[59] In a detailed study of the word *nenia* John Heller has tried to discredit this meaning of *nenia* as well as the application of the term *nenia* to funeral song and to suggest instead that the word's "original and core meaning" was something like "plaything" or "trifle."[60] In fact, Heller's comprehensive collection of testimonia pertaining to *nenia* points in exactly the opposite direction of his conclusions. Nor should we be surprised that this is the case, since a semantic progression from the more general "trifle" to "funeral song" to "end of the intestine" is surely much harder to explain and defend than one that moves the other way around.

In any case, the earliest attestations of the term *nenia* all accord with the meaning "end," either concretely, as in "last bit of the entrails" or "funeral song," or more abstractly, as in "finale." Thus Plautus uses the term almost certainly to refer to the anus of a shrewmouse, when he has a character threaten to stab another (interestingly enough, expressly not with a *machaera*, the Greek term for the knife used for killing and carving animals), thereby rendering him "more full of holes than a shrewmouse's ass" (*confossiorem soricina nenia*, Bacch. 889). As Heller himself informs us, there was an ancient folk belief that a hare acquired an additional anus for each year of its life: this passage may refer to a similar, albeit otherwise unattested belief concerning mice[61]—or perhaps just to the extraordinary and telltale production of feces on the part of mice and other rodents. In another Plautine passage a character describes a slip and fall as the "*nenia* of his dance" (*id fuit nenia ludo*, Pseud. 1278); in yet another a prostitute is said to have "pronounced the *nenia*" (*neniam dixit*, Truc. 213) for the property of an admirer.[62] The second-century BC poet Afranius makes a fairly explicit association between *nenia* and last rites (*exequiales*).[63] Cicero describes the performance of a *nenia* as Roman funeral custom, and adds the remark that the word *nenia* is used in Greek as well for "lugubrious songs" (*Leg.* 2.62). Such a Greek word is unattested, but, curiously, other ancient writers associate *nenia* with

Greek *nētē*, meaning last string on a lyre, presumably made of animal innards.[64]

In the imperial period, the association of *nenia* with the end of the intestines and thus, potentially, with sacrificial procedure is implied by a passage of Petronius as well. In an episode that Heller finds puzzling, Petronius has Trimalchio refer to the food of rustics as *gallum galli-naceum, penthiacum et eiusmodi nenias*, "cockish cock, penthiacum? and suchlike oddments" (*Sat.* 47.2), then add the remark that "my cooks are even accustomed to cook calves in a bronze pot" (*mei coci etiam vitulos aeno coctos facere solent,* 47.2.). The point seems to be that, while even poor country folk might boil up a hot pot of bits and pieces of small fowl, Trimalchio's cooks have cauldrons big enough to cook whole pigs (mentioned earlier) or calves. Whatever *neniae* are, they apparently are cooked up in a boiling pot, as would also be the case for the entrails and add-ons in animal sacrifice. Centuries later the Christian polemi-cist Claudius Edictius Mamercus can play on the specific connection of *nenia* with a portion of the entrails of an animal when he comments on those who (metaphorically, it would seem) enjoy a "striking abun-dance of steaming entrails" (*perpellente copia tepentium naeniarum, Anim.* 2.8)[65] — "steaming" being just the word to apply to remains of a freshly slaughtered animal.[66]

The association of *nenia* simultaneously with animal entrails and funeral song (we will get to the trifling aspect soon enough), rather than being a metaphorical extension from one domain to another, in fact seems to be grounded in the practice of funeral song itself. That is, the *nenia* led by the *praefica* is conceived of as the last bit of song shared by the inner circle of mourners and the commencement of the distri-bution of mourning to a wider set of participants. Thus we are told by Servius (*Aen.* 6.216) that the *praefica* is the *princeps planctuum* — the "first dibs-taker of lamentation."[67] That is, she starts the process of distribu-tion of the funeral song by "setting forth" (*praeficio*) the lament that will be taken up by others.[68] Her function is described by Varro, citing an earlier grammarian, as "presiding over the female slaves, as to how they would lament" (*quae praeficeretur ancillis quemadmodum lamentaren-tur, Ling.* 7.70). Suetonius, in describing the funeral of Augustus, men-tions that one feature of the proceedings was the "singing of the *nenia* of the principes by free citizens of both sexes" (*canentibus neniam princi-pum liberis utriusque sexus, Aug.* 100.2).[69] The expression *nenia principum*, far from implying a eulogy of multiple emperors — which would make no sense at the funeral of the first emperor — must refer, as does the pas-sage from Servius, to the leading role in lamentation taken by specific individuals. A characteristic of *neniae*, even when not specifically funeral songs, seems to be the repetition by a larger group of a refrain set forth (*prae-*) by one person.[70] This feature is apparent even in a seemingly disparate use of *nenia*, such as Horace's description of a children's jingle, "sung down" or "repeated" (*decantata, Epist.* 1.1.59), from one person to another through the ages.

As for the finality, or lastness, of *nenia*, the point is emphasized by a number of ancient sources: the grammarian Diomedes calls it the "last and ultimate song that, together with lamentation, is sung to the dead" (*id carmen quod cum lamentatione extremum atque ultimum mortuo accinitur, GLK* 1.484–85). Ovid refers to the occasion of a strike by Rome's flute players, which led to the absence of the (otherwise expected, it would seem) *nenia* leading the "final choruses" (*supremos choros, Fast.* 6.668) at the funeral.[71] A late gloss calls *neniae* "the very last songs sung to the deceased" (*nenias, novissima cantica quae ad mortuum dicuntur, CGL* 5.226.4).[72] Indeed, we find a sophisticated evocation of *nenia* as the "last song" in a passage of Horace otherwise not well understood. In an ode addressed to one Lyde, Horace invites her to join him in a musical celebration of the feast of Neptune. But his invitation implies more than a day passed in song, since the final stanza imagines Lyde singing of the goddess of love, then simply asserts "Night too will be hymned in a merited *nenia*" (*dicetur merita Nox quoque nenia, Carm.* 3.28.16). The *nenia* is not so much a lullaby, as some would have it, as a farewell song to a night well spent. As often, Horace expects his reader to understand more erotic activity than he describes: a whole night of sex is implied in the asyndetic transition between Lyde's songs of Venus and the *nenia* she — or he — performs at dawn.

Uses of *nenia* to refer to funeral song or to an ending of whatever sort are thus consistent with what I take to be an underlying, perhaps original, association with the last bit of the entrails, the last addition to the sacrifice. In a sense, both the name and the practice of the *nenia* reinforce the association of song and sacrifice in the Roman tradition. Not only does song teach the forms of sacrifice (and by implication, of distribution and ordering more generally), but song itself is an offering to the forces beyond the here and now, an entity to be carved up and shared, sometimes by an inner circle, at other times by a wider group of participants. If language estranges humanity from nature, song restores the connection in part, as we have seen in earlier chapters, by imitating birds and other natural phenomena, but also, paradoxically, by objectifying language as something that can be cut up, analyzed, and reassembled, perhaps especially via rhythm. But just as sacrifice carries with itself questions of inclusion and exclusion with respect to the distribution of the dismembered victim, so too song raises questions of distribution as well: Will it be limited to a solo performer, to a finite convivial

circle or chorus whose membership is clearly delimited, or will it be
available for anyone to pick up, join in, repeat, reuse? If the last-named,
then what, after all, has the song founded? Where are the boundaries
of the community it seeks to define? Precisely such questions seem to
have preoccupied those in Roman society whose interest lay in making
song finite, in empowering some voices at the expense of others. And
so we find the song of the *praefica* trivialized, marginalized, excluded
through various political and rhetorical strategies. But the anxiety of
those who would contain the *nenia* was not without basis: the grief of
survivors can overwhelm the orderly processes of bequeathal and surrogation, and the type of song the *praefica* apparently led, the chanting
of a refrain, would have been particularly susceptible to widespread imitation.[73] The latter seems to have been part of the point of the *nenia*,
which Wille describes as, among other things, designed to generate as
much noise as possible in order to protect the living from the spirits of
the deceased.[74] In other words, we are beginning to see, in the realm
of Carmentis, as well as in that of Nenia (the goddess associated with
nenia),[75] the internal contradictions of the Romans' attempts to found a
particular social order on song. Indeed, the bits and pieces of evidence
that we can assemble about these goddesses and, more important, the
practices they oversee suggest that they were conceived by at least some
Romans as a kind of revenge of the body on the voice.

Let us begin with the marginalization of the *nenia*, which is easy
enough to observe. While various testimonia point to the antiquity and
continuing significance of the *nenia* (after all, the lament is expressly associated with the funeral of more than one emperor,[76] Horace uses it
to describe the poems of Simonides on the dead at Thermopylae and
Marathon,[77] and various authors assimilate it to funeral laudation),[78]
others speak of it and its performers in what can at best be described as
disparaging terms. Thus Phaedrus calls *neniae* "vile" (*Fab.* 3 prol. 10), an
accusation resumed by later glossographers.[79] Nonius Marcellus, citing
Varro, refers to *nenia* as an "inept and unformed type of song" (*ineptum
et inconditum carmen*, 145.24) The emperor Septimius Severus associated
neniae disparagingly with old women (*neniis quibusdam anilibus*, *Epist.*
Capitol. Alb. 12.12 = Heller 1943: 240), while Horace and Petronius attributed them to boys (Hor. *Epist.* 1.1.59–64; Petr. *Sat.* 46.4). Horace
once groups *neniae* with "shameful lamentations" (*Carm.* 2.20.21–22).
And, as we shall discuss shortly, *neniae* can be attributed to witches,
specifically those of Marsian origin: see Hor. *Epist.* 17.29; Ov. *Ars Am.*
2.11, *Fast.* 6.142 (in which the witch is expressly described as an *anus*,
or old woman). As for the performer—or, perhaps better, leader—of
the *neniae*, we hear of her being "hired" (*conductae*) as early as a fragment of Lucilius, which mentions "the *praeficae*, who for a price weep

at the funeral of another" (or of someone outside the household?: *mercede quae conductae flent alieno in funere praeficae*, Lucil. 995–96 W). Varro, citing the earlier grammarian Aurelius, also indicates that the *praefica* is hired (*quae conduceretur*), in this case "to sing the praises of the deceased in front of his house" (*quae ante domum mortui laudes eius caneret, Ling.* 7.70). Nonius too says she is hired (*conducta*, 145), although the Latin of his passage leaves it unclear as to whether this is in his view always the case or only on occasions when the deceased lacks appropriately qualified relatives.[80] From the elite male perspective, apparently part of what was offensive about the *praefica* was that she was, at least by the classical period, a paid professional. While the formation of her title, *praefica*, from *prae* and *facio*, the one who sets up in front of (others), parallels that of the archaic *praesul* of the Salian college (the one who dances in front of others, who sets out the patterns for imitation),[81] and while at least one testimonium explicitly indicates that she predates Rome's conflict with Carthage,[82] nevertheless she—and her song—come to be disparaged as representative of the low-class activities more generally associated with alien cultural innovators.

Not entirely clear is whether the *praefica*'s hired status causes elite males to treat her with disdain, or their disdain for her and her song causes them to describe her as, or call attention to her status as, hired help. The intonement of a refrain that is picked up and repeated by a larger group constitutes a type of music familiar to the other ancient peoples besides the Romans but subject to derision as "Asiatic" or "effeminate." Thus M. L. West speaks of the *linos*, familiar among Greeks, as a possible example of a distinct Asiatic singing style, one that was antiphonal or responsorial and from its "oriental" or pre-Hellenic origin eventually evolved into Christian ritual.[83] But it is equally possible that such antiphonal or responsorial singing was widespread in Greece as in Rome and merely identified as primitive, Oriental, or womanly because it was contrary to the musical style preferred by elite males, indeed, as I have been suggesting throughout this book, constitutive of their elite status. The *nenia* is dismissed as trivial, shameful, disgusting, meaningless precisely because it isn't. It is the remnant of an alternative musical system that, because of its association with as highly charged an event as the funeral, cannot be entirely eliminated and must be contained instead.

As I have suggested, this containment of funeral lament takes the form of rhetorical disparagement, as well as of more familiar strategies such as limitation on time of mourning, especially for women,[84] and on expenses associated with funerals.[85] Recognizing the extent of this disparagement in the ancient record helps us to avoid taking various testimonia at face value (e.g., the suggestion that *neniae* are ipso facto trivial, a trap into which far too many scholars fall). It also gives us access to an even deeper nexus of ideas linking *nenia,* as both song type and goddess, to Carmentis, and identifying both as aspects of a system of song always in tension with the song of free men.

Carmen, it will be recalled, gains its force from its ability to transcend the boundary between play, or *ludus,* and the external world, between bodily dependency and vocal autonomy. *Carmen* is privileged by and in turn privileges the voice over the body. Carmentis and Nenia also raise questions of the relationship between voice and body, but as female deities, associated with types of song that are either female or at least gender-inclusive—*vates,* for example, being male and female, *neniae* being sung, on at least some occasions, by mourners of both sexes—they personify a different relationship between body and voice than that carried by masculinist ideologies of song. For one thing, Carmentis and Nenia are goddesses of what we might call the materiality of the body. Carmentis is associated with birth, Nenia with death. To the degree that Carmentis's name brings to mind apportionment or distribution, whether of the lifetime of the newborn or of the parts of the sacrificial victim, it speaks to the finiteness and particularity of bodily existence. Nenia, too, whether concerned with the last bit of the *augmenta,* or the commencement of mourning for the newly deceased, is associated as well with the concrete particulars of an individual body. This association is reinforced in the case of Carmentis by the names of her "companions" Antevorta (or Prorsa) and Postverta, whose names are sometimes interpreted as referring to foresight and hindsight (e.g., Ov. *Fast.* 1.633–36), but can just as easily (if not more so) be applied to the position of the fetus within the womb (Serv. *Aen.* 8.51, citing Varro; Gell. *NA* 16.16.2) or the arrangement of entrails within the sacrificial victim.[86] Even more specifically, to the extent that Carmentis concerns herself with birth, she is inevitably associated with female, as opposed to male bodies, and more particularly, with the birth canal and vaginal opening. And Nenia, as we have seen, has a name that from early through late Latin, refers as well to the end of the intestinal tract and the anus. In his discussion of the carnivalesque inversion of the "classical body," Bakhtin calls attention to the repeated invocation by nonelite texts and practices of bodily effusions, especially through openings other than the mouth, that is, of menstruation, micturation, and excretion.[87] Such effusions find a textual counterpart in other images of excess and superfluity, especially common in works of a satirical or parodic outlook.[88] Yet, as Bataille argues, for all that all societies must develop strategies for managing excess or superfluous energy, it is through observation of the different techniques of management that we come to understand the differences between societies and cultures.[89] It is my contention that

Carmentis and Nenia are traces of an alternative system of management of excess to that found elsewhere in Roman culture, evidence, as
it were, of instability and alterity within the otherwise self-contained
world of Roman song. Their alterity cannot be regarded as exactly coextensive with gender differentiation, or status differentiation, or bodily
difference between men and women, young and old. And yet all of these
aspects and more—such as the difference between limited sacrifice and
unlimited distribution of lament, or between univocal song (whether in
fact performed by one or by many) and reciprocal or alternating song—
figure in the contrast between the song of Carmentis and Nenia and the
song of elite adult males. Indeed, a primary reason that scholars have
found it so difficult to provide a unified account of the wide-ranging
testimonia pertaining to Carmentis and Nenia is that they are, in effect,
figures of and about complex particularity.

As far as I can tell, Carmentis and Nenia/nenia do not occur together in any single passage of Latin literature. But one anecdote, told
by Aulus Gellius, comes close to uniting them and is therefore worth
examining in some detail. As Gellius tells the story, his friend Favorinus
encountered the "learned and famous grammarian" (*docto celebrique* . . .
grammatico, NA 18.7.1) Domitius at, of all places, the shrine of Carmentis
(*fanum Carmentis*, 18.7.2). There Favorinus asks Domitius for his advice
on the correct Latin translation of the Greek word *dēmēgoriai*, to which
Domitius responds, with "an even more ferocious than usual voice and
countenance" (*voce atque vultu atrociore*, 18.7.3):[90]

> Surely no hope of salvation remains, when even you, the most illus-
> trious of philosophers, take nothing to heart but words and the differ-
> ent forces of words! Yet I will send you a book in which you will find
> what you are looking for. For I, although a grammarian, seek reasoned
> teachings concerning life and morals, while you philosophers are, as
> M. Cato says, mere *mortualia,* or winding-sheets: you collect word lists
> and favorite little expressions, things that are disgusting, useless, and
> frivolous—just like the sounds of those women known as *praeficae.* And
> would that all human beings were mute! Shamelessness would have
> less means of expressing itself.

> Nulla, inquit, prorsus bonae salutis spes reliqua est, cum vos quoque,
> philosophorum inlustrissimi, nihil iam aliud quam verba auctorita-
> tesque verborum cordi habetis. Mittam autem librum tibi, in quo id
> reperias quod quaeris. Ego enim grammaticus vitae iam atque morum
> disciplinas quaero, vos philosophi mera estis, ut M. Cato ait, "mortu-
> alia"; glosaria namque conligitis et lexidia, res taetras et inanes et frivo-
> las, tamquam mulierum voces "praeficarum." Atque utinam, inquit,

muti omnes homines essemus! minus improbitas instrumenti haberet. (Gell. *NA* 18.7.3)

Domitius beats Favorinus at his own game, citing two unusual but interrelated words, *mortualia* and *praeficae,* in the course of his answer. As the chapter proceeds, we learn that the book he supplied did in fact explain, among other things, the meanings of *contiones,* which is the word Favorinus had proposed as a possible Latin equivalent of *dēmēgoriai.* The grammarian, despite his outburst, is master of his craft. Yet the choice of terms with which to insult — and top — the philosopher hardly seems accidental. We know nothing more of the fragment from Cato; indeed, we cannot be sure whether it extends only to the word *mortualia* or perhaps (as seems more likely) includes the association of that term with philosophers, in which case Domitius would be citing the highest moral and lexical authority for both form and content of his attack. But we do know that the term *mortualia* was familiar enough for Plautus to play upon it in a passage in *Asinaria,* where, after reading a letter he has drafted on behalf of a lovestruck youth, a parasite proclaims, "this is no gibberish, no *mortualia*" (*haec sunt non nugae, non enim mortualia,* Plaut. *Asin.* 808).[91] *Mortualia* here seems to mean either winding-sheets, that is, useless, disgusting pieces of cloth wrapped around the corpse (a meaning attested by Naevius in Nonius) or something like *nenia* — the useless, trivial song sung on the occasion of the funeral. If the parasite emphasizes the materiality of the letter he is reading out, the former makes more sense; if the performance, the latter. But then *mortualia* seems to have the same ambiguity in the fragment from Cato as cited by Domitius: the philosophers, conceived of as producers of text, might better be likened to winding-sheets; but as linguistic performances, their verbal productions might more appropriately be insulted as funeral dirges.

Unexpected as this ascription of deliberate ambiguity to Domitius might seem, it is confirmed by the contents of the book he later sends to Favorinus, which demonstrates, according to Gellius, how *senatus* was used for a place and persons, *civitas* for locale, town, constitution, and a multitude of people, and so on. Domitius's use of the peculiarly ambiguous insult *mortualia* thus looks forward to the contents of the book he will send, which is all about ambiguity, but also, it would seem, backward to his use of the plural *auctoritates,* in referring to the interests of philosophers: they are interested not just in words but in the multiple forces or meanings of individual words.

Now, Domitius's citation of Cato for the term *mortualia* is followed by the further (or elaborated) insult of philosophers as gatherers of word lists, disgusting, inane, frivolous things, "like the utterances of women (known as) *praeficae.*" Up to this point we have regarded the utterances of *praeficae* as *neniae,* a word Domitius does not use. But then he does not exactly say either what we might have expected him to say — namely, that *mortualia* is a term for the utterances of *praeficae*. It seems quite possible, that even as he resolves one puzzle (i.e., the multiple meanings of the term *contio*) with another puzzle (the ambiguity of *mortualia*), he introduces still another linguistic conundrum, namely, the use of *mortualia* and *nenia* for the same performance. Yet even without attributing such deviousness to Domitius or Gellius, we are still left with an explicit set of references linking the trivial verbal obsessions of philosophers with the utterances of the *praeficae* in an anecdote specifically placed at the temple of Carmentis and followed by discussion of a grammatical treatise that demonstrates the ambiguity of the very terms that define the political community of the Romans, namely *senatus* and *civitas* (as mentioned previously), as well as *tribus, decuriae,* and finally, the original culprit, *contio*. What is more, we are told by Favorinus, via the narrator Gellius, that Domitius himself either is or is not insane and may or may not be speaking a profound truth. The whole episode is beginning to seem less like a neutral anecdote of one-upmanship and more like the manifestation of multiple notions of voice and its authority. In effect, it crystallizes in a deceptively simple narrative the tension between different constructions of verbal performance — male and female, local (Domitius is a famous grammarian at Rome) and foreign (Favorinus, we know from elsewhere in the text, is a speaker of Greek from Gaul), univocal and polyvalent, spoken and written, one-directional (e.g., *disciplinas*) and playfully responsive, old (Cato) and new — not to mention different constructions of the very community the verbal performance seeks to found. And all of this is due to an encounter at the shrine of Carmentis. The anecdote brings to the fore the very forces that the marginalization of Carmentis, Nenia, and the figure of the *praefica* seek to contain.

If Gellius, writing in the second century AD, illuminates the self-deconstructing potential of Roman strategies of containing without effacing alternative systems of song, a much earlier story makes clear what at least one sector of the population regarded as being at stake in the struggle over ritualized speech. As he prepares to begin his catalog of Roman orators, Cicero suggests that oratorical prowess can be inferred even about republican leaders who left no written legacy. Brutus, he argues, could not have expelled the last king and founded the republic had he not used the "persuasive force of oratory" (*oratione persuasum,* Cic. *Brut.* 53). The dictator Marcus Valerius must have used eloquence when he persuaded the plebs to end their legendary secession. Lucius Valerius Potitus, Appius Claudius, Gaius Fabricius, Tiberius Coruncanius, Manius Curius, Appius Claudius — all settled difficulties domestic or foreign in such a manner as to imply the use of skillful oratory. But the figure who, after Brutus, receives the longest discussion is Marcus Popilius (known elsewhere as Marcus Popilius Laenas, cos. 348).[92] "Of his talent," Cicero writes, "something can be inferred" (*licet aliquid etiam de M. Popili ingenio suspicari,* 56):

> Once during his consulship he was performing public sacrifice, dressed in a *laena* in his capacity as the *flamen Carmentalis.* He received the news that the plebs were rising in sedition against the aristocrats. So, still dressed in his *laena,* he went to the *contio* and, relying on both charisma and oratory, put an end the rebellion.

> qui cum consul esset eodemque tempore sacrificium publicum cum laena faceret, quod erat flamen Carmentalis, plebei contra patres concitatione et seditione nuntiata, ut erat laena amictus ita venit in contionem seditionemque cum auctoritate tum oratione sedavit. (Cic. *Brut.* 56)

If considered strictly from the standpoint of the history of oratory, the episode of Popilius illustrates the continuing attempt to assign religious authority to the nominally secular figure of the orator. If considered in terms of the struggle between song and oratory for political ascendancy, the episode counts as one of several illustrating the gradual rise of oratory as a distinct practice. But in terms of the particular role we have identified for Carmentis and all that she, together with *nenia,* implies concerning the interrelationship of song, sacrifice, the materiality of the body, as well as the potential multiplication of voices and authorities, the episode can be understood as asserting the privileged status of the elite male voice — even, or perhaps especially, the voice of a plebeian consul seeking to quell the sedition of his fellow plebeians. Just as the authoritative male voice seeks to subsume the ability of *ludus* to fashion reality and thereby joins the homosocial chorus of legitimate voices, so here the male, singular, political figure quite literally wraps himself in the mantle of Carmentis to secure the integrity, the oneness, of the political community of Rome.

Magic and the State

Carmentis and Nenia, whether we conceive of them as anthropomorphic deities or as synecdoches for a complex set of practices, discourses, and beliefs, are figures of boundaries or transitions: between nonbeing and being, life and death, the interior and the exterior of the body, and the interior and exterior of the state. Carmentis presides over birth, fate, and the triumphal entry into the city (the *porta Carmentalis* also being known as the *porta triumphalis*). As *vates* she inaugurates correct sacrificial procedures. In the calendar she is linked with Janus; in legend with the founding of civilization on the site of Rome. Nenia, on the other hand, marks the end. She is the end of the intestines, the last song, a lullaby, a farewell, a conclusion. And yet at the same time, she and, to a lesser extent, Carmentis are associated with the unboundability of the body, with expulsion, surplus, penetrability, disembowelment. Because of their association with the real as opposed to the ideal body (or, in Bakhtinian terms, the grotesque as opposed to the classical), Carmentis and Nenia are marginalized in the song and practice of elite males. But they cannot be eliminated entirely. In fact, the Roman state requires Carmentis and more so Nenia to secure precisely the boundedness of the body and of time that are necessary for the state to come into being and at any given to moment remain so.

The funeral at which *nenia* is performed is only an end for those who believe that the dead cease to exist. As Gil points out, in many tribal societies, death is not an end, but the beginning of a different state of being.[93] The dead dwell — sometimes comfortably, sometimes uneasily — among the living.[94] The belief in the finality of death is a necessary condition for the development and maintenance of a sense of history as unidirectional, which is itself an enabling condition and central tenet of the state. But how is the finality of death to be secured except by the laying to rest of the dead in body and in spirit? This creation of an impenetrable boundary between the dead and the living seems to be what G. Wille has in mind when he describes the noise of the Roman *nenia* as an attempt to keep the spirits of the dead at bay.[95] And the ancient sources sometimes speak of *nenia* in precisely this way. Thus, Martianus Capella has the goddess Harmonia declare that it is through her that "human beings have attracted assistance [perhaps medical cures?] and calmed infernal wrath through *nenias*" (*Per me . . . homines illexere succursum irasque inferas per nenias sedavere*, Phil. 9.925). Such a belief would also account for the recurrent claim that the *nenia* "praised" the deceased.[96] Rather than constituting a confusion between the *nenia* and the funeral laudation, such claims might well acknowledge potential differences in the purpose of praise: in one case, to establish a pattern for imitation or surrogation, to validate the authority of the *imago;* in the other case, to keep the dead at bay, to make it clear that their life has been consummated, to block their access to the world of the living. Indeed, a scholiast on Horace *Odes* 3.28 makes an interesting distinction between the newly deceased and those already below the earth when he defines *nenia* as "a song that is sung to (or for) the dead in honor of those below" (*carmen est, quod mortuis cantabatur in honorem inferorum*, Schol. Hor. *Carm.*

3.28.16).[97] We are perhaps to form an image, similar to that inspired by the passage from Ausonius, of the undead, or the no-longer-dead, surging forward as access to the underworld is temporarily opened in order to accommodate the newly deceased. Elsewhere as well the *nenia* is described as an "honor" or a "duty" toward the dead, apparently with the implication that the dead will remain unsettled without it.[98] In one of several prophecies of poetic immortality Horace orders away "*neniae* and shameful grieving and lament" (*absint . . . neniae/luctusque turpes et querimoniae*, Carm. 2.20.21–22). "Restrain all outcry," he continues, "and chase superfluous honors from my tomb" (*compesce clamorem ac sepulcri/mitte supervacuos honores*, 2.20.23–24). Apart from confirming the association of *nenia* with loud noise and with honor for the deceased, the Horatian passage also points, by implication, to the function of *nenia* in keeping the dead at bay: such an attempt is futile, he suggests, for he (Horace) will already have been transformed into a swan, a "twin-shaped *vates*" (*biformis vates*, 2.20.2–3), and carried aloft into the upper atmosphere. Horace's announcement of poetic immortality draws upon a more disturbing belief in the incompleteness of death. He both promises and threatens death as "a mode of being."[99]

This tension between two versions of death—and the consequent notions of history—explains the coexistence in the Roman funeral rite of two types of verbal performance, namely the *laudatio*, spoken by the young male making his debut in public life, and the *nenia*, led by the *praefica* and joined by a gathering chorus. Cicero expressly states that it is a Roman custom at the funeral of "honored men" (*honoratorum virorum*, Leg. 2.62) for *laudes*, or speeches of praise, to be delivered in an assembly, and then for a funeral song, or *nenia*, to be performed to the accompaniment of a flute (*Leg.* 2.62). Horace, in the first ode of the second book, implies that the *nenia* (Carm. 2.1.38) is the musical or poetic counterpart to the prose narrative of recent battles and deaths composed by Asinius Pollio. While Horace alludes to the poems for the Greek war dead attributed to Simonides and thus provides a Hellenic literary point of reference for his mention of *nenia*, nonetheless the contrast between Pollio's narrative and Horace's poetic possibilities (*nenia* or something less lugubrious) seems to depend on the audience's awareness of the double performance of *laudatio* and *nenia* at the elite funeral. The *Apocolocyntosis* attributed to Seneca is also structured in part around a contrast or division between *laudatio* (in this case, an anti-*laudatio*) and *nenia*. The speech of the deified Augustus, who expressly presents himself as speaking among the gods for the first time (*Apocol.* 10.1), and proceeds to list both his own positive achievements (with ample use of the colon-final perfective form of the verb that is characteristic of surviving *laudationes*) and Claudius's negative accomplishments, takes the place of the *lau-*

datio, while the dirge Claudius hears on his way back to the underworld is identified as a *nenia* being sung by a large chorus (*ingenti enim megaloi khorikoi nenia cantabatur*, 12.10). A similar double performance, without explicit use of the term *nenia*, is recorded for other imperial funerals as well.[100]

Heller would see the coexistence of "serious" *laudatio* with "trivial" *nenia* as an extension of the early practice of incorporating parody into serious triumphal and other processions.[101] But this is to put the cart of triviality before the horse of mourning. None of the passages that describe the actual performance of *nenia* presents it as other than serious, sincere, and meaningful: "emotional work," as one scholar has described it.[102] Retrospectively the apparently simple nature of the chants, the gender of the *praefica*, the potential boundlessness of the circle of mourners and of the expressions of grief can and do lead to the identification of the *nenia* as "trivial" or "trifling"—as no doubt does the concrete application of the term *nenia* to the last bit of entrail. But apart from serving as a form of emotional expression (for surely the elite males, who seem not to partake of the *nenia*, have emotions as well), the *nenia* must also be understood in its relationship to the *laudatio* with which it is paired. In the commemorative oration delivered by the male ingenue, we see the ritual instantiation of the power of the voice, the separation of the vocal from the bodily, and, to be sure, passionate aspects of human existence. It is not that the *praeficae* do not use their voices as well but that their vocalizations, their *neniae*, are regarded as vile, tawdry, even repulsive. The crucial moment of transition from one generation to the next thus contains within it the reproduction and transmission of the divide between body and voice that we have observed as built into the systematic distinction between play and song. *Nenia*, although it is a type of song, takes the participant and the audience in the direction of the body, *laudatio* in the direction of the voice and mind. What we have had to understand through a long process of philological analysis is lived by the participants in the Roman funeral, male and female, elite and nonelite, volunteers and hirelings.

But, as I have suggested, there is more. *Nenia* settles the spirits of the dead. It allows for, even as it tries to prevent, the possibility that death is just another mode of being. It opposes the *laudatio* along axes of gender and class, but it ultimately supports the overall social function of the *laudatio*. For it is only by laying the dead to rest that they can become ancestors, that they can become the history that the elite male calls upon to authorize his own status, and that, on the political level, the state requires if its own authority is to be seen as transcending time. Without *nenia*, there is no divide between living and dead, past and present; there is no ancestor to be emulated, no need for a state to transmit the *mos maiorum* from one generation to the next, because there are in effect no *maiores*.

In its role as creator of ancestors, *nenia* forms a partnership with Carmentis and her divinatory skills. For while Carmentis is not explicitly concerned with ancestors, the skills she bears give her access to two conflicting modes of the interpretation of signs, which are not unrelated to conflicting approaches to the status of the dead. Much as Nenia, in laying to rest the dead simultaneously allows for the possibility of their continuing existence, so the *vates* Carmentis is a figure of metaphysical and semiotic duality. From the standpoint of the state, she possesses dangerously direct access to the meanings inscribed in nature (entrails, places, etc.). Hence she must be marginalized, her skills co-opted by colleges of pontiffs, her mortal avatars excluded from the *civitas* through force or ideology or both.[103] But at the same time as she resists the estrangement from nature brought about by language, as she emblematizes the irreducible complexity of material existence, she also makes possible the decorporealization of language by introducing writing. For we are told, in source after source, that Carmentis, or the Arcadians more generally as led by her and her son Evander, introduced writing to Italy—and not just any writing but the Greek alphabet as adapted to the needs of the Latin language.[104] In other words, Carmentis has access to natural phenomena that are signs in themselves, but also to a phonetic alphabet that is, in effect, a reanimation of the prototype of speech.

In a rich and suggestive discussion of the interrelationship of art, script, and ancestor worship in early China, David Keightley draws a connection between the development of script that represents speech (as opposed to representing things in themselves), and the creation of "ancestors" through the practice of secondary burials.

> Chinese characters may thus be thought of as a form of aural commemoration, of revivification that functioned in ways analogous to the mortuary treatment of skeletons. Just as religious rituals turned the deceased, once alive, into an ancestor with whom one could communicate and who had certain religious tasks and duties, so did the use of graph strokes turn the word that had once been spoken into a written form of communication, with its semiotic tasks and duties. Just as the living heard the sounds of their ancestors in the divination cracks, so did the Chinese characters provide the means to hear the sounds of the original words, bringing those words, as it were, back to life.[105]

While the Roman view of the ancestors, or *maiores*, certainly differs from that of the Chinese, both cultures imagine a process of reanimation made possible, paradoxically, by the finality of death. In Roman terms, the work of Carmentis and the work of Nenia presuppose one another. And while some may wish to interpret the story of Carmentis and the alphabet as late republican guesswork, or, in the case of Dionysius of Halicarnassus, part of an ongoing effort to assign all things Roman a Greek origin, it has to be admitted that the story fits—both with the rest of the legend and cult of Carmentis, concerned as it is with the reading of signs, and with historical evidence concerning the relationship between the Latin alphabet and the Greek and the great antiquity of writing in the vicinity of Rome, which predates even the eighth-century founding.[106] Moreover, the relationship between writing and song implied by the story of Carmentis is the same as that to be inferred from the Roman record more generally as analyzed throughout this study. Far from diminishing the importance of song, writing is a prompt to its further production. Writing remains dependent on and secondary to speech. To regard writing as providing direct access to objects or ideas represented would be to construe it as equivalent to the reading of entrails or the magical interpretation of natural signs, something the elite Roman tradition will remain reluctant to do. For the Romans, writing is coextensive with the history of the state—not as a means of bureaucratic control, although that in time will come, but as one more manifestation of the gap between the dead and the living, between the prototype and its reanimation or revivification. The writing of Carmentis, like *nenia*, makes history possible. And yet, as we have seen, that history is, from its commencement, co-opted by song: for the song of the *salii*, too, as well, one imagines, as the song of the *sodales*, is coincident with if not prior to the coming into being of the state. The process of marginalization of Carmentis and Nenia is not one that follows a simple historical trajectory: rather it is one that must be engaged in at each and every moment if history is to continue.

And so we find throughout Roman history an attempt to contain the negative powers associated with Carmentis and Nenia: explicitly in the rhetorical trivialization of *nenia*, implicitly in the reassignment of *vates* and *nenia* to socially excluded or disreputable sectors of the population. It is something of a chicken-and-egg problem to determine whether it is the social marginality of women and foreigners that leads to the exclusion of *vates,* or the need to exclude *vates* that leads to their identification as women and foreigners. No doubt both forces are at work simultaneously. Yet the Romans' willingness to acknowledge Carmentis's status as *vates* and her role in the founding, their acknowledgment, as in the Twelve Tables, of the possibility of enchantment, and their use of the terms *carmen* and *cantus* indiscriminately of song and incantation suggest an underlying acknowledgment of the continuing role of what we would call sorcery or magic in political and social affairs. As with so much else, the Romans prefer to subsume or deport rather than destroy.

It would be an interesting exercise to try to relate the outbursts of rhetorical and other types of violence against the *vates*, the *sacrificuli*, the *praeficae*, and the *neniae* to other developments in the cultural history of Rome. Certainly scholars have demonstrated various ways in which the suppression of the vatic-inspired Bacchanals in 186 BC served the needs of an embattled elite seeking to secure its hold over post-Hannibalic Italy. We can read the upsurge of Dionysiac activity and its ferocious repression as delayed reaction to the depredations of the Second Punic War. More compelling is the view that the Roman elite takes advantage of genuine threats in preceding generations to manufacture a rhetorical threat to social stability in the 180s.[107]

A similar pattern obtains in the flurry of accusations against the Marsi and association of them with the dangerous powers of *nenia* generations after their acquiescence in the Social Wars of the early first century BC. To be sure the Marsi had presented a problem for the Romans and had been associated with magical practices long before the so-called Bellum Marsicum of 90–87 BC. For an extended period during the Samnite Wars their territory was treated by the Romans as a safe passage to Samnium, not always reliably: indeed, Livy refers to two separate rebellions by the Marsi during the late fourth century (Livy 8.29.4, 9.41.45).[108] These, combined with their leadership in the Social Wars, led the Marsi to be regarded, in the view of one scholar, as the enemy of Rome "per eccellenza,"[109] ideal figures of alterity. But this is perhaps to miss the specificity of the implied accusation against the Marsi. In Livy's account, the Marsi start out providing safe passage, then defect. During the Hannibalic Wars, they remain loyal to Rome (Livy 28.45), yet they become ringleaders during the Social Wars. Rather than the enemy par excellence, the Marsi constitute the danger within—a fifth column, to invoke a twentieth-century image.[110]

Against this background, the specific claims with respect to the magical powers of the Marsi begin to take on new significance. Already in Lucilius we find the prediction (made by whom, we can't tell) that someone

> will burst in two, as happens when a Marsian makes snakes burst
>   open,
> having stretched all their veins with his incantation.

> iam disrumpetur medius, iam, ut Marsus colubras
> disrumpit cantu venas cum extenderit omnes.

> (Lucil. 605–6 W)

While Marsians' skillful handling of snakes and other natural entities can sometimes be presented in a more positive light,[111] their assault on bodily integrity figures in some memorable appearances in Augustan poetry. When Horace has the witch Canidia ponder the failure of her magic, she ascribes it to a rival's greater skill in incantation (*veneficae/ scientioris carmine*, Epod. 5.71–72). As she exclaims:

> Not by the customary potions, Varus,
>> O head about to weep much!
> will you run back to me, nor will your mind return
>> recalled by Marsian spells.

> Non usitatis, Vare, potionibus,
>> o multa fleturum caput,
> ad me recurres, nec vocata mens tua
>> Marsis redibit vocibus.
>>> (Hor. *Epod.* 5.73–76)

The exclamation comes at a moment of dramatic recognition on Canidia's part (*a! a!*, she cries out, 5.71), the implication being that what she has tried so far has been the equivalent of Marsian spells, and therefore unexpectedly ineffectual. That prior attempt, as described earlier in the poem, has consisted of a double assault on bodily integrity, from within and without, for we have been shown how Canidia and her assistants have buried a prepubescent boy so deep in the ground that only as much of his face is exposed as stays above water when a body is suspended by the chin (5.35–36: a very strange image indeed). The aim of the witches is to starve the boy to death, then use his innards and liver to make a love-potion—but only after his eyes have started to ooze (*intabuissent pupulae*, 5.40). Horace imagines a bodily betrayal from within and an assault on the innards from without. Indeed, the whole scenario, with its young boy, lead witch and assistants, head protruding from fluid just a bit, and oozing eyes, is a weird inversion of a scene of birth, with Canidia (whose name perhaps evokes the *can-* of *cano*, despite the difference in vowel quantity) and her sidekicks standing in for a midwife and helpers or even Carmentis, Postvorta, and Antevorta. Even Varus, the target of Canidia's erotic attentions, is described only as "a head about to weep much" (*multa fleturum caput*, 5.74). While "head" can be a term of endearment, especially in Greek poetry, it hardly seems such here, and the image of a weeping head reinforces that of the buried boy, with only head exposed, and eyes dripping, whether from disintegration or birth fluids or both.[112]

Horace never gets around to telling us what kind of magic Canidia will cook up that is worse than all of this, more powerful even than

Marsian spells, but his recantation of his attacks on her in epode 17 reinforces the association between the Marsi and the rupture of bodily integrity, while also assigning their chants the specific name *nenia*. As Horace concedes,

> And so I am forced to admit what I had denied,
> that Sabellan songs make a heart beat loud
> and Marsian *nenia* can cause a head to leap apart.

> Ergo negatum vincor ut credam miser,
> Sabella pectus increpare carmina
> caputque Marsa dissilire nenia.
>
> (Hor. *Epod.* 17.27–29)

Ovid, too, describes the Marsian use of magical language as *nenia*, fitting the ethnic to the verbal performance as readily as he unites "Medean" to herbs and "Haemonian," or Thracian, to magical arts (*Ars Am.* 2.99–102). Whatever it is that leads Marsian incantation to be given the same term as Roman funeral lament, the connection is a strong one, for no other ethnic group, besides the Marsi and the Romans themselves, is associated with *nenia*.

The dangers to be ascribed to Marsian *nenia* receive fullest discussion in Ovid's account, in book 6 of the *Fasti*, of the festival and story of Carna. There we learn of Carna's rape by Janus, of her power to ward off screech owls who prey on infant boys, and of the honors she receives in the form of a sacrifice of beans. Carna herself is a virtual doublet of Carmentis. Her name is built on the same verbal root for carving or dividing,[113] she is closely linked to Janus (in her case through a story that he raped her and rewarded her with special powers),[114] and she figures in yet another story of foundation and foundation sacrifice. As Macrobius tells it, Junius Brutus, who took the lead in expelling the Tarquins, celebrated the success of the venture by making a sacrifice to Carna on the Caelian mount in fulfillment of an oath (*pulso Tarquinio sacrum Carnae deae in Caelio monte voti reus fecerit*, *Sat.* 1.12.31).[115] While Macrobius thinks Brutus picked Carna because as protectress of the vital organs (*vitalibus humanis praeesse*, 1.12.32) she had helped him to disguise his own internal strength, it seems more likely that she, like Carmentis, presides over the vital organs of (among others) sacrificial victims and thus, like Carmentis, is to be associated with the founding (or, in this case, refounding) of Rome and its attendant religious practices. Indeed, as Sabbatucci sees, Carna's sharing of her feast, in Ovid and in the Roman calendar, with Juno Moneta, makes sense in that the cult of Juno Moneta is itself associated with yet another refounding of Rome, this time by Camillus in the aftermath of the Gallic invasion and sack of the city.[116] Like Carmentis before them, so Carna and Juno Moneta seem to speak to a concern with foundational knowledge of the inner workings of the body, particularly as ascribed to the female.

But if Carna resembles Carmentis, she also has much in common with *nenia* as well. In Ovid's story, it is Marsian *nenia* that transforms old women into the dangerous screech owls, whom Carna must ward off. They seek to devour the entrails of the king's baby son; she seeks to appease them with the sacrifice of a baby pig. Moreover, while *nenia* marks the passage between life and death and keeps the dead at bay, Carna is the eponymous goddess of the Carnaria, a feast at which survivors and heirs commemorate the deceased by strewing roses.[117] While the connection with Carmentis, with Juno, or with the laying down of the dead more generally is not articulated in Ovid's legend, nonetheless his poetic narrative displays deep, one might say tender concern with the entrails of baby boys and the need to protect them from the dangerous ways of women. As clearly as any of the passages we have considered thus far, his tale gives expression to the foundational knowledge associated with song, sacrifice, and magic, once again grounding such knowledge in the materiality of the body, and once again acknowledging its potential both to create and to destroy a *civitas* based on the hegemony of elite males.

As Ovid explains it, in exchange for having slept with Carna, Janus makes her goddess of hinges, but also grants to her a white thorn "through which she would be able to repel sad harm from doors" (*qua tristes pellere posset / a foribus noxas, Fast.* 6.129–30). The hinges and the doors don't concern Ovid much, but the white thorn and in particular the damage it can foreclose receive full discussion. It turns out that the power of the thorn is to be directed against the attack of screech owls, hideous nocturnal birds that were either born that way or "came about through song, when Marsian *nenia* transformed crones into creatures of flight" (*seu carmine fiunt, / naeniaque in volucres Marsa figurat anus,* 6.141–42). These screech owls, or *striges,* are literary relatives of Harpies, as Ovid himself acknowledges, but they also resemble Canidia and her collaborators. They prey upon unguarded boys, snatching them from their cribs, violating (*vitiant,* 6.) their bodies, tearing out their milky entrails with their beaks (*carpere . . . lactentia viscera rostris,* 6.137), and filling their own maws with the infants' blood. When the *striges* attack the infant son of King Proca of Alba Longa, they caress his baby breast with their tongues, but he cries out, and his nurse, who comes upon the birds now ripping the baby's cheeks with their hard claws, rushes to tell Carna (under her alternative name Grane). Carna performs the appropriate apotropaic ritual, touching the doors with an arbutus frond, sprinkling helpful water, and offering up the raw innards (*exta . . . cruda*, 6.158) of a two-month-old pig, expressly proposing them as a substitute for the sought-after entrails of the boy:

> And so, birds of the Night, spare the boyish innards (says she):
>   a small victim perishes for the sake of a small child.
> Heart for heart, entrails for entrails, I beseech you, carry them off!
>   We offer this life in exchange for one that is better.

> Atque ita, Noctis aves, extis puerilibus, inquit,
>   parcite: pro parvo victima parva cadit
> cor pro corde, precor, pro fibris sumite fibras
>   hanc animam vobis pro meliore damus.

>   (Ov. *Fast.* 6.159–62).

Having completed her libation, Carna sets out the entrails (*prosecta*), forbids anyone to look back at them, and places a branch of the white thorn near the window of the nursery. Thereafter, the birds stay away and the baby's healthy color returns.

Carna fights magic with magic, sacrifice with sacrifice. Although a victim of rape, she sides with the principle of patriarchy, indeed enables its continuation by rescuing the king's son. Having deceived men, tantalizing them with the prospect of withheld sex, and having in her turn been deceived by the male god Janus, she now openly invites the *striges* to accept the trick, the deceit of sacrificial substitution. If her own body is not especially interesting to the poet, certainly that of the king's son is—his baby's breast, his cheeks marked by scratches, his milky entrails, a sign, to be sure, that he is not yet weaned, but also a macabre invitation to the reader to visualize his disembowelment. And yet the relationship of the *striges* to the baby's body is not altogether hostile, for at first, before he cried out, they "were sucking on his infant breast with greedy tongues" (*pectoraque exsorbent avidis infantia linguis*, 6.145)—an image expressive of their own infantile eroticism, their own momentary regression to a stage where harmless gratification is all that is sought. "But the unlucky boy wails" (*at puer infelix vagit*, 6.146): unlucky, to be sure, as the potential target of claws and beaks, but unlucky, too, in the fate that awaits him, in the need to separate from the caress, from pleasure undifferentiated by gender, and to assume his role in the continuation of the state, the forward march of history.[118] And an important role it is, for while Ovid says no more here of Procas's son but continues with the honors owed to Carna, other texts expatiate on the two sons of Procas, Numitor and Amulius, one the maternal grandfather, the other the tyrannical opponent, of Rome's founder Romulus and his ill-fated twin.

Back to the Labyrinth

I have argued that *nenia* settles the dead and thereby makes history possible, a history created by the reanimation of ancestral prototypes. At the same time, *nenia* has the power to rupture bodies, to expose the innards, and in so doing to deny the distinctiveness of human beings, to resituate them, male and female, within nature. While the power of *nenia* can be construed as magical, it is also clearly political in nature; indeed it is foundational of politics in its etymological sense of the activity of members of an abstract, transtemporal community, that is, to use the term loosely, the state.

The tension between the deadness of the dead, their categorical difference from the living, and the materiality of the body, its embeddedness in a nature from which neither language nor ideology has estranged it, is manifest as well in the rite of the *salii*, with which our study began. But there, rather than constituting a source of anxiety, the triumph of culture over nature is cause for celebration, for *exultatio*. Whereas Nenia, together with Carmentis, Carna, *vates*, magicians, and so on, skew the dichotomy reanimation-materiality in the direction of the material (the natural, the ungendered), the Salian rite emphasizes the cultural, the abstract, the masculine, the voice. We can grasp the difference by considering the way concrete representations of the body figure in the Salian rite, only to be transcended. Here the key image is that of the labyrinth, or *truia*, the modified spiral incised on the Tragliatellan oinochoe, the dance pattern of the *salii*, and, more generally, both a creator of a boundary between living and dead and a sign of the materiality of the body.

Of the labyrinth as threshold between life and death much has been written.[119] Perhaps the clearest ancient indication is to be found in Vergil's *Aeneid*. Book 6 opens with a depiction of the Daedalan labyrinth on the Gates at Cumae: an anticipation of the poet's own more general depiction of the underworld as labyrinthine. The association of labyrinth with difficult access to the dead (and difficult egress for the dead) is widespread, in antiquity and in later periods. The four model labyrinths identified by the ancient literary tradition all have something to do with the boundary between life and death: the Egyptian labyrinth described by Herodotus is also a tomb of the pharaohs; the Etruscan labyrinth guards access to the grave of Lars Porsenna; the Cretan labyrinth hides the Minotaur, whose task is to finish off the young men and women offered as tribute to the tyrant; and Troy, as labyrinth, is the quintessential site of heroic combat and death.[120]

But Troy is a labyrinth in another sense as well: it hides the prized female, Helen, as the Cretan labyrinth seems to have hidden Ariadne in some versions of that story.[121] If it means death for many, it also marks the transition to full, adult status for others. The penetration of the labyrinthine walls of Troy by the horse is an image of heterosexual intercourse[122] and coincides in myth with mass rape. And the Cretan labyrinth is for Theseus the occasion of initiation into adulthood: indeed, his adventures in the labyrinth and subsequent escape in the company of the fourteen youths are the mythical counterpart of the ritual celebration of the initiatory crane dance, or *geranos*, on the island of Delos.[123] The knowledge acquired by the journey into and return from the labyrinth can be represented as psychological or ethical or cultural: but it is also knowledge of the innards of the body, whether construed as entrails or female sexual organs or both.

Babylonian tablets from about 1000 BC that pertain to the reading of entrails depict them as labyrinthine spirals. (Indeed one such tablet contains the inscription "palace of the intestines.")[124] And the term *trua,* which is the probable base of the Salian verbs *amptruare* and *redamptruare,* describes, according to Festus, the pattern produced by entrails as they are agitated while cooking (*truam quoque vocant, quo permovent coquentes exta,* 9 L).[125] Scholars have noted the evocation of the Cretan labyrinth in Vergil's account of Dido and Aeneas's ill-fated hunt.[126] The cave they enter may recall any of a number of labyrinthine caves,[127] but ultimately it is the main characters' sexual encounter, figured as a kind of hierogamos, or cosmic marriage, that matters, not their spelunking. Is the labyrinth also a figure for a part of the female anatomy, then? Certain representations of the Theseus-Ariadne-Minotaur triangle suggest as much, although exactly which part is less clear: in one the thread dangles from the trim of Ariadne's robe and coils in front of her chest; in another it comes from the top of her head and coils near ground level, beneath Theseus's uplifted foot. But in each instance, the ball is distinctly a coil or labyrinth, not the more compressed sphere we might imagine.[128] All of which returns us to the oinochoe from Tragliatella, with its evocation of *lusus Troiae* in the figure of horsemen; of *salii* in the dancing of the armed men; of initiation in the different types of clothing and in the depiction of sexual intercourse; and, of course, its depiction of a labyrinth captioned TRVIA.

When Theseus defeated the Minotaur, he rescued young women as well as men. His crane dance was performed by both sexes. Women are present in the Tragliatella oinochoe, as sex partners, and in other roles harder for us to understand. And they were present in the Salian rite as well. We hear of a Salian *praesula,* that is, female lead dancer, from Tusculum (*ILS* 5018). Perhaps more important, we learn from Festus, who attributes the tidbit to both Cincius Alimentus and Aelius Stilo that there were also *saliae virgines.* According to Cincius they were hired (*conducticias,* much like the *praeficae*) and added to, or brought to, or summoned (as guests?) to the male *salii* (*quae ad salios adhibebantur,* Fest. 439 L). Cincius makes it seem as though the Salian maidens were geishas or *hetairai.* But Aelius assigns them a different role, reporting that "they make sacrifice in the *regia* with the *pontifex* while dressed in military garb with *apices* in the manner of the *salii*" (*sacrificium facere in regia cum pontifice paludatas cum apicibus in modum Saliorum,* Fest. 439 L). They look like *salii,* they act like *salii,* they are associated with the *regia,* like *salii.* But there is perhaps one problem: they perform their sacrifice in the company of the pontiff (which one we don't know), a figure of the republican reorganization of Roman religion. We may see here yet again a practice of effacing without entirely suppressing the involvement of women in the foundational activities of the state, with the Salian maidens maintaining some, but not all, of the aspects of an early initiation rite that continued in fuller form for young men.[129] Vergil performs a similar act of effacement, as he has Daedalus depict Theseus's rescue only of seven youths, not of the otherwise canonical set of seven youths and seven maidens.[130] And yet, in the final analysis, Roman ritual could no more dispense with the knowledge of women than Vergil could allow his hero to enter the labyrinth of the underworld without a *vates* to guide him.

EPILOGUE· AT THE
THRESHOLD OF HISTORY

T HIS STUDY OPENED WITH A WARNING AGAINST THE RETRO-
active imposition of contemporary categories of cultural
organization onto the remains antiquity. Instead, it has
used the language of the Romans, in particular, terms pertaining to song, speech, play, imitation, and sacrifice to
gain access to the practices and concepts that shaped Roman verbal
production. It would be a mistake, however, to go to an opposite extreme of philological determinism and suggest that only those categories and concepts that are represented by specific terms with easily
circumscribed meanings are relevant to our own understanding of ancient Rome. Indeed, one of the key arguments of this book has been
that the privileging of language, especially the disembodied vocal performance of the elite male, is a self-interested maneuver on the part of
a segment of the Roman population, a highly successful strategy that
nonetheless cannot efface traces of other, more explicitly embodied,
practices. If emphasis on the "literariness" of Roman texts is an anach-
ronistic privileging of one aspect of Roman cultural practice, a privileging that blinds us to the rich and suggestive remains of Roman song, so
too, overemphasis on song, especially if it is reduced to a component
of a system, can obscure both the bodiliness of vocal performance and
the pervasiveness of the mimetic faculty that informs it. In her study
of mimetic performance of the BaAka of central Africa Michelle Kisliuk has made rich use of Raymond Williams's suggestion that "we have
to break from the common procedure of isolating the object and then
discovering its components. On the contrary we have to discover the
nature of a practice and then its conditions" — to which we might add,
"its conditions as they evolve and differ across time and space."[1] In this

study I have attempted to grasp the nature of the practice of song and to begin to comprehend its conditions.

Yet one of the paradoxes of studying the history of Roman song is that the production of song is itself a condition of the history that preserves evidence of it. By this paradox I refer not only to the relatively obvious point that writing, the promptbook and aide-mémoire of ancient song, is the bulk of what remains for us to analyze, but also to Horkheimer's and Adorno's conception of the "threshold of history" as the point where "mimesis as a practice for living with nature blurs with the transformation of mimesis into an instrument for dominating."[2] We recall that for Horkheimer and Adorno this crossing of the threshold begins the "long march to Enlightenment civilization." It represents the "liquidation of magic" by language, of which Benjamin wrote, and the first step in the organization of mimesis, which he dreaded.

Rome, I submit, was obsessed with this very threshold of history. It retrojected song to the foundation (or foundations, following our discussion of Carmentis and Carna), and it made possible its own continuous refounding through song, individually through the prophecies of Carmentis and the passage song of the *praefica,* communally through ritual song of the Salian priests, and the widespread historical practice of song that participated in and derived its significance from the timelessness of their performance of founding. Rome struggled continuously with the duality of mimesis, its potential to take hold of the power of the other and yet its inevitable yielding into the other. As Vergil writes of farmers, they "imitate decayed soil by plowing" (*putre solum — namque hoc imitamur arando, G.* 2.204) — that is, they lay claim to the fertile power of naturally decayed soil through the human activity of plowing, and at the same time they press the plow into the soil, they yield into the very soil they seek to dominate. In a strictly physical sense, the unputrified soil is not the object imitated but rather the material of which the imitation is fashioned. Yet this is not what the Latin says: it regards the natural substance imitated and the thing of which the imitation is fashioned as both the objects of mimesis.

Nietzsche says (somewhere) that once an idea is put into words it is dead. For the Romans, death was not such a bad thing, because only the dead could make history. This observation is no mere word game, playing on our own language's vacillation between history as that which is past and gone and history as the inscribed and incorporated survival of the past into the present. For the Romans, really and truly, only the dead made history.

And they made it through imitation, through being re-presented in the rite of the *imagines,* those fragile waxen death masks reanimated by subsequent generations. Consider: the mask is the product of wax being pressed onto and pulled off the face of the deceased. It is a souvenir of the life of the ancestor, then a prompt for reanimation, and then, once again, a souvenir of performance, that is, the ritual reanimation of the deceased. The *imago* exists at the threshold of history, both in the sense that it is made at the moment at which the deceased becomes a historical figure, an ancestor, but also in that it allows his successors to make history, to have authority and legitimacy over subsequent generations. Again, Vergil makes the point brilliantly clear, this time in the sixth book of the *Aeneid,* where he depicts those souls — and only those souls — who don the *imagines* of Romans as escaping the endless cycle of death and rebirth, that is, as entering history.

To sing is to leave the realm of play, the timelessness of ritual, the in-betweenness of adolescence, the pleasurable release of sex, and to don the mask of the dead, thereby seeking to make history. It is to reanimate any of a number of prototypes and yet, at the same time, to expose the gap between the imitator and the imitated, to admit the impossibility of a given subject's ever partaking of the history he makes. It is the singer's attempt to deposit a miniature in his own grave, to leave an imitation and a souvenir of the performance that is his life, to commence the distribution of lament. It is to undertake the impossible yet necessary feat of leaving the body behind, to make of language an archive, to fix a limit on a process that can never be completed. Winnicott writes with respect to artistic production that "the finished creation never heals the underlying lack of sense of self."[3] The Romans lived this insight, as individual subjects and as a collectivity. And so they kept on singing.

NOTES

Abbreviations

Abbreviations of periodicals and journals are from *L'Année Philologique*. Abbreviations of classical authors and texts from the *Oxford Classical Dictionary* are used wherever possible.

CAH   *The Cambridge Ancient History*. Ed. J. Boardman et al. 2d ed. Cambridge, 1984–.

CIL   *Corpus Inscriptionum Latinarum*. Akademie der Wissenschaften. Berlin, 1862–.

DS   *Dictionnaire des antiquités grecques et romains d'après les textes et les monuments*. Ed. C. Daremberg and E. Saglio. 5 vols. in 10. Paris, 1877–1919.

EV   *Enciclopedia virgiliana*. 5 vols. in 6. Rome, 1984–91.

FPL   *Fragmenta poetarum latinorum epicorum et lyricorum praeter Ennium et Lucilium*. Ed. K. Büchner. Stuttgart, 1995.

GLK   *Grammatici Latini*. Ed. H. Keil. 7 vols. Leipzig, 1857–80.

OCD   *Oxford Classical Dictionary*. Ed. S. Hornblower and A. Spawforth. 3d ed. Oxford, 1996.

OLD   *Oxford Latin Dictionary*. Oxford, 1982.

RE   *Paulys Real-Encylopädie der classischen Altertumswissenschaft*. 2d. ed. Stuttgart, 1893–1963.

Introduction

1. On Greek song-culture, see Calame 1977; Gentili 1988; Nagy 1989, 1990. On oral and performative dimensions of Latin literature there is a large and growing body of scholarship, e.g., Quinn 1980; Vogt-Spira 1989, 1990; Wille 1989; Horsfall 1996; Gamel 1998; Markus 2000; Rüpke 2000; Campbell 2001; Green 2002. Two works in particular merit more attention than they have received: Valette-Cagnac 1997, which analyzes reading as a social practice in the Roman world, and Wachter 1998, whose short but convincing demonstration of the elements of oral composition in written poems raises new and important questions about the compositional techniques of Augustan poets. In general, the simplistic distinction between oral and literate cultures is no longer considered valid, for Rome or for any other society that has encountered writing. Scholars focus instead on a variety of literacies as situated within a broader framework of cul-

tural and social practices: see Ong 1982; Morrison 1987; Calinescu 1993; Gee 1990, 1992; Maybin 2000. As Cameron puts it for the ancient world: there is "no conflict between song and book" (1995: 87); "[i]t is a gross oversimplification to think of an age of reading succeeding an age of listening" (1995: 102). W. Johnson 2000 confirms the applicability of such observations to the Roman republic and early principate. Even in the analysis of individual poems as verbal artifacts, it is rarely helpful to conceive of singing and writing as irreconcilably opposed processes. I have not been able to consult Guittard 1996.

2. E.g., Dupont 1985; Bartsch 1994; Feldherr 1995, 1998. On the relationship between practice and performance as categories of analysis, see Bell 1992: 37–46.

3. Rappaport 1999; Bell 1992; Taussig 1993, 1999.

4. For the expression "peeling away," see M. Johnson 1987: 138.

5. Comte 1973 (orig. 1851–53), 1.233; Vico 1999 (orig. 1744). .

6. Comte 1973 2.188, 2.195ff.

7. For this summary expression, see Taussig 1993: 70. Of particular relevance are the essays of Benjamin translated as "On the Mimetic Faculty" and "Doctrine of the Similar" in Benjamin 1999 and "The Work of Art in an Age of Mechanical Reproduction" in Benjamin 1968. See also Rochlitz 1996; Hansen 2000.

8. Schwartz 2001.

9. Taussig 1993: 47, summarizing and paraphrasing Horkheimer and Adorno.

10. Bell 1992: 98.

11. On which, see Taussig 1997, 1999.

Chapter 1. Song and Foundation

1. The reading and interpretation of the fragment follows the analysis of Radke 1981: 121. For alternatives, which still contain the plural imperative of *cano, canere*, see *FPL, Carmen Saliare*, frag. 1; Pighi 1958: 24; Capdeville 1973: 404–6. On choral self-address in ancient song, see Norden 1939: 193–99.

2. Varro *Ling.* 7.3; Colonna 1991. See also Calvetti 1987, who describes a bronze sculpture from Bisenzio that he believes depicts *salii* already in the eighth century BC.

3. Rappaport 1999; Donald 2001. See also M. Bloch 1973 and Tambiah 1985: 17–59, albeit with different emphases. Bell 1992 problematizes the very concept of ritual and proposes instead that we focus on the practice of ritualization. My contention is that in Roman culture language is ritualized in part through its association with events such as the Salian performance that can be understood as ritual. Bell has little to say about the place of language in ritual, but her description of "ritual mastery" as entailing "the ability . . . to (1) take and remake schemes from the shared culture that can strategically nuance, privilege, or transform, (2) deploy them in the formulation of a privileged ritual experience, which in turn (3) impresses them in a new form upon agents able to deploy them in a variety of circumstances beyond the circumference of the rite itself" (1992: 116) closely corresponds to my account of the transformation of everyday speech into song as part of a "privileged ritual experience" that "impresses it in a new form upon agents able to deploy it in a variety of circumstances beyond . . . the rite itself." For a similar account of the "ritualization" of language, or as he puts it, "the making special of everyday speech," see Nagy 1990 on song in archaic Greece.

4. Rappaport 1999: 322.

5. Rappaport 1999: 76.

6. Rappaport 1999: 405.

7. Ibid.

8. For description of the rite, see material gathered at *RE* 2.1.1874–99, esp. Dion. Hal. 2.70 and Plut. *Vit. Num.* 13.4–5. On the *ancilia*, see R. Bloch 1963; Schäfer 1980; Colonna 1991; Borgna 1993. They are explicitly identified as *pignora imperii* at Ov. *Fast.* 3.346

and Florus *Epit.* 1.2.3. Torelli 1984 thinks that the Salian accoutrements (tunic, armor, dagger, and apex) constitute a fossilization of military garb of the eighth and seventh centuries BC. The fragments of the Salian hymn are collected at *FPL*, pp. 2–9. Pighi 1958 includes a translation of some of the fragments into classical Latin.

9. Rüpke 1990: 23–25, 61ff.

10. On Romulus and Numa as representing complementary components of Roman notions of sovereignty, see Scheid 1990: 279–80, following Dumézil 1948 and 1977. Testimonia attributing the foundation of the Salian rite to Numa include Cic. *Rep.* 2.26; Varro *Ling.* 7.3; Livy 1.20.4; Hor. *Epist.* 2.1.86–87; Dion. Hal. *Ant. Rom.* 2.71.1; Plut. *Vit. Num* 16; Ov. *Fast.* 3.259ff.; Terentius Scaurus, *GLK* 7.28. Gabba's radically skeptical view, that Augustan and later references to a religion of Numa are contemporary fictions driven by ideology, has not won widespread support (Gabba 1984).

11. The *salii* or their performance are associated with Quirinus (Stat. *Silv.* 5.2.129–31, Livy 5.52.7), with Jupiter, Mars, and Quirinus (Serv. *Aen.* 8.663), with Janus (Varro *Ling.* 7.26), and with Mars (Lucian *Salt.* 20; Porphyry *Hor. Carm.* 1.36.12; Livy 1.20.4; Aur. Vict. *De Vir. Ill.* 3.1). The old view of the Salian rite as preparation for war and of the Salian priesthood as dedicated primarily or exclusively to Mars has been debunked in recent years: see Rüpke 1990, 1998 anticipated by Piganiol 1930.

12. Taussig 1999 (quoted phrases from pp. 2 and 191, respectively). See also Taussig 1997: 120ff.

13. Benjamin 1977: 31, cited by Taussig 1999: 2.

14. The legend is most fully recounted at Ov. *Fast.* 3.259–390. See also Paul. 117 L; Dion. Hal. *Ant. Rom.* 2.71.1–2; Plut. *Vit. Num* 16.

15. The phrase *pignora imperii* occurs at Ov. *Fast.* 3.346 and Florus *Epit.* 1.2.3. Serv. *Aen.* 7.88 lists the *ancilia* collectively as one of the seven *pignora* of Roman power. Vergil addresses the problem of one versus many by presenting all of the *ancilia* as "fallen from the heavens" (*lapsa ancilia caelo, Aen.* 8.664). Livy uses the phrase *caelestia arma,* "heavensent armor," of the *ancilia* as a group (1.20.4). For ancient attempts to establish an etymology of the term *ancile*, see Serv. *Aen.* 7.188; Varro *Ling.* 7.43; Fest. 117 L; Ov. *Fast.* 3.377; plus discussion by Bömer 1957–58, commentary on *Fasti* 3.160–61.

16. Julius Obsequens *De Prodigiis* 104; Flor. *Epit.* 68. In like manner, Serv. *Aen.* 2.166 says that the "true" Palladium could be differentiated from the copies due to its ability to "move its spear and eyes" (*verum tamen agnoscitur hastae oculorumque mobilitate*). For the marble reliefs of the *ancilia* in the so-called Regia Calviniana of 36 BC, see Schäfer 1980.

17. For the legend and its interpretation, see Hung 1995.

18. Fest. 117 L refers to the Salian refrain *mamuri veturi* and says it was named after the craftsman. Ov. *Fast.* 3.389–94 does not cite the refrain, but indicates that the name of Mamurius is invoked by the priests as reward for his accomplishment. Plut. *Vit. Num.* 16 simply indicates that some believe the refrain is *mamuri veturi* while others think it is *memoriam veterem*. Vergil presents the *salii* in Evander's town as singing the legendary accomplishments of Hercules (*Aen.* 8.285–302). While it is customary to associate the content and style of the Vergilian passage with surviving Greek hymns, it does not seem out of the question that Vergil was also reflecting actual practice in indigenous rites. Certainly the hymning of an individual god would not be out of the question, given what we have been told about Salian *axamenta*. And Hercules himself seems to have been the focus of a Salian rite in the Latin town of Tibur: see the material gathered at *RE* 2.2.1893.

19. I refer to the Nietzschean aphorism "the 'apparent' world is the only one: the "real' world has only been lyingly added," cited from *Twilight of the Idols* by Taussig 1999: 99.

20. Lydus *Mens.* 4.49. On Mamurius as scapegoat, see Dumézil 1948: 207ff., who also wishes to see his expulsion as a symbol of the driving out of the old year.

21. E.g., Bömer 1957–58, commentary on *Fasti* 3.161; Porte 1985.

22. Serv. *Aen.* 2.166. Mamurius is also the name of the sculptor, in this instance Oscan, of a talking bronze statue of Vertumnus at Prop. 4.2.61.

23. Illuminati 1961, following Norden 1939: 231–34 and Deroy 1959.

24. Colonna 1991, fig. 26, a fourth-century BC Etruscan vase. See also Borgna 1993, fig. 25, a sixth-century BC vase from Sala Consilina.

25. Calvetti 1987.

26. Colonna 1991: 100.

27. Cf. Non. 58 L, which attributes to Nigidius Figulus the use of the verb *tintinnire* (= *sonare*) to describe the sound of the bronze in the Salian performance.

28. The object is discussed by Calvetti 1987. The suggestion that the chained mammal may be a human being in disguise is my own.

29. Stern 1966; Foucher 1974.

30. To further complicate matters, there is a manuscript variant of *pelta,* a type of shield, for *pellem,* the word translated in the text as "hide."

31. Blakely (Westover) 1997; Blakely 2001. Illuminati 1961: 71–76 also points to a connection with African rites. He argues that the role of a *collegium* of metalworkers would have declined in significance as Rome switched to a slave-based economy; but such a development does not affect the continuing reliance of society on the proper management of transformational crafts.

32. Helms 1993: 69–87.

33. Blakely (Westover) 1997.

34. E.g., Eluére and Cottier-Angeli 1993; Giardino 1995.

35. Plin. *HN* 34.1.1; Plut. *Vit. Num.* 17.

36. Concern with the relationship between metallurgy and political power is apparent in other aspects of early Italian ritual and myth, such as the story of Cacus (see Camassa 1983) and cults of Vulcan (see Capdeville 1995). See also Massa-Pairault's discussion (1992: 15ff.) of a Würzburg amphora (dating to around 670 BC) that she believes depicts five *daktyloi,* a nonmortal harpist, and a weasel (as sign of chthonic aspect). She suggests that the amphora may commemorate the founding of a *collegium,* and links the depiction of the *daktyloi* to the myth of Mamurius Veturius. On the association of *collegia, sodalitas,* and conviviality (for which an amphora might prove useful), see Chapter 2.

37. Helms 1993: 19, anticipated by Illuminati 1961: 73, who also stresses the politically disruptive power of the craftsman.

38. On the metallurgical *daimones* and the invention of music, see Wille 1967: 540, citing Solinus 11.56; Germ. *Arat.* 34–38; Lucr. 2.629–35, 637ff.; and Verg. *G.* 4.150. Notice that Dion. Hal. *Ant. Rom.* 2.70 explicitly likens the *salii* to the *curētes.*

39. Kügler 1977: 115–44. Also useful on *Meistergesang* is A. Taylor 1966, emphasizing the tradition's development by representatives of sedentary crafts in developing urban centers. Taylor also discusses the list of twelve masters, the membership in which changes over time.

40. Kügler 1977: 179, from the English summary.

41. Oddly Sabbatucci 1988: 95 says the song was inscribed in fourth century BC but gives no evidence. Note that the Arval brothers carry *libelli* at the time of the performance of their song: *CIL* 6.2104a line 32 (= Scheid 1998b: 100a).

42. See Ov. *Ars Am.* 3.345, where *compono* seems to mean "apply a melody" to a preexistent text; on the fitting together of voice and rhythm, see Marius Victorinus, *GLK* 6.184.

43. Lomax 1968: 224. But cf. Tambiah's (1985: 134) description of ritual as the "disciplined rehearsal of 'right attitudes.'"

44. Taussig 1999: 239.

45. Tambiah 1985: 155, criticizing (among others) M. Bloch 1973.

46. Rappaport 1999: 350.

47. As Gros and Torelli (1988: 23–24) observe, initiation "is a condition for the genesis and development of the archaic city," because it constitutes passage to full membership in the citizen body.

48. E.g., Illuminati 1961; Torelli 1984, 1990; Sabbatucci 1988: 93–98; Ceccarelli 1998: 150–57. Versnel 1993: 329 accepts the initiatory aspect of the Salian rite.

49. For details on the Liberalia, see Illuminati 1961: 58–61.

50. Illuminati 1961; Sabbatucci 1988: 53–60, 93–98.

51. Torelli 1984: 76, 107–8, 111–12. Cf. Versnel 1993, who speaks of "role reversal" (158n104) perhaps in the context of initiation (327n125).

52. Torelli 1984: 109, citing Scarpi 1979 and Brelich 1961: 78.

53. Illuminati 1961: 74–75.

54. Dion. Hal. *Ant. Rom.* 2.70.5; Plut. *Vit. Thes.* 21.1. The verbal similarity was noted by Norden 1939: 185ff. For more on the relationship between crane dance and initiation, see chapter 6.

55. As indicated by Lucilius 348 W (320 M): *praesul ut amptruet inde, ut volgus redamptruet inde* ("the *praesul* performs the figure on one side, and the crowd reperforms it on the other"), a passage quoted and amplified by Fest. 334 L: *Redantruare dicitur in Saliorum exultationibus: "cum praesul amptruavit," quod est, motus edidit, ei referuntur invicem motus* ("the term *redantruare* is chanted in the exultations of the Salians, 'when the praesul has performed the figure,' that is, given movements, the movements are in turn given back to him." On the complexity of the movements of the *salii*, see also Plut. *Vit. Num.* 13.5.

56. For various interpretations of the inscription TRVIA, which is perhaps best taken as referring to both the form of the labyrinth and the city of Troy, see Carandini 1997: 160. On such double etymologies as a form of cultural translation, see Kingsley 1993.

57. In discussing the oinochoe of Tragliatella, I rely on Giglioli 1929, Menichetti 1992, and Massa-Pairault 1992: 1–34.

58. Menichetti 1992.

59. On the recurrence and multiple significance of armed dancing in archaic Italy, see R. Bloch 1958; Camporeale 1987; Ceccarelli 1998: 141–58.

60. Calvetti 1987: 3.

61. On the *lusus Troiae*, see *RE* 13.2.2059–67. The possible connection with the oinochoe has been noted by Helbig 1915; Norden 1939: 231; Heller 1946; Jackson Knight 1967: 202–14; Menichetti 1992: 7–30; P. Miller 1995.

62. For this definition of Troia, see also Fest. 504 L: *Troia et regio Priami et lusus puerorum equestris dicitur et locus in agro Laurente, quo primum Italiae Aeneas cum suis constituit.*

63. See, e.g., Borgeaud 1974: 5: "The labyrinth in this context [initiation] is the very image of the place of withdrawal where the transformation of the initiates was effected, the 'symbolic milieu that represented both a grave and a womb.'" The internal quotation is from V. Turner 1966: 96. On the association of labyrinth with initiation, see also Versnel 1993: 326.

64. Also supportive of the association with initiation is the occurrence of armed dancing in comparable contexts elsewhere. See Ceccarelli 1998: 41–42 (Athens), 99–108 (Sparta), 178 (Crete). See also Scarpi 1979.

65. E.g., Verg. *Aen.* 8. 287: *hic iuvenum chorus, ille senum;* also Macrob. *Sat.* 3.14.14 reports that "Appius Claudius, a man who was awarded a triumph, nonetheless remained a Salius until old age and held it as something worth boasting about that he was the best dancer of the members of the collegium" (*cum Appius Claudius, vir triumphalis, qui Salius usque ad senectutem fuit, pro gloria optinuerit, quod inter collegas optime saltitabat*); and Diom., *GLK* 1.476, refers to *salios iuniores,* a phrase that implies the existence of *seniores* as well.

66. Rüpke 1990: 25; see also Rüpke 1998.

67. Dionysius says that it is Numa who selected twelve patrician youths for the first company of Salii, but it is more generally assumed that the Salii were assigned to patricians as part of a series of reorganizations of priesthoods during the early to middle republic.

68. See Fest. 439 L on *saliae virgines;* and *ILS* 5018 (from Tusculum) mentions a *praesula,* or female lead dancer.

69. Thus Torelli 1984: 109 translates *vulgus* in the fragment from Lucilius as "tutto il popolo."

70. See O'Neill 2003.

71. This is the suggestion of Norden 1939: 185ff.

72. On this process of spectacularization within *Aeneid* 5, see Feldherr 1995.

73. Bell 1992: 92.

74. Gunderson, personal communication, June 2003.

75. Borgna 1993.

76. On the association of distance with sovereignty, see Helms 1993: 28ff.

77. Fest. 386 L: *Sollistimum, Ap. Pulcher in Auguralis disciplinae lib. I. ait esse tripudium, quod !aut! excidit ex eo, quod illa fert: saxumve solidum, aut arbos viviradix ruit, quae nec prae vitio !humani! caedanturve iacianturve, pellanturve.*

78. Ernout 1994: 703 defines *tripudare* as "sans doute 'danser à trois temps'" and Walde and Hoffmann 1980, s.v., compares Greek *tripodizare* and *dipodia.* Ernout explains Cicero's ascription of an etymology *terripavium* or *terripudium* (*Div.* 2.72) as an attempt to make sense of the practice of looking for feed to fall from the mouth of the sacred fowl and calling the result *tripudium sollistimum* or *sonivium* (*Div.* 2.20, *Fam.* 6.6). More likely, as Ernout points out, the augury was based on the dancing or leaping movement of the designated bird. Cicero himself seems aware of the peculiarity of the practice of announcing a *tripudium sollistimum* on the basis of the spewing of chicken feed, since he several times refers to it as a "forced" (*coactum*) type of augury (i.e., *Div.* 1.27, 2.73). Pliny's reference to *tripudium sollistimum* (*HN* 10.49) leaves it unclear whether he thinks the omen consists in the dropping of food (not mentioned) or the dance of the cock (which would more closely fit the spirit of the passage, in which Pliny develops an elaborate comparison between cocks and adult human males). A fragmentary entry in Festus reads: *Tripudium . . . ⟨au-⟩spiciis in exultatione tripudiat . . . a terra pavienda sunt dicta. Nam pavire . . .* (498 L, lacunae in text). Does it perhaps explain the proper understanding of the augural *tripudium* as having to do with some creature's exultant dance? It is hard to imagine bouncing grain being described in quite this way. Finally, Apul. *Met.* 7.16 applies the word *tripudium* to the movements of a donkey at last let out to pasture. Pighi 1958: 84 rightly sees that the term *tripudium* has an augural significance, but wrongly concludes that it therefore has nothing to do with a three-beat or triple-step dance.

79. Bell 1992: 116. See also note 3.

80. Bell 1992: 83–84.

81. Bell 1992: 85.

82. Pighi 1965; Quintilian 1.6.40. Cf. Hor. *Epist.* 2.1.86. For a parallel to the recitation of an incomprehensible text, see Tambiah's description of Buddhist monks reciting closed chants neither they nor the members of their congregation understand (1968: 179–80).

83. *SHA* 2.104; cf. Illuminati 1961: 45–46.

84. Fest. 3 L (= *FPL* frag. 13). On the etymology and meaning of the term *axamenta,* see Ernout 1994, s.v. *aio.* It is also possible, as Sabbatucci 1988: 95 points out, to interpret the passage from Festus as suggesting that *axamenta* were assertions about all the gods, and that individual verses were named after individual deities. In addition to Janus, Juno, and Minerva, other gods referred or alluded to include Jupiter (with the epithet *Leucesie* in *FPL* frag. 2, following the interpretation of Macr. *Sat.* 1.15.4), Saturn (Fest.

432 L = *FPL* frag. 7), and perhaps Ceres, or a masculine version thereof (Varro *Ling. Lat.* 7.26 = *FPL* frag. 3).

85. Rappaport 1999: 396ff. On song as a substitute for argument, indeed a silencing of argument, see M. Bloch 1973.

86. On cosmological song and dance in antiquity, see Lucian *Salt.* 17, 37; more generally J. Miller 1986.

87. On number of *salii* corresponding to months of the year, see Lydus *Mens.* 4.2, discussed by Dubourdieu 1989: 239–40. Scheid's description of Lydus as "un antiquaire mediocrement informé" seems beside the point here, especially in the light of the links with Fonteius and Varro. Nor, given the testimonium from Varro referred to in the text, does Scheid's (1990: 282) further suggestion, that to the contemporaries of Varro and Augustus the number twelve had no significance, seem persuasive, at least with respect to the *salii*.

88. On European versus African music, see Snead 1984. On bourgeois versus folk music, Marothy 1974. Less important for our purposes than the ethnic or class associations is recognition of the different types of music and their possible association with different concepts of time and cosmology. Kisliuk 1998: 146ff. is right to warn against reductionism, yet acknowledges that musical performance can, indeed must, be interpreted in terms of other categories relevant to a given performative context. See also Lomax 1968, who seeks to develop an explicit typology linking musical performance types to dominant modes of production.

89. Snead 1984: 72.

90. Lott 1993: 177.

91. Snead 1984: 67.

92. Cf. Helms 1993: 248: "Repetition constitutes reassurance that the energizing link between society and its cosmological realm and ancestral creative centers is still effective, still functioning."

93. Let it be noted that Snead himself calls attention to the prevalence of a cyclical approach to history and cosmology throughout the premodern history of the West. As he writes, "[t]he now suppressed (but still to be found) recognition of cycles in European culture has always resembled the beliefs that underlie the religious conceptions of black culture, observing periodic regeneration of biological and agricultural systems" (1984: 65).

94. Snead 1984: 65.

95. On this aspect of warrior psychology, see the fascinating account of Grossman 1995. Grossman summarizes his analysis of historical evidence for soldiers' reluctance to kill by stating that "the vast majority of combatants throughout history, at the moment of truth when they could and should kill the enemy, have found themselves to be 'conscientious objectors'" (1995: xv).

96. Bataille 1955: 28ff.

97. Grossman 1995: 5–16.

98. This, too, is an important aspect of Grossman's argument: a society that trains its soldiers to ignore the human impulse against killing has a difficult time reintegrating those soldiers into the community at peace.

99. Attali 1985: 30.

100. Attali 1985: 19.

101. Taussig 1993: 46–47.

102. On the theme of marriageability in this poem, see Habinek 1986.

103. The quotation is from Helms 1993: 19.

Chapter 2. Song, Ritualization, and Agency

1. Bell 1992:16.

2. Bell 1992: 116.

3. Bell 1992: 141.

4. Bell 1992: 141.

5. For early convivial practice, see de Marinis 1961; Rathje 1983; and especially Peruzzi 1998. On the prehistory of drama, the inferences of Wiseman 1988, 1998 are useful. But equally important is the language of drama itself, which presupposes both a dramatic tradition (see, e.g., Wright 1974; McCarthy 2000) and prior recognizable song types (to be discussed later).

6. McCarthy 2000 considers comedy's construction of the "arts of authority" without reference to *sodalitas*.

7. On the range of applications of the term *sodalis*, still useful is Waltzing 1968 (originally published 1895-1900). Drummond in *CAH* 7.2.158 typifies scholarly tendencies to reduce sodalities to their institutional dimension. Scheid 1990: 699ff. is concerned to understand the *sodalitas* of the Arval brothers as an institution of Roman political and religious life; but his arguments should not be construed to deny the relevance of *sodales* in other than such formal contexts. See also Scheid 1998a: 116-18. For the songs of the *fetiales* and the Arval brothers, see Pighi 1958: 27-51. Almar 1990: 374 makes the interesting suggestion that *sodalicia* and *sodalitates* consist of individuals of higher rank than are to be found in *collegia*. See also De Robertis 1981.

8. For the etymology of *sodalis*, see Ernout 1994, s.v. As De Simone 1980 notes, the spelling *suodales* on the Lapis Satricanus would seem to confirm the etymology, which was in any event not seriously in doubt prior to the publication of the Lapis.

9. E.g., Bremmer 1982; Murray 1991.

10. In addition to being applied to the notoriously convivial *salii* and to other groups who reinforced social bonds through conviviality, the term *sodalis* becomes a signpost of conviviality in a wide variety of literary texts and genres. See, e.g., Catull. 12.13, 47.6; *Rhet. Her.* 4.64; Cic. *Sen.* 44-45; Hor. *Carm.* 1.25.19, 1.27.7, 1.36.5, 1.37.4, 2.7.5, 3.18.6; Ov. *Tr.* 4.10.46; Livy 2.3.2 (aristocratic life-style more generally), 40.7.1 (conviviality); Plin. *Ep.* 7.4.8. On trust and obligation among *sodales*, see Cic. *Verr.* 1.94; Plin. *Ep.* 2.13.6. On the expectation of harmonious "fraternal" relations, see Hellegouarc'h 1963: 110; Scheid 1990: 699; Bannon 1997: 191; Catull. 100.4; Cic. *Cael.* 26. The wording of the passage from Catullus suggests that the association of *sodales* with fraternal relations is proverbial: *quod dicitur, illud / fraternum vere dulce sodalicium* (100.3-4). According to Cic. *Planc.* 29, Plancus fears his father like a god but loves him "like a *sodalis*, a brother, a peer" (*ut sodalem ut fratrem ut aequalem*). Scheid, in speaking of the renewed interest in *sodalitates* as a form of social and religious organization under Augustus refers to "une fraternisation artificielle" (1990: 706) and writes of the newly selected Arval brothers: "Dévenus 'frères,' ils formaient autour du nouveau Romulus une nouvelle élite de compagnons solidaires comme des parents" (1990: 707). For *sodales* and dining, see Almar 1990. *CIL* 12.5811, with discussion by King 1998, provides interesting extra-literary evidence of the connection between *sodalitas* and song.

11. Rappaport 1999: 322.

12. The original publication and analysis were by a group of scholars under the auspices of the Nederlands Istituut te Rome (The Hague, 1980). Another early use of the term *sodal-*, in the Twelve Tables of Roman law, already suggests the possible tension between sodalician and civic ties, since the law in question entitles *sodales* to pass regulations for themselves provided they in no way violate public law (*ne quid ex publica lege corrumpant*: Tables VIII, frag. 27 W = Gaius ap Dig. 47.22.4). In the later republic, the term *sodalicium* comes to designate a potentially disruptive subset of society:

see Hellegouarc'h 1963: 109ff. The identification of men as *sodales* of one another can assume positive or negative connotations in the same author: e.g., Cic. *Sen.* 45 versus *Planc.* 46. Cicero expresses shock when conditions of *sodalitas* are violated, even by criminals like Verres (*Verr.* 1.93), yet regards it as plausible that a *sodalis* would be called on to abet criminal activity (*Verr.* 1.158).

13. For differing theories as to the specific circumstances under which the temple was destroyed and rebuilt, see Stibbe 1980; Versnel 1980, 1996; Momigliano in *CAH* 7.2.98–99; Waarsenburg 1996b; deWaele 1996. But all situate the destruction and reconstruction of the temple in the context of the turmoil that convulsed Latium in the late sixth and early fifth centuries BC.

14. "Funeral" is the description of Stibbe 1980: 36. Throughout his discussion Stibbe talks of "reverence" and "great care" with which the stone was placed. But the net effect was that the inscription remained hidden for almost 2,500 years.

15. There is no dispute over the transcription of the text: Waarsenburg 1996a confirms that the first legible letter is I. Versnel 1996 indicates that an early photo may suggest that an N preceded it: if so, Coarelli's supplement of the first word as MANIEIS receives further corroboration.

16. Coarelli 1995: 209ff. Other reconstructions or interpretations (e.g., Cornell 1995: 144) tend to take the word *sodales* with *Publii Valerii* on the dubious analogy of the association of *sodales* with other followers of the *gens Fabia* in the failed expedition against Veii described by Livy at 2.49.6. Coarelli's analysis has the advantage of grammar, parallel institutions, and colometry. On the later history of *sodalitates* dedicated to gods, see Waltzing 1968: 47. Scheid 1990: 252 notes a possible parallel between *sodales* of Publius Valerius at Satricum and *luperci* Fabiani and Quinctiales, which he takes as evidence that "leading Roman families . . . founded religious sodalities independent of curiae, but recognized by the city." These parallels are more plausible than the one suggested by Bremmer, but they still only point to a one possible interpretation of the Satrican *sodales*, not a necessary one. Versnel's attempt (1996) to restore I(O)VNIEI as the first word, while possible on palaeographical grounds, is implausible in the context of the inscription: it requires taking *steterai* as a verb form without parallel in Latin and turns *sodales* into the object of an unparalleled action, "the setting up" of *sodales*.

17. For colometry, see Habinek 1985a, 1985b: in the present instance we have an extended dative followed by a dependent genitive and by the extended subject of an unexpressed verb. As for meter, each colon also fits the pattern of bimoraic trochees and hierarchical binarism that Parsons 1999 regards as definitive of third- and second-century BC Saturnian.

18. On the iconology of the rebuilt temple, see Massa-Pairault 1992: 77–79.

19. On conviviality beyond death, see Pontrandolfo 1995. In the light of the steady stream of archaeological discoveries pertaining to the convivial culture of archaic Italy, it is strange indeed to continue to read of the practice as a Hellenistic borrowing at Rome in the second century BC (e.g., Krostenko 2001). The accumulated evidence suggests that eating and drinking in groups, with accompanying musical performance, is as old a practice as Rome itself. What varies over time and between sectors of the population are the nature and form of convivial entertainment and the social significance attached thereto (a matter on which Krostenko is more helpful, at least for the late republic). Even the transformation of convivial practice in the second century BC, with concomitant attempts at state control via sumptuary legislation, is only the intensification of a struggle that is ongoing. Those who are still in doubt about the antiquity of convivial practice in Rome and neighboring areas are invited to peruse the numerous books and articles mentioned in this and subsequent notes. As for Horsfall's argument (1994) that archaeological remains are "voiceless," the same point could be applied to the text and fragments he exploits: no data exist as such without an interpretive framework.

20. Pontrandolfo 1995.

21. Numerous examples are on display in the Florence Archaeological Museum.

22. E.g., *CIL* 1.2 8–9: *honc oino ploirume cosentiont;* Cato *Agr.* 1: *maiores nostri sic habuerunt;* parody at Plaut. *Amph.* 55–56: *quod omnes mortales sciunt / Pyrgopolinicem te unum in terra vivere/virtute et forma et factis invictissumis.* For discussion, see Habinek 1998a: 45–59. Kruschwitz 2002: 53–54 and 62–63 also notes parallels between the commemorative epitaphs and the language of early comedy, but does not observe the shared interest in the commemorating community.

23. For recent assessments of Cato's references to *carmina convivalia,* see Zorzetti 1990, Coarelli 1995: 204ff., and, in particular, Sciarrino 2004. On the meaning of *clari,* see Habinek 2000.

24. Surviving *skolia* are found at Aristophanes *Wasps* 1222–48 and Athenaeus 15.694. For discussion and analysis, see Vetta 1983. See also Cameron 1995: chap. 3. To my knowledge the association of Cato's *carmina convivalia* with the Greek tradition of *skolia* was first made by Zorzetti 1990.

25. Bell 1992: 140.

26. Debate over the nature and provenance of the Saturnian continues to rage: for an update, see Kruschwitz 2002; also relevant (but not mentioned by Kruschwitz) are Freeman 1998 and Parsons 1999. To my knowledge, no scholar has discussed the implications of the Saturnians' replacement by both hexameter and elegiac couplet for an understanding of the Saturnian itself. The use of elegiac couplet in inscriptions is generally assumed to be an imitation of Greek practice: but is it plausible to assume that Romans would have imitated Greek practice in such a traditional context if the Greek practice seriously violated the *Sprachgefühl* of the preexisting tradition?

27. Ennius *Ann.* 232–34 W and Skutsch 1985: ad loc.

28. *CIL* 1.2.7, 1.2.8, 1.2.10, 1.2.11 are in Saturnians, but *CIL* 1.2.15, part of the same complex, is in elegiac couplets. For discussion and interpretation, see Coarelli 1972; van Sickle 1987; Kruschwitz 2002 (with extensive further bibliography). On the connection between elegy and symposium in the Greek world, see Bowie 1990 and Murray 1991.

29. Rüpke 2002.

30. This point is made most clearly by Ovid, who in writing from exile suggests that the presence of *sodales* is a condition of poetic production: see Habinek 1998a: 153ff. But most elegies are addressed to "boon companions" who may or may not participate in a convivial life-style with the poet. See, e.g., Prop. 1.10, 1.13, 3.17, 3.25, 4.8; Ov. *Am.*1.4.

31. Landolfi 1990, despite its title (to be translated as "Banquet and Roman Society from the Origins to the First Century BC") in fact says little about the new discoveries pertaining to convivial culture in archaic Rome.

32. Saller 1991: 163.

33. Carandini 1997: 11 refers to the discovery of a private house with *triclinium* at Rome from the late sixth century BC. Interestingly, he also observes that the house (like much else in Rome) survived the Gallic invasion of 390 and was thus available for use by much later generations of Romans. It seems increasingly clear that physical environment, cultural practice, and historical knowledge did not undergo a disastrous rupture at the time of the invasion, as had been earlier believed.

34. Rathje 1994, on banqueting as generative of aristocracy; Sinos 1994; Rystedt 1984. Note the remarks of Ampolo 1984: 475: "la poesia greca arcaica, più utile a capire il modo di vivere e le suppellettili degli aristocratici d'Occidente nell'età arcaica che le pagine di Livio o Dionigi."

35. Burial of convivial ware: see, e.g., Rathje 1990, 1994, 1995.

36. On the last-mentioned, see Cristofani 1984.

37. Hedeager 1992: 31.

38. For varying views on the reality (or not) of fifth-century decline, see discussion by A. Drummond in *CAH* 7.2.130–43.

39. On conviviality as part of the lived experience of early elites, see Cristofani 1984; Gras 1984; Massa-Pairault 1992: 126; Lombardo 1988; Rathje 1995; Cornell 1995: 90–91; C. Smith 1996: 233ff.; Carandini 1997: 11, 525; Peruzzi 1998.

40. For date of the material from Murlo, see De Puma and Small 1994; Coarelli 1995: 212. For interpretation of the plaques, see Massa-Pairault 1992: 38–42; Rathje 1994; Sinos 1994; Small 1994. For date of the material from Acqua Rossa, Coarelli 1995: 213; for discussion, Small 1971 and 1994.

41. Small 1971, item XXIVB, although she interprets the gesture as one of greeting.

42. R. L. Lacy reports, in the catalog from the exhibition *Case e palazzi di Etruria* (1985) that one of the unpublished frieze plaques from Murlo (#403 = Inventory 112640) shows one of the four reclining guests at a banquet turned toward a standing flute player; the guest has an open mouth, as if singing ("ed ha la bocca aperta, come se cantasse").

43. Sinos 1994: 113.

44. Sinos 1994 on assembly scenes and gods; also Massa-Pairault 1992: 38ff.

45. On the Mezentius legend, see Coarelli 1995: 199ff, following Versnel 1970: 285–86. Also LaPenna in *EV* 3.510–15. The seventh-century Caeretan inscription is discussed by Briquel 1989.

46. Livy 4.2; brief discussion by Beard, North, and Price 2000: 1.64.

47. On the *epulum Iovis*, see *RE* 2.2.1552–53; *DS* 2.1.736–79; North in *CAH* 7.2.597. *Epulo* occurs as an epithet of Jupiter at *CIL* 6.36756 and 6.30932; as an epithet of Mercury at *CIL* 6.522.

48. On controversies over *epula* and other forms of banqueting in the aftermath of the Second Punic War and as part of elite in-fighting of the second century BC, see Livy 39.6.78; Polybius 31.25.4; perhaps Cic. *Q. Rosc.* 134; also Montanari 1990: 59; Gruen 1990: 170ff.; Gruen 1992: 304–9; Sciarrino 2004.

49. Cic. *Mur.* 76; Sen. *Ep.* 95.72–73, *Ep.* 98.13.

50. Bell 1992: 197.

51. Sciarrino 2004.

52. Sciarrino 2004.

53. "Nous comprénons alors que le syssition est l'instrument efficace d'un pouvoir qui pour mieux s'incrire dans l'imaginaire s'impose aux quotidiens" (Schmitt Pantel 1992: 76).

54. For further discussion of internal and external evidence for *convivia* as the scene of literary performance in the third and second centuries BC, see Rüpke 2000a.

55. The relationship between the two passages was first analyzed by Handley 1968.

56. With reference to Fraenkel's famous study, *Plautinisches im Plautus.* For more recent attempts to situate Plautus in an Italian context, see Wright 1974; Benz, Stark, and Vogt-Spira 1995; McCarthy 2000.

57. Even though all comedy is, in effect, song, the boundary between *diverbia* and *cantica* reproduces within a play the boundary between speech and song in the broader cultural context. For a comparable phenomenon in Greek song, see Nagy 1989: 5ff.

58. On the relationship between *convivium* and *comissatio,* see Dupont 1999.

59. The joining of men of different ages in the context of *sodalitas* seems to have some basis in external reality. At *Sen.* 45 Cicero's Cato discusses his participation in *convivia* with *sodales,* despite his advanced age. Evidence pertaining to membership in the Salian *sodalitas* also points simultaneously in two directions: sometimes we are given the impression of a group of young men (i.e., adolescent or younger) initiates; other times it is clear that older men are also involved. Is it possible that one retained a strong sense of identification with peers (*aequales*) with whom one was admitted to the *so-*

dalitas, while at the same time being open to sodalician relations across generational boundaries? If so, then at least some Roman *sodalitates* would be akin in structure to contemporary college alumni associations. Indeed, one argument for shared living space and academic experience during freshman year is the likelihood that students thus initiated will bond to both the class and the institution, thus facilitating fundraising further down the road of life.

60. Cf. Plaut. *Bacch.* 1105, where, before turning convivial, one father describes another as "companion of my sorrow and my misfortune" (*socium aerumnae et mei mali*).

61. See papyrus discussed by Cameron 1995.

62. On precept giving as a form of wisdom associated with conviviality, see Bielohlawek 1983; Kurke 1990; Zorzetti 1990 (with respect to the sayings of Appius Claudius). The tension between convivial and professional (i.e., philosophical) wisdom is exploited to great effect by the Roman satirists. See in particular the *virtus* fragment of Lucilius (1196–1208 W) and Hor. *Sat.* 2.7. On the relationship between *dicta* and *carmina*, see chapter 3.

63. Pl. *Bacch.* 816–17 = Men. *Dis Ex.* frag. 111 K-T.

64. On *sententiae* as precepts in Plautus, and their concentration in scenes of deception, see Moore 1998: 67ff.

65. For the fragmentary sayings of Appius Claudius, see *FPL*, pp. 11–13. In addition to the fragment discussed in the text, note also the structure of fragment 1 (Fest. 418 L):

... ⟨?⟩ qui animi compotem esse
ne quid fraudis stuprique ferocia pariat
(frag. 1 = Fest. 418 L)

On background, style, and meter of the Appian *carmina*, see Tar 1975: 15–30. Marx (as reported by Tar 1975: 17) notes the similarity between the Appian *sententia escit suas quisque faber fortunas* and Plaut. *Trin.* 363, *nam sapiens quidem pol ipsus fingit fortunam sibi*, and concludes therefore that both are to be traced to an original expression of Philemon. This may or may not be the case. My point is simply that Plautus's Latin-speaking audience would have heard expressions like those quoted in the text as proverbs, regardless of their origin in or similarity to Greek expressions. For further discussion of the *carmina* of Appius Claudius, see Dufallo 2001: 132–34 with earlier bibliography.

66. On circulation by time of Panaetius, see Cic. *Tusc.* 4.2.4. The association of "wisdom" with conviviality is implicit in the Roman use of term "taste" (*sapientia*) in both contexts.

67. Note the similarity of the first two verses to the famous comic fragment of Naevius: *alii adnutat alii adnictat alium amat alium tenet*, etc.: 74–79 W.

68. *operam dare*: Plaut. *Merc.* 621. At Plaut. *Merc.* 288 the phrase is used of an *amicus*.

69. Social dimensions of Roman comedy are addressed by Konstan 1986, Habinek 1998: 55–59, McCarthy 2000, Richlin 2005. My own approach is perhaps closest to that of Konstan, who emphasizes the civic context of comedy and its role in the formation and transmission of the ideology of the Roman state. Krostenko 2001 underestimates the social aspect of comic conviviality (see note 74). The work of all of these scholars stands in contrast to the still common tendency to overlook the social and ideological function of comedy in favor of inquiry into its generic history.

70. On the ritual context of Roman comedy, see L. R. Taylor 1937. Also relevant is Goldberg 1998.

71. This is implied by Livy's account of the development of Roman drama at *Ab Urbe Condita* 7.2: see Morel 1969 and my discussion in chapter 4. Montrose 1996 presents an excellent account of the ways in which Elizabethan drama replaces and subsumes earlier performances and rituals, especially relating to rites of passage. Elizabethan drama, like Plautine, is officially sanctioned by the state and, also like Plautine, seems to play

in important role in fostering the shift in allegiances from local identities to a broader national identity.

72. McCarthy 2000.

73. For the social transformation that characterizes Plautus's era, see Habinek 1998a: 34–59 with further bibliography. On the relationship between soldiers and civilians, several plays feature a military rival to the lead *sodalis*. We might recall the argument of Murray 1991 to the effect that *symposia/convivia* originate in the need to keep off-duty soldiers occupied. While this view is a bit simplistic (see Lombardo 1988), the possible overlap between military and convivial groups figures prominently in the Roman imagination: e.g., Cic. *De Or.* 2.200; Verg. *Aen.* 10.386; Livy 2.49.5.

74. Krostenko 2001 has noted the lack of parody of approbatory terms applying to elite performance at *convivia* in Plautus. Far from testifying to the nonexistence of certain convivial practices, such omission reflects the political force of Plautine comedy. In a sense, conviviality is the unchallenged value of Plautine comedy, which at least metaphorically invites all citizens to adopt its spirit and practice.

75. Cèbe 1966.

76. On parody or reuse of other song types (or literary genres) in Plautine comedy generally, see Cèbe 1966. Passages that imply the preexistence of the love song include *Pseud.* 647–71 (on which Cole 1991), *Cas.* 837, *Poen.* 363ff; see more generally Flury 1968. Passages using tragedy include *Pseud.* 772, *Curc.* 317, *Pers.* 12, *Cas.* 621ff., *Rud.* 664, *Amph.* 186–212, *Pseud.* 704–5, *Bacch.* 933 (some but not all are discussed at Fraenkel 1962: 307–53). For aristocratic braggadocio, see *Stich.* 274–304, *Pers.* 753–54 (on which Gomez Pallares 1993: 132), *Miles* 32, 55, 56, 88–89 (Gomez Pallares 1993: 148), *Men.* 466ff. (Gratwick 1993: ad loc.). For use of prayer form, see *Cist.* 519ff., also Guittard 1998. On military language, see Herescu 1959. Instances of adaptation of precepts are discussed in the text.

77. On the structure of blackface minstrel performance, see Engle 1978. On parody within minstrelsy of other verbal and musical performances, such as Shakespearean plays, recitals, etc. see also Lott 1993: 62ff.

78. Goldberg 1986 discusses Terence's tendency to make the context and allusions of the Greek originals vaguer in his Latin adaptation.

79. For a concise discussion of this key distinction, see Pearce 1989: 60ff.

80. See the excellent discussion of rhetorical culture along these lines in Gunderson 2000.

81. On this important topic, see Richlin 2005, amplifying McCarthy 2000.

82. This is the summary of the late Durkheim by Gane 1998: 95.

83. Bell 1992: 197, 215.

84. *Satura quidem tota nostra est:* Quintilian 10.1.93.

85. For the relationship between the satirist and the city, see Hor. *Sat.* 1.10.3–4 and Persius 1.114 on Lucilius; also Hor. *Sat.* 1.4.69, 1.10.64 and Cic. *De Or.* 1.72 for Lucilius's *urbanitas;* also Mariotti 1960: 10–12. Satire's association with the city of Rome has become programmatic by the time of Persius and Juvenal, both of whom emphatically locate their opening satires there (e.g., Persius 1.4, 1.7; Juvenal 1.31). Even the prospect of leaving Rome becomes a vehicle for commentary on the city, from Lucilius's description of shunning Rome to escape gladiatorial shows (636–37 W) to Juvenal's account of his encounter with the departing Umbricius in satire 3.

86. Oliensis 1998. Satire's association with conviviality is as old as Ennius (6–7 W, 14–19 W) and continues through Horace (e.g., satire 2.8) and Juvenal (satire 4). The connection seems especially strong in the case of Lucilius, who is treated by later satirists as the prototype. Lucilius refers to specialists in convivial performance (e.g., the *dominus* at 285–86 W), to convivial fare (470–71 W, 596–97 W), to specific *convivia* at Athens (815–51 W) and in a military camp (1221–1233 W). Even his obsession with phallic male sexuality, with the exclusion of *cinaedi,* with *pueri* and *puelli* (166, 308–9, 311–12, 324–25, 450–52, 453, 639, 959–60, 1048), his interest in anal sex (1180) in *stuprum* or abusive sex

(1181), and his speaker's boastfulness with respect to women (892ff., 923–24, 974–75) recall both the Athenian sympotic environment and second-century Roman debates over convivial protocol. Other critics tend to interpret satire's conviviality as synecdoche for subjects ranging from decorum to bodily necessity; but it is worth recalling that conviviality is a lived practice and not just a metaphor.

87. It may also replicate the architectural practice of aristocratic tombs, whose *laudationes* were not necessarily open to all passersby, as Enrica Sciarrino reminds me.

Chapter 3. Song and Speech

1. As discussed by Cahoon 1996.

2. Ov. *Tr.* 2.453, Catull. 4.12, and Apul. *Met.* 5.15, respectively.

3. For the derivation of *carmen* from *cano* see Ernout 1994, s.v. *carmen*. For further discussion of the lexical relationship among *cano*, *dico*, and *loquor*, see Habinek 1998b.

4. On the relative importance of competence versus ideology in ritual practice, see Bell 1992: esp. 187ff.

5. For this meaning of *dico*, see Habinek 1998b, as well as additional examples discussed later.

6. For this understanding of the relationship between *cano* and *canto*, see Valette-Cagnac 1997: 158–59, correcting W. Allen 1972. Markus 2000 notes that forms of *cantus* and *cantare* are often used negatively by poets, although not in reference to religious performance. This pattern makes perfect sense: to sing someone else's song is to be defective as a Roman man but observant as a participant in a religious rite. Quinn 1980: 158 notes that from Catullus onward "*cantare* . . . always implies some kind of mimetic performance of the text." This may be, but what is being mimed is someone else's original performance acknowledged as such. *Canto* feigns or borrows the authority of song, whereas *ludo*, as we shall see in a later chapter, is a type of mimesis with no intrinsic claim to authority: indeed transcendence of it grounds the authority of song.

7. We might compare Valette-Cagnac's demonstration of how it is the pronouncement of the law by the appropriate magistrate that gives it its force rather than its preservation as a written text: Valette-Cagnac 1997: 181ff.

8. On *cano* and *carmen* in the poetry of Vergil, see *EV* 1.648–49 and 665–66.

9. Jaeger 1990.

10. As Valette-Cagnac 1997 notes, oralization was an important but not necessary component of ancient reading. Still, the preponderance of the evidence she and others have assembled indicates that most "reading" of poetry or other special speech (i.e., "song") involved some degree of oralization.

11. *OLD*, s.v. *condico*.

12. Ernout 1994, s.v. *eloquor*.

13. On *e-* as referring to transformation from one state to another, see Brachet 2000. Brachet provides an unnecessarily complicated explanation for the force of the prefix in words such as *eloqui* and *enarrare*, seeing it as an "irradiation" of its use in verbs like *exhaurire*, in which it implies totality or completeness. In fact, Brachet's own core understanding of *e-* as referring to transformation works here as well. See Habinek 2003.

14. Citations in the text are from DS 1.2.922 and G. Williams 1982: 54 respectively.

15. For an interesting discussion of this magical formula, see Tupet 1976: 171, 1986: 2597–99. Note that Plin. *HN* 28.21 refers to Cato's chant for dislocated limbs as a *carmen auxiliare*, or helpful carmen.

16. *OLD*, s.v. *carmen*.

17. Conte 1994: 20.

18. Zorzetti 1990, 1991 is one of the few scholars to have applied this basic insight rig-

orously. Teleological accounts of Roman cultural history, often based on self-serving presentations by individual ancient authors, are still widespread.

19. The Arval brothers use *carmen* of their own performance at *acta* 218/19, p. 26; *FPL*, pp. 9–11.

20. On the *carmina* of the *vates*, see, e.g., Livy 1.45.5, 1.55.6, 4.30.9, 5.15.1–4; of the fetial priests, Livy 1.32.9, 7.24.6–7, Pighi 1958: 27–47. On the historical evolution of the role of fetiales at Rome and elsewhere in Italy, see Rüpke 1990: 97–117.

21. On the difference between *malum carmen*, magical incantation, and *carmen famosum*, defamatory accusation, and the Twelve Tables' concern to limit both, see Tupet 1976: 166–69, 1986: 2592–97. But see also Baistrocchi 1987: 259–63, who rightly observes that the social impact of verbal abuse and magical incantation is essentially the same: i.e., a diminution of the target's public standing.

22. Ernout 1994, s.v. *kalator*.

23. *FPL*, pp. 11–13; Tar 1975; Dufallo 2001: 132–34.

24. On the reproduction within drama of the distinction between song and speech, see Nagy 1989, 1990.

25. See note 21.

26. Other uses of *can-* in Lucilius are 605–6 W, 1128 W, and 1168 W.

27. A similar pattern obtains in the writings of Seneca the Younger, who uses *carmen* or verbs based on the root *can-* to refer to pontifical prayer (*Marc.* 13.1), a selection from Vergil's *Georgics* (*Brev. Vit.* 9.2), unspecified *carmina* that are clearly being sung (*Brev. Vit.* 12.4), a poem attributed to Maecenas (*Ep.* 101.13), the sound of a tuba (*Ep.* 108.10), and a love chant (*Ep.* 9.6).

28. This key point is missed by Newman 1965, who tries to make their practice the rule, and the rest of Latinity the exception.

29. For *memoro*, see *Annales* 35, 106, 149, 166, 314, 357, 487, 543, 551. For *poemata*, see the expression *poemata nostra cluebunt* at *Annales* 12, and discussion by Skutsch 1985: 168, 472. Even as he tries to excise his epic from the realm of song, he ends up emphasizing the importance of verbal performance, as use of the word *cluebunt*, "will be heard of," indicates.

30. Newman 1965, having persuaded himself that describing the poet as a singer in Lucretius's day is an Alexandrian affectation (this despite the ample evidence otherwise discussed previously) must explain away Lucretius's application of *cano* to Ennius as an attempt to defend him from the Roman Alexandrians. Newman's further attempt to explain the Ciceronian phrase *cantores Euphorionis* and the Horatian expression *nil praeter Calvum et doctus cantare Catullum* as referring to the alleged "cacozelia" of Catullus's expression *"Dianam . . . canamus"* is equally strained. The insult in describing someone as a *cantor*, as we have seen already, is in the implication that he cannot *"cano"* or sing his own song.

31. Lucil. 401–10 W; Cic. *Div.* 1.66.

32. Cato, *Carmen de moribus*, frag. 2 Jordan, with discussion by Habinek 1998a: 37–38.

33. E.g., Morris 1968 ad loc., who cites Quint. *Inst.*10.1.99: "Although Varro avers that the Muses, in the judgment of Aelius Stilo, if they were willing to speak Latin would speak in the language of Plautus . . ." (*licet Varro Musas, Aelii Stilonis sententia, Plautino dicat sermone locuturas fuisse, si Latine loqui vellent . . .*). More generally on Horace's terminology for poetry and its Hellenistic antecedents, see Brink 1982.

34. Traube 1986: 16.

35. Traube 1986: 17.

36. Traube 1986: 17.

37. Traube 1986: 19.

38. On these passages, see Herington 1985.

39. Jourdan-Hemmerdinger 1988.

40. Jourdan-Hemmerdinger 1988: esp. 150.

41. Lawler 1946, 1952; Lonsdale 1981.

42. Cf. Jourdan-Hemmerdinger 1988: 155, who refers to the "micro-intervals" that characterize Greek *nomoi* based on the song of birds.

43. Plut. *De Soll. An.* 973b–e. Discussed by West 1992: 120, whose translation of Plutarch is quoted.

44. Unparalleled in antiquity, that is. On the campus of the University of California, San Diego, artificial eucalyptus trees are interspersed with natural ones. One of the artificial trees is programmed to recite selections from Milton's *Paradise Lost* at random intervals. What better example could we have of the continuing human urge to mime nature, of the mimetic faculty as "the nature that culture uses to control nature," of language, especially in the intensified form of "sung" poetry as the "greatest archive of non-sensuous similarity"? An informant tells me of being startled and delighted by the intoned poetry while passing through the forest late at night: a reminder that even under advanced capitalism art can have the power to enchant, to provide "energizing links" with the world beyond the here and now.

45. Burkert 1972: 375–76.

46. See the discussion of Pythagorean musical theory by Fideler 1987 (clearest); McClain 1978; and Burkert 1972: 369ff.

47. The expression *tympana tenta* (Lucr. 2.619) would seem to refer to skins stretched at different intervals to produce different sounds when struck.

48. Gabba 1984.

49. On Greek theory and Roman action, or Romans' sense of themselves as putting into practice Greek theory, see Habinek 1987, 1989.

50. See Zorzetti 1991 on the "music of Numa."

51. Burkert 1972: 378.

52. Cic. *Rep.* 6.18. On the voices of the stars in various ancient traditions, see Colace 1995. On the Pythagorean notion of cosmic harmony, Burkert 1972: 351ff.; J. Miller 1986.

53. McClary 1995—although she is perhaps too ready to attribute the "disembodiment" to Pythagoras himself.

54. See Volk 2002: 196ff. for a brief summary of earlier views of Manilius, both favorable and unfavorable. Volk's work is in general helpful on Manilius's relationship to other didactic poems, but it suffers from the "conceit of scholars" in assuming that this is all that is interesting about Manilius. On Manilius's relationship to Stoic cosmology, see Lapidge 1989; Neuburg 1993. Neuburg argues that despite his demonstrable interest in Stoic cosmology as well as Stoic pedagogy, these are subordinated to a "deistic, almost mystic vision of the astrological adept's relationship with the stars."

55. For other parallels, see Liuzzi 1991–97. Volk 2002: 222–24 regards the relationship between sorcerer and poet as one in need of resolution in favor of the latter, thus imposing on Manilius precisely the dichotomy his proem is constructed to avoid. Her argument that the activity Manilius ascribes here to himself (*deducere mundum*) is described as impious (*nefas*) later in the poem ignores the fact that in the later passage the universe (*mundus*) is described as unwilling (*invitus; Astr.* 2.127) while the one seizing it is presented as doing so for his own benefit (*velut in semet captum deducere orbem, Astr.* 2.128—a far cry from what Manilius is up to in the proem and throughout his song).

56. Goold 1977.

57. On the secondariness of prose with respect to song, see Nagy 1990 (Greek); Godzich and Kittay 1987 (French); Habinek 1998b (Latin): all anticipated, to be sure, by Comte, who argued that prose developed in each and every language as a result of a "differentiation in the language of Poetry" (Comte 1973 = 1852: 2.196).

58. For Manilius as "composer," see also Volk 2002: 208.

59. Cf. the remarks of Volk 2002: 217: "It is not that the poet has chosen his topic out of

many and for the sole, purely literary, reason that it has not been treated before. On the contrary, it is the topic that has literally chosen the poet: he sings about the cosmos because it is the wish of the cosmos, or put differently, of fate, that he should do so."

60. As, e.g., Hardie 1986 reads the *Aeneid*.

61. Of course, it is possible to understand the expression *caelo descendit carmen ab alto* as meaning that "the topic of my song takes its start in the lofty heavens," as Goold seems to interpret it. But such a rendering makes metaphorical what is conveyed literally as the descent of song from the sky.

62. For further discussion of the relationship between specialized, often Hellenized, practices in the late republic and the general discourse of the aristocracy, see Wallace-Hadrill 1997; Moatti 1997.

63. On the figure of the *Romanus sapiens* in Quintilian, see Habinek 1987.

64. Roach 1996: 2ff.

65. Cf. Quint. *Inst.*1.10.27, which adds the detail that the *fistula* was called a *tonarion* in Greek. For this instrument, see West 1992: 113–14. Aulus Gellius (*NA* 1.11.10–16) implies that the story was sometimes (wrongly in his view) taken to mean that Gracchus was accompanied throughout his entire speech by a piper. Other versions of the story: Plut. *Gracch.* 2.4–5.825b, *Ir. Cohib.* 456a; Val. Max. 8.10.1. See also De Martino 1995: 35–36.

66. Helpful on the fraught relationship between oratory and song is Richlin 1997. Her analysis emphasizes the orators' fear of being associated with the figure of the actor, who gives pleasure to others through use of his body. But this fear is mixed with a desire on the part of the orator to lay claim to the cultural and social power long ascribed to singers. See also Connolly 1998.

67. *EV* 1.648–49.

68. For further discussion of manhood and performance style, see chapter 5.

69. Indeed at 11.3.167 he recommends imitation of song (*cantici quiddam*) and at 11.3.170 "flexibility of voice" (*flexum vocis*), an expression familiar from discussions of song.

70. I cannot improve on the Loeb translation offered in the text.

71. An observation Tony Corbeill shared with me many years ago.

72. One of many reasons why the renown of Seneca became central to the reproduction of the Roman elite: see Habinek 2000.

73. To be sure, as Hinds 1987 points out, the abstruse and convoluted content of the Muses' song more closely fits the aesthetic and, we might add, political aims of the Alexandrian Roman poet; but there is nothing categorically unpoetic or unsonglike about the Ovidian verses ascribed to the Emathides. Indeed, how could there be, given that they too are part of Ovid's own *carmen perpetuum?*

74. Taussig 1993: 72ff.

75. Taussig 1993: 81 citing Darwin's *Journal,* p. 209.

76. Taussig 1993: 81.

77. Taussig 1993: 74–75, apparently quoting Darwin's *Journal,* p. 119.

78. Benjamin 1968: 223, as cited and discussed by Taussig 1993: 20. The German original of Benjamin's essay dates to 1936.

79. Traditional scholarship (e.g., Hendrickson 1894) dismisses the Livian narrative as an imitation of Aristotle's account of the origins of Greek drama. Arguments in favor of this point of view have been much overstated: for criticism, see Habinek 2004. Moreover, whatever the "source" of Livy's account, the use of the mimetic faculty described therein is characteristically Roman. See also Morel 1969 and Dupont 1993 on connections between the narrative and other aspects of Roman thought or practice.

80. On the significance of the term *iuventus* in this episode, see Morel 1969.

81. Kingsley 1993 discusses the ancient use of double etymologies as a strategy of "intercultural absorption." It is interesting to note the extent to which such etymologies in Latin cluster around the description of performance practices.

82. Parodic performances in art: Cèbe 1966; Szilágyi 1981; Thuilliers 1997. Ancient accounts of such parody include Dion. Hal. *Ant. Rom.* 7.72, drawing on the Roman annalist Fabius Pictor. See also Wiseman 1988.

83. Bell 1992: 200.

Chapter 4. Song and Play

1. *Pace* Huizinga 1955: 42, who considers song irrelevant to play because the terms for the two concepts do not overlap.

2. Piccaluga 1965, whose discussion of the semantic field of *ludus* is still the best available, comes close to making this claim in her insistence on the relationship between *ludus* and movement or dynamism of various sorts. Her study of the ludic element in Roman culture complements my own since she examines historical instances of festivals from the earliest days onward, whereas I focus on the systemic relationship between play and song as carried by linguistic usage.

3. On the privileging of the voice more generally in the Western philosophic tradition, see A. Cavarero, *For More than One Voice* (Stanford, 2005).

4. Huizinga 1955: 28. Cf. Dupont 1985: 44–94 for a description of the self-contained character of *ludus* at Rome and of the arena as locus of play.

5. Thus Caillois's influential definition of *ludus* as "le gout de la difficulté gratuite" (1967: 75) is in no way based on the uses of the term in the Latin language. But his overall concept of play, or *jeu*, as consisting of an activity that is free, circumscribed, unproductive, rule-bound, fictive ("accompagné d'une conscience spécifique de realité seconde ou de franche irrealité par rapport a la vie courante" [1967: 43]) and uncertain of outcome, is virtually coextensive with the semantic field of *ludus*.

6. On the important difference between *eloquor* and *loquor,* see discussion in chapter 3.

7. On *ludo* of sexual play, see Adams 1982: 162, 223, 225; and Piccaluga 1965: 38–40, perhaps overdelicately.

8. The last example is from Adams 1982: 162.

9. Ehrmann 1968: 55. Huizinga 1955: 4 defines play as "a well-defined quality of action which is different from 'ordinary' life."

10. Huizinga 1955: 176. Ehrmann, too, criticizes both Huizinga and Caillois for the claim that play can "be isolated as an activity without *consequences*" (Ehrmann 1968: 42). On the related Roman duality of violence and lyricism, see Seel 1964.

11. Winnicott 1971: 2.

12. Winnicott 1971: 64. For the application of Winnicott's ideas to broader cultural processes, see Jacobus 1999; Purchase 2003.

13. This would seem to be the general implication of Gunderson 2000: esp. chaps. 2 and 3.

14. On the psychological significance of Roman school exercises, see Bloomer 1997a; also Gunderson 2003, who rightly emphasizes that declamation continues as a ludic activity of adult males at Rome. Habinek 2005 discusses in general terms the role of education in the constitution of elite values.

15. Huizinga 1955: 177.

16. E.g., C. Barton 1993; Gunderson 1996.

17. Although it is possible for an individual to represent such play as continuing well into adulthood, as Ovid seems to in his role as *praeceptor amoris.* See, e.g., *Ars Am.* 3.62.

18. On elite, adolescent participation in *lusus Troiae,* see Piccaluga 1965: 135–46. Because the *lusus Troiae* does not apply to all Roman youths, Piccaluga is reluctant to understand it, at least in its Augustan form, as a rite of initiation. But, as we have seen, ritual delegation is a characteristic of Roman religious practice—indeed, one of the abstractions materialized by rites such as the performance of the *salii* and the public performance of elite youths.

19. Fear 2000.
20. E.g., Ov. *Tr.* 5.1.7: *et laetus laeta iuvenalia lusi,* "and happily I played the happy play of youth," refers to literary as well as sexual play.
21. V. Turner 1966.
22. For Nero's engagement in musical and mimetic performance, see material collected at Griffin 1984: 160–63.
23. It is also interesting to note that Aulus Gellius refers to his treatise as *commentationes* (*NA praef.* 4), a term that refers to written aids to memory and is thus separate from the realm of oral performance. On writing as a characteristic of *ludus,* see the discussion later in this chapter.
24. Gunderson 2003 on declamatory play is highly instructive here.
25. The ideas on satire and *ludus,* on the origins of satire, and on satire's social function contained in this paragraph are developed more fully in Habinek 2004.
26. Henderson 1989; Freudenburg 2001; Habinek 2004.
27. Henderson 1989.
28. Dion. Hal. *Ant. Rom.* 7.72.
29. Cf. Naev. *Com.* 75 W for use of *datatim* in the context of a challenge dance.
30. Although we shouldn't rule out the possibility that the dancing of the slaves advertises their sexual skills: see Gurlitt 1921: 167.
31. On *scurrae,* see Corbett 1981 and Habinek 2004.
32. Compare the presentation of what appears to be parodic dancing on the Karlsruhe vase discussed by Szilágyi 1981 and Habinek 2004. See also Thuilliers 1997, who rightly points out that the presence of such parodic performers on Etruscan reliefs of athletic competition sharply differentiates the Italian context from the Greek *palaistra.*
33. Tertullian, however, states that receptive intercourse is preparation for dancing: *pantomimus a pueritia patitur ex corpore ut artifex esse* (*De spect.* 17).
34. The text of the relevant fragment, Accius 213–14 W is uncertain, but it seems clear that some form of *lud-* is to be read.
35. Morel 1969.
36. The traditional view, articulated by Hendrickson 1894, that Livy is merely echoing Aristotelian doctrine on the origins of Greek drama is controverted by archaeological evidence (on which see Szilágyi 1981 and Thuilliers 1997), in addition to being based on an inaccurate reading of the Latin of the Livian passage (on which Habinek 2004). P. Smith 1989 provides a sophisticated analysis of the passage and of its relationship to Varro's research with the aim of uncovering the prehistory of certain Latin literary forms.
37. Piccaluga 1965: 135ff.; Camporeale 1987; Ceccarelli 1998.
38. The association of dance with military training is often overlooked by scholars who wrongly assume hostility to dance on the part of dominant elements of Roman culture. Thus Corbeill 1996: 128ff. (also Corbeill 1997) misinterpets Cicero's rhetorical attacks on the Catilinarian conspirators as representative of a generalized hostility to dance. From Cicero's vantage point, the problem is not that the conspirators dance — indeed, such can be taken as evidence of their desire to form a counterstate to the aristocratic republic — but that they dance naked at *convivia* rather than armed in the Campus Martius.
39. Cf. Piccaluga 1965: 43ff. on the play of animals; also *TLL,* s.v. *ludere.*
40. E.g., Naev. *Trag.* frags. 5–6 W.
41. See examples collected at *TLL* 5.2.1948.
42. Séchan 1930; Lonsdale 1981; Dupont 1985; also relevant is Berard 1983.
43. On themes of mimes, see Jory 2002; also Lucian *Salt.* 37ff., esp. the reference to "all the fabulous transformations, the people who have been changed into trees or beasts or birds" (*Salt.* 58, Loeb trans.).

44. "For it seems to me that the ancient myth about Proteus the Egyptian means nothing else than that as a dancer, an imitative fellow, he was able to shape himself and change himself into anything, so that he could imitate even the liquidity of water and the sharpness of fire in the liveliness of his movement; yes, the fierceness of a lion, the rage of a leopard, the quivering of a tree, and in a word whatever he wished. Mythology, however, on taking it over, described his nature in terms more paradoxical, as if he became what he imitated. Now just that thing is characteristic of the dancers to-day, who certainly may be seen changing swiftly at the cue and imitation Proteus himself. And we must suppose that in Empusa, who changes into countless forms, some such person has been handed down by mythology" (Lucian *Salt*. 19, Loeb trans.). Cf. Sil. *Pun*. 7.423: *Proteus per varias lusit formas;* and Lonsdale 1981.

45. Ov. *Met*. 8.845–878. Notice the use of the verb *eludo* to describe the unnamed daughter's shift in appearance from that of a fisherman to "her own form" (*elususque abiit. illi sua reddita forma est*, 8.870). The story also implies an association between the bodiliness of *ludus* and the condition of slavery, inasmuch as Erisychthon sells (*vendit*) his daughter, and she in her prayer for release, describes him as *dominus*, or master (*Met*. 8. 847–50): see Feldherr 2002. Corporeality, play, and slavery will figure in our later analysis of Hor. *Epist*. 2.2. For more on Ovid's *Metamorphoses* in relation to dance, see Habinek 2002, building on Galinsky 1996: 265–66. The topic deserves a more ample discussion.

46. Caillois 1967: 252 rightly differentiates between masking that "protects an identity" and "masking that imposes a presence," associating the latter with a premodern outlook. In a sense Venus's appearance here serves both purposes.

47. Verses 327 and 328—*o quam te memorem, virgo? namque haud tibi vultus / mortalis, nec vox hominem sonat; o dea certe*—echo both the language and the scenario of Anchises' greeting to Aphrodite in the *Homeric Hymn to Aphrodite*. Also relevant to the erotics of the mother-son encounter is the allusion to Sappho—and whole tradition of love poetry—in the reference to flight (*fugientem*) and pursuit (*secutus*) in the passage quoted in the text.

48. Daut 1975; Lahuson 1982.

49. On the use of *imagines* in Roman funeral processions and as an aspect of aristocratic display more generally, see Flower 1996; Dufallo 2001; Højte 2002.

50. Flower 1996: 281–332; Daut 1975 is especially concerned to trace the evolution of the term in the direction of "artistic portrait" or *Kunstbild*.

51. L. Afranius Vopiscus frag.; Cic. *Cael*. 34, *Leg. Agr.;* Hor. *Epod*. 8.11–12, respectively.

52. See discussion in Daut 1975, confirmed by Lahuson 1982.

53. Indeed the sources sometimes describe the Romans as "imitating" the *imagines:* Cic. *De Or*. 2.225; Val. Max. 5.8.3.

54. For a good discussion of the literary background to this ode, see Harrison 1993. Lowrie 1997: 297–316 helpfully discusses interpretive problems and indeterminacies; but I find it hard to accept her claim (shared by most critics) that Horace omits the scene of rape. In contrast to Moschus who narrates the event (*Europa* 162–66), Horace dramatizes it.

55. On dreams and play, see the suggestive remarks of Winnicott 1971: 20ff. Winnicott differentiates between fantasy, which he regards as a "dead end," and dreams, which, due to their symbolic nature, open up possibilities, as does play.

56. Although, as Harrison 1993: 151 notes, the expression *multum amati* (3.27.47) may indicate that this is not the first instance of sexual intercourse between Europa and the bull. Lowrie (1997: 308–10) notes that Europa's story seems to combine two patterns, one in which the maiden is raped by a god, another in which she runs off willingly with an appealing stranger.

57. Freud 1960.

58. Again, Harrison rightly sees that "the quotation of the reproach of another which is then turned into self-reproach by the speaker is a common feature of tragic rhetoric"

(1993: 153). But literary precedent hardly invalidates psychological effect in context. As a consequence I have some difficulty accepting Harrison's overall interpretation of Europa's panic as "a storm in a tea-cup" (1993: 153).

59. Daut 1975: 73.

60. See, e.g., the important collection of material from Osteria dell' Osa, near ancient Gabii, discussed and illustrated in Bietti Sestieri 1992.

61. Ehrmann 1968: 34: "[T]o pretend that play is mimesis would suppose the problem solved before it had even been formulated."

62. The expression is Susan Stewart's description of miniatures (Stewart 1997: 77). As she goes on to explain, in a passage highly suggestive for the interpretation of the archaic Roman miniatures and waxen *imagines*, "Small works are fragile and reflect the fragility of the human just as they are themselves instances of human making. One must take care and yet one can never take enough care—each life will end, human life on earth may well end" (1997: 83).

63. Mann, "Freud and the Future," quoted by Connerton 1989: 62.

64. Winnicott 1971: 144.

65. Winnicott 1971: 64.

66. Fink 1968: 27.

67. Fink 1968: 28.

68. Wagenvoort 1956 (= Wagenvoort 1935).

69. My argument thus situates in each and every movement from ludic to serious poetry the trajectory Muth 1972 ascribes to ancient literary history more generally. For Muth, the marginality of poetry effected by the Alexandrians is imitated by Catullus, whose merging of poetry and life-style in turn makes possible the career of a figure like Vergil. Muth's historical narrative, although influential, is at best reductive. It ignores the existence of politically engaged (i.e., "serious") court poetry in Hellenistic Greece, the nonludic poetry of Catullus and his contemporaries, and the movement from *ludus* to epic in the careers of both Vergil and Ovid. In a different but related vein, scholars such as Nisbet and Hubbard 1970: 361 ascribe the use of *ludo/ludus* to Roman poets' imitation of Greek *paizein*. While there is no reason to doubt that in specific cases, poets may have chosen the guiding term *ludus* as a translation of or allusion to a Greek expression (see also McDonnell 2003: 242–43), it is equally the case that their use of the word cannot be isolated from its broader significance in nonliterary discourse. Special speech is an intensification, not a repudiation of everyday speech.

70. For discussion, see also Muth 1972; Büchheit 1976; Burgess 1986; Selden 1992: 463ff.; Fitzgerald 1995: 37ff, with additional work cited in each case.

71. Varro cited at Nonius 342: *risi multum lusi modice;* Ov. *Am.* 3.1.27–28: *quod tenerae cantent, lusit tua Musa, puellae / primaque per numeros acta iuventa suos;* Ov. *Tr.* 2.59: *bucolicis iuvenis luserat ante modis;* Ov. *Fast.* 2.6: *lusit numeris; Culex* 1: Lusimus, Octavi, *gracili modulante Thalia; Ciris* 19–20: *quamvis interdum ludere nobis / et gracilem molli liceat pede claudere versum.* Of passages such as these Wagenvoort 1956: 37 writes that "the guiding thought in this is that the words are playfully rounded off into a verse by means of the metre." But it would be more accurate to say that the guiding thought is that play consists of voluntary submission to arbitrary convention. Muth 1972, discussing several of these passages, ignores the metrical issue altogether.

72. Dupont 1999.

73. Fitzgerald 1995: 37 describes Calvus and Catullus as "swapping verses back and forth in an analog of foreplay."

74. Skutsch 1985: 459.

75. Burgess 1986, with good comparanda on responsive poetry in Greece and Rome.

76. For *munus* as sex, see Friedrich 1908: 475; Adams 1982: 164. For *conficio,* Adams 1982: 159.

77. See Thomas 1988: ad loc.

78. Suet. *Vita Verg.* 26. The term used by Suetonius, *pronuntiare,* is a technical term for the performance of actors: see Varro *Ling.* 6.58; Plin. *Ep.* 5.19.3–6 uses the term to describe the activity of his freedman Zosimus in presenting comedies and seems to differentiate this performance via impersonation from the simple oral reading (*legit*) of orations, histories, and poems.

79. As noted, e.g., by Clausen 1994: 179.

80. On *meditor* Traina (*EV* 3.450) writes "La semantica virgiliana di *meditor* . . . e tutta compresa nelle accezioni di 'esercitare,' 'prepararsi' e infine 'pensare a fare qualcosa.'"

81. Clausen 1994: 182 explains that *non* is to be taken with *cano* rather than constituting a litotes with *iniussa:* "V. will not sing of what Apollo has forbidden."

82. The quoted phrase is Stewart's description of the opening of Walt Whitman's poem "Vocalism": see Stewart 2002: 143.

83. "Vocalism," quoted from http://www.daypoems.net/plainpoems/2077.html, accessed September 1, 2003. On language as a kind of co-optation of the divine power of naming, see Benjamin, "On the Mimetic Faculty," in Benjamin 1999: 2.720–22 and the analysis thereof by Rochlitz 1996: 42–46.

84. For the reverse sequence, see Hor. *Sat.* 1.1.27, where the poet proposes "setting aside play" in order to commence serious business (*sed tamen amoto quaeramus seria ludo*).

85. Clausen 1994: 216 aptly cites the remark of the ancient commentator Servius, to the effect that "they could recite a continuous song . . . or exchange responses" (*qui possent et continuum carmen dicere . . . et amoebaeum referre*).

86. See, e.g., Ov. *Tr.* 4.10.59; also Hor. *Sat.* 1.10.18–19, which attacks one rival as a "monkey . . . learned only in doing covers of Calvus and Catullus" (*simius iste / nil praeter Calvum et doctus cantare Catullum*). In the passage under discussion from eclogue 7, *canto* may refer to the borrowing of melody that makes of their performance something less than *carmen;* or it may simply be an instance of *canto* to emphasize the musicality of a song.

87. Clausen 1994: 232.

88. Pace Mynors 1990: ad loc.

89. Della Corte 1986: 1.136–37.

90. See now I. Rutherford 2001.

91. Stewart 2002: 143.

92. Whitman: see note 83.

93. Huizinga 1955: 42–43.

94. Oliensis 1998: 8ff. discusses Horace's relationship to Florus in the poem while also arguing that the poet's rebuke of the relatively insignificant Florus is intended to be "overread" by Augustus, who is reported to have complained that Horace did not mention him in his poetry (Suet. *Vita Hor.*).

95. The dating of the second book of the epistles is disputed. I have argued elsewhere that *Epistles* 2.1 cannot be earlier than 12 BC (see Habinek 1998a: 196–97). If, as Oliensis suggests, *Epistles* 2.2 is meant to be read in tandem with 2.1, then it too must be fairly late. Some scholars argue that because *Epistles* 2.2 is thematically similar to 1.1, it should be dated to roughly the same time (i.e., 19 BC), and further suggest that 2.2 could not have been written before the fourth book of *Odes,* since it presents Horace as unwilling to return to lyric poetry. The former argument is insubstantial, the latter insufficient: could not Florus's request have come after book 4 of the *Odes?* Indeed, Horace's self-presentation through the allegory of the slave suggests that he once stopped work but then resumed.

96. Oliensis 1998: 9; Leach 2002.

97. Feldherr 2002.

98. *RE* Suppl. 5.186–219, art. "Epistolographie."

99. On the philosophical background to this and other arguments in *Epistles* 2.2, see Rutherford 1981.

100. The quotations are from Hansen's adaptation of Benjamin's comments on midcentury reproductive technologies to contemporary developments. Hansen 2000, cited at http://www.mimetics.com/theory.html, accessed May 10, 2004.

101. On writers' dependence on slaves, see Habinek 2005 and other works cited there. Enrica Sciarrino reminds me that the craft metaphor implicit in the terms *poema* and *poeta* implies a kind of subservience that the poet-singer seeks to overcome, both as a historical enterprise (Augustan versus early poetry) and as a biographical endeavor.

102. See note 95.

103. Recent discussion of the *Carmen Saeculare,* with further bibliography, in Putnam 2000. Cancik 1996 is especially good on the integral relationship between the song and the ritual, in contrast to Feeney 1998 and Scheid 1998a: 85ff.

104. Feeney 1998.

105. *Pace* Scheid 1998a: 85–86. What Scheid seems to be saying is that in the classical period a *precatio* is sufficient language to make a religious performance complete. But this is not the same as saying that the *carmen* is therefore irrelevant or superfluous? On what basis can we deem any element of a religious ritual superfluous? Moreover, given the semantic inclusiveness of the term *carmen,* we might hypothesize that *precatio* itself comes into being through a process of differentiation and segmentation within the realm of song.

106. Thus Feeney 1998: 34 writes "The eclipse of the old Capitoline deities by the Palatine gods of the princeps is most remarkable, and it is exposed more nakedly in ten minutes of singing than it had been in three days of ritual action."

107. Coarelli 1993 (not cited by either Feeney 1998 or Putnam 2000). On the archaic association with Apollo and Artemis, see also Baistrocchi 1987: 96ff.

108. Coarelli 1993: 219–20. As Coarelli notes, the proper restoration of the phrasing of the *precatio* with respect to the subject *Latinus* could not be made until the discovery of fragments of the Severan *acta* in 1931.

109. Plut. *Vit. Poplic.* 21.1, discussed by Coarelli 1993: 222.

110. Gabba 1984.

111. As reported by the Greek historian Phlegon of Tralles, *Fragmente der griechischen historiker,* 257 F 37. See also Zetzel 1989 on the relationship of the oracle to the secular games and to Vergil's *Aeneid.*

112. Phlegon of Tralles, 257 F 37, verse 5. Cf. Rutherford 2001: 33, who suggests that the *Carmen Saeculare* be understood as just such a "Latin paean."

113. It is worth noting that the Salian performers, at least in the era of Augustus, were evidently *patrimi et matrimi* as well: Dion. Hal. *Ant. Rom.* 2.71.4.

114. See discussion in chapter 1 and, in particular, the iconological studies of Massa-Pairrault 1992.

115. Fraenkel 1957: 364ff. following earlier discussions by Mommsen and Vahlen. The point is well taken but interpretation of the word *vestrum,* as of the phrase *dis, quibus septem placuere colles,* should not be made overly restrictive. While the first half of the hymn focuses on Apollo and Diana and the second on Jupiter and Juno, neither is excluded from the others' portion.

116. Ernout 1994, s.v. *mos, moris.*

117. The echo of the title of Danto 1981 is not accidental.

118. Feeney 1998: 34.

119. I say "return" to Jupiter because he is present in the phrase *dis quibus septem placuere colles* of verse 7, a phrase that, more precisely than the opening address to Phoebus and Diana, defines the dedicatees of the song.

120. Cancik 1996 correctly notes that the expression *sacrificio perfecto* refers to the sacrifice to Apollo and Diana.

Chapter 5. Song and the Body

1. Connerton 1989; Gil 1999.
2. Connerton 1989: 102.
3. For this process within antiquity, see Habinek 1998; after antiquity, see Farrell 2001; Waquet 2001.
4. Connerton 1989: 100–101. In effect, inscribing practices have been the beneficiary of what Vico calls "the conceit of scholars."
5. Connerton 1989: 102.
6. *Letyat Zhuravlij,* dir. M. Kalatazov.
7. For a natural history of cranes, see Matthiessen 2001. Further discussion of cranes and crane dances, including photographs of the latter, can be found in Lonsdale 1981. Moving images of cranes and other birds migrating and dancing can be found in the documentary film *Winged Migration,* which was showing in American theaters in the summer of 2003. My own reflections on birds as natural analogues of soldiers were inspired in part by an image from a television documentary on USO performances in Vietnam: hundreds of soldiers, seated on a beach for a concert, lifted their arms above their heads in applause, giving the appearance of a flock of sea-birds about to take flight. On the relationship between birds and soldiers in Greek art and literature see Shanks 1999: esp. 90–95. On Vergil's association of the Trojans, in their return to their ancient homeland of Italy, with migrating cranes, see Baistrocchi 1987: 73.
8. Matthiessen 2001: 210.
9. Matthiessen 2001: 220, with internal citation of Alice M. Moyle, *Songs from the Northern Territory* (Canberra, 1974). On imitation of the brolga (a type of crane) by aboriginal children, see Lonsdale 1981: fig. 21.
10. Matthiessen 2001: 178. Lonsdale 1981: fig. 32 depicts adolescent girls in Zaire performing a crane dance.
11. Matthiessen 2001: 155.
12. Gil 1998: 251, summarizing and paraphrasing M. Gauchet. The use of animals as a substitute for exteriority helps explain the prevalence of the story of pygmies doing battle with cranes throughout ancient literature and art. Animal analogies are commonplace in ancient physiognomic literature: see T. Barton 1994: 105ff.
13. The dance and song of women in ancient Rome deserve their own study, as does the gendering of certain types of performance. For preliminary suggestions, see Richlin 1992, 1997, 2000 and Gamel 1998. In the present study I focus on men because it is the disembodiment of their voices that becomes authoritative within Roman culture. Also, I find the constructedness of male bodily practice still somewhat less readily accepted and understood by contemporary students and scholars and therefore perhaps in need of more immediate attention. In chapter 6 we consider song as an incorporating practice for women as well.
14. For metaphorical projection as characteristic of human thought, see M. Johnson 1987; Lakoff 1987; M. Turner 1991, 1996. These and other proponents of "metaphor theory" are confirming through discourse analysis Walter Benjamin's essential insight concerning language as "the highest level of mimetic behavior and the most complete archive of nonsensuous similarity" (Benjamin 1999: 2.722).
15. Connerton 1989: 102.
16. Connerton 1989: 22. See also chapter 3.
17. The expression "spiraling upward on thermals" is a rephrasing of Matthiessen 2001: 223. This bit of information renders the intellectual gymnastics of a long line of Vergilian commentators unnecessary. On the meaning of the Latin words *polus,* see *OLD,* s.v.
18. Bourdieu 1992: 200ff.

19. The tension between individual and flock may also explain the use of crane dances in marriage rituals, since cranes pair off and remain "loyal" to their mates. On the mating practices of cranes see Matthiessen 2001.

20. The phrase, "keeping together in time" supplies the title of William McNeill's account of the role of group drill and dance in the development of Western military dominance. See McNeill 1995.

21. Vegetius 1.4 speaks of the *alacritas* and *velocitas* expected of the legions. Josephus 3.102 writes of the soldiers' movement as one body: "This perfect discipline makes the army an ornament of peace-time and in war welds the whole into a single body — so compact are their ranks, so alert their movements in wheeling to right or left, so quick their ears for orders, their eyes for signals, their hands to act upon them."

22. On military conscription in the Roman world, see Grant 1974; Webster 1998; more generally, Chambers 1987.

23. On birds as fourth realm, see Schnapp-Gourbeillon 1981; Shanks 1999: 95ff.

24. As Shanks notes, following Schnapp-Gourbeillon 1981, in Homer, "the epiphanies of gods occur not as animals, but exclusively as birds. Their otherness and association with divinity makes of birds a sign of the beyond" (1999: 95).

25. Excellent photographs of the disks can be found at Colonna 1991. As Shanks writes of depictions of hoplites on Protocorinthian pottery, "[i]f the designs upon the shields of painted hoplites are considered to indicate something of the soldier behind, then the bird, particularly the flying bird of prey, is the mirror of the hoplite infantryman. . . . Birds go with the soldier" (1999: 91).

26. Visible in photographs in Giglioli 1929 and Menichetti 1992.

27. Massa-Pairault 1992: chap. 1.

28. Massa-Pairault 1992 emphasizes the need to consider the context in which objects were employed in considering their "iconology." For her the critical contexts of early Italian art are the *convivium* and marriage.

29. Downey 1995: 7.

30. Downey 1995: 7.

31. Colonna 1991.

32. For other mythological heroes named Cycnus, see Ahl 1982. Ahl also discusses the migratory habits of swans and the fact that mute swans do not breed in Italy and Greece.

33. I owe this observation to a speaker (whose name I have forgotten!) at a meeting of the American Philological Association some ten years ago.

34. Hinds 1987: 47–48 discusses the programmatic nature of the passages about the Cayster.

35. Hinds 1987: 47 with n. 64.

36. Cf. Manil. *Astr.* 5.364ff. where the man born under the sign of Cycnus is said to pursue luxurious items for the table as far afield as men of old traveled for military conquest.

37. C. Barton 1993; Habinek 1997. For a differing view, see C. Williams 1999.

38. Gil 1998: 158.

39. Cf. the remarks of Robert Drews (1993: 225), who is discussing the development of new social and political structures in the early Iron Age, based on male solidarity: "The solidarity of an Iron Age community, whether of a polis or of a nation, stemmed from the recognition that in war the fortunes of the community would depend on every man playing his part."

40. This association, as Erik Gunderson reminds me, also seems to be the basis of the practice of augury or divination. Cf. the use of *tripudium* to describe birds and men, as discussed in chapter 1.

41. Attali 1985.

42. For the connection, see Galinsky 1996: 265–66; Habinek 2002.

43. Lucian *Salt.* 37. For an interpretation of the treatise as a whole, see now Lada-Richards 2003.

44. The phrase "Rome's cultural revolution" was introduced by Wallace-Hadrill 1989, its use and meaning expanded by Habinek and Schiesaro 1997 and Wallace-Hadrill 1997.

45. See, e.g., Grant 1974; Webster 1998.

46. Dio goes so far as to reconstruct a debate on the topic between Maecenas and Augustus: Dio 52.14.3–52.27.3.

47. Webster 1998.

48. Webster 1998.

49. Connerton 1989: 3. McNeill 1995: 86 notes with respect to the legions of the Roman Empire that "prolonged practice drills created a sustained intense fellow-feeling among soldiers, insulating them from surrounding society in a fashion antithetical to the political involvement of the citizen-soldier of an earlier age."

50. There was a massive call-up of Italians, including freedmen, during the Pannonian revolts of AD 6 and 9, perhaps to be understood as the momentary exception that proves the rule.

51. It is perhaps worth reflecting on the quickly changing concepts of masculinity that have swept the United States in the aftermath of the abolition of conscription in 1972. On the history of military conscription in Europe and the United States, see Gooch 1980; Chambers 1987; Flynn 2002.

52. For Athenian society, see the classic discussion of Winkler 1990: 45–62. For Roman, Walters 1997 and C. Williams 1999 set out the ideological framework of the dominant sector.

53. Brief, but misleading, discussion of the *cinaedus* in Walters 1997; Corbeill 1997. Fuller presentation of sources in *RE* 21.459–60. For the later empire, see Gleason 1995. Richlin 1993 contains much useful material but blurs the boundaries between the discursive category of the *cinaedus* and participants in homosexual acts. For recent criticism of her approach see C. Williams 1999: 209–17. On cinaedic dance in Greece and Rome, see Bettini 1982; Benz 1999.

54. On which see Gleason 1995.

55. On miming alongside plays or other presentations during the late republic and empire, see Jory 1996. On parodic dancing at early *ludi,* see Szilágyi 1981, Thuilliers 1997, and pp. 104–9 above.

56. Some discussion of homoerotic aspects of Plautine comedy can be found in Gurlitt 1921; Lilja 1982, 1983. Specific discussion of the *cinaedus* in Bettini 1982, 1995 and Benz 1999 focuses on a single episode in Plautus's *Amphitruo* (see my subsequent discussion).

57. See Gratwick 1993 ad loc; also *CIL* 1.626.

58. The use of the accusative object *scortum* of the *accubui,* which, as Gratwick 1993 notes, is otherwise difficult to explain, seems due to a desire to mimic epigraphic style. Cf. *Bacch.* 1080, where the expression *duxi, habui scortum, potavi, dedi, donavi, et enim id raro,* also seems to parody epigraphic style.

59. Gratwick 1993 moves *hanc* to the end of line 476 and inserts *pallam* at the beginning of 477, thereby ruining the both the epigraphic and the comic effect.

60. Here Gratwick usefully notes that the *palla* "is going to disappear entirely by liquidation as cash, not even leaving her name to anyone." Gratwick 1993: ad loc.

61. Delatte 1950. Foucault (as reported in Martin, Gutman, and Hutton: 1988) makes much of this habit of introspection and self-scrutiny, attributing it to major changes in subjectivity during the empire. But it seems possible that such customs were already familiar to Plautus's audience, especially since they seem to have their clearest articulation in the writings of earlier Hellenistic philosophers.

62. Is it relevant that *contumelia* is a punishment for adultery? See Walters 1997: 39 and Digest 8.5.23(22).3.

63. Gratwick 1993: 187.

64. Serv. *Aen.* 8.3 and Dion. Hal. *Ant. Rom.* 14.2.2.

65. On which Guittard 1998; Moore 1998: 61 on Plaut. *Epid.* 182–84; also Plaut. *Cist.* 519–21.

66. Thus C. Williams 1999 and Habinek 1997 in contrast to, e.g., Richlin 1993; R. Taylor 1997; Corbeill 1996. For further discussion of cinaedic dancing, see *RE* 21.459–62; Colin 1952–53; Binsfeld 1956: 49ff.; Cèbe 1963: 358n5; Bettini 1982, 1995; and Benz 1999. While C. Williams is right to challenge the view of *cinaedi* as historical agents who preferred the receptive role in anal intercourse, I have reservations about his reconstruction of them as equally "real" historical agents who actively chose to resist the gender protocols of the Roman world. It is hard enough to reconstruct practices in the ancient world without retroactively ascribing contemporary motivations. Halperin 2002 regards the *cinaedus* as expressing a distinct "sexual morphology" without a correspondingly distinct sexual identity, but does not explore the theatrical component of cinaedism in Rome.

67. Benz 1999.

68. For the Chariton mime, see Santelia 1991.

69. "Uncorked" is the translation of Christenson 2000: ad loc, who fails, however, to note the sexual and cinaedic implications of the passage. For another obscene use of the verbal root *prom-*, see Plaut. *Pseud.* 608 (on which Gurlitt 1921: 112).

70. Adams 1982: 145–46 notes that the verb *caedo* frequently refers to anal rape. Christenson 2000: ad loc. speaks only of the "bizarre imagery."

71. Bettini 1982, 1995. Martial 2.86 refers to "reading Sotades cinaedus backwards" (*nec retro lego Sotaden cinaedum*), but it is unclear what exactly he means by that. On Sotades and *versus sotadeus*, see also Cameron 1995: 98ff. and Santelia 1991: 75–80.

72. Bettini 1982, 1995.

73. Adams 1982: 149, citing only Hor. *Sat.* 2.7.49. C. Williams 1999 seems to regard the use of the verb *verbero* in this sense as widespread. It is also worth noting that flogging and slashing (*verbero, caedo* in their nonmetaphorical sense) are actions that can legally be taken by a master against a slave but not against a citizen: hence outrage attendant upon the scourging of a veteran at Livy 2.23, or the flogging of free allies, as reported in Cato the Elder's speech against Q. Minucius Thermus (*ORF* 8.58).

74. An observation I owe to an unpublished seminar paper by David Engel. See also the brief discussion at Adams 1982: 49.

75. Gurlitt 1921: 120 calls it "eine häufiges Wortspiel."

76. Interestingly, the first line of their new song is an iambic octonarius, a rhythm that, according to Tobias 1979, is especially associated with "comic or heroic exaggeration."

77. Conte 1994: 53.

78. Kroll, *RE* 21.459–62; Bettini 1982, 1995.

79. For purposes of my argument it little matters whether the singular expression *mei sodalis* at Catull. 12.13 applies to one or both of the amiable duo Veraniolus and Fabullus.

80. See also Habinek 1998a: 154, 164 on the relationship in Ovid's exile poetry between physical absence of *sodales* and (alleged) poetic ineptitude. Cf. King 1998 on the relationship between *sodalitas*, cult, and song in Ov. *Tr.* 4.10.

81. Cic. *Cael.* 26 speaks of the *germani Lupercorum* as *sodales*; at *Planc.* 29 he describes the defendant as fearing his father like a god, but loving him "like a *sodalis*, like a brother [*frater*], like a peer." And Ovid, writing from exile, says that he "loved his *sodales* in a brotherly way" (*quosque ego fraterno dilexi more sodales, Tr.* 1.3.65), a point noted by Friedrich in his comment on Catull. 100.4 (Friedrich 1905).

82. Or, as Thomson puts it, "This is an example of the proverbial truth (a true example of the saying) that devoted friendship between brothers [and sisters] is a pleasant thing" (Thomson 1997: 536).

83. There is much anxiety among historians over the exact institutional nature of *sodali-*

tates and *sodalicia*. But the words merely turn into abstractions the relationships among *sodales*. The moral, political, and legal status of groups of *sodales* depends not on the relationship per se, which is always in essence one of conviviality, or "boon companionship," but on the activities undertaken by a given group of *sodales* and the interpretation of those activities by others. See discussion in chapter 2.

84. Habinek 1998a: 69–87.

85. On silencing of the opponent's voice as the goal of invective, see the closing paragraphs of Cicero's speech against Piso; also Kelly 1994.

86. Thus Thomson 1997: 267.

87. Thomson 1997 thinks that the poem is structured around a surprising contrast between Thallus's softness, or effeminacy, and his rapaciousness. But the poem as a whole, especially when read in relationship to other references to *cinaedi*, suggests that the apparent contrast is not so surprising after all. Indeed, sexual voraciousness seems to be characteristic of *cinaedi*.

88. Mynors's Oxford Classical Text (1990) prints *manus* for the *nates* of earlier editors.

89. Winkler 1990: 45–62.

90. On which, see chapter 1, note 10.

91. Habinek 1998a: 69–87, esp. 84ff.

92. C. Williams 1999: 172ff. is good on the ways in which the *cinaedus* is constructed as violating various protocols of normative masculinity, not just the taboo against the "passive" role in intercourse. Halperin 2002 emphasizes the association of the *cinaedus* with unbridled pleasure.

93. Doves were associated with the goddess Venus, and "dovie" is a term of endearment, e.g., Pl. *Cas.* 148.

94. Ganymede, or Catameitus, typifies the handsome "foreigner abducted by a potentate to be his slave" (C. Williams 1999: 59, with further discussion of the popularity of the figure at Rome). Adonis, as the target of female lust, and a free man, raises more complex issues of intentionality.

95. Cf. the remarks of C. Williams 1999: 177 on the persistence of the association of the *cinaedus* with the "image of the effeminate Eastern dancer."

96. Interestingly, along with *cinaedus*, words for thief, glutton, drunk, fool, and pathic (*fur, ebrio, fatue, pathicus*) are the ones that show up on small tiles that may have served as tokens in games at *convivia*: see C. Williams 1999: 179 with earlier bibliography.

97. Cf. *Pseud.* 1275, where the title character says he has just performed *ionica*, that is like a *cinaedus*, by dancing with a *palla* at a *convivium*.

98. Leach 2002.

99. Quotation from C. Williams 1999: 59. On the anxieties attendant upon exposure of the slave's body, see the material presented by Bodel 2002.

100. While I do not rule out the possibility that some men in the ancient world self-identified as *cinaedi* and assumed the role of sexual or gender deviants, I think it more productive to consider elite discourse about cinaedism as one of "the collective fantasies that infuse and often generate the frameworks that define and regulate normative ethical communities" (quotation from Dean 2000: 20, writing on the social and cultural function of attacks on homosexuality and pornography in interwar France). Discussion of sex and gender in the ancient world sometimes seems driven by projection of modern subjectivity onto the ancient material. Thus C. Williams 1999: 153 writes of ancient Rome that "men must have been fighting urges that dwelt within them." Perhaps, but how can we know whether they were fighting urges for sexual contact with other men, or whether they developed a discourse about urges for sexual contact with other men as a way of dealing with entirely different psychological, social, and cultural needs and wants? Dean's analysis of twentieth-century France would suggest the latter.

101. Shackleton Bailey translates *morio* not as "buffoon" but as "cretin." Cèbe 1966: 356–57 and pl. 16 describes two hyperphallic statues from Pompeii as *moriones*. Is it possible that the *morio* is the reification of the *cinaedus* as oversexed as an active, as opposed to passive, partner? Martial's list of potential fathers also includes a *lippus,* or "blear-eyed man." At first glance this term may seem to describe a condition rather than a performance type, but the frequent references to the *lippus* in comedy and satire suggest that he too is a stock character in other performance contexts that are largely lost to us.

102. H. G. Liddell, R. Scott, and H. S. Jones, *A Greek-English Lexicon* (Oxford, 1968), s.v.

103. On scratching the head with a single finger as sign of membership in a subculture, see Richlin 1993; R. Taylor 1997: 339.

104. Gleason 1995: 55–81 is especially good on this topic.

105. On the poem, see Henderson 2001: 151–62. Of course, as Henderson rightly points out, there is no way of telling in what spirit we are to take Demetrius's volte-face.

106. Habinek 1997. Wechsler's discussion (1988) of physiognomy in revolutionary France as a way of sorting out the urban mass parallels my analysis of newly cosmopolitan Rome. See also T. Barton 1994: 96. The claim of C. Williams 1999: 13 that the ideology of cinaedism "never changed" during the hundreds of years of Roman civilization strikes this reader as unlikely.

107. Cf. the comparable tension between birth and performance in Quintilian's account of the education of the orator, well analyzed by Gunderson 2000. On birth versus performance in the writings of Seneca the Younger, see Habinek 1998a: 136–50.

108. Gleason, too, notes the shift to a culture of "individualistic performance" (1995: 121), albeit in the Greek cities. Certainly the competition among rhetorical stars of the Greek "second sophistic" is a spectacular manifestation of concern with virtuosity. But it is my contention that shifting models of manhood, from the corporate to the individualistic, had an impact on more specifically Roman discourse as well. It is interesting to note, too, that even as the *cinaedus* becomes less important as a figure of bodily expressivity, writers persist in manifesting anxiety about his voice: see Gleason 1995: 103–30.

109. Zorzetti 1991: 316n18. Zorzetti also makes a connection between Roman and Hellenistic expressivity, following Gentili 1977. I do not disagree that what comes to be considered expressionistic by the Romans may have resembled and, in some cases, been dependent on Hellenistic style. But explanation of the popularity of expressive performance styles at Rome and their ideological significance must come from within Roman culture itself and not simply be attributed to Greek influence. On modes of performance, see also Hall 2002.

110. In fact, this is Macrobius's slight but revealing paraphrase of Scipio. In the direct quotation Scipio denounces "dancing with castanets" (*cum crotalis saltare*), which Macrobius rewords as "to dance while gesturing with castanets" (*crotala gestantes saltare*).

111. "Striking little poses" is the translation Krostenko 2001: 25 offers for *staticulos dat,* and is surely correct.

112. E.g., Beacham 1999: 237–38; Corbeill 1997: 105; Krostenko 2001: 49–50.

113. Zorzetti 1991: 315–16 cites the passage from the *Laws* as an example of Cicero's concern with Hellenistic expressionism at Rome. But it seems worth noting that Cicero's concern is with the impact on the audience rather than on the performer. As Gleason notes of Cicero, "While he clearly harbors qualms about certain vocal techniques, what is absent in Cicero is any impassioned concern that the excesses of the stage are infecting rhetorical practice" (1995: 108).

114. Cf. Gunderson 2000: 111ff. for an excellent discussion of the implications and afterlife (including this passage of Gellius) of the Ciceronian definition of orators as "performers of truth" (*veritates ipsius actores, De Or.* 3.214).

115. Beacham 1999 cites this passage as evidence of pantomime performance of philosophi-

cal dialogue, but his application of the term pantomime seems imprecise. Pantomime is generally understood to involve a separation of the bodily performance from the vocal; Plutarch's language is more easily understood as suggesting that the same slaves spoke and gestured.

116. See Schertz 2004 on the iconography of Marsyas in Roman art.

117. A paradox well analyzed by Gunderson 2000: esp. 149–86. On the more widespread tendency in imperial Rome to displace discussion of elite subjectivity and political power (or lack thereof) into consideration of the actions of slaves, see Roller 2001: 213ff.

118. This and other translations in this paragraph from Loeb, Plutarch's *Moralia*, vol. 9.

119. Beacham 1999: 30, following the argument of E. Gruen.

120. Following Martin 1993 on the seven sages as "performers of wisdom."

121. On the political implications of Phaedrus's fables, see more generally Bloomer 1997b: 73–109 and Henderson 2001.

122. For the application of *fractus/infractus* to the voice of *cinaedi*, see Gleason 1995: 112. Gleason argues that the terms "connote effeminacy through a kind of semantic double-determination. Words or voices that are 'broken' are weak, and therefore feminine; rhythms that are 'broken' (in Greek, *keklasmenoi*) soil the dignity of prose with the unmanly ethos of certain lyric meters." While I don't disagree with Gleason's analysis, I prefer to focus on the literal meaning of *fractus:* broken into pieces or, in the case of bodies, disarticulated. On the terminology of badly gendered performance, vocal or otherwise, see also Richlin 1997 and C. Williams 1999: chap. 4. Of course Maecenas's cultural performance is *infractus* in another sense, inasmuch as he is deemed responsible for introducing Bathyllus, whose style of mime separated, once and for all, verbal from kinetic performance.

123. The idea of birth is expressed earlier in the sentence with the word *nata*. The passage quoted is part of a lengthier discussion of characteristics that are owing to birth rather than imitation. Birth is also an issue for Juvenal, who in satire 2, differentiates between deviants by choice and deviants by birth.

124. With the mention of the *pallium* we are back to the issue of the *cinaedus*'s greed: for Maecenas to be described as "the fugitive slave of a rich man" implies alienation, at the least, of the rich man's property. The recurrent matter of the *pallium* also suggests that the *cinaedus* of mime stole a *pallium* as a part of his routine.

125. For analysis of Tacitus's account of Messalina as a figure of "excessive desire," see Joshel 1997: esp. 242ff.

126. Cf. Joshel 1997: 243, who links this fluidity with similar descriptions of the flow of "money, goods, and bodies" at Rome. On fluidity and pleasure more generally, see Edwards 1993: 174–75.

127. On play as the characteristic activity of the Roman satirist, see Habinek 2004. On Juvenal's performance as in effect "boundary work" for an embattled masculinity, see Henderson 1989; Freudenburg 2001.

128. On which Gunderson 2000.

129. On the association of elegy with *mollitia* and with youth, see Fear 2000.

130. Dupont 1997: 55.

131. My argument can thus be understood as complementing that of Matthew Roller, who suggests that Pliny seeks to expand the "arena for aristocratic competition" (Roller 1998: 289) even to include recitation of trivial, playful poetry.

132. On the negative connotations of rigidity, see Quint. *Inst.* 11.3.76, there speaking specifically of the eyes.

133. For the continuing performance of lyric and, it would seem, elegiac poetry to musical accompaniment, see Gell. *NA* 19.9.1–14.

134. On the relationship between Pliny's writing and the poetry of Catullus, see Gunderson 1997; Roller 1998.

135. Fear 2000.

136. On which, see Svenbro 1993: 187ff.; Habinek 1998a: 163.

Chapter 6. Magic, Song, and Sacrifice

1. Twelve Tables VIII.8b W = Plin. *HN* 28.17.

2. Twelve Tables VIII.1a = Cic. *Rep.* 4.12. Scholars are in the habit of citing Momigliano 1942 for the differentiation between enchantment and defamation; but as Baistrocchi 1987: 259–63 notes, *occentatio* itself is a kind of "furto della fama" through the transformative power of song.

3. See the helpful discussion of Phillips 1986. Versnel 1991 takes the extreme view that only definitions imposed from the outside are useful in scholarship — a position contradicted by his own patient use of philological method!

4. Garosi 1976: 13 (translation mine).

5. Bell 1992: 170.

6. Cf. Bell 1992: 201, summarizing Foucault: "A power relationship undoes itself . . . when it succeeds in reducing the other to total subservience or in transforming the other into an overt adversary."

7. See the excellent discussion of Dido's Punic antecedents in Hexter 1992.

8. She is called Carmentis by Varro (*Ling.* 6.6.12), Vergil (*Aen.* 8.335–41), Ovid (*Fast.* 1.499, 6.529), Aulus Gellius (*NA* 16.16.1–4, 18.7.2), and Servius (*Aen.* 8.336); Carmenta by Dionysius of Halicarnassus (*Ant. Rom.* 1.31), Strabo (5.30), and Plutarch (*Vit. Rom.* 21.2, *Quaest. Rom.* 56). There is clearly some crossing of the Greek and Latin traditions, as both Strabo and Servius give the goddess's Greek name as Nikostrate while Dionysius of Halicarnassus says it is Themis. Livy seems to call her both Carmenta (1.7.8) and Carmentis (5.47.2), the former when he is telling her story, the latter in reference to a rock named after her. Good collection of references to Carmenta/Carmentis by S. Fasce at *EV* 1.666–68.

9. Plut. *Vit. Rom.* 21.2 describes her as Evander's wife.

10. E.g., Fantham 1992; Newlands 1995; Herbert-Brown 1996.

11. For Carmentis as nymph, see Verg. *Aen.* 8.336 and 339, where the word *nympha* accompanies each of the two occurrences of her name.

12. E.g., Herbert-Brown 1996: 159–62. Even Wiseman, who is at first inclined to dismiss the story of Carmentis as Hellenistic etiologizing (as if no one etiologized before Callimachus!), "a story for the 'Carmentalia' festival and the shrine of Carmenta by the Porta Carmentalis" (1995: 40), two pages later backs off and acknowledges with respect to Herakles that "the exploit, the prophecy, the altar — now seem to be much more ancient than previously thought" (1995: 42). Of course, the prophecy in question is the one ascribed to Carmentis and the altar site of sacrifice that Strabo and Dionysius ascribe to Evander at her instruction.

13. "[U]n fondaco greco precoloniale" (Coarelli 1997: 302). For further discussion of the Ara Maxima in relation to the founding of Rome, see Grandazzi 1997; Carandini 1997.

14. For dating of pottery from Euboea and Ischia to the eighth century BC, see Coarelli 1997: 305. He also says there is bronze age (fourteenth to thirteenth centuries BC) "ceramica 'appenninica.'"

15. Baistrocchi 1987: 95–104, who also collects extensive testimonia for ancient views of the Palatine as center of the city and, as he puts it, "il riflesso ombelicale terrestre del Polo e degli altri 'colli' siderei dell'Orsa Minore" ("the umbilical reflex on earth of the Polestar and of the other sidereal 'hills' of the constellation Ursa Minor") (1987: 104).

16. *hos esti nyn en mesoi malista tēs Romaiōn poleos,* Dion. Hal. *Ant. Rom.* 1.31.3.

17. For a good discussion of the calendrical significance of Carmentis and the Carmentalia, see Sabbatucci 1988: 26–29.

18. For Carmentis as goddess of birth, see Plut. *Vit. Rom.* 21.1; Gell. *NA* 16.16.1–4, with reference to Varro. For Janus as *princeps in sacrificando*, see Cic. *Nat. D.* 2.67. Cf. Fest. 45 L on supplication of Janus at the beginning of a new life. For Janus in the Salian hymn, see Fest. 3 L; Varro *Ling.* 7.26.

19. On Janus more generally, with extensive prior bibliography, see Capdeville 1973. On Janus as match for Carmentis, Sabbatucci 1988: 25ff.

20. Sabbatucci 1988: 41–47, 70–73.

21. Rappaport 1999: esp. 4–22, building on Rappaport 1979. See also chapter 1.

22. See in particular Scheid 1988. A number of scholars, at least as far back as Daremberg and Saglio, have interpreted Varro *Ling.* 7.84 as indicating that no blood sacrifices were made to Carmentis. But the passage merely records a prohibition against the bearing of any objects made from an animal that died of its own accord (*morticina*) or such an animal itself into Carmentis's sanctuaries.

23. Ancient sources pertaining to Numa as religious founder are gathered by Gabba 1984, but he interprets them hypercritically as traces of Augustan-era invention.

24. On Vergil's use of the term *vates*, see M. Massenzio in *EV* 5.2.456–58. Note that Servius emphasizes Carmentis's status as *vates*, writing "she isn't really a nymph, but a female singer of vatic prophecies" (*haec autem non vere nympha fuit sed vaticinatrix, Aen.* 8.336).

25. I have translated both *exta* and *fibra* as entrails, although in fact *exta* seems to refer to a subset thereof: see Santini 1988.

26. The syntactic pattern *cuius . . . is* seems to be a variant of the "if . . . then" response characteristic of vatic and oracular "responders."

27. Garosi 1976: 36–52 discusses the role of *vates* in the introduction of new, and potentially subversive, religious practices. Earlier discussions neglect this aspect of *vates*, part of a more general neglect of sacrificial practice at Rome.

28. Graf 1994: 61.

29. On *Carmentis* from *carmen*, see Ov. *Fast.* 1.467; Serv. *Aen.* 8. 336; Plut. *Vit. Rom.* 21.2; Dion. Hal. *Ant. Rom.* 1.31; Aug. *Civ. Dei* 4.11, *Origo Gentis Romanae* 5.

30. On *Carmentis* as *carere mentis*, see Plut. *Vit. Rom.* 21.2.

31. Bömer 1957–58, commentary on *Fasti* 1.499; Porte 1985: 201, 253; Ernout 1994: 101; Walde and Hoffmann 1980: 170.

32. Peruzzi 1978: 50.

33. See Bömer 1957–58, commentary on *Fasti* 1.499.

34. Perrot 1961: 102.

35. Perrot 1961: 297n3. Schilling 1960 accepts the parallel with *semen/sementis*, but Perrot's rejection seems decisive.

36. Radke 1979: 82.

37. "[D]essen, was Zuteilung verschäfft oder bringt" (Radke 1979: 82).

38. On this meaning of *caro*, see Scheid 1988: 271; Ernout 1994: 101.

39. Scheid 1988: 271. On this use of *caro/carnis*, cf. Livy 32.1.9, 37.3.4, and Serv. *Aen.* 2.211 — all cited by Scheid.

40. On the past as a version of externality comparable to distance, see Helms 1993.

41. Dion. Hal. *Ant. Rom.* 1.33.4, Loeb trans.

42. Svenbro 1988.

43. Schol. Pind. 1.3.18–19; *Hymn Herm.* 437–42; Athen. 8.347e; Phld. *De Mus.* 4 col. 21.6–13 van Krevelen: all cited from and discussed by Svenbro 1988.

44. With respect to weight cf. the Greek tendency "to divide sacrificial meat according to weight" (Svenbro 1988: 236).

45. *CIL* 6.2104a line 32 (= Scheid 1998b: 100a32). For discussion and earlier bibliography, see Scheid 1990: 620n104. The term *descinderunt* also appears at *CIL* 6.2066 (Scheid 1998b: 57.69) in a fragmentary context that makes reference to the wearing of garlands after a sacrifice.

46. On the etymological link between *scindo* and other Indo-European words for "cut," see Ernout 1994: 602; Walde-Hoffmann 1980: 3.493.

47. On the force of the preverb *de-*, see Brachet 2000.

48. See note 43. Also relevant here is Hor. *Carm.* 1.15.15, which refers to division (*divides*) of song. The passage seems to suggest the breaking up of a song (accompanied by a cithara) into portions to be performed by women and portions to be performed by a man, but interpretation is controversial. Horace's indication that Paris will perform on a cithara suggests that he has in mind a large-scale, public performance, one in which division or distribution (another possible meaning of *divido*) of song might be especially appropriate. On the contexts for use of the cithara, see West 1992: 49ff.

49. On the use of the term *magus* in this poem, Graf 1994: 47–48; on the sacred fire, Thomson 1997: 519–20 (following Kroll).

50. Thomson 1997: 519. Graf 1994: 47 describes the invective as "assez froide."

51. Thomson 1997: 520.

52. Suetonius, *De viris illustribus*, fr. 104 Reifferscheid.

53. Santini 1988. For the etymological association with *induo, exuo*, see Ernout 1994: 461. For the burning of song upon an altar, see also Manil. *Astr.* 1.20–22, as interpreted by Schrijvers 1983.

54. For the allusion to Orpheus, see Kiessling 1959: 78 as cited by Svenbro 1988: 250n112.

55. Svenbro 1988: 240.

56. This distancing of the *vates* is apparent in imperial references, which place them on the geographical and social margins of society, e.g., Plin. *HN* 30.13, *Ep.* 6.20.19; Tac. *Hist.* 2.78.

57. On *vates* and the state, see Zorzetti 1991, Wiseman 1994.

58. Previous discussions of the *nenia* include Kroll, *RE* 32.2390–93; DS, s.v. *nenia;* Heller 1939, 1943; Tupet 1976; Richlin 2000.

59. Santini 1988.

60. Heller 1943.

61. Heller 1939: 363n12, following the interpretation of Sedgwick 1930. The alternative view, perhaps hinted at in Donat. *Ter. Eun.* 1024 and accepted by, among others, Tupet 1976: 177, that the *nenia* here is "le cri aigu de la souris" makes no sense in context.

62. Harder to understand is the expression *neque umquam lavando et fricando scimus facere neniam* (Plaut. *Poen.* 231) as sung by a group of women complaining of the effort involved in self-adornment. The phrase *facere neniam* seems to reflect the expression *facere finem*, "to make an end of," except that Latin would ordinarily use a genitive for the dependent gerunds, not the dative. It is also possible that the gerunds are ablatives, but in what sense could a *nenia*, regardless of meaning, be said to be composed "by means of" washing and exfoliating? Most likely there is a pun of some sort here, perhaps dependent on the underlying notion of "setting forth" implicit in the root shared by *praefica* (the leader of the *nenia*, according to Nonius 67.8 and 145.24–27; cf. Varro *Ling.* 7.70; Serv. *Aen.* 6.216) and *facere*.

63. The fragmentary passage from Fest. 154.20–22 L seems to link *nenia* with *exequias*. See Heller 1943: 228. Cf. Pacat. *Paneg. Theodos.* 37.3 (121 B) for the juxtaposition of *funebres nenias* and *carmen exequiale.*

64. On *nenia* and *nētē*, see Diomedes, *GLK* 1.484–85; Fest. 156–7L.

65. The whole passage, which is somewhat obscure, is rife with images of butchery or sacrifice (*abstrusas rationes*), banqueting (*cubiculariis disputationibus*), and entrails (*visceribus*), not to mention the "lethargic guesses of cronish opinions" (*veternosas anilium opinionum suspiciones*).

66. E.g., Plin. *HN* 29.78 on the "warm flesh of plucked roosters" (*carnes gallinaceorum ut tepebant avulsae*).

67. On the sacrificial significance of the term *princeps*, see Scheid 1988.

68. This process of leadership, or distribution, of mourning, may be depicted on a bas relief from Amiternum, discussed by Flower 1996: 98–99 (with plate VI) and Richlin 2000: 244–45.

69. Note as well the choral performance of a *nenia* at the funeral of Claudius in Sen. *Apocol.* 12.3, and the interpretation of the triumph song for Theodosius as simultaneously *funebres neniae* for the usurper Magnus Maximus (Pacat. *Paneg. Theodos.* 37.3).

70. The parallel to the *praesul* of the Salian performance is noted later.

71. Some manuscripts read *toros* for *choros*. In either case, the reference to finality (*supremos*) and to performance at a funeral (*funeribus*, Ov. *Fast.* 6.660) is secure. The *nenia* seems to have been designed to encourage performance by as large a group as possible: for the use of choruses, see Sen. *Apocol.* 12.3 and, probably, Suet. *Aug.* 100.2.

72. Cited at Heller 1943: 235. It is possible at least in the case of Diomedes that the emphasis on finality is an attempt to link *nenia* etymologically to Greek *neaton*, "latest" or "last," as he goes on to discuss, while also allowing for an etymology from *nētē*, which he describes as the last string on a lyre (Diom., *GLK* 1.484–85). But already at *Aen.* 6.231 Vergil had referred to the pronouncement of "last words" (*novissima verba*) by the otherwise insignificant character Corynaeus at the funeral of Misenus. In his somewhat scrambled note on the passage, Servius seems to link this action to the performance of the *praefica*.

73. D. Allen 2002 comments on the threat mourning posed to continuation of military action: cf. the decision of the Roman Senate, in the aftermath of the catastrophe at Cannae, to limit women's mourning to a period of thirty days (Val. Max. 1.1.5 and Richlin 2000: 232).

74. Wille 1967: 71, where he speculates that the sound of the funeral procession was designed to create "das akustische Maximum." This view is perhaps implied at Mart. Cap. 9.925: *irasque inferas per nenias sedavere.*

75. For sources pertaining to the goddess Nenia and her shrine just beyond the porta Viminalis, see Radke 1979: 227. Wissowa 1912: 197 thinks the location of her shrine distant from the early center of Rome suggests that she is not an early deity. But it is just as likely that her worship beyond the Servian (and by implication earlier) walls relates to her association with burial, that is, with establishing a boundary between the living and the dead: see Carandini 1997: 406n75 and, in particular, Colonna 1996, who seeks to associate a necropolis for Latial era IIB (i.e., 830–770 BC) with the worship of Nenia at the site.

76. The term specifically arises in connection with the funerals of Augustus (Suet. *Aug.* 100.2) and Claudius (Sen. *Apocol.* 12.3). Cf. Amm. Marc. 19.1.10. on the singing and dancing of neniae for aristocratic youth.

77. Hor. *Carm.* 2.1.38. Horace toys with the possibility of assimilating his own lyric reflections on recent history to the *nenia* of Simonides, but ends up rejecting death in war as fit only for the prose works of Pollio, which are the primary subject of praise in the ode.

78. Fest. 161 L describes the *nenia* as being sung "for the sake of praise" (*laudandi gratia*). Cic. *Leg.* 2.24.62 describes the *neniae* as accompanying or following up (*prosequatur*) the spoken praises of the dead. Sidonius *Epist.* 2.8.2–3 presents a *nenia* as fit for inscription on a gravestone.

79. See examples collected by Heller 1943: 240.

80. *Nenia, ineptum et inconditum carmen, quod a conducta muliere, quae praefica diceretur, is, quibus propinqui non essent, mortuis exhiberetur.*

81. On the etymology of *praefica*, see Ernout 1994: 212. On the *praesul*, see chapter 1.

82. Non. 67.8: *haec mulier vocitata olim praefica usque ad Poenicum bellum.*

83. West 1992: 388. Notice that Linos is said to have invented the threnos: Heraclid. Pont. in ps-Plut. *De mus.* 3, as reported at *OCD* 868.

84. Richlin 2000: 231–32. Treggiari 1991: 493–95.

85. See, e.g., Habinek 1998a: 8, 61–62, with further bibliography.

86. Indeed the double significance of the names may be taken to reinforce Bettini's linking of them with the "spatial localization of time" (Bettini 1988–91: 154–56).

87. Bakhtin 1984: esp. pp. 303–436.

88. See, e.g., Eilberg-Schwartz 1995 on invective's association of the vagina and the mouth.

89. Bataille 1988–91.

90. I take "even more than usual" to be the force of the comparative in *atrociore*, which is otherwise unmotivated.

91. It seems just barely possible that *mortualia* here means, as elsewhere, "winding-sheets," i.e., useless pieces of cloth wrapped around the body. Does *mortualia*, like *nenia*, cross between object and song? with *mortualia* describing a trashy object included with the body, as *nenia* is trashy object included with the sacrifice? A late antique gloss, *CGL* 5.226, associates *nenia* with *mortualia* as follows: *nenias dicuntur carmina senilia et mortualia*.

92. See discussion by Vanggaard 1988: 45–49, including broader reflection on the political significance of the *flamines*.

93. Gil 1998: 54: "The social organization of traditional peoples presupposes the idea of a 'nonannihilating' time. It is in this sense that one can say that traditional societies 'have no history.' They have no historicity, they do not build themselves up by introducing nothingness, as we do, into the very heart of the social project."

94. On ancient notions of the "restless dead," see Johnston 1999; Ogden 2001: 163–90, 202–16.

95. Wille 1967: 51–67.

96. For *nenia* as a type of praise, see Non. 67.8 (citing Varro *De vita populi romani lib. iv*); Cic. *Leg.* 2.62, on *nenia* as following or perhaps extending the *laudes*. On the *nenia* being sung "for the sake of praise," see Fest. 154.20 L and Fest. 155 L. Praise seems implied as well by Horace's use of the term *merita* in reference to the night that receives a *nenia* in *Odes* 3.28: *dicetur merita Nox quoque Nenia, Carm.* 3.28.16).

97. In contrast to most sources, which describe the *nenia* as being sung "in the direction of" the dead (in + accusative), a scholiast on Hor. *Epod.* 17.29 describes it as a song "of the dead" (*mortuorum*), perhaps testimony to the principle that *similia similibus curantur*.

98. Auson. *Com.* 4.5, *Par.* 17.1–3, 28.6. For *nenia* as duty, see Auson. *Par.* Praef. 5–6.

99. Gil 1998: 54.

100. See the passages assembled by Heller 1943: 232.

101. Heller 1943: esp. 254ff.

102. Richlin 2000.

103. Hence the hostility to *vates* and other workers of magic attested by the historians.

104. On Carmentis and the alphabet: Hyginus *Fab.* 277; Isid. *Et.* 1.4.1, 5.39.11.

105. Keightley 1996: 75.

106. Peruzzi 1998.

107. Habinek 1998a: 41, 76 with earlier bibliography.

108. Whether these rebellions are historically true or not, Livy's recounting of them conforms to the image of the Marsi as the "enemy within." For passage through the territory of the Marsi, see Livy 8.6.8.

109. Piccaluga 1976: 209. I have not yet consulted Dench 1995.

110. It may also be relevant that the Marsi were alleged to be descended from Circe: see Gell. *NA* 16.1. As Piccaluga 1976 notes, the Marsi were regarded as being and remaining Marsi by nature, as opposed to other peoples who became Romans by convention.

111. Piccaluga 1976: 208, with ancient testimonia.

112. Stramaglia 1995: 227–28 discusses the ancient story attributed to Hippolitus of Rome in which a prophetic head composed of *omentum* begins to melt.

113. Radke 1979: 83–84.

114. Ov. *Fasti* 6.105–30 tells the story of Carna's rape by Janus. On Carmentis's association with Janus, see Sabbatucci 1988: 29. McDonough 1997 discusses the myth and ritual of Carna and the *strix* as expressive of Roman attitudes toward misfortune, liminality, and infant death in particular. He also suggests that the *strix* may be not so much a specific species of bird as an imaginary hybrid monster of the sort depicted on surviving curse tablets. His assessment of Carna in terms of the "anthropology of misfortune" is not incompatible with my emphasis on foundational knowledge. On Carna, see also Pettazzoni 1940.

115. See also Tertullian *Nat.* 2.9.

116. Sabbatucci 1988: 182–92.

117. For roses at the Carnaria, see *CIL* 3.3893; Illuminati 1961: 47; McDonough 1997: 340n79.

118. In Lacanian terms, we might say that the boy leaves the realm of the Imaginary and enters the Symbolic, the latter marked by a ritual of substitution and differentiation.

119. E.g., Jackson Knight 1967; Bourgeaud 1974; Fitzgerald 1984; P. Miller 1995. Doob 1990 emphasizes instead the epistemological aspects of the labyrinth, the tension between confusion when perceived from within and order when perceived from without. She dismisses concern with "anthropological origins" as a "search for the Ur-labyrinth" (1990: 3)—an odd claim that does not jibe with my reading of the literature, which tends to emphasize the multivalence of the image.

120. On Troy as labyrinth, see in addition to the works cited in the previous note Heller 1946. For Pliny the fourth labyrinth is not Troy, but one at Lemnos.

121. Clark 1979: 125–45.

122. On Trojan War as hierogamos, see Baistrocchi 1987: 23–27.

123. Plut. *Vit. Thes.* 21, with discussion by Lawler 1946; Calame 1977. Cf. Pollux 4.101; Schol. Il. 18.590–606. On initiatory aspects of the Theseus cycle, see Borgeaud 1974, with further works cited there. Lawler points out that no ancient author explicitly describes the dance as mimetic of cranes; on the other hand, no ancient author seems troubled by the use of the word "crane" (*geranos*) to refer to it. The evidence presented by Lawler is compatible with a dance in two stages—one twisting and winding, as if in imitation of a snake or the movement through the labyrinth, the other "a crisp, rapid circle dance, followed by a forward and backward dance of two lines in opposition to teach other" (1946: 114).

124. Jackson Knight 1967: 231–32, following Weidner 1917 and Müller 1935.

125. Cf. also *trulla*, meaning "cooking pot," which Jackson Knight 1967: 231 connects to *trua*.

126. P. Miller 1995 points to the references to Delos and Crete in the simile describing Aeneas's appearance at Verg. *Aen.* 4.143–46.

127. On caves and labyrinths, see Jackson Knight 1967; Clark 1979: 136–37, 140; P. Miller 1995.

128. Jackson Knight 1967: 249–52, following Shear 1923. Cf. Müller 1935 who refers to both intestines and vulva.

129. According to Torelli 1984: 73–74, Deubner suggested that the *Saliae virgines* performed sacrifice while the men were away at war.

130. Cf. Vergil's omission of women from among the inhabitants of the field of the blessed despite their presence in the corresponding Orphic poetry: Habinek 1989.

Epilogue. At the Threshold of History

1. Kisliuk 1998: 15, citing and paraphrasing R. Williams 1980.

2. Taussig 1993: 46–47.

3. Winnicott 1971: 55.

REFERENCES

Adams, J. 1982. *The Latin Sexual Vocabulary*. Baltimore.

Ahl, F. 1982. "Amber, Avalon, and Apollo's Singing Swan," *AJPh* 103: 373–411.

Aldrete, G. 1999. *Gestures and Acclamations in Ancient Rome*. Baltimore.

Allen, D. 2002. "The Trump Card: Plato's Strong Claim for Rhetoric in the *Menexenus*," lecture, University of Southern California, January 27.

Allen, W., Jr. 1972. "Ovid's *Cantare* and Cicero's *Cantores Euphorionis*," *TAPA* 103: 1–14.

Almar, K. 1990. *Inscriptiones Latinae: Eine illustrierte Einführung in die lateinische Epigraphik*. Odense. Odense university classical studies, 14.

Ampolo, C. 1984. "Il lusso nelle società arcaiche: Note preliminari sulla posizione del problema," *Opus* 3.2: 469–76.

Attali, J. 1985. *Noise: The Political Economy of Music*. Trans. B. Massumi. Minneapolis. Theory and History of Literature, 16. (Originally, *Bruits: Essai sur l'économie politique de la musique*, n.p., 1977.)

Baistrocchi, M. 1987. *Arcana Urbis: Considerazioni su alcuni rituali arcaici di Roma*. Genoa.

Bakhtin, M. 1984. *Rabelais and His World*. Trans. H. Iswolsky. Bloomington.

Bannon, C. 1997. *The Brothers of Romulus: Fraternal Pietas in Roman Law, Literature, and Society*. Princeton.

Barton, C. 1993. *The Sorrows of the Ancient Romans*. Princeton.

Barton, T. 1994. *Power and Knowledge: Astronomy, Physiognomics, and Medicine under the Roman Empire*. Ann Arbor.

Bartsch, S. 1994. *Actors in the Audience: Theatricality and Doublespeak from Nero to Hadrian*. Cambridge, Mass.

Bataille, G. 1955. *Prehistoric Painting: Lascaux or the Birth of Art*. Trans. A. Wainhouse. Lausanne.

Bataille, G. 1988–91. *The Accursed Share: An Essay on General Economy*. Trans. R. Hurley. 3 vols. in 2. New York.

Baudot, A. 1973. *Musiciens romains de l'antiquité*. Montreal. Etudes et commentaires 82.

Beacham, R. 1999. *Spectacle Entertainments in Early Rome*. New Haven and London.

Beard, M., J. North, and S. Price. 2000. *Religions of Rome*. 2 vols. Cambridge.

Bell, C. 1992. *Ritual Theory, Ritual Practice*. Oxford.

Benjamin, W. 1968. *Illuminations: Essays and Reflections*. Ed. and introd. Hannah Arendt, trans. Harry Zohn. New York.

Benjamin, W. 1977. *The Origin of German Tragic Drama*. Trans. J. Osborne. London.

Benjamin, W. 1999. *Selected Writings*. Vol. 2: *1927-1934*. Trans. R. Livingstone et al., ed. M. Jennings et al. Cambridge, Mass.

Benz, L. 1999. "Dramenbearbeitung und Dramenparodie im antiken Mimus und in plautinishcen *Amphitruo*," in *Studien zu Plautus' Amphitruo*, ed. T. Baier. Tübingen. ScriptOralia 116, Reihe A: Altertumswissenschaftliche Reihe, Bd. 27. Pp. 51-96.

Benz, L., E. Stark, and G. Vogt-Spira (eds.). 1995. *Plautus und die Tradition des Stegreifspiels*. Tübingen. ScriptOralia 75. Reihe A: Altertumswissenschaftliche Reihe, Bd. 19.

Berard, C. 1983. "Le corps bestial," in *Le corps et ses fictions*, ed. C. Reichler. Paris. Pp. 43-54.

Bettini, M. 1982. "A proposito dei versi sotadei, greci e romani," *MD* 9: 59-105.

Bettini, M. 1991. *Anthropology and Roman Culture: Kinship, Time, Images of the Soul*. Baltimore and London.

Bettini, M. 1995. "*Amphitruo* 168-72: *Numeri innumeri* und metrische Folklore," in *Plautus und die Tradition des Stegriefspiels*, ed. L. Benz, E. Stark, and G. Vogt-Spira. Tübingen. ScriptOralia 75. Reihe A: Altertumswissenschaftliche Reihe, Bd. 19. Pp. 89-96.

Bielohlawek, K. 1983. "Precettistica conviviale e simposiale nei poeti greci (da Omero fino alla silloge teognidea e à Crizia)," in *Poesia e simposio nella Grecia antica*, ed. M. Vetta. Rome. Pp. 96-116.

Bietti Sestieri, A. 1992. *The Iron Age Community of Osteria dell'Osa*. Cambridge.

Binsfeld, W. 1956. "Grylloi, ein Beitrag zur Geschichte der antiken Karikatur." Diss. Cologne.

Blakely (Westover), S. 1997. "Myth and Models of Production," lecture, Swedish Institute of Archaeological Research, Athens, December 7.

Blakely, S. 2001. "Black Hephaistos: Greek Daimones and African Metal Working," lecture, Johns Hopkins University, March 15.

Blakely, S. Forthcoming. *Black Hephaistos: Greek Daimones and African Metal Working*.

Bloch, M. 1973. "Symbols, Song, Dance and Features of Articulation," *European Journal of Sociology* 15: 55-81.

Bloch, R. 1958. "Sur les dances armées des Saliens," *Annales: ESC* 13: 706-15.

Bloch, R. 1963. *Les prodiges dans l'antiquité classique*. Paris.

Bloomer, W. M. 1997a. "Schooling in Persona: Imagination and Subordination in Roman Education," *CA* 16: 57-78.

Bloomer, W. M. 1997b. *Latinity and Literary Society at Rome*. Philadelphia.

Bodel, J. 2002. "*Caveat emptor*: Slave Traders in Ancient Rome and the American South," lecture, Berkeley, November 2.

Bömer, F. 1957-58. *Die Fasten*. 2 vols. Heidelberg.

Borgeaud, P. 1974. "The Open Entrance to the Closed Palace of the King: The Greek Labyrinth in Context," *History of Religions* 14: 1-27.

Borgna, E. 1993. "*Ancile e arma ancilia*. Osservazioni sullo scudo dei Salii," *Ostraka* 2.1: 9-42.

Bourdieu, P. 1992. *The Logic of Practice*. Trans. R. Nice. Stanford.

Bowie, E. 1990. "*Miles Ludens*? The Problem of Martial Exhortation in Early Greek Elegy," in *Sympotica: A Symposium on the Symposion*, ed. O. Murray. Oxford. Pp. 221-29.

Brachet, J.-P. 2000. *Recherches sur les préverbes de- et ex- du latin*. Brussels. Collection Latomus, 258.

Brelich, A. 1961. *Guerre e agonale nella Grecia arcaica*. Bonn.

Bremmer, J. 1982. "The suodales of Poplios Valesios," *ZPE* 47: 133-47.

Bremmer, J. 1993. "Three Roman Aetiological Myths," in *Mythos in mythenlöser Gesellschaft*, ed. F. Graf. Colloquium Rauricum Band 3. Stuttgart. Pp. 158-74.

Brink, C. O. 1982. *Horace on Poetry. Epistles Book II: The Letters to Augustus and Florus*. Cambridge.

Briquel, D. 1989. "Á propos d'une inscription rédecouverte au Louvre: Remarques sur la tradition relative à Mézence," *REL* 67: 78-93.

Brommer, F. 1982. *Theseus: Die Täten des griechischen Helden in der Antiken kunst und literatur.* Darmstadt.

Buchheit, V. 1976. "Catulls c. 50 als Programm und Bekenntnis," *RhMus* 119: 162–80.

Burgess, D. 1986. "Catullus c. 50: The Exchange of Poetry," *AJP* 107: 576–86.

Burkert, W. 1972. *Lore and Science in Ancient Pythagoreanism.* Trans. E. L. Minar Jr. Cambridge, Mass.

Cahoon, L. 1996. "Calliope's Song: Shifting Narrators in Ovid, *Metamorphoses* 5," *Helios* 23: 43–66.

Caillois, R. 1967. *Les jeux et les hommes: Le masque et le vertige.* Paris.

Calame, C. 1977. *Les choeurs des jeunes filles en Grece archaïque.* 2 vols. Rome. Filologia e critica, 20 and 21.

Calinescu, M. 1993. "Orality in Literacy: Some Historical Paradoxes of Reading," *Yale Journal of Criticism* 6: 175–90.

Calvetti, A. 1987. "Rappresentazioni 'saliari' nella decorazione plastica di un vaso bronzeo à Bisenzio (VIII sec. a.C.)," *Studi romani: Rivista trimestrale dell'Istituto nazionale di studi romani* 35: 1–11.

Camassa, G. 1983. *L'occhio e il metallo: Un mitologema greco à Roma?* Genoa.

Cameron, A. 1995. *Callimachus and His Critics.* Princeton.

Campbell, B. G. 2001. *Performing and Processing the Aeneid.* New York. Berkeley Insights in Linguistics and Semiotics, 48.

Camporeale, G. 1987. "La danza armata in Etruria," *MEFRA* 99: 11–42.

Cancik, H. 1996. "carmen und sacrificium: Das Saecularlied des horaz in den Saecularakten des Jahres 17 v. Chr.," in *Wörte, Bilder, Töne. Studien zur Antike und Antikerezeption,* ed. R. Faber and B. Seidensticker. Festschrift B. Kytzler. Würzburg. Pp. 99–113.

Capdeville, G. 1973. "Les epithetes cultuelles de Janus," *MEFRA* 85: 395–436.

Capdeville, G. 1995. *Volcanus: Recherches comparatistes sur les origines du culte du Vulcain.* Rome. Bibliothèque des Ecoles françaises d'Athènes et de Rome, 288.

Carandini, A. 1997. *La nascità di Roma: Dei, Lari, eroi e uomini all'alba di una civiltà.* Turin. Biblioteca di cultura storica 219.

Cèbe, J.-P. 1966. *La caricature et la parodie dans le monde romain antique des origines à Juvenal.* Paris. Bibliothèque des Ecoles françaises d'Athènes et de Rome, 260.

Ceccarelli, P. 1998. *La pirrica nell'antichità greco-romana. Studi sulla danza armata.* Pisa and Rome.

Chambers, J. W., II. 1987. *To Raise an Army: The Draft Comes to Modern America.* New York.

Christenson, D. 2000. *Plautus Amphitruo.* Cambridge. Cambridge Greek and Latin Classics.

Clark, R. 1979. *Catabasis: Vergil and the Wisdom-Tradition.* Amsterdam.

Clausen, W. 1994. *A Commentary on Virgil* Eclogues. Oxford.

Coarelli, F. 1972. "Il sepolcro degli Scipioni," *Dialoghi di archeologia* 6: 36–106.

Coarelli, F. 1993. "Note sui ludi saeculares," in *Spectacles sportifs et scéniques dans le monde étrusco-italique.* Rome. Collection de l'Ecole française de Rome, 172. Pp. 211–45.

Coarelli, F. 1995. "Vino e Ideologia nella Roma Arcaica," in *In Vino Veritas,* ed. O. Murray and M. Tecusan. London. Pp. 196–213.

Coarelli, F. 1997. *Roma. Guide Archeologiche Mondadori.* Rome.

Colace, P. Radici. 1995. "Le voci delle stelle," in *Lo spettacolo delle voci,* ed. F. De Martino and A. Sonnenschein. Bari. Pp. 231–42.

Cole, T. 1991. "In Response to Nevio Zorzetti," *CJ* 86: 377–82.

Colin, J. 1952–53. "Juvenal, les baladins et les rétiaires d'après le manuscrit d'Oxford," *Atti delle Scienze di Torino, Classe di scienze morali, storiche e filolgoiche* 87: 315–85.

Colonna, G. 1991. "Gli scudi bilobati dell'Italia centrale e l'*ancile* dei Salii," *Archeologia classica* 43: 55–122.

Colonna, G. 1996. "Roma arcaica, i suoi sepolcreti e le vie per i Colli Albani," in *Alba Longa: Mito, storia, archeologia,* ed. A. Pasqualini. Rome. Pp. 335–50.

Comte, A. 1973. *System of Positive Polity*. 4 vols. New York. Reprint of 1875 English translation by J. H. Bridges. (Originally in French, 1851–53.)

Connerton, P. 1989. *How Societies Remember*. Cambridge.

Connolly, J. 1998. "Mastering Corruption: Constructions of Identity in Roman Oratory,"
in *Women and Slaves in Greco-Roman Culture: Differential Equations*, ed. S. Murnaghan and
S. Joshel. London and New York. Pp. 130–51.

Conte, G. 1994. *Latin Literature: A History*. Trans. J. Solodow, rev. D. Fowler and G. Most.
Baltimore and London.

Corbeill, A. 1996. *Controlling Laughter: Political Humor in the Late Roman Republic*. Princeton.

Corbeill, A. 1997. "Dining Deviants in Roman Political Invective," in *Roman Sexualities*, ed.
J. Hallett and M. Skinner. Princeton. Pp. 99–128.

Corbett, P. 1981. *The Scurra*. Edinburgh.

Cornell, T. 1995. *The Beginnings of Rome, 753–264 B.C.* London and New York.

Cristofani, M. 1984. "Iscrizioni e bene suntuari," *Opus* 3.2: 319–324.

Danto, A. 1981. *The Transfiguration of the Commonplace*. Cambridge, Mass.

Daut, R. 1975. *Imago: Untersuchungen zum Bildbegriff der Römer*. Heidelberg. Bibliothek der
klassischen Altertumswissenschaften N.F. Reihe 2, Bd. 56.

Dean, C. 2000. *The Frail Social Body: Pornography, Homosexuality and Other Fantasies in Interwar France*. Berkeley.

Delatte, A. 1950. "Le cas de Pacuvius," *Bulletin Classe des Lettres de l'Académie Royale de Bel-
gique* 36: 95–117.

della Corte, F. 1986. *Le Georgiche di Virgilio*. 2 vols. Genoa. Pubblicazioni dell'Istituto di filo-
logica classica e medievale, Universita di Genova, Facolta di lettere, 97 and 98.

de Marinis, S. 1961. *La tipologia del banchetto nell'arte etrusca arcaica*. Rome. Studia archaeologica, 1.

De Martino, F. 1995. "La voce degli autori," in *Lo spettacolo delle voci*, ed. F. De Martino and
A. Sonnenschein. Bari. Pp. 17–59.

Dench, E. 1995. *From Barbarians to New Men: Greek, Roman, and Modern Perspectives of Peoples
from the Central Apennines*. Oxford.

De Puma, R., and J. P. Small (eds.). 1994. *Murlo and the Etruscans: Art and Society in Ancient
Etruria*. Madison, Wisc., and London.

De Robertis, F. 1981 *Il fenomeno associativo del mondo romano*. Bari. Reprint of 1955 edition.

De Simone, C. 1980. "L'aspetto linguistico," in *Lapis Satricanus*, publication of Nederlands
Instituut te Rome. The Hague. Pp. 71–94.

Deroy, L. 1959. "Les noms latins du marteau et la racine étrusque "mar,'" *L'Antiquité Classique* 28: 5–31.

deWaele, J. 1996. "Salii, Satricum en de chronologie van de tempels van Mater Matuta,"
Lampas 9: 10–26.

Donald, M. 2001. *A Mind So Rare: The Evolution of Human Consciousness*. New York.

Doob, P. 1990. *The Idea of the Labyrinth from Classical Antiquity through the Middle Ages*. Ithaca
and London.

Downey, S. 1995. *Architectural Terracottas from the Regia*. Ann Arbor. Papers and Monographs of the American Academy in Rome, 30.

Drews, R. 1993. *The End of the Bronze Age*. Princeton.

Dubourdieu, A. 1989. *Les origines et le développement du culte des penates à Rome*. Rome. Collection de l'Ecole française de Rome, 118.

Dufallo, B. 2001. "Appius' Indignation: Gossip, Tradition, and Performance in Republican
Rome," *TAPA* 131: 119–42.

Dumézil, G. 1948. *Mitra Varuna. Essai sur deux representations indo-européennes de souveraineté*.
Paris.

Dumézil, G. 1977. *Les dieux souverains des Indo-Européens*. Paris.

Dupont, F. 1985. *L'acteur-roi ou le théâtre dans la Rome antique.* Paris.

Dupont, F. 1993. "Ludions, *lydioi:* Les danseurs de la *pompa circensis.* Exegèse et discours sur l'origine des jeux a Rome," in *Spectacles sportifs et scéniques dans le monde étrusco-italique.* Rome. Collection de l'Ecole française de Rome, 172. Pp.189–210.

Dupont, F. 1997. "*Recitatio* and the Reorganization of the Space of Public Discourse," in *The Roman Cultural Revolution,* ed. T. Habinek and A. Schiesaro. Cambridge. Pp. 44–60.

Dupont, F. 1999. *The Invention of Literature: From Greek Intoxication to the Latin Book.* Trans. J. Lloyd. Baltimore.

Edwards, C. 1993. *Politics of Immorality in Ancient Rome.* Cambridge.

Ehrmann, J. 1968. "Homo Ludens Revisited," *Yale French Studies* 41: 31–57.

Eilberg-Schwartz, H. 1995. "The Nakedness of a Woman's Voice," in *Off with Her Head! The Denial of Women's Identity in Myth, Religion, and Culture,* ed. H. Eilberg-Schwartz and W. Doniger. Berkeley and Los Angeles. Pp. 165–84.

Eluére, C., and D. Cottier-Angeli. 1993. "Early Metallurgy in Italy," in *The Art of the Italic Peoples, from 3000 BC to 300 BC.* Joint exhibition by the Museum of Art History, Municipal Department of Cultural Affairs of the City of Geneva, and the Association Hellas et Roma, Geneva. Trans. by Bruce Gollan. Geneva. Pp. 71–83.

Engle, G. (ed.). 1978. *This Grotesque Essence: Plays from the American Minstrel Stage.* Baton Rouge, La.

Ernout, A. 1994. *Dictionnaire étymologique de la langue latine.* 4th ed. Paris.

Fantham, E. 1992. "The Role of Evander in Ovid's Fasti," *Arethusa* 25: 155–71.

Farrell, J. 2001. *Latin Language and Latin Culture from Ancient to Modern Times.* Cambridge.

Fear, T. 2000. "Love's Economy: Aesthetics, Exchange, and Youthful Poetics in Roman Elegy." Ph.D. diss., University of Southern California.

Feeney, D. 1998. *Literature and Religion at Rome: Culture, Contexts, and Beliefs.* Cambridge.

Feldherr, A. 1995. "Ships of State: *Aeneid* V and Augustan Circus Spectacle," *CA* 14: 245–65.

Feldherr, A. 1998. *Spectacle and Society in Livy's History.* Berkeley and Los Angeles.

Feldherr, A. 2002. "Upward Mobility? Daedalus, Status, and Metamorphosis," lecture, Berkeley, November 2.

Fideler, D. 1987. Introduction to *The Pythagorean Sourcebook and Library.* Compiled and trans. K. Guthrie. Grand Rapids, Mich.

Fink, E. 1968. "The Oasis of Happiness: Toward an Ontology of Play," *Yale French Studies* 41: 19–30.

Fitzgerald, W. 1984. "Aeneas, Daedalus and the Labyrinth," *Arethusa* 17: 51–65.

Fitzgerald, W. 1995. *Catullan Provocations: Lyric Poetry and the Drama of Position.* Berkeley and Los Angeles.

Flower, H. 1996. *Ancestor Masks and Aristocratic Power in Roman Culture.* Oxford.

Flury, P. 1968. *Liebe und Liebessprache bei Menander, Plautus und Terenz.* Heidelberg.

Flynn, G. Q. 2002. *Conscription and Democracy: The Draft in France, Great Britain and the United States.* Westport, Conn. Contributions in military studies, 210.

Foucher, L. 1974. "Sur un image du mois de Mars," *Annales de Brétagne et des Pays de l'Ouest* 81: 3–11.

Fraenkel, E. 1922. *Plautinisches im Plautus.* Berlin.

Fraenkel, E. 1957. *Horace.* Oxford.

Freeman, P. 1998. "Saturnian Verse and Early Latin Poetics," *Journal of Indo-European Studies* 26: 61–90.

Freud, S. 1960. *The Ego and the Id,* trans. J. Rivière. New York.

Freudenburg, K. 2001. *Satires of Rome: Threatening Poses from Lucilius to Juvenal.* Cambridge.

Friedrich, G. 1905. *Catulli Veronensis Liber.* Leipzig and Berlin.

Gabba, E. 1984. "The Collegia of Numa: Problems of Method and Political Ideas," *JRS* 74: 81–86.

Galinsky, K. 1996. *Augustan Culture: An Interpretive Introduction*. Princeton.

Gamel, M.-K. 1998. "Reading as a Man: Performance and Gender in Roman Elegy," *Helios* 25: 79–95.

Gane, M. (ed.). 1998. *The Radical Sociology of Durkheim and Mauss*. London and New York.

Garosi, R. 1976. "Indagine sulla formazione del concetto di magia nella cultura romana," in *Magia: Studi di storia delle religioni in memoria di Raffaela Garosi*. Rome. Pp. 13–93.

Gee, J. 1990. *Social Linguistics and Literacies: Ideology in Discourse*. London.

Gee, J. 1992. *The Social Mind: Language, Ideology and Social Practice*. New York.

Gentili, B. 1977. *Lo spettacolo nel mondo antico. Teatro ellenistico e teatro romana arcaico*. Rome and Bari.

Gentili, B. 1988. *Poetry and Its Public in Ancient Greece: From Homer to the Fifth Century*. Trans. and introd. A. T. Cole. Baltimore.

Giardino, C. 1995. *Il Mediterraneo occidentale fra XIV ed VIII secolo à.C.: Cerchie minerarie e metallurgiche* (The West Mediterranean between the 14th and 8th Centuries B.C.: Mining and metallurgical spheres). British Archaeological Reports International Series no. 612. Oxford.

Giglioli, G. 1929. "L'Oinochoe di Tragliatella," *Studi Etruschi* 3: 111–59.

Gil, J. 1998. *Metamorphoses of the Body*. Trans. S. Muecke. Minneapolis and London. Theory Out of Bounds, 12.

Gleason, M. 1995. *Making Men: Sophists and Self-Presentation in Ancient Rome*. Princeton.

Godzich, W., and Kittay, J. 1987. *The Emergence of Prose: An Essay in Prosaics*. Minneapolis.

Goldberg, S. 1986. *Understanding Terence*. Princeton.

Goldberg, S. 1998. "Plautus on the Palatine," *JRS* 88: 1–20.

Gómez Pallarés, J. 1993. "Aspectos epigraficos de la poesia latina," *Epigraphica* 55: 129–58.

Gooch, J. 1980. *Armies in Europe*. London.

Goold, G. 1977. *Manilius Astronomica*. With an English translation. Cambridge and London. Loeb Classical Library.

Graf, F. 1994. *La Magie dans l'antiquité gréco-romaine: Idéologie et pratique*. Paris.

Grandazzi, A. 1997. *The Foundation of Rome: Myth and History*. Trans. J. M. Todd. Ithaca and London.

Grant, M. 1974. *The Army of the Caesars*. London.

Gras, M. 1984. "Canthare, societé etrusque et monde grec," *Opus* 3.2: 325–31.

Gratwick, A. 1993. *Plautus Menaechmi*. Cambridge.

Green, R. 2002. "Towards a Reconstruction of Performance Style," in *Greek and Roman Actors: Aspects of an Ancient Profession*, ed. P. Easterling and E. Hall. Cambridge. Pp. 93–126.

Griffin, M. 1984. *Nero: The End of a Dynasty*. New Haven and London.

Gros, P., and M. Torelli. 1988. *Storia dell'urbanistica: Il mondo romano*. Rome and Bari.

Grossman, D. 1995. *On Killing: The Psychological Cost of Learning to Kill in War and Society*. Boston.

Gruen, E. 1990. *Studies in Greek Culture and Roman Policy*. Leiden 1990. Cincinnati Classical Studies, n.s., 7.

Gruen, E. 1992. *Culture and National Identity in Republican Rome*. Ithaca, N.Y. Cornell Studies in Classical Philology, 52.

Guittard, Ch. 1996. "Récherches sur le 'carmen' et la prière dans la littérature latine et la religion romaine." 6 vols. Paris. Thèse pour le doctorat d'Etat. Université de Paris-IV.

Guittard, Ch. 1998. "Invocations et structures theologiques dans la prière a Rome," *REL* 76: 71–92.

Gunderson, E. 1996. "The Ideology of the Arena," *Classical Antiquity* 15: 113–51.

Gunderson, E. 1997. "Catullus, Pliny, and Love-Letters," *TAPhA* 127: 201–31.

Gunderson, E. 2000. *Staging Masculinity: The Rhetoric of Performance in the Roman World*. Ann Arbor.

Gunderson, E. 2003. *Declamation, Paternity, and Roman Identity: Authority and the Rhetorical Self.* Cambridge.

Gurlitt, L. 1921. *Erotica Plautina: Eine Auswähl erotischer Szenen aus Plautus.* Munich.

Habinek, T. 1985a. *The Colometry of Latin Prose.* Berkeley and Los Angeles. California Studies in Classical Philology, 25.

Habinek, T. 1985b. "Prose Cola and Poetic Word Order," *Helios* 12: 51–66.

Habinek, T. 1986. "The Marriageability of Maximus: Horace *Ode* 4.1.13–20," *AJP* 107: 407–16.

Habinek, T. 1987. "Greeks and Romans in Book 12 of Quintilian," *Ramus* 16: 192–202.

Habinek, T. 1989. "Science and Tradition in *Aeneid* VI," *HSCP* 92: 223–56.

Habinek, T. 1997. "The Invention of Sexuality in the World-City of Rome," in *The Roman Cultural Revolution,* ed. T. Habinek and A. Schiesaro. Cambridge. Pp. 23–43.

Habinek, T. 1998a. *The Politics of Latin Literature: Writing, Identity, and Empire in Ancient Rome.* Princeton.

Habinek, T. 1998b. "Singing, Speaking, Making, Writing: Classical Alternatives to Literature and Literary Studies," *Stanford Humanities Review* 6: 65–75.

Habinek, T. 2000. "Seneca's Renown: *Gloria, Claritudo,* and the Replication of the Roman Elite," *Classical Antiquity* 19: 264–303.

Habinek, T. 2002. "Ovid and Empire," in *The Cambridge Companion to Ovid,* ed. P. Hardie. Cambridge. Pp. 46–61.

Habinek, T. 2003. Review of J.-P. Brachet, *Recherches sur les préverbes de- et ex- du latin.* Brussels 2000. *Gnomon* 75: 560–62.

Habinek, T. 2004. "Satire as Play," in *The Cambridge Companion to Roman Satire,* ed. K. Freudenburg. Cambridge.

Habinek, T. 2005. *Ancient Rhetoric and Oratory.* Oxford. Blackwell Introductions to the Classical World.

Habinek, T., and Schiesaro, A. 1997. Introduction to *The Roman Cultural Revolution,* ed. T. Habinek and A. Schiesaro. Cambridge. Pp. xv–xxi.

Halperin, D. 2002. "Forgetting Foucault: Acts, Identities, and the History of Sexuality," in *The Sleep of Reason: Erotic Experience and Sexual Ethics in Ancient Greece and Rome,* ed. M. Nussbaum and J. Sihvola. Chicago. Pp. 21–54.

Hall, E. 2002. "The Singing Actors of Antiquity," in *Greek and Roman Actors: Aspects of an Ancient Profession,* ed. P. Easterling and E. Hall. Cambridge. Pp. 3–38.

Handley, E. 1968. *Menander and Plautus: A Study in Comparison.* London.

Hansen, M. 2000. *Embodying Technesis: Technology beyond Writing.* Ann Arbor. Selections on the Internet, available at http://www.mimetics.com/theory.html.

Hardie, P. 1986. *Virgil's Aeneid: Cosmos and Imperium.* Oxford.

Harmon, A. 1972. *Lucian.* With an English translation. London and Cambridge, Mass.

Harris, W. 1989. *Ancient Literacy.* Cambridge, Mass.

Harrison, S. 1993. "The Literary Form of Horace's Odes," in *Horace: L'oeuvre et les imitations: Un siècle d'interprétation,* ed. W. Ludwig. Geneva. Fondation Hardt pour l'étude de l'Antiquité classique, Entretiens 39. Pp. 131–62.

Hedeager, L. 1992. *Iron-Age Societies: From Tribe to State in Northern Europe, 500 BC to AD 700.* Trans. J. Hines. Oxford.

Helbig, W. 1915. *Sur les attributs des saliens.* Extract. *Memoires d l'Académie des inscriptions et belles-lettres* 37.2. Paris.

Hellegouarc'h, J. 1963. *Le vocabulaire latin des relations et des partis politiques sous la République.* Paris. Publications de la Faculté des letteres et sciences humaines de l'Universitée Lille, 11.

Heller, J. 1939. "Festus on Nenia," *TAPhA* 70: 357–67.

Heller, J. 1943. "Nenia 'paignion,'" *TAPhA* 74: 215–68.

Heller, J. 1946. "Labyrinth or Troy Town?" *CJ* 42: 123–39.

Helms, M. 1993. *Craft and the Kingly Ideal: Art, Trade, and Power.* Austin, Tex.

Henderson, J. 1989. "Satire Writes 'Woman': Gendersong," *PCPhS* 35: 50–80.

Henderson, J. 2001. *Telling Tales on Caesar: Roman Stories from Phaedrus*. Oxford.

Hendrickson, G. L. 1894. "The Dramatic Satura and the Old Comedy at Rome," *AJP* 15: 1–30.

Herbert-Brown, G. 1996. *Ovid and the Fasti: An Historical Study*. Oxford.

Herescu, N. I. 1959. "Les traces des épigrammes militaires dans le 'Miles Gloriosus' de Plaute," *Revue Belge de Philologie et d'Histoire* 37: 45–51.

Herington, J. 1985. *Poetry into Drama: Early Tragedy and the Greek Poetic Tradition*. Berkeley. Sather Classical Lectures, 49.

Hexter, R. 1992. "Sidonian Dido," in *Innovations of Antiquity*, ed. R. Hexter and D. Selden. New York. Pp. 332–84.

Hinds, S. 1987. *The Metamorphosis of Persephone: Ovid and the Self-Conscious Muse*. Cambridge.

Højte, J. (ed.) 2002. *Images of Ancestors*. Aarhus. Aarhus Studies in Mediterranean Antiquity, 5.

Horsfall, N. 1994. "The Prehistory of Latin Poetry: Some Problems of Method," *RIFC* 172: 50–75.

Horsfall, N. 1996. *La cultura della plebs romana*. Barcelona. PPU-Littera-Departament Filologia Latina UB, Series Cornucopia.

Huizinga, J. 1955. *Homo Ludens: A Study of the Play-Element in Culture*. Boston.

Hung, Wu. 1995. *Monumentality in Early Chinese Art and Architecture*. Stanford.

Illuminati, A. 1961. "Mamurius Veturius," *SMSR (Studi e materiali di storia delle religioni)* 32: 41–80.

Jackson Knight, W. F. 1967. *Vergil: Epic and Anthropology*. Ed. J. Christie. London.

Jacobus, M. 1999. *Psychoanalysis and the Scene of Reading*. Oxford.

Jaeger, M. 1990. "The Poetics of Place in Augustan Literature." Ph.D. diss. Berkeley.

Johnson, M. 1987. *The Body in the Mind: The Bodily Basis of Meaning, Imagination and Reason*. Chicago.

Johnson, W. 2000. "Toward a Sociology of Reading in Classical Antiquity," *AJP* 121: 593–627.

Johnston, S. I. 1999. *Restless Dead: Encounters between the Living and the Dead in Ancient Greece*. Berkeley.

Joplin, P. K. 2002. "The Voice of the Shuttle Is Ours," in *Sexuality and Gender in the Classical World: Readings and Sources*, ed. L. McClure. Oxford. Pp. 259–86. Reprint of *Stanford Literature Review* 1 (1984): 25–53.

Jory, E. J. 1996. "The Drama of the Dance: Prolegomena to an Iconography of Imperial Pantomime," in *Roman Theater and Society: E. Togo Salmon Papers I*, ed. W. Slater. Ann Arbor. Pp. 1–28.

Jory, E. J. 2002. "The Masks on the Propylon of the Sebasteion at Aphrodisias," in *Greek and Roman Actors: Aspects of an Ancient Profession*, ed. P. Easterling and E. Hall. Cambridge. Pp. 238–53.

Joshel, S. 1997. "Female Desire and the Discourse of Empire: Tacitus' Messalina," in *Roman Sexualities*, ed. J. Hallett and M. Skinner. Princeton. Pp. 221–54.

Jourdan-Hemmerdinger, D. 1988. "L'epigramma di Pitecusa e la musica della Grecia antica," in *La musica in Grecia*, ed. B. Gentili and R. Pretagostini. Rome and Bari. Pp. 145–82.

Keightley, D. 1996. "Art, Ancestors, and the Origin of Writing in China," *Representations* 14: 68–98.

Kelly, A. 1994. "Damaging Voice: Language of Aggression for the Athenian Trial." Ph.D. diss., Berkeley.

Kiessling, A. 1959. *Horace. Satiren*. Berlin.

King, R. 1998. "Ritual and Autobiography: The Cult of Reading in Ovid's *Tristia* 4.10," *Helios* 25: 99–119.

Kingsley, P. 1993. "Poimandres: The Etymology of the Name and the Origins of the Hermetica," *JWCI* 56: 1–24.

Kingsley, P. 1995. *Ancient Philosophy, Mystery, and Magic: Empedocles and Pythagorean Tradition*. Oxford.

Kisliuk, M. 1998. *Seize the Dance! BaAka Musical Life and the Ethnography of Performance*. New York.

Konstan, D. 1986. *Roman Comedy*. Ithaca, N.Y.

Krostenko, B. 2001. *Cicero, Catullus, and the Language of Social Performance*. Chicago.

Kruschwitz, P. 2002. *Carmina Saturnia Epigraphica*. Stuttgart. *Hermes* Einzelschriften, 84.

Kügler, H. 1977. *Handwerk und Meistergesäng: Ambrosius Metzgers Metamorphosen-Dichtung und die Nürnberger Singschüle im frühen 17. Jahrhundert*. Göttingen. Palaestra, Bd. 265.

Kurke, L. 1990. "Pindar's Sixth *Pythian* and the Tradition of Advice Poetry," *TAPA* 120: 85–107.

Lada-Richards, I. 2003. "Controlling Theater," unpublished essay.

Lakoff, G. 1987. *Women, Fire, and Dangerous Things: What Categories Reveal about the Mind*. Chicago.

Lakoff, G., and M. Johnson. 1980. *Metaphors We Live By*. Chicago.

Lahuson, G. 1982. "Statuae et imagines," in *Praestant Interna: Festschrift für Ulrich Hausmann*, ed. B. von Freytag gen. Löringhoff et al. Tübingen. Pp. 101–9.

Landolfi, L. 1990. *Banchetto e società romana: Dalle origini al I sec. a.C. Roma*. Rome. Filologia e critica 64.

Lapidge, M. 1989. "Stoic Cosmology and Roman Literature, First to Third Centuries AD," *ANRW* 2.36.3: 1379–1429.

Lawler, L. B. 1946. "The Geranos Dance: A New Interpretation," *TAPA* 77: 112–30.

Lawler, L. B. 1952. "Dancing Herds of Animals," *CJ* 47: 317–24.

Leach, E. 2002. "Amorini Domestici: Desire, Servitude and Liberation in Imperial Representation," lecture, Berkeley, November 1.

Lilja, S. 1982. "Homosexuality in Plautus' Plays," *Arctos* 16: 57–64.

Lilja, S. 1983. *Homosexuality in Republican and Augustan Rome*. Helsinki. Commentationes Humanarum Litterarum, 74.

Liuzzi, D. 1983. *M. Manilio: Astronomica*. Lecce.

Lomax, A. 1968. *Folk Song Style and Culture*. Washington, D.C. American Association for the Advancement of Science, Publication No. 88.

Lombardo, M. 1988. "Pratiche di commensalità e forme di organizzazione sociale nel mondo greco: Symposia e syssitia," *ASNP* 3.18: 263–386.

Lonsdale, S. 1981. *Animals and the Origin of Dance*. London.

Lonsdale, S. 1993. *Dance and Ritual Play in Greek Religion*. Baltimore and London.

Lott, E. 1993. *Love and Theft: Blackface Minstrelsy and the American Working Class*. Oxford.

Lowrie, M. 1997. *Horace's Narrative Odes*. Oxford.

Mariotti, I. 1960. *Studi Luciliani*. Florence. Scuola normale superiore di Pisa: Studi di lettere, storia, e filosofia, 25.

Markus, D. 2000. "Performing the Book: The Recital of Epic in the First Century C.E. Rome," *CA* 19: 138–79.

Marothy, J. 1974. *Music and the Bourgeois, Music and the Proletarian*. Trans. E. Rona. Budapest.

Martin, L., H. Gutman, and P. Hutton (eds.). 1988. *Technologies of the Self: A Seminar with Michel Foucault*. Amherst, Mass.

Martin, R. 1993. "The Seven Sages as Performers of Wisdom," in *Cultural Poetics in Archaic Greece: Cult, Performance, Politics*, ed. C. Dougherty and L. Kurke. Cambridge. Pp. 108–30.

Massa-Pairault, F.-H. 1992. *Iconologia e politica nell'Italia antica: Roma, Lazio, Etruria dal VII al I secolo A.C.* Milan. Biblioteca di Archaeologia 18.

Matthiessen, P. 2001. *The Birds of Heaven: Travels with Cranes*. Paintings and drawings by R. Bateman. New York.

Maybin, J. 2000. "The New Literacy Studies: Context, Intertextuality and Discourse," in *Situated Literacies: Reading and Writing in Context*, ed. D. Barton, M. Hamilton, and R. Ivanic. London. Pp. 197–209.

McCarthy, K. 2000. *Slaves, Masters, and the Art of Authority in Plautine Comedy.* Princeton and Oxford.

McClary, S. 1995. "Music, the Pythagoreans, and the Body," in *Choreographing History,* ed. S. L. Foster. Bloomington. Pp. 82–104.

McDonnell, M. 2003. "Roman Men and Greek Virtue," in *Andreia: Studies in Manliness and Courage in Classical Antiquity,* ed. R. Rosen and I. Sluiter. Leiden and Boston. Pp. 235–62. *Mnemosyne* suppl., 238.

McDonough, C. 1997. "Carna, Proca and the Strix on the Kalends of June," *TAPA* 127: 315–44.

McNeill, W. 1995. *Keeping Together in Time: Dance and Drill in Human History.* Cambridge, Mass.

Menichetti, M. 1992. "L'oinochoë di Tragliatella: Mito e rito tra Grecia ed Etruria," *Ostraka* 1.1: 7–30.

Miller, J. 1986. *Measures of Wisdom: The Cosmic Dance in Classical and Christian Antiquity.* Toronto.

Miller, P. 1995. "The Mintoaur Within: Fire, the Labyrinth, and Strategies of Containment in *Aeneid* 5 and 6," *Classical Philology* 90: 225–40.

Moatti, C. 1997. *La raison de Rome: Naissance de l'ésprit critique à la fin de la République (IIe–Ier siècle avant Jesus-Christ) .* Paris.

Momigliano, A. 1942. Review of L. Robinson, *Freedom of Speech in the Roman Republic, JRS* 32: 120–24.

Montanari, E. 1990. *Mito e storia nell'annalistica romana delle origini.* Rome. Filologia e critica 65.

Montrose, L. 1996. *The Purpose of Playing: Shakespeare and the Cultural Politics of the Elizabethan Theatre.* Chicago and London.

Moore, T. 1998. *The Theater of Plautus.* Austin, Tex.

Morel, J. P. 1969. "La *Iuventus* et les origines de la théâtre romain," *REL* 47: 208–52.

Morris, E. P. 1968. *Horace: Satires and Epistles.* With introductions and notes. Norman, Okla.

Morrison, K. 1987. "Stabilizing the Text: The Institutionalization of Knowledge in Historical and Philosophic Forms of Argument," *Canadian Journal of Sociology* 12: 242–74.

Müller, F. 1935. "Studia ad Terrae Matris cultum pertinentia," *Mnemosyne* 3.2: 37–50.

Murray, O. (ed.). 1990. *Sympotica: A Symposium on the Symposion.* Oxford.

Murray, O. 1991. "War and the Symposium," in *Dining in a Classical Context,* ed. W. Slater. Ann Arbor. Pp. 83–104.

Murray, O., and M. Tecusan (eds.). 1995. *In Vino Veritas.* London.

Muth, R. 1972. "Poeta ludens: Zu einem Prinzip der alexandrinisch-hellenistischen und der römisch-neoterischen Dichtung," in *Serta Philologica Aenipontana* II, ed. R. Muth. Innsbruck. Innsbrucker Beiträge zur Kulturwissenschaft, 17. Pp. 65–82.

Mynors, R. 1990. *Virgil. Georgics.* Edited with a commentary. Oxford.

Nagy, G. 1989. "Early Greek Views of Poets and Poetry," in *The Cambridge History of Literary Criticism. 1. Classical Criticism,* ed. G. Kennedy. Cambridge. Pp. 1–71.

Nagy, G. 1990. *Pindar's Homer: The Lyric Possession of an Epic Past.* Baltimore.

Neuburg, M. 1993. "Hitch Your Wagon to a Star: Manilius and His Two Addressees," in *Mega nepios: Il destinatario nell'epos didascalico,* ed. A. Schiesaro, P. Mitsis, and J. S. Clay. Pisa. Materiali e discussioni per l'analisi dei testi classici, 31. Pp. 243–82.

Newlands, C. 1995. *Playing with Time: Ovid and the Fasti.* Ithaca, N.Y.

Newman, J. K. 1965. "De verbis *canere* et *dicere* eorumque apud poetas Latinos ab Ennio usque ad aetatem Augusti usu," *Latinitas* 13: 86–106.

Nietzsche, F. 1990. "Twilight of the Idols," in *Twilight of the Idols and the Anti-Christ.* Trans. R. J. Hollingdale. London.

Nisbet, R., and M. Hubbard. 1970. *A Commentary on Horace: Odes, book I.* Oxford.

Norden, E. 1939. *Aus altrömischen Priesterbüchern.* Lund and Leipzig.

Ogden, D. 2001. *Greek and Roman Necromancy.* Princeton.

Oliensis, E. 1998. *Horace and the Rhetoric of Authority*. Cambridge.

O'Neill, P. 2003. "Going Round in Circles: Popular Speech in Ancient Rome," *CA* 22: 135–65.

Ong, W. 1982. *Orality and Literacy: The Technologizing of the Word*. London.

Pallottino, M. 2000. *Origini e storia primitiva di Roma*. Milan.

Parsons, J. 1999. "A New Approach to the Saturnian Verse and its Relation to Latin Prosody," *TAPA* 129: 117–38.

Pearce, F. 1989. *The Radical Durkheim*. London.

Perrot, J. 1961. *Les derivés latins en* -men *et* -mentum. Paris. Etudes et Commentaires 37.

Peruzzi, E. 1978. *Aspetti culturali del Lazio primitivo*. Florence. Accademia Toscana di Scienze e Lettere "La Colombaria" 47.

Peruzzi, E. 1998. *Civiltà greca nel Lazio preromano*. Florence. Accademia Toscana di Scienze e lettere "La Colombaria" Studi 165.

Pettazzoni, G. 1940. "Carna," *Studi Etruschi* 14: 163–72.

Phillips, C. R. 1986. "The Sociology of Religious Knowledge in the Roman Empire to A.D. 284," *ANRW* 2.16.3: 2677–2773.

Piccaluga, G. 1965. *Elementi spettacolari nei rituali festivi romani*. 1965. Studi e materiali di storia delle religioni, Quaderni 2.

Piccaluga, G. 1976. "I Marsi e gli Hirpi. Due diversi modi di sistemare le minoranze etniche," in *Magia: Studi di storia delle religioni in memoria di Raffaela Garosi*. Rome. Pp. 207–32.

Piganiol, A. 1930. "Le sens religieux des jeux antiques," *Scientia* 48: 395–404. Reprint, *Scripta varia*, ed. R. Bloch. 3 vols. Brussels, 1973. 2.158–74.

Pighi, G. B. 1958. *La poesia religiosa romana*. Bologna.

Pontrandolfo, A. 1995. "Simposio e elites sociali nel mondo etrusco e italico," in *In Vino Veritas*, ed. O. Murray and M. Tecusan. London. Pp. 176–95.

Porte, D. 1985. *L'étiologie religieuse dans les Fastes d'Ovide*. Paris. Collection d'études anciennes.

Purchase, P. 2003. "Death and the Dying Subject in Ancient Pastoral and Elegy." Ph.D. diss., University of Southern California.

Putnam, M. 2000. *Horace's* Carmen Saeculare: *Ritual Magic and the Poet's Art*. New Haven and London.

Quinn, K. 1980. "The Poet and His Audience in the Augustan Age," *Aufstieg und Niedergang der römischen Welt*, 2.30.1: 75–180.

Radke, G. 1979. *Die Götter Altitaliens*. 2. Durchgesehene und erganzte Auflage. Münster. Fontes et Commentationes, 3.

Radke, G. 1981. *Archaïsches Latein*. Darmstadt.

Rappaport, R. 1979. *Ecology, Meaning, and Religion*. Richmond.

Rappaport, R. 1999. *Ritual and Religion in the Making of Humanity*. Cambridge. Cambridge Studies in Social and Cultural Anthropology 110.

Rathje, A. 1983. "A Banquet Service from the Latin City of Ficana," *ARID* 12: 7–29.

Rathje, A. 1990. "The Adoption of the Homeric Banquet in Central Italy in the Orientalizing Period," in *Sympotica: A Symposium on the Symposion*, ed. O. Murray. Oxford. Pp. 279–88.

Rathje, A. 1994. "Banquet and Ideology: Some New Considerations about Banqueting at Poggio Civitate," in *Murlo and the Etruscans*, ed. R. De Puma and J. P. Small. Madison and London. Pp. 95–99.

Rathje, A. 1995 "Il Banchetto in Italia Centrale: Quale Stile di Vita?" in *In Vino Veritas*, ed. O. Murray and M. Tecusan. London. Pp. 167–75.

Richlin, A. 1992. "Julia's Jokes, Galla Placidia, and the Roman Use of Women as Political Icons," in *Stereotypes of Women in Power: Historical Perspectives and Revisionist Views*, ed. B. Garlick, S. Dixon, and P. Allen. New York. Pp. 65–91. Contributions in Women's Studies, 125.

Richlin, A. 1993. "Not before Homosexuality: The Materiality of the Cinaedus and the Roman Law against Love between Men," *Journal of the History of Sexuality* 3: 523–73.

Richlin, A. 1997. "Gender and Rhetoric: Producing Manhood in the Schools," in *Roman Eloquence: Rhetoric in Society and Literature*, ed. W. Dominik. London. Pp. 90–110.

Richlin, A. 2000. "Emotional Work: Lamenting the Roman Dead," in *Festschrift for Gordon Williams*, ed. E. Tylawsky. N.p. Pp. 229–47.

Richlin, A. 2005. *Plautus and the Mysterious Orient*. Berkeley and Los Angeles.

Roach, J. 1996. *Cities of the Dead: Circum-Atlantic Performance*. New York.

Rochlitz, R. 1996. *The Disenchantment of Art: The Philosophy of Walter Benjamin*. Trans. J. M. Todd. New York and London.

Roller, M. 1998. "Pliny's Catullus: The Politics of Literary Appropriation," *TAPhA* 128: 265–304.

Roller, M. 2001. *Constructing Autocracy: Aristocrats and Emperors in Julio-Claudian Rome*. Princeton.

Rüpke, J. 1990. *Domi militiae. Die religiöse Konstruktion des Krieges in Rom*. Stuttgart.

Rüpke, J. 1998. "Kommensalität und Gesellschaftstruktur. Tafelfreu(n)de im alten Rom," *Saeculum* 49: 193–215.

Rüpke, J. 2000. "Räume literarischer Kommunikation in der Formierungsphase römischer Literatur," in *Moribus antiquis res stat romana: Römische werte und römische Literatur im 3. und 2. Jh. v. Chr.*, ed. M. Braun, A. Haltenhoff, and F.-H. Mutschler. Munich and Leipzig. Pp. 31–54. Beiträge zur Altertumskünde, 134.

Rutherford, I. 2001. *Pindar's Paeans: A Reading of the Fragments with a Survey of the Genre*. Oxford.

Rutherford, R. 1981. "Horace Epistles 2.2: Introspection and Retrospective," *CQ* 31: 375–80.

Rystedt, E. 1984. "Architectural Terracotta as Aristocratic Display—The Case of Seventh-Century Poggio Civitate (Murlo)," *Opus* 3.2: 367–71.

Sabbatucci, D. 1988. *La religione di Roma antica: Dal calendario festivo all'ordine cosmico*. Milan.

Saller, R. 1991. Review of *Cambridge Ancient History*, vos. 7.2 and 8, *JRS* 81: 157–63.

Santelia, S. 1991. *Chariton Liberata*. Bari.

Santini, C. 1988. "Il lessico della spartizione nel sacrificio romano," in *Sacrificio e società nel mondo antico*, ed. C. Grottanelli and N. F. Parise. Rome and Bari. Pp. 293–302.

Scarpi, P. 1979. "Le pyrriche o le armi della persuasione," *Dialoghi di Archeologia* 1: 78–97.

Schäfer, T. 1980. "Zur Ikonographie der Salier," *Jahrbuch des Deutschen Archaeologischen Instituts* 95: 342–73.

Scheid, J. 1988. "La spartizione sacrificiale a Rome," in *Sacrificio e società nel mondo antico*, ed. C. Grottanelli and N. F. Parise. Rome and Bari. Pp. 267–92.

Scheid, J. 1990. *Romulus et ses frères: Le collége des frères arvales, modéle du culte public dans la Rome des empereurs*. Rome. Bibliothèque des Ecoles françaises d'Athènes et de Rome, 275.

Scheid, J. 1998a. *La religion des Romains*. Paris.

Scheid, J. 1998b. *Commentarii fratrum arvalium qui supersunt/ Les copies épigraphiques des protocoles annuels de la confrèrie arvale* (21 av–304 ap J.-C.). Avec la collaboration de P. Tassini et J. Rüpke. Rome and Paris.

Schertz, P. 2000. Schertz, P. 2004. "Seer or Victim?: The Figure of Marsyas in Roman Art, Politics, and Religion." Ph.D. diss., University of Southern California.

Schilling, R. 1960. Review of Tels-de Jong, *Sur quelques divinités romaines de la naissance de la prophétie* (Delft, 1959), *Latomus* 32: 650–53.

Schmitt Pantel, P. 1992. *La cité au banquet: Histoire des repas publics dans les cités grècques*. Rome. Collection de l'Ecole française de Rome, 157.

Schnapp-Gourbeillon, A. 1981. *Lions, héros, masques: Les représentations de l'animal chez Homère*. Paris.

Schrijvers, P. H. 1983. "Le chant du monde: Remarques sur *Astronomica* I 1–24 de Manilius," *Mnemosyne* 36: 143–50.

Schwartz, V. 2001. "Walter Benjamin for Historians," *American Historical Review* 106: 1721–43.

Sciarrino, E. 2004. "Putting Cato the Censor's *Origines* in Its Place," *CA* 23: 323–57.

Séchan, L. 1930. *La danse grècque antique*. Montpellier.

Sedgwick, W. B. 1930. "Confossiorem soricina nenia," *CR* 44: 56–57.

Seel, O. 1964. *Romertüm und Latinität*. Stuttgart.

Selden, D. 1992. "*Ceveat lector:* Catullus and the Rhetoric of Performance," in *Innovations of Antiquity*, ed. R. Hexter and D. Selden. New York and London. Pp. 461–512.

Shanks, M. 1999. *Art and the Greek City State: An Interpretive Archaeology*. Cambridge.

Shear, T. 1923. "A Terra-Cotta Relief from Sardes," *AJA* 27: 131–50.

Sinos, R. 1994. "Godlike Men: A Discussion of the Murlo Procession Frieze," in *Murlo and the Etruscans*, ed. R. De Puma and J. P. Small. Madison and London. Pp. 100–120.

Skutsch, O. 1985. *The Annals of Quintus Ennius*. Oxford.

Small, J. P. 1971. "The Banquet Frieze from Poggio Civitate (Murlo)," *Studi Etruschi* 39: 25–61.

Small, J. P. 1994. "Eat, Drink, and Be Merry: Etruscan Banquets," in *Murlo and the Etruscans*, ed. R. De Puma and J. P. Small. Madison and London. Pp. 85–94.

Smith, C. 1996. *Early Rome and Latium: Economy and Society c. 1000 to 500 BC*. Oxford.

Smith, P. 1989. "Postquam ludus in artem paulatim verterat. Varro und die Frühgeschichte des römischen Theaters," in *Studien zur vorliterarischen Periode im frühen Rom*, ed. G. Vogt-Spira. Tübingen. Pp. 77–134.

Snead, J. 1984. "Repetition as a Figure of Black Culture," in *Black Literature and Literary Theory*, ed. H. L. Gates Jr. New York and London. Pp. 59–80.

Stern, H. 1966. "La représentation du mois de mars d'une mosaïque d'el-Djem," *Mélanges d'archéologie et d'histoire offerts à André Piganiol*. Paris. 1.597–609.

Stewart, S. 1997. "At the Threshold of the Visible," in *At the Threshold of the Visible: Minuscule and Small-Scale Art, 1964–1996*. Essays by Guest Curator Ralph Rugoff and Susan Stewart. Independent Curators Incorporated. New York. Pp. 73–84.

Stewart, S. 2002. *Poetry and the Fate of the Senses*. Chicago.

Stibbe, C. 1980. "The Archaeological Evidence," in *Lapis Satricanus*, publication of Nederlands Instituut te Rome. The Hague. Pp. 21–40.

Stramaglia, A. 1995. "Le voci dei fantasmi," in *Lo spettacolo delle voci*, ed. F. De Martino and A. Sommerstein. Bari. Le Rane: Studi 14. Pp. 193–230.

Svenbro, J. 1988. "Il taglio della poesia. Note sulle origini sacrificali della poetica greca," in *Sacrificio e società nel mondo antico*, ed. C. Grottanelli and N. F. Parise. Rome and Bari. Pp. 231–52.

Svenbro, J. 1993. *Phrasikleia: An Anthropology of Reading in Ancient Greece*. Trans. J. Lloyd. Ithaca, N.Y.

Szilágyi, J. 1981. "Impletae modis saturae," *Prospettiva* 24: 2–23.

Tambiah, S. 1968. "The Magical Power of Words," *Man: Journal of the Royal Anthropological Institute* 3: 175–208.

Tambiah, S. 1985. *Culture, Thought, and Social Action: An Anthropological Perspective*. Cambridge, Mass., and London.

Tar, I. 1975. *Uber die Anfänge der römischen Lyrik*. Szeged. Acta Universitatis de Attila Jozsef Nominatae, Acta Antiqua et Archaeologica.

Taussig, M. 1993. *Mimesis and Alterity: A Particular History of the Senses*. New York and London.

Taussig, M. 1997. *The Magic of the State*. New York and London.

Taussig, M. 1999. *Defacement: Public Secrecy and the Labor of the Negative*. Stanford.

Taylor, A. 1966. *The Literary History of Meistergesang*. New York. Reprint of 1937 edition.

Taylor, L. R. 1937. "The Opportunities for Dramatic Performances in the Time of Plautus and Terence," *TAPA* 68: 284–304.

Taylor, R. 1997. "Two Pathic Subcultures in Ancient Rome," *Journal of the History of Sexuality* 7: 319–71.

Thomas, R. 1988. *Virgil. Georgics.* Cambridge.

Thomson, D. F. S. 1997. *Catullus.* Edited with a Textual and Interpretative Commentary. Toronto. Phoenix suppl. vol. 34.

Thuilliers, J-P. 1997. "Un relief archaïque inédit de Chiusi," *Revue Archéologique,* ser. 6, 46: 243–60.

Tobias, A. J. 1979. "Bacchiac Women and Iambic Slaves in Plautus," *CW* 73: 9–18.

Torelli, M. 1984. *Lavinio e Roma: Riti iniziatici e matrimonia tra archeologia e storia.* Rome.

Torelli, M. 1990. "Riti di passagio maschili di roma arcaica," *MEFRA* 102: 93–106.

Traube, E. 1986. *Cosmology and Social Life: Ritual Exchange among the Mambai of East Timor.* Chicago and London.

Treggiari, S. 1991. *Roman Marriage: Iusti coniuges from the Time of Cicero to the Time of Ulpian.* Oxford.

Tupet, A.-M. 1976. *La magie dans la poésie latine, I: Des origines à la fin du règne d'Auguste.* Paris.

Tupet, A.-M. 1986. "Rites magiques dans l'antiquité romaine," *ANRW* 2.16.3: 2592–2675.

Turner, M. 1991. *Reading Minds: The Study of English in the Age of Cognitive Science.* Princeton.

Turner, M. 1996. *The Literary Mind.* New York and Oxford.

Turner, V. 1966. *The Ritual Process: Structure and Anti-structure.* Chicago.

Valette-Cagnac, E. 1997. *La lecture à Rome: Rites et pratiques.* Paris.

van Sickle, J. 1987. "The *Elogia* of the Cornelii Scipiones and the Origin of Epigram at Rome," *AJP* 108: 41–55.

Vanggaard, J. H. 1988. *The Flamen: A Study in the History and Sociology of Roman Religion.* Copenhagen.

Versnel, H. 1970. *Triumphus: An Inquiry into the Origin, Development, and Meaning of the Roman Triumph.* Leiden.

Versnel, H. 1980. "Historical Implications," in *Lapis Satricanus,* publication of Nederlands Instituut te Rome. The Hague. Pp. 95–150.

Versnel, H. 1991. "Some Reflections on the Relationship Magic-Religion," *Numen* 38: 177–97.

Versnel, H. 1993. *Inconsistencies in Greek and Roman Religion II: Transition and Reversal in Myth and Ritual.* Leiden. Studies in Greek and Roman Religion, 6.2.

Versnel, H. 1996. "SALIEI of I(O)VNIEI?" *Lampas* 9: 46–61.

Vetta, M. 1983. "Un capitolo di storia di poesia simposiale (per l'esegesi di Aristofane, 'Vespe' 1222–1248)," in *Poesia e simposio nella Grecia antica,* ed. M. Vetta. Rome. Pp. 119–55.

Vico, G. 1999. *New Science: Principles of the New Science Concerning the Common Nature of Nations.* Trans. D. Marsh and introd. A. Grafton. London.

Vogt-Spira, G. (ed.). 1989. *Studien zur vorliterarischen Periode im frühen Rom.* Tübingen.

Vogt-Spira, G. (ed.). 1990. *Strukturen der Mündlichkeit in der römischen Literatur.* Tübingen.

Volk, K. 2002. *The Poetics of Latin Didactic: Lucretius, Vergil, Ovid, Manilius.* Oxford.

Waarsenburg, D. 1996a. "Lapis Satricanus: Nieuw lucht op een oude foto," *Lampas* 29: 5–9.

Waarsenburg, D. 1996b. "Satricum, de tempels en de Lapis," *Lampas* 29: 27–45.

Wachter, R. 1998. "'Oral Poetry' in ungewöhntem Kontext: Hinweise auf mündliche Dichtungstechnik in der pompejanischen Wandinscrhiften," *ZPE* 121: 73–89.

Wagenvoort, H. 1956. "Ludus poeticus," in *Studies in Roman Literature, Culture and Religion.* Leiden. Pp. 30–42. Reprint of "Ludus poeticus," *Les Etudes Classiques* 4 (1935): 108–20.

Walde, A., and J. B. Hoffmann. 1980. *Lateinisches etymologisches Wörterbuch.* 5th ed. Heidelberg.

Wallace-Hadrill, A. 1989. "Rome's Cultural Revolution." Review article on P. Zanker, *The Power of Images in Augustan Rome, JRS* 79: 157–64.

Wallace-Hadrill, A. 1997. "*Mutatio morum:* The Idea of a Cultural Revolution," in *The Roman Cultural Revolution,* ed. T. Habinek and A. Schiesaro. Cambridge. Pp. 3–22.

Walters, J. 1997. "Invading the Roman Body: Manliness and Impenetrability in Roman Thought," in *Roman Sexualities,* ed. J. Hallett and M. Skinner. Princeton. Pp. 30–43.

Waltzing, J.-P. 1968. *Etude historique sur les corporations professionelles chez les romaines depuis les origines jusqu'à la chute de l'Empire d'Occident.* Bologna. Reprint of Louvain, 1895–1900 edition.

Waquet, F. 2001. *Latin, or the Empire of the Sign: From the Sixteenth to the Twentieth Century.* Trans. J. Howe. London and New York.

Webster, G. 1998. *The Roman Imperial Army of the First and Second Centuries A.D.* 3d ed. Norman, Okla.

Wechsler, J. 1988. *A Human Comedy: Physiognomy and Caricature in Nineteenth Century Paris.* Chicago.

Weidner, E. F. 1917. *Orientalistische Studien Fritz Hommel.* Leipzig. 1.192–93.

West, M. L. 1992. *Ancient Greek Music.* Oxford.

Wille, G. 1967. *Musica Romana: Die Bedeutung der Musik im Leben der Römer.* Amsterdam.

Wille, G. 1989. "Quellen zur Verwendung mündlicher Texte in römischen Gesängen vorliterarischen Zeit," in *Studien zur vorliterarischen Periode im frühen Rom,* ed. G. Vogt-Spira. Tübingen. ScriptOralia 12. Pp. 199–225.

Williams, C. 1999. *Roman Homosexuality: Ideologies of Masculinity in Classical Antiquity.* New York and Oxford.

Williams, G. 1982. "Carmina," in *Cambridge History of Latin Literature,* ed. E. Kenney and W. Clausen. Cambridge.

Williams, R. 1980. *Problems in Materialism and Culture.* London.

Winkler, J. 1990. *The Constraints of Desire.* New York.

Winnicott, D. 1971. *Playing and Reality.* New York.

Wiseman, T. 1987. *Roman Studies Literary and Historical.* Liverpool.

Wiseman, T. 1988. "Satyrs in Rome? The Background to Horace's *Ars Poetica,*" *JRS* 78: 1–13.

Wiseman, T. 1994. *Historiography and Imagination: Eight Essays on Roman Culture.* Exeter. Exeter Studies in History, 33.

Wiseman, T. 1995. *Remus: A Roman Myth.* Cambridge.

Wiseman, T. 1998. *Roman Drama and Roman History.* Exeter. Exeter Studies in History. (Unnumbered series).

Wissowa, G. 1912. *Religion und Kultus der Römer.* Munich.

Wright, J. 1974. *Dancing in Chains: The Stylistic Unity of the Comoedia Palliata.* Rome. Papers and Monographs of the American Academy in Rome, 25.

Zetzel, J. 1989. "*ROMANE MEMENTO:* Justice and Judgment in *Aeneid 6,*" *TAPA* 119: 263–84.

Zorzetti, N. 1990. "The *Carmina Convivalia,*" in *Sympotica: A Symposium on the Symposion,* ed. O. Murray. Oxford. Pp. 308–20.

Zorzetti, N. 1991. "Poetry and the Ancient City: The Case of Rome," *CJ* 86: 311–29.

SUBJECT INDEX

Acqua Rossa, 41, 271
acting, 140
actio, 99
actor(s), 70, 85, 121, 130, 195, 202, 210, 277, 282
adolescent(s), 114–15, 122–23, 130–31, 147, 152, 271, 278
Adonis, 192–94, 288
Adorno, T., 31–32, 258
adulescens, 181
Aelius Stilo, 25, 81, 255–56, 275
Aeneas, 32, 90, 123–25, 128, 131, 153, 162–66, 170
aequales, 271
Aesop, 204–5
aestimatio, 187
Africa, metalworking in, 13–14
agents (*also* agency), 2, 4, 6, 34–35, 43, 55, 57, 110, 124, 149, 262
aggression, 130–31
agmen, 164
Ahl, F., 285
Ainu, of Hokkaido, 161
akanere, 26
akephalon, 230
Alcaeus, 144
Alcman, 83
Alexandrianism, Roman, 275, 277
Alexandrian poets, 281
Allen, D., 294
alphabet, 230, 247–48
alterity, 104–9, 240, 249
Amiternum, relief from, 294

amorini, 147
Ampolo, C., 270
amptruare, 18, 108
Anacreon, 103, 144
ancestors, 124–25, 127, 129–30, 246–47; creation of, 247–48; worship of, 247
ancestral songs, 140
Anchises, 141, 280
ancile (pl. *ancilia*), 8–10, 12, 16–17, 19–22, 24, 28, 54, 93–94, 124–25, 128–29, 168–69, 222, 263
animals, imitation of, 12, 122, 140, 284, 292
Antevorta, 239, 250
antiphonal style, 238
anus (= old woman), 136, 237, 252
apices, 23, 28
Apollo, 19, 69, 137–38, 140, 151–53, 155–56, 283
Appius Claudius Caecus, 49, 76
Ara Maxima, 223–24, 291
Aratus, 78
archaeological remains, interpretation of, 40–42, 269
Ariadne, 18, 254–55
aristocracy, 40–44, 55–56, 82, 95, 109, 200, 270, 277. *See also* social status
aristocrats, 89–90, 131, 199, 243, 272–73, 280; boasts of, 53, 179–80
Aristotle, 277, 279
armor, 172–73
art, 6, 82, 97, 129, 131; archaic, 176; plastic, 122

immortality, 145, 245
impersonation, 124, 127–28, 130, 136, 149, 282
incantation, 1, 25, 78, 90, 172, 220, 248–50, 275
incedo, 117, 124
incisum, 230
incorporating practice(s), 158–60, 162, 168–69, 171, 176–78, 208, 284
inflection, vocal, 99–100
infractus, 205, 290
initiates, 94, 176, 271
initiation, 130–31, 138, 148, 168–69, 172, 255, 275; *Carmen Saeculare* and, 152–53; comedy and, 52; Salian rite as, 16–19, 26, 32–33
inscribing practices, 158, 174, 217, 284
intestines, 234–35, 244, 255
intonation, 101–2
invective, 191, 288, 293, 295
ionica, 288
Italians, conscription of, 176, 286
iuvenis, 171, 220
iuventus, 107, 120–21, 277

Janus, 26–27, 223–24, 244, 251–52, 263, 266, 292
Johnson, W., 262
Juno, 26, 151–52, 155–56, 251–52
Jupiter (*also* Jove), 86–87, 121, 125, 149, 223, 271; and *Carmen Saeculare*, 152, 155, 283; in Salian rite, 10, 26, 263, 266
Juvenal, 56, 115, 205, 208–10, 273

kabeiroi, 13
kalator, 76
Kandinsky, W., 1, 7, 63
Keightley, D., 247
kinaidologoi, 187
kinaidos, 191
King, R., 268, 287
Kingsley, P., 265, 267
kōlon, 230
komma, 230
kourētes (*also* Curetes), 13, 20, 29, 87, 267
korybantes, 13
Krostenko, B., 269, 272–73

labyrinth, 18–19, 32, 94, 153, 169, 221, 254–56, 265, 296
laena, 243
lament, 84, 104–5, 245. *See also* funeral(s)
language: disruptive potential of, 9, 28,

37, 225, 236; ritualization of, 9, 262; semiotic aspect of, 150
Latins, 151, 156
Latium, 9, 13, 37–38, 41, 156, 259
latus, 184
laudatio (*also* eulogy), 6, 39, 43, 76, 183, 212, 245–46
law, 61, 122, 221
laxus, 198
Leach, E., 194
legions, 167, 176, 285–86
lego, 282
letters (*epistulae*), 148
Liber, 143, 186
Liberalia, 17, 265
libellus (pl. *libelli*), 230–31, 264
liminal experience, 115
linos, 238
Linos, 294
literacy, 262
literature, 150–51, 157, 159, 262, 268, 273
living, the, 244, 248, 254, 294
Livius Andronicus, 81, 107–8, 200
Livy, 222, 227–28, 279
locuta, 61, 75, 79
locutio, 5
loquax, 166
loquor: *dico* and, 70–74; used of everyday speech, 59–61, 63–65, 79, 81–82, 105, 134, 136, 144, 148, 173
Lomax, A., 15, 267
love song, 53, 183, 273, 275, 280
lubricus, 182, 193, 201
Lucilius (addressee of Seneca's letters), 104, 273
Lucilius (satirist), 55–56, 115
ludi, 6, 35, 139, 155; *circenses*, 121; *plebei*, 42; *Romani*, 42, 116; *saeculares*, 6, 150–57, 283; *scaenici*, 107–8, 120–21
ludio (pl. *ludiones*), 107–8, 120–21
ludo, 112–13, 117, 119, 121, 126, 128, 133, 144, 274, 281
ludus, 5, 67, 106–8; bodies and, 116–22, 127–28, 136–40, 142–48, 159, 169, 175; images and, 122–28; seriousness and, 111–14; sex as, 112, 118–19, 123–24, 126–28; of youth, 114–15, 204–5, 213
ludus poeticus, 122, 130, 132–50
lullaby, 78–79, 236, 244
luperci, 17, 28–29, 36, 269
lust, 191, 210, 288
lusus Troiae, 19–21, 114–15, 120–21, 153, 255, 265, 278

invention of, 82–84, 86–87; in oratory, 97–102; power of, 31, 41, 52, 175; song and, 61, 162, 203, 215, 218, 230

musical theory, 90, 276

musical training, 97

musicus, 215

musso, 166

myth, 11, 107, 112, 122, 125, 130, 152, 156; Greek, 13–15, 222; Italian, 264; and metalworking, 13–15, 186–87

Naevius, Cn., 200

Nagy, G., 2, 262

narro, 73

nemein, 230

nenia (pl. neniae), 6, 228, 233–43, 245–46, 249, 251–52, 254, 293–95

Nenia, 237, 239–40, 242–44, 247–48, 254, 294

Nero (emperor), 29, 102, 115, 279

nervi, 230

Nestor, 173

nētē, 293–94

Newman, J., 275

Nietzsche, F., 11, 258, 263

noisemaking, 82–83

nomino, 71

nomos (pl. nomoi), 83, 230, 276

Norchia, 13, 168

Numa: music of, 70, 276; Pythagoreanism and, 87–89; as sacrificer, 224, 226; in Salian legend and rite, 9–10, 20, 81, 93, 111, 263, 266, 292

numerus (pl. numeri), 70, 99, 102, 203

oaths, 189

objects: in drama, 36, 54; everyday, 129; in ritual, 8, 15–16, 24, 43; slaves as, 54; transformation of, 11–16

occentatio, 61, 77, 220, 291

Old Comedy, 202

Oliensis, E., 147, 282

olios, 53

omens, 163, 166–67, 168

omentum, 232, 295

oracle(s), 1, 10, 152, 154, 230, 283

orality, 2, 262, 274, 279, 282

orator, 47

orators: characteristics of, 85, 97, 113, 229, 289; at funerals, 130; and song, 2, 111, 157, 220

oratory, 53, 70; authority of, 73–74, 159, 242–43; performance of, 191, 198, 201,

205, 213–15; rivalry with song, 77, 94–102, 277

organica, 84

"orientalizing" art, 41

oro, 134

Orpheus, 5, 58, 90–91, 103, 140, 172, 233

Osteria dell'Osa, 281

oura, 230

Ovid: career of, 59, 281; on conviviality, 215, 287; *Metamorphoses*, 14, 84, 104, 171, 176; on song, 59, 166, 174, 176, 277; as source of legends, 11, 222, 224

paean, 140–41, 152, 230, 233, 283

paizein, 281

palaestra, 67, 279

Palatine hill, 155

palla, 179–80, 193, 288

palladium, 11, 263

pallium, 190, 205, 290

pantomime, 119, 210, 289–90

parallaks, 18

parasite, 178, 181, 241

parody, 116, 178, 246, 278–79; Plautine, 53, 117, 181, 272–73, 286

Parsons, J., 269

passage, 152, 213, 225, 252, 258. *See also* rites of passage

pastoral poetry, 136–37

pathicus, 189–90

patricians, 266

Paullus Maximus (L. Aemilius Paullus), 33, 36

percrepo, 78

performance: as category of analysis, 2, 80, 128, 162, 195, 241, 262; of *cinaedi*, 195–98; embodiment and, 175–78, 290; genres of, 53, 95, 144; musical, 79, 99, 267; oratorical, 70, 99, 205; ritual, 8, 75, 108, 131, 154–57; of song, 62, 82, 105, 108, 136–37, 175–77, 205, 213, 246, 257; styles of, 199–219; of texts, 56, 116, 212–13

Persius, 56, 115, 210, 273

persona(e), 56, 122

Peruzzi, E., 273

Philemon, 49, 272

philosophia, 103

philosophy, 23, 112, 241–42, 286; contrasted with play, 132, 145, 148; parody of, 53, 116; performance of, 289–90; as profession, 272; as rival to song, 94–97, 102–4; Stoic, 93

INDEX OF SOURCES

328

·

Index of

Sources